Place
Matters

Place Matters

METROPOLITICS FOR THE TWENTY-FIRST CENTURY

PETER DREIER, JOHN MOLLENKOPF & TODD SWANSTROM

UNIVERSITY PRESS OF KANSAS

Published by the

University Press of Kansas

(Lawrence, Kansas 66049),

which was organized by the

Kansas Board of Regents and

is operated and funded by

Emporia State University,

Fort Hays State University,

Kansas State University,

Pittsburg State University,

the University of Kansas, and

Wichita State University.

Library of Congress Cataloging-in-Publication Data
Dreier, Peter
Place matters : metropolitics for the twenty-first century /
Peter Dreier, John Mollenkopf, and Todd Swanstrom.
p. cm. — (Studies in government and public policy)
Includes bibliographical references (p.   ) and index.
ISBN 0-7006-1134-7 (cloth : alk. paper) —
ISBN 0-7006-1135-5 (pbk. : alk. paper)
1. Urban poor — United States.   2. Urban policy —
United States.   3. Federal-city relations — United States.
4. Metropolitan areas — United States.   I. Mollenkopf,
John H., 1946–   II. Swanstrom, Todd.   III. Title.
IV. Series
HV4045 .D74   2001
307.76′0973 — dc21
2001002313

British Library Cataloguing in Publication Data
is available.

Printed in the United States of America

10 9 8 7 6 5 4 3 2 1

Figures 1.1 and 1.2 on pages 14 and 15 are reprinted by
permission of Cornell University Press from Lawrence Mishel,
Jared Bernstein, John Schmitt, and the Economic Policy
Institute, *The State of Working America, 1998–1999,* copyright
1999, Cornell University.

The paper used in this publication meets the minimum
requirements of the American National Standard for
Permanence of Paper for Printed Library Materials
Z39.48-1984.

For Bennett Harrison

Contents

Tables and Illustrations

Preface

This book grew out of our frustration with the current stalemated debate about the condition of cities and our conviction that we can move beyond it. All three of us have spent more than two decades studying and taking part in the real world of urban politics. *Place Matters* reflects our view that the problems presently facing America's cities are primarily political in nature. Since their origin lies in politics, so does their solution. New political coalitions and public policies could make a big difference in the social and economic conditions in metropolitan areas and in the lives of those who live in them. To achieve these changes, however, we need to rethink our basic ideas about neighborhoods, cities, metropolitan areas, and the federal role in addressing urban problems. We view this book, therefore, not only as a synthesis of research findings but also as a road map for reform.

Some observers have been arguing recently that cities are now doing fine on their own and do not need another wave of federal urban policy. It is true that many urban social indicators improved during the second half of the 1990s. In most cities, unemployment, poverty, and crime rates declined, while the home ownership rate, particularly among blacks and Hispanics, increased. Banks made more loans in urban neighborhoods, and private investors built office buildings, retail stores, sports complexes, and other facilities. At the end of the decade, the long decline in wages among unskilled workers finally seemed to have stopped. Even air pollution got better in many urban areas. More suburbanites expressed concern about "suburban sprawl," and more city dwellers cared about revitalizing old neighborhoods. These trends have led the media to herald an incipient urban revival.

This message is certainly preferable to the widespread stereotype that America's cities are cauldrons of social pathology that are beyond the "point of no return." Although the urban condition has recently improved, however, this trend is neither inevitable nor even robust. It stems largely from an unprecedented national economic expansion, reinforced by national policies that reduced unemployment, spurred productivity, lifted up the working poor, and targeted private investment to low-income urban areas. None of these factors substantially changed the most fundamental urban problem—namely, the growing concentration of poverty in central cities (and now inner suburbs) and the growing separations between the poor and the well-to-do. Nor can we be assured that any of these positive trends will continue into the first decade of the new century, especially if the country experiences a prolonged recession.

Our central cities and inner-ring suburbs are still plagued with serious problems, and many are in worse shape now than two decades ago. Decline has accelerated in many older suburbs, a troublesome trend, because they typically have even fewer institutional resources than do central cities to respond to the problems that have crept up on them. In the midst of enormous prosperity, we have missed an opportunity to do a better job of reducing urban and inner suburban poverty. We accept as "normal" levels of poverty, crime, and homelessness that would cause national alarm in Canada, Western Europe, or Australia.

Building a political majority in support of new policies to address metropolitan poverty and inequality will require several elements: a favorable climate of public opinion, vigorous leadership from elected officials and citizen activists, a workable set of programs, and an accurate diagnosis of the root causes of our situation. We think the political climate is now more favorable than in the past. As Americans see their cities improving and more of the poor working to make ends meet, they are more willing to support policies to help the "deserving" working poor. In the closely contested November 2000 presidential election, Al Gore and Ralph Nader together received over 51 percent of the vote, indicating majority support for a liberal or progressive agenda. Sensing the national mood, George Bush campaigned as a "compassionate conservative." Though he seeks to govern as a traditional conservative, with tax cuts, increased military spending, and less regulation of big business, he has also emphasized "faith-based" approaches to helping the urban poor and improving urban education. If a prolonged recession occurs, national concern for the social safety net will grow rapidly.

We believe that a new political majority must be built around identifying and building on concerns that unite those who live in central cities with residents of the suburbs. We do not believe their concerns are antithetical to each other. But finding common ground between them requires elected officials and organized citizens alike to show political leadership. This book sketches out that common ground and proposes ideas about how to meld it into a new majority. We understand that half of America's voters live in the suburbs of our metropolitan areas. We know that we must explain to them why they should see their interests as joined to the interests of those who live in central cities. We think that they will reach this conclusion when they come to understand three fundamental realities: outer metropolitan areas cannot prosper as much as they might without healthy central cities; the interests of inner suburbs are now closer in many respects to those of central cities than to those of better-off outer suburbs; and many problems that vex suburbanites as well as central-city residents have their roots in and are exacerbated by the metropolitan political fragmentation and competition that now characterize our metropolitan areas.

Place Matters provides the analysis necessary to make a convincing case for a metropolitan agenda. We have been impressed by the wide variety of elected officials, business and labor leaders, civic and community activists, environmentalists, journalists, and philanthropists who recognize these realities, are forging new approaches that cross the boundaries between cities and suburbs, and are building new kinds of political coalitions to pursue them. We hope this book contributes to accelerating the pace of change.

We began this collaboration by organizing a small conference on the future of urban America in May 1994. Sponsored by the Spivack Program on Applied Social Research and Social Policy of the American Sociological Association (ASA), it took place at the Belmont Conference Center in Maryland. We invited some of the nation's leading scholars and practitioners to spend a weekend discussing the current condition of urban life and the public policies and political strategies needed to ameliorate cities' problems and build on their strengths. We warmly thank the participants for their insights and candor. They include William Barnes (National League of Cities), Robert Embry (Abell Foundation), Elaine Fielding (University of Michigan), Ted Hershberg (University of Pennsylvania), Edward Hill (Cleveland State University), Mark Alan Hughes (Public/Private Ventures), Pam Karlan (Stanford University), John Logan (State University of New York at Albany), Guy Molyneaux (Peter Hart & Associates), Manuel Pastor (University of California, Santa Cruz), Neal Peirce (syndicated columnist), Nestor Rodriguez (University of Houston), Margery Austin Turner (Urban Institute), and Margaret Weir (University of California, Berkeley). We particularly thank our three energetic and enthusiastic colleagues at the ASA who made an early commitment to the conference and helped us organize it: Felice Levine (ASA executive officer), Carla Howery (deputy executive officer), and Paula Trubisky (special assistant).

We initially intended to write a modest report summarizing the discussion that took place at the 1994 conference. It gradually grew into a book-length study as we wrote and reconsidered various drafts over the years. As a result, this project took much longer than we initially anticipated, but the delay allowed us to consider the remarkable resurgence of scholarly concern with the problems and potentials of urban areas, especially the growing interest in regional approaches to urban issues. We have also been heartened by the resurgence of progressive politics among unions, community organizations, environmental groups, and others. We drew on these promising trends in developing this book.

Our argument builds on the work of hundreds of scholars, whose contributions we acknowledge in our many notes. A few people deserve special mention, however. On two separate occasions, Rich DeLeon read the entire manuscript and provided extensive comments that immeasurably improved it. We presented a preliminary version of our ideas at the Urban Affairs Association annual meeting in Los Angeles in May 2000 and received thoughtful and constructive comments from panelists Paul Jargowsky, Fred Seigel, and Phil Thompson. Many other colleagues reviewed earlier versions of the manuscript, provided data and examples, and shared their thoughts about the political and policy issues we address. They include Richard Brown, Sang Chi, Frances Frisken, John Goering, David Imbroscio, Neil Kraus, Leslie McCall, Michael Leo Owens, Timothy Ross, Richard Rothstein, Richard Sauerzopf, Ray Seidelman, Margaret Weir, Hal Wolman, and Elvin Wyly. Research assistance was provided by Sylvia Chico, Mine Doyran, Victoria Hyzer, Rachel Josil, Chris Latimer, and Danielle Croce. Elizabeth McDaniel and Nicole Radmore of the Russell Sage Foundation provided critical editorial assistance in the closing stage of our work. Fred Woodward, director of the University Press of Kansas, was enormously supportive during the entire process. We appreciate his faith in our ideas. We also benefited from the caring professionalism of Rebecca Giusti and Susan Schott.

We could not have managed to write this book without a large supply of patience and love from our families. We thank them for their understanding. Peter wishes to thank his wife, Terry Meng, and his twin daughters, Amelia and Sarah, who were born while the book was still a jumble of memos and e-mails on his computer's hard drive. John thanks his always stimulating and unfailingly supportive spouse and daughter, Kathleen Gerson and Emily Mollenkopf.

Todd thanks his wife, Katie, and daughters Jessica, Madeleine, and Eleanore for their love and patience.

One of the last things Bennett Harrison did before he died in early 1999 at the age of fifty-six was to provide us with extensive comments on an early draft of our work. We will always cherish Ben's exuberant scrawls of "terrific" and "explain this" on these manuscript pages. We hope our work is informed by the insight, political commitment, and generosity that Ben radiated. We miss him dearly and dedicate this book to his memory.

I am tempted to believe that what we call necessary

institutions are often no more than institutions to which

we have grown accustomed, and that in matters of social

constitution the field of possibilities is much more extensive

than men living in their various societies are ready to imagine.

—*Recollections of Alexis de Tocqueville*

Place Still Matters

This book has a simple thesis: place matters. Where we live makes a big difference in the quality of our lives, and how the places in which we live function has a big impact on the quality of our society. The evidence shows that places are becoming more unequal. Economic classes are becoming more spatially separate from each other, with the rich increasingly living with other rich people and the poor with other poor. The latter are concentrated in central cities and distressed inner suburbs, and the former are in exclusive central-city neighborhoods and more distant suburbs.

This rising economic segregation has many negative consequences, ranging from reinforcing disadvantage in central-city neighborhoods to heightening the cost of suburban sprawl as families flee deteriorating central cities and inner suburbs. This trend in the spatial organization of American metropolitan areas is not the simple result of individuals making choices in free markets. Rather, federal and state policies have biased metropolitan development in favor of economic segregation, concentrated urban poverty, and suburban sprawl. We need new policies for metropolitan governance that will level the playing field and stop the drift toward greater spatial inequality. We also need a political strategy for uniting residents of central cities and suburbs in a new coalition that will support these policies.

It may seem odd to argue that place matters when technology appears to be conquering space and Americans are so mobile. Cars and planes have made it possible for us to move about more quickly than ever before. More importantly, cable television, telephones, faxes, computers, and, above all, the Internet enable us to access many of society's benefits without leaving our homes. With a satellite dish or cable service, we can choose from a menu of entertainment options ranging from tractor pulls to Tolstoy, from rap to Rachmaninoff. Distance learning is growing rapidly, with "virtual" universities enabling students to pursue college degrees from their homes. With e-commerce, we hardly even need to drive to the mall anymore, and more people are working at home instead of commuting to the office every day. Where you live, in short, seems to have less and less of an effect on the type of person you are and what you do. Technology has eclipsed the traditional reasons people gathered together in cities: to be close to jobs, culture, and shopping. Cities, it seems, are becoming obsolete.[1]

In fact, this idea is nonsense.[2] As places of intense personal interaction, cities are as important as ever. If technology were truly abolishing the importance of space and place, real estate values would flatten out. Soaring house prices in Silicon Valley, Boston, and New York City are proof positive that people will pay dearly to live in certain places. Indeed, the vast majority of Americans, over 80 percent, have chosen to live within metropolitan areas and have not spread themselves across the countryside.

It is true that mass ownership of automobiles has made it possible for people to live farther from where they work within these metropolitan areas than they could fifty years ago. If they can afford it, Americans generally prefer to live in low-density suburbs. But people still care about where they live, perhaps more than ever. Higher-income professionals have geographically dispersed networks that transcend their neighborhoods and cities, sometimes extending to the entire globe. They use these "weak" ties, or dispersed networks, for gathering information, seeking opportunities, and finding jobs.[3] But where they choose to live still affects how much they pay in taxes, where their children go to school, and who their friends are.

Place becomes more important as one moves down the economic ladder. On the wrong side of the "digital divide," poor and working-class families are less likely to own a computer, have Internet access, or send and receive e-mail.[4] They rely more on local networks to find out about jobs and other opportunities. Often lacking a car (and adequate mass transit), they must live close to where they work. Unable to send their children to private schools, they must rely on local public schools. Unable to afford day care, lower-income families must rely on informal day care provided by nearby relatives and friends.

In short, whether we are highly skilled professionals or minimum-wage workers, where we live matters. Place affects our access to jobs and public services (especially education), our access to shopping and culture, our level of personal security, the availability of medical services, and even the air we

TABLE 1.1. Comparison of Three Congressional Districts

	Median Family Income, 1989	Families in Poverty, 1990 (%)	White Voting-Age Population, 1990 (%)	Population per Square Mile, 1990	Democratic Vote for President, 2000 (%)
New York's 16th Central City	$16,683	39.5	21.4	37,567	92.9
Ohio's 10th Inner Ring	$37,053	8.2	95.1	3,667	52.5
Illinois' 13th Outer Ring	$55,481	1.8	92.3	1,415	42.4

Source: Demographic characteristics from U.S. Census Bureau, 1990 Census of Population and Housing, Summary Tape Files 3D, Congressional Districts of the United States; 1996 voting data from Michael Barone and Grant Ujifsa, *The Almanac of American Politics 1998* (Washington, D.C.: National Journal, 1997); 2000 election results from POLIDATA, a private political and demographic research firm.

breathe. People still care deeply about where they live. The adage still holds true: the three most important factors in real estate are location, location, location.

THE POWER OF PLACE

To illustrate this point, we examine three different congressional districts, chosen to show how places differ within American metropolitan areas. We begin with a poor central-city district in the South Bronx section of New York City, proceed to a district that spans the West Side of Cleveland and its suburbs, and conclude with a wealthy outer-ring suburban district west of Chicago. Although very different, they each illustrate the point that no matter where we live, economic segregation, concentrated poverty, and suburban sprawl have tremendous impacts on our lives.

New York's Sixteenth Congressional District: Inner-City Ghetto on the Rebound

The Sixteenth Congressional District in the South Bronx is the poorest and one of the most Democratic congressional districts in the nation. This was not always so. Located just north of Manhattan in New York City, the Bronx was, until 1960, a haven for Italian, Irish, and Jewish working- and middle-class families, many of whom had fled the immigrant slums of the Lower East Side of Manhattan. Home to the New York Yankees and a thriving manufacturing sector, the Bronx prospered until manufacturing jobs began leaving in the 1960s. Between 1969 and 1996, manufacturing jobs in the Bronx fell from 51,788 to 14,134.[5] The influx of poor Puerto Ricans and the blight caused by the con-

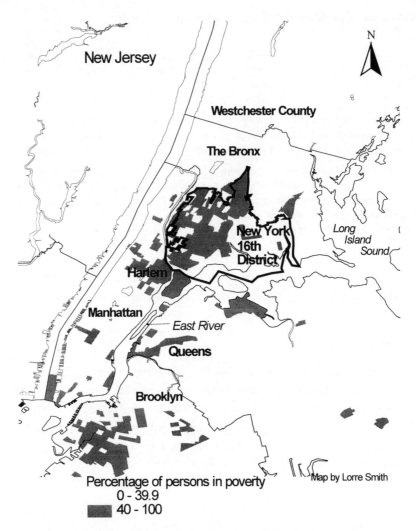

New Jersey

Westchester County

The Bronx

New York
16th
District

Long
Island
Sound

Harlem

Manhattan

East River

Queens

Brooklyn

Percentage of persons in poverty
  0 - 39.9
  40 - 100

Map by Lorre Smith

MAP 1.1. New York's Sixteenth Congressional District

struction of the Cross-Bronx Expressway hastened massive white flight from the Bronx to the suburbs. In the 1970s, the population of the Bronx fell by about 300,000 people, to 1.17 million. In October 1977, President Jimmy Carter made an unannounced walking tour of Charlotte Street in the South Bronx. Pictures of the president strolling through a devastated landscape resembling a bombed-out European city after World War II made the South Bronx a worldwide symbol of urban decay.[6]

What sets the Sixteenth Congressional District apart from others is not just its poverty but its high percentage of children. Over one-third of the population was under the age of eighteen in 1990, the highest percentage of any congressional district in New York State. Life has not been kind, however, to many of these children. In *Amazing Grace*, Jonathan Kozol documented the hardscrabble life of many children living in Mott Haven, an area in the South Bronx with a population of about 48,000 in 1990. With a 1991 median household income of only $7,600, Mott Haven is an area of extreme concentrated poverty. Still, a majority of those who are able to work do so. A major reason for the high poverty rate is that the city government relocated thousands of homeless families there. As one formerly homeless woman observed bitterly: "Nobody thought that they was goin' to put us into fancy neighborhoods on the East Side. You're not goin' to put poor people in neighborhoods like that. But no one believed that they would concentrate us in the place that were most diseased because this would amount to a death sentence." [7] The area is indeed beset with high rates of infectious diseases, including tuberculosis and AIDS. Lead paint poisoning, common in older apartment buildings, strikes a large number of children, who suffer brain damage and develop learning disabilities. Asthma is rampant, often triggered by cockroach droppings. The rate of violent crime is so high that parents are afraid to let their children go outside. Kozol ends his book by listing twenty-three children with whom he became acquainted who died violently in the neighborhood between 1990 and 1994.

The odds that the surviving children of Mott Haven will make it to middle-class communities are slim. No matter what standards are used, the neighborhood schools rank near the bottom of public schools in New York City. The students come from home environments that are not conducive to educational achievement. Students often lack quiet, orderly places to study. Kozol interviewed one little boy who was forced to study with a flashlight in the closet of his brother's bedroom. Socially, economically, and psychologically isolated from the mainstream society thriving only a few miles away in Manhattan, Mott Haven sends the message to its children that they are not wanted and will not succeed. The children feel stigmatized by the squalor and the ugliness. As a school psychologist put it: "Many of the ambitions of the children are locked-in at a level that suburban kids would scorn. It's as if the very possibilities of life have been scaled back." [8]

Not all the news about the South Bronx is negative. Parts of it enjoyed a remarkable revival in the 1980s and 1990s. Over 57,000 housing units have been built or rehabilitated in the past eleven years. Violent crime is down sharply, as it is throughout New York City. The population decline has been stemmed by an influx of immigrants who have brought new energy and entrepreneurial skills to the area. Businesses, including grocery stores, are making a comeback.

The New York Yankees, 1998 and 2000 World Series Champions, are a source of great pride to the community. Still, its voters cast only 132,061 ballots in the 2000 presidential election, one of the lowest rates of any congressional district in the nation. Those who do go to the polls vote overwhelmingly Democratic, handily electing Jose Serrano to his sixth term in Congress in 2000.

The stereotype that people in poor neighborhoods lack positive values and do not care for one another does not apply to the Bronx. Even in the poorest areas, the churches, immigrant associations, tenant organizations, and neighborhood associations are vibrant. Indeed, the Bronx is home to some of the most dynamic and successful community development corporations (CDCs) in the nation.[9] Working with neighborhood representatives, the New York City Partnership helped build 5,161 new housing units in the Bronx. Most are duplexes that include a rental unit, thus mixing home owners and renters. Subsidized with government money and free land, the projects inject working-class home owners into devastated neighborhoods, creating islands of renewal in seas of decay. They sell for up to $185,000, demonstrating that working families are, once again, willing to invest in the Bronx.[10]

Although racially and economically diverse neighborhoods in the Bronx are succeeding, the odds are still stacked against a larger revival for the South Bronx. In evaluating two successful Bronx CDCs, Mid-Bronx Desperados and Banana Kelly, urban analyst and former Albuquerque mayor David Rusk found that between 1970 and 1990, the CDCs were able to reverse population losses in their neighborhoods, but poverty rates continued to rise and buying power in the neighborhoods fell. Rusk concluded that if the outward movement to the suburbs continues in the New York region, the neighborhoods of the South Bronx will not be able to stem decay, no matter how hard they work.[11]

Ohio's Tenth Congressional District: Spreading Urban Problems

Ohio's Tenth Congressional District stretches from the West Side of Cleveland through inner working-class suburbs out to middle-class suburbs. The population center of the district is rapidly moving west, away from the city. More than half its electorate now lives outside the city limits, most in older suburbs that are themselves threatened by population loss and disinvestment. The district is over 94 percent white, with a strong ethnic flavor. Germans and Irish are the largest ethnic groups, but the district also has large numbers of Poles, Italians, and Slovakians. The largest suburb, Parma, has been mocked by affluent snobs for white socks, cheap beer, and pink flamingos in the front

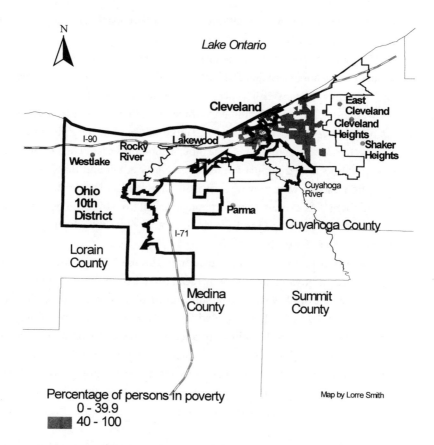

MAP 1.2. Ohio's Tenth Congressional District

Map labels: N, Lake Ontario, Cleveland, East Cleveland, Cleveland Heights, Shaker Heights, I-90, Rocky River, Lakewood, Westlake, Cuyahoga River, Ohio 10th District, Parma, Cuyahoga County, I-71, Lorain County, Medina County, Summit County

Percentage of persons in poverty
0 - 39.9
40 - 100

Map by Lorre Smith

yards of tidy bungalows. The district's voters tend to be socially conservative and economically liberal. For this reason, it is known as a swing district, voting alternately Republican and Democrat in presidential elections. It has sent mostly Democrats to Congress, but a Republican won two terms before the present incumbent, Dennis Kucinich, the controversial former mayor of Cleveland, captured the seat in 1996.

Immigrants were originally attracted to the area by jobs at the steel mills on Cleveland's West Side along the Cuyahoga River. Like many Rust Belt cities, deindustrialization hit the West Side of Cleveland and its suburbs hard. Between 1979 and 1983, the Cleveland region lost one-quarter of all its manufacturing jobs.[12] The district retains a substantial Chevrolet plant in Parma, a nearby Ford plant, and many small metalworking shops serving larger manufacturers. Economic restructuring led to a tremendous increase in low-wage jobs, especially in the service sector. As a result, income inequality increased dramatically in the 1970s and early 1980s.[13]

The pain of economic restructuring was unevenly distributed across the Tenth Congressional District. The part within the city of Cleveland suffered precipitous population losses. The people left behind are poor. The poverty rate on the West Side of Cleveland climbed to three times that of the district as a whole (25 percent versus 8 percent) by 1987. Home values in the city plummeted by 50 percent or more in the 1990s. The inner-ring suburbs fared better, but many of them also suffered population losses. A 1993 study found that five times as many home sellers were moving away from Cleveland and its nearby suburbs as toward them.[14] As a result, Parma's population fell from over 100,000 in 1970 to less than 86,000 in 2000, and Lakewood, another older suburb, dropped from about 70,000 to fewer than 57,000.

The outward movement of population in the Tenth Congressional District has not been motivated primarily by racial fears, because most minorities live on the East Side of Cleveland. To be sure, busing of white students in Cleveland to black East Side schools accelerated flight. And Parma was one of only two cities in the country to be subject to a federal court order because it had intentionally excluded minorities. (The other was Yonkers, New York.) Ten years after the remedial order was issued, however, the black population in Parma was still less than 1 percent.[15] The steady outward movement of families within the Tenth Congressional District was thus flight from blight, not flight from blacks.

Notwithstanding their small minority populations, the inner-ring suburbs in the Tenth Congressional District are all concerned about urban decline. By 1990, Lakewood's poverty rate had risen to 10 percent. Between 1983 and 1995, its assessed property values increased only 10 percent (controlling for inflation), but they jumped 100 percent in Westlake, an outer-ring suburb in the district. In the mid-1990s, Parma became known for gang activity. According to a survey of Parma schools, one in eleven students belonged to a gang, and 60 percent said that they could get drugs in their school. A July 1995 *Life* magazine cover story reported that gangs were recruiting at the Parmatown Mall. Gang activity even spread to the more affluent suburb of Seven Hills.[16] In spite of these problems, the area is politically involved. A significantly larger number of voters (227,885) went to the polls in the 1996 presidential election than did in the South Bronx.

Government actions heavily influenced the outward movement of population in the Tenth Congressional District. Most important was highway construction. The interstate highways in the area represent an investment of over

$1 billion (in 1991 dollars). In 1968, Interstate 71 aided migration from Parma south to Strongsville and Medina. In 1978, Interstate 90 opened up, traversing the Tenth Congressional District from east to west and spurring movement first from Cleveland to Lakewood and then further out to Rocky River and West-lake.[17] Aware of the negative effect of public policies, the inner-ring suburbs of Cleveland formed a coalition, the First Suburbs Consortium, to lobby the state government for better treatment. Some leaders of outlying suburbs responded critically to the new group. The mayor of North Royalton, Gary Barma, said that the inner-ring mayors were "pointing their finger at someone else for their problems" and should not get a greater share of state funds.[18]

In short, Ohio's Tenth Congressional District spans the range of contemporary urban conditions, from concentrated inner-city poverty to threatened inner-ring suburbs to privileged outer suburbs. To keep ahead of urban decline, families are rapidly migrating outward, and this process shows no signs of slowing down anytime soon. This presents a problem for Congressman Kucinich, for Ohio will lose one of its nineteen seats in the next reapportionment, and the Republicans who currently control the Ohio legislature could decide to eliminate the Tenth Congressional District.

Illinois' Thirteenth Congressional District: Rapidly Developing Suburbs

The Thirteenth Congressional District in Illinois lies directly west of Chicago, covering southern DuPage County and exurban parts of Cook and Will Counties. With excellent interstate connections, the area is rich with gleaming glass corporate headquarters and research centers. In 1966, AT&T built Bell Labs along the new Interstate 88. A few years later, Amoco moved its main research and development facility to the area. The corporate headquarters of McDonald's, Ace Hardware, Federal Signal Corporation, and the Spiegel mail-order company are located in the area around Interstates 88, 294, and 290. Given the many business executives and scientists who live in the area, the district's median family income in 1990 ($55,481) was the second highest in Illinois and twenty-second highest out of 435 in the country. Not surprisingly, the district also gave a higher percentage of its votes to Republican Robert Dole in 1996 than did four-fifths of the other districts. The district has consistently sent Republicans to Congress, including the current incumbent, Judith Biggert.

The Thirteenth Congressional District is growing rapidly because families are fleeing Chicago and its inner-ring suburbs in search of communities with low crime, less congestion, and good schools. The most rapidly growing com-

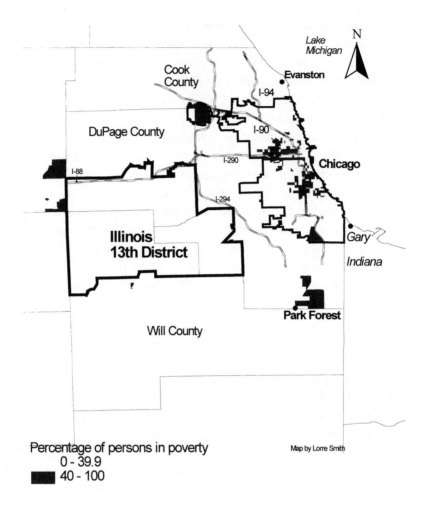

Lake
Michigan

N

Cook
County

Evanston

I-94

DuPage County

I-90

I-290

Chicago

I-88

I-294

Gary

Illinois
13th District

Indiana

Park Forest

Will County

Percentage of persons in poverty
0 - 39.9
40 - 100

Map by Lorre Smith

MAP 1.3. Illinois' Thirteenth Congressional District

munity is Naperville. A sleepy town of 7,000 in 1950, Naperville had a population of 128,358 in 2000.[19] Naperville is not primarily a commuter suburb for Chicago. Only about 5,000 people take the train into downtown Chicago's Loop each day. Most work in Naperville or other suburbs. Joel Garreau calls the Illinois Research and Development Corridor, including Naperville, Oak Brook, Lisle, Aurora, and the East-West Tollway, an "edge city."[20] Garreau defines an edge city as an area built up in the past thirty years that has at least 5 million square feet of office space and 600,000 square feet of retail space and that residents perceive as a destination. With its extensive office and commercial development, Naperville is a quintessential example of the urbanization of the suburbs. The district's high levels of income and education are reflected in the relatively large number of votes cast in the 1996 presidential election, 232,541.

As a place to grow up in, Naperville has many strengths. A 1997 study by Zero Population Growth (ZPG) ranked Naperville the most "kid friendly" city out of 219 studied (Chicago ranked 200th). The ZPG study used twenty key statistics, including crime, teen pregnancies, school dropout rates, and the number of children living in poverty, to compute its rankings. A key difference between Naperville and Chicago was the percentage of children who lived in poverty: 1.1 percent for the former, 33.6 percent for the latter. This prompted Brian Dixon, ZPG's director of government relations, to comment, "When you have these booming edge cities, they tend to suck the life out of the inner cities." Naperville's mayor, George Pradel, disagreed: "It's not a competition. There's an interdependence between the city and Naperville."[21]

Naperville is not without problems. Rapid growth in the town and its surrounding areas requires voters to constantly pass bond issues to build new schools. The only way to pay for them without steeply raising taxes is to capture new commercial development, which can provide more of a fiscal surplus than residential development can. For this reason, Thomas Scullen, superintendent of Naperville's School District 204, noted, "Some residents would like to see a moratorium on growth, but that's not going to happen."[22] So, in order to enhance commercial development and tax ratables, the people who move to the Thirteenth Congressional District searching for more greenery and less congestion end up reproducing some of the urban ills they had fled. As Will County's planning director Tyson Warner put it, "The more people that come in looking for the rural atmosphere, the less rural atmosphere there is."[23]

Despite well-performing high school students, rising incomes, and soaring home values, many stresses and anxieties trouble Naperville residents. Perhaps the leading complaint is a lack of community or a sense of belonging—hardly surprising for a suburb that recently added 9,000 people in one year. Naperville is a city of transferees, with perhaps one-third of the people transferring every three years. The turnover rate in the schools is anywhere from 15 to 35 percent a year.[24] In addition, most households need two full-time incomes to afford the average house. Stories of latchkey kids abound; day care centers specialize in taking care of children after school.

In the 1950s, academic critics viewed suburbs as places of suffocating conformity. In an article on Naperville subtitled "Stressed Out in Suburbia," Nicholas Lemann argues that the new outer-ring suburbs are different.[25] "The suburban psychological force that occasionally overwhelms people," Lemann writes, "is not the need to fit in, but the need to be a success." Striving to make it in one of the most privileged suburbs in the United States takes its toll on families. The great shortage in Naperville is not money but time.

THE PROBLEM OF ECONOMIC SEGREGATION

Clearly, place matters. Where people live makes a big difference in the quality of their lives. The residents of these three congressional districts experience widely different living conditions, uneven access to amenities and opportunities, and disparate levels of political influence. The fundamental reality is one of growing economic segregation in the context of rising overall inequality. People of different income classes are moving away from each other not just in how much income they have but also in where they live. America is breaking down into economically homogeneous enclaves. Our argument, in a nutshell, is that although growing economic inequality is bad, it is greatly worsened by growing economic segregation. This dynamic harms the quality of life for the working and middle classes as well as for the poor, imposes costs on society as a whole (including the rich), and lessens American society's capacity to engage in vigorous democratic debate and to act collectively to address its pressing problems.

Rising Inequality

In terms of raw consumption, the United States is the richest country in the world, perhaps the richest country ever. Factoring in the low prices of consumer goods in the United States, the United States had the highest per capita income out of thirteen advanced industrial countries in 1996.[26] Household incomes are rising, and technological advances enable Americans to buy more and more value with each dollar.[27] After nine years of continuous economic expansion (1991–2000), the "great American job machine" had driven the unemployment rate to its lowest level since the 1960s. By the turn of the century, the inflation rate remained low, home ownership was the highest in history, and new homes were bigger and better equipped than ever. The bull run on Wall Street and soaring corporate profits enabled those at the top to accumulate massive fortunes. The computer and telecommunications industries created new fortunes overnight (though technology stock prices plummeted in value in 2000). The Internet has revolutionized the way we do business, and the United States leads the world in information technology. The unusually strong U.S. economy created huge budget surpluses, and the federal government began paying down its massive debt. Americans as a whole have never been as prosperous as they are now at the beginning of the twenty-first century.

TABLE 1.2. Household Income Inequality in Developed Countries (Ratio of 90th Percentile of Household Income to 10th Percentile)

Country	Year	90th/10th
United States	1997	5.57
Italy	1995	4.77
United Kingdom	1995	4.57
Australia	1994	4.33
Ireland	1987	4.18
Japan	1992	4.17
Spain	1990	4.04
Canada	1997	4.01
Austria	1995	3.73
Switzerland	1992	3.62
France	1994	3.54
New Zealand	1987–88	3.46
Belgium	1996	3.20
Germany	1994	3.18
Netherlands	1994	3.15
Denmark	1992	2.86
Norway	1995	2.83
Finland	1995	2.69
Sweden	1995	2.61
Average without U.S.		3.43

Source: Luxembourg Income Study, Income Inequality Measures, at lisweb.ceps.lu/key/ineqtable.htm.

This abundance has not flowed proportionately to all segments of American society, however. In fact, the United States has the distinction of having the greatest income and wealth disparities of any advanced industrial society. Table 1.2 shows that American households in the top 10 percent make more compared with those in the bottom 10 percent than in any other advanced industrial country. By almost every other measure (Gini coefficients of inequality, wage inequality, poverty rates, and exit rates out of poverty), the United States ranks at the bottom of developed countries.[28] In the 1980s, both *Time* and *Business Week* published articles debating whether the wage structure had a missing middle that is, whether the low- and high-wage jobs of the new service economy were replacing the solid middle-class jobs of the fading industrial economy. The debate is now over. *Business Week*'s 1994 cover story "Inequality: How the Gap Between the Rich and the Poor Hurts the Economy" pointed out that the rich and super-rich had monopolized most income growth and almost all wealth accumulation.

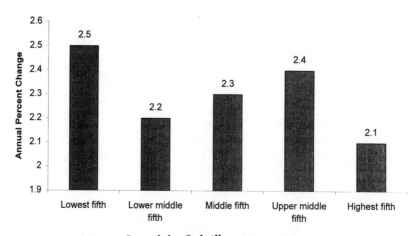

FIGURE 1.1. Income Growth by Quintiles, 1947–1979

Source: Lawrence Mishel, Jared Bernstein, and John Schmitt, *The State of Working America, 1999* (Ithaca, N.Y.: ILR Press, an imprint of Cornell University Press, 2000), p. 52.

Unlike previous economic expansions, during the economic boom of the mid-1990s, workers in the bottom half of the income scale actually saw their real incomes fail to regain their previous heights. Only since about 1996 have tight labor markets finally begun to pull those at the bottom into the wake of the speeding economy. This is good news. There is also bad news, however: low-wage workers are still falling further behind those at the top.[29]

Historically, American society has been based on an implicit social contract: if you work hard, you will get ahead. Substantiating this contract was not only the belief but also the experience that economic growth would benefit all social classes. In President Kennedy's memorable words, "A rising tide lifts all boats." As Figure 1.1 shows, every income class of Americans benefited from economic growth between 1947 and 1979, with those in the bottom 20 percent actually enjoying faster income growth than those above them.

In the 1980s, however, this foundation of the American social contract began to crumble. Bennett Harrison and Barry Bluestone called this the "great U-turn," when the country suddenly changed directions on the long road of continuously improving material conditions for most people.[30] Between 1979 and 1998, real family incomes for the bottom 20 percent of families (those making less than $22,077 in 1998) actually fell, as Figure 1.2 shows. Only the top 60 percent enjoyed significantly rising incomes, with most of the gain flowing to the "fortunate fifth," as Robert Reich calls them—the top 20 percent of income earners (those making over $85,541 in 1999 dollars)—who enjoyed a healthy 38 percent increase in real income.[31]

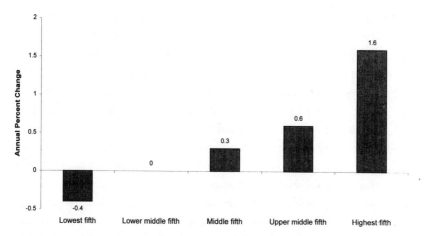

FIGURE 1.2. Income Growth by Quintiles, 1979–1998
Source: Lawrence Mishel, Jared Bernstein, and John Schmitt, *The State of Working America, 1999* (Ithaca, N.Y.: ILR Press, an imprint of Cornell University Press, 2000), p. 52.

By just about every measure, income inequality has increased significantly in the United States in the past twenty years.[32] The share of the nation's total income of the bottom 80 percent of families fell between 1979 and 1998; only the top 20 percent enjoyed an increase. Those at the very top did especially well. During those years, the top 5 percent of families (those making over $148,406 in 1998) saw their share of total income increase from 15.3 to 20.7 percent; at the same time, the bottom 20 percent saw their share of total income fall from 5.4 to 4.2 percent. And as the gap between the rich and the poor widened, the middle class shrank. Between 1979 and 1998, the proportion of persons living in families making 50 to 200 percent of the median income—the broad middle class—declined from 68 to 61.5 percent. At the same time, the groups at the bottom (with less than 50 percent of median income) and at the top (over 200 percent) grew.

The enormous pay increases for America's corporate chief executive officers (CEOs) are one cause of rising inequality. Between 1989 and 1998, when median hourly wages grew by just 2.4 percent, CEO compensation nearly doubled, growing 90.6 percent (including all components of CEO compensation, such as bonuses and stock options) to an average of $3,528,000. In 1978, the average CEO made 29 times what the average worker made; by 1999, the average CEO made 109 times what the average worker earned. American CEOs earn over twice the average pay of CEOs in other developed countries. Moreover, CEO pay is not closely tied to corporate performance; CEOs often get big raises even when their firms lose money.[33]

The distribution of wealth is even more unequal than the distribution of income. The top 1 percent earned 16.6 percent of total income in 1998, but they owned 38.1 percent of all wealth (the value of assets minus debts), averaging over $10.2 million. By contrast, the middle fifth of the population held a mere 4.5 percent of wealth, and those in the bottom fifth actually owed more than they owned. Although wealth inequality increased more slowly in the 1990s than it did in the 1980s, the trend is still toward greater inequality. In the 1990s, the top 1 percent of households grew in wealth by an average of over $1 million, the middle 20 percent of households grew only marginally (from $58,800 to $61,000), and the poorest one-fifth improved significantly but still finished the decade on average $8,900 in debt. The 1990s also witnessed an explosion in the number of very rich households, with the number of millionaires climbing by 54 percent between 1989 and 1998; the number of decamillionaires ($10 million or more in net worth) nearly quadrupled.[34]

Unlike the other periods of sustained economic expansion in the United States, the 1990s provided few, if any, benefits to those at the bottom early in the decade. Beginning in 1995, tight labor markets finally began to pull poor people into the wake of the speeding economy. After fifteen years of decline or stagnation, wages increased by 6.4 percent (adjusted for inflation) from 1995 to 1999. Beginning in 1997, the poverty rate finally began to fall, reaching 11.8 percent in 1999, the lowest rate since 1979.[35] Household income grew faster in cities than in suburbs from 1992 to 1998, and four-fifths of the 2.2 million households that moved out of poverty in 1999 lived in cities.[36]

The 1990s boom and tight labor markets had finally provided real benefits to those at the bottom of the economic ladder. But the national statistics exaggerate the progress in attacking poverty and inequality. Once again, place matters: the economic boom left many parts of the United States behind, and in prosperous regions, those at the bottom saw rising housing prices eat up their wage gains.

In 2000, the federal government classified one in eight cities as "doubly burdened," defined as having at least two of the following three conditions: an unemployment rate 50 percent higher than the national average, a poverty rate 20 percent or higher, and a population loss exceeding 5 percent since 1980. Although New York and Los Angeles are on this list, most are middle-sized cities located in the interior of the country, such as Dayton, Ohio, and Flint, Michigan.[37] As we shall see, central-city residents continue to lag behind suburban residents in jobs and income, although this trend bottomed out in the last decade. Within central cities, residents of disadvantaged neighborhoods bear substantial burdens, such as higher grocery prices and inferior schools, that do not show up in the income statistics.

The claim that the economic boom has reduced poverty also overlooks the fact that the federal government defines poverty in a way that severely underestimates the problem. This definition, devised back in the 1960s, assumes that the average family pays one-third of its income for food. The poverty formula takes the Department of Agriculture's minimum food budget for different-sized families and multiplies it by three. Since the 1960s, however, the cost of food has gone up much more slowly than other necessary expenditures, especially housing. This means that the poverty line is set too low, especially in booming regions. One study found that the actual cost of a "bare bones" budget in New York City was up to five times the poverty level for families with children.[38] Similarly, in the Los Angeles area, a two-parent family with two children needs to earn at least $44,700 simply to meet basic needs such as housing, food, child care, health care, and transportation. This is almost three times the official poverty line. If the poverty rate is revised to two times the official poverty threshold, then at least one out of four workers in Los Angeles County is poor.[39]

The cruel irony is that the economic boom has actually hurt low-income renters, especially in overheated, high-tech regions such as New York, Boston, and San Francisco. From 1997 to 1999, rents increased by 9.9 percent nationwide, compared with the general inflation rate of 6.1 percent. But rent increases were higher in cities than in suburbs.[40] Housing planners use the standard that households should pay no more than 30 percent of their income for rent and utilities. By 1999, 41 percent of renter households paid more than that, with nearly one in five paying more than half their incomes.[41] Nowhere in the country can a family with one full-time minimum-wage worker (earning $5.15 per hour) afford the cost of a two-bedroom apartment at the "fair-market rent." [42] In Marin, San Francisco, and San Mateo Counties in California, a worker would have to earn $28.06 per hour to afford the average apartment.[43]

So, when the economic boom of the late 1990s finally provided some lift for the incomes of households at the bottom, it did not decrease inequality. In fact, inequality increased throughout the 1990s. Worse, many families are stuck in stagnating regions or poverty-stricken neighborhoods, which handicaps their ability to advance economically. Those living in booming regions may find it easier to increase their incomes, but they usually have to spend these gains on rising housing, transportation, and other costs.

Conservative economists and commentators such as George Will and Thomas Sowell often pooh-pooh the inequality problem. They charge that the statistics on inequality exaggerate the problem, because a snapshot of in-equality at one point in time overlooks the fact that people earn different in-comes at different stages of their lives (young people always earn less).[44] Life-time earnings, therefore, are more equally distributed than are annual earnings. Indeed, if people were more mobile over their life spans, so that class inequali-ties were not so entrenched, then rising inequalities would be less worrisome. Significant mobility among classes would mean that the same people would not always be stuck in poverty or guaranteed wealth and privilege. The United States has a long tradition of offering penniless immigrants the chance to rise from rags to riches. We have always viewed ourselves as less class-bound than Europe.

The evidence shows, however, that increased mobility has not compensated for the pulling apart of the income and wealth distributions. A careful review of the research found that America is indeed a mobile society, with anywhere from 25 to 40 percent of the population moving out of an income quintile (the income scale divided into five groupings of 20 percent each) every year.[45] But because young people are earning less than their parents, mobility in the United States is no higher than that in other countries and shows no signs of increasing. Economic mobility, in fact, declined after the 1960s.[46] In the United States, the "escape rate" of poor people out of poverty is second worst among the coun-tries studied; only Canada is worse.[47] Rags-to-riches stories are rare. In short, America is becoming more of a class-bound society, and we cannot count on mobility to diminish the negative effects of rising inequality.

If we can therefore put aside the claims of some that rising inequality is exaggerated, what about those who say that although inequality may truly be rising, we do not need to worry about it? If the processes that create in-equality are fair to all participants, this argument goes, then the outcomes, however unequal, are also fair. Equal opportunity is what matters, not equal results. Free-market conservatives argue that present inequalities fairly reflect people's different abilities and work efforts. As two writers for the journal of the conservative American Enterprise Institute put it, "For the most part, upper-income American families do better than lower-income families because they toil harder."[48] In this view, income differences are justifiable if they are propor-tional to differences in hours worked and productivity. Some have even gone so far as to argue that economic success is largely determined by IQ.[49]

The argument that increasing inequality reflects differences in work effort or productivity does not stand up to scrutiny. To give but one example, the per-centage of the employable poor who worked increased from 64.8 to 70.3 percent between 1979 and 1998.[50] People at the bottom are not falling behind because they are working less; in fact, between 1979 and 1998, the average poor family increased its total annual working hours by 15.7 percent, to 1,112 hours.[51] Nor is it plausible to argue that the huge incomes flowing to corporate CEOs reflect disproportionately higher contributions to productivity. The average American is working longer hours and is more productive than ever, yet wage increases have not reflected this. Corporations are not sharing their productivity gains through proportionate wage increases. Corporate profits were at a forty-five-year high in 1996, but wages increased at less than half the pace typical of previous economic expansions. Commenting on this wage squeeze, *Business Week* warned, "The sight of bulging corporate coffers coexisting with a continuous stagnation in Americans' living standards could become politically untenable."[52] Moreover, as we will show later, rising economic segregation has undermined equal opportunity in the United States, making it more difficult for many poor people to achieve the American dream.

Finally, many people say that we should not care about the gap between the rich and the poor, but only about whether the poor are materially better off than they used to be. The availability of cheaper and better consumer goods, they argue, makes the poor better off than ever.[53] According to this view, if the American poor lived in a Third World country, they would be considered well-off, at least in terms of consumption. The problem, of course, is that they actually live in a society where almost everybody makes more than they do—and this makes a big difference. Rising inequality not only has negative material effects on the poor; it also eats away at social cohesion, the foundation of our democracy. The belief that "in the long run, we are all in the same boat" holds American society together. Rising inequality sends the message that we are in different boats and that, contrary to President Kennedy's famous statement, the rising tide will lift some and not others. When the most negative impacts of economic change are confined to the poor and near poor, the main political effect may be growing middle-class enmity or indifference toward these poor. When the negative effects spread to the working and middle classes, however, the potential exists for an unwinding of American democracy.

Political theorists from Aristotle to the present have argued that democracies cannot survive with large inequalities. Writing in the fourth century B.C., Aristotle warned: "[I]t is the duty of a genuine democrat to see to it that the masses are not excessively poor. Poverty is the cause of the defects of democracy."[54] A healthy democracy depends on a strong middle class, which functions as a moderating force between the potentially divisive demands of the rich and the poor. Fearing the inequalities generated by an urban industrial society, Thomas Jefferson reflected "that an equal distribution of property is impracticable but [because of] the consequences of enormous inequality producing so much misery to the bulk of mankind, legislators cannot invent too many devices for subdividing property." [55]

Politically, the problem is not so much the existence of poverty but the gap between the rich and the poor. This gap enables the rich to dominate (and potentially corrupt) the poor. The possibility of blatant class legislation unfairly favoring the rich becomes more likely. Rising inequality makes a mockery of the democratic principle of one person, one vote. The flood of billions of dollars into the 2000 presidential and congressional elections, driven by large contributions made possible in part by Wall Street's boom, demonstrates the corrupting potential of soaring inequality. Efforts to wall off the political system from the corroding effects of large contributions have been frustrated by the Supreme Court's ruling in *Buckley v. Valeo* (1976) equating campaign contributions with free speech. If the gap between the rich and the poor continues to widen, not even a carefully crafted constitutional amendment and laws constraining the influence of money on politics can save our political system from the corrupting effects of concentrated wealth.

American presidents from Jefferson to Jackson, from Teddy Roosevelt to Truman, have spoken out against that corrosive effect of economic inequality on democracy. As Franklin Roosevelt put it in his Third Inaugural Address (January 6, 1941): "There is nothing mysterious about the foundation of a healthy and strong democracy. The basic things expected by our people of their political system are simple. They are: equality of opportunity; jobs for all those who can work; security for those who need it; the ending of special privilege for the few." [56]

Place-Based Inequalities

Missing from the debate about rising inequality has been an understanding of the critical role of place. The Nobel Prize–winning economist Amartya Sen provides a broader way of understanding inequality. He argues that we should understand inequality not simply in terms of income or wealth but in terms of our ability to achieve the good life, by which he means being active members of society and realizing our full potential as human beings. According to Sen, "relevant functionings can vary from such elementary things as being adequately nourished, being in good health, avoiding escapable morbidity and premature mortality, etc., to more complex achievements such as being happy, having self-respect, taking part in the life of the community, and so on." [57] Sen adds that we must also be concerned about "capabilities," or our ability to choose different activities or functionings. For example, a starving person is very different from one who has chosen to go on a hunger strike. Other things being equal, people are better off if they have real choices in life.

Sen would be the first to admit that having money, or access to jobs, services, and credit, is essential to free choice and a high quality of life. But he argues that equality of income cannot be equated with true equality. A focus on income or wealth confuses the means to the good life with the good life itself. People's ability to convert income into the good life, Sen observes, varies tremendously. A person who suffers from severe kidney disease, for example, cannot enjoy the same quality of life as a perfectly healthy person with the same income, because of the daily monetary and emotional costs of dialysis. Thus, Sen argues, we cannot look at inequality simply in terms of income; we must take into account the actual situations and activities of people. Health, age, gender, race, education, and many other conditions besides income affect our ability to function effectively.

The thesis of this book is that where we live has a powerful effect on the choices we have and our capacity to achieve a high quality of life. Following Sen, we examine inequality in light of how place shapes and constrains our opportunities not only to acquire income and convert it into quality of life but also to become fully functioning members of the economy, society, and polity. As one example, the increasing devolution of public functions from the federal government to state and local governments means that geographical location has become more important in determining what we pay in taxes and what public goods and services we enjoy. The segregation of income groups into different local governments means that supposedly equal citizens have unequal access to public goods such as schools, parks, and clean air. In chapter 3, we show how the places we live also shape our access to jobs, retail goods and services, healthy environments, medical services, and safety (freedom from crime).

The national debate on rising income inequality has largely missed the spatial dimension of the problem. One exception has been the scholarly and media focus on the so-called underclass, often defined as areas with poverty rates of 40 percent or higher. The underclass is usually viewed as confined to minorities—blacks and Hispanics—but the number of whites living in areas of concentrated poverty grew by 145 percent between 1970 and 1990.[58] Underclass areas are usually characterized by a wide range of negative conditions, including high rates of unemployment, drug use, crime, teen pregnancies, out-of-wedlock births, single-parent families, and school dropouts. Because those at the bottom of the income distribution are increasingly forced to live in poor central-city neighborhoods, they face a more negative environment and greater obstacles to mobility than if they lived among better-off neighbors.

The publication of William Julius Wilson's seminal book *The Truly Disadvantaged* in 1987 kicked off a lively scholarly debate on the causes and consequences of concentrated urban poverty.[59] This debate has shed light on how place matters for poor people, but it also has serious defects. First, it is important to remember that most poor people do not live in neighborhoods characterized by concentrated poverty. In 1990, only 17.9 percent of all poor people (3.7 million out of 20.9 million) lived in census tracts where the poverty rate exceeded 40 percent.[60] Research on these areas has often exaggerated their problems and overlooked their strengths. Most people living in such areas are hardworking, law-abiding citizens. As Katherine Newman points out, most residents of even the worst neighborhoods studied by Wilson are working, looking for work, or going to school.[61] Only a small minority engages in criminal behavior.

The research on concentrated poverty has also suffered from tunnel vision. It focuses on one extreme — concentrated poverty neighborhoods — while ignoring the broader dynamics that distribute classes across places. By so doing, underclass research on the poor has unintentionally reinforced media stereotypes of low-income neighborhoods as basket cases whose problems stem from internal causes. Underclass neighborhoods are not distinct islands disconnected from the rest of society; their problems are closely connected to regional dynamics, in particular, the migration of upper-income households and jobs to exclusive outer-ring suburbs. The problems associated with the growing spatial concentration of poverty also beset many inner-ring suburbs. Many older suburbs are in worse shape fiscally and in other ways than their central cities. One study of 554 suburbs found that poverty increased in half of them, and real family income declined in a third of them, during the 1980s.[62]

The destructive factors associated with the underclass are not a world set apart from the rest of society. Problems such as single-parent families, drug use, and crime rose throughout metropolitan areas in the 1970s and 1980s. To be sure, the problems are worst in concentrated poverty areas, and the gap between "good" and "bad" neighborhoods has widened. But there was an across-the-board deterioration in many social indicators in the 1970s and 1980s. (In the 1990s, some of these social indicators, such as out-of-wedlock births and crime, improved.)[63] Areas of concentrated poverty, therefore, are merely the most pronounced and visible manifestations of problems that extend throughout society. To attribute them only to a local "subculture of poverty" in poor neighborhoods ignores the strengths of these neighborhoods and their connection to the broader society.[64] Although cities have serious problems, they also have great strengths and perform essential functions for society.

Conditions in outer-ring suburbs often appear ideal, but they are not. Wealthy outer-ring suburbs have different problems from inner-ring suburbs, central cities, and concentrated poverty neighborhoods, but they are related. In a sense, they are two sides of the same coin. The low rates of labor force participation in the South Bronx stem in part from the location of many entry-level jobs on the urban fringe, far from the inner city. In contrast, residents of outer-ring suburbs such as Naperville work long hours and commute long distances, leaving little time for family life and community responsibilities, partly because they want to live on the urban fringe far from urban problems. Their family stresses and lack of leisure time are related to the fact that an acceptable form of more urbanized living is not available to them. The environmental problems of outer suburbs and inner cities also stem from the same source. The polluted air and lack of green space in central cities may be abominable, but the flight of households to greener pastures on the urban fringe gobbles up farmland and spews additional automobile emissions into the air. In short, the problems of the different parts of metropolitan areas are interconnected; no part occupies the moral high ground. We can make progress only when the different parts of metropolitan areas work together.

Above all, discussions of concentrated poverty among researchers, public officials, and the news media have largely ignored the political causes and consequences of economic segregation. Scholars have carefully analyzed the relative contributions of economic factors, such as deindustrialization and foreign competition, and social factors, such as racial discrimination or countercultural values and underclass behaviors, to the growth of concentrated poverty. Neither side has said much, however, about how federal, state, and local policies produce and reproduce economic segregation. Nor have many researchers examined the profoundly negative effects of the geographical separation of income classes on city, state, and national politics. The growing political distance between central cities and the surrounding middle- and upper-class suburbs has made it increasingly difficult to assemble political support for policies designed to address rising inequality.

These place-based inequalities would be less worrisome if places, like people, experienced more mobility, with poor places becoming rich, and vice versa. According to market economics, economic inequalities between geographical areas should have a natural tendency to correct themselves. As an area becomes poor, land prices and wages should fall until they entice entrepreneurs to come back in and take advantage of the differentials. In 1968, Edward Banfield argued in *The Unheavenly City* that this "logic of metropolitan development" would induce "the well-off" to "move from the suburbs to the cities, causing editorial

writers to deplore the 'flight to the central city' and politicians to call for programs to check it by redeveloping the suburbs."[65] More than thirty years later,
we are still waiting.

The evidence suggests, to the contrary, that the United States is facing a
vicious circle of geographically rooted income inequalities. Over half a century ago, Gunnar Myrdal's magisterial study of race relations, *An American Dilemma,* developed the theory of "cumulative causation."[66] According to Myrdal,
racial segregation nurtures the qualities in blacks that lead whites to discriminate against them, fueling more segregation. The idea of cumulative causation,
or a vicious circle, applies to place-based inequalities in the United States today.
Increasing economic inequality leads to a greater concentration of poverty in
certain neighborhoods, which in turn undermines the efforts of the residents
to escape from poverty. The geographic concentration of the wealthy has the
opposite effect, encasing residents in a privileged environment, especially with
respect to local public education. Not only do children in rich school districts
get a better education; they also make contacts (through internships, jobs, and
college admission connections) that help them to succeed.

Democracies do not require perfect equality, but they do require that economic inequalities not invade and corrupt politics, or vice versa. Economic
inequality should not mean that some people automatically have more political influence than others. Nor should people be able to use political power
to gain privileged access to economic wealth. Political philosopher Michael
Walzer calls this the "art of separation."[67] Today, growing spatial segregation
means that economic, political, and social inequalities are piling on top of one
another. As rich people gather in privileged places, they enhance their political power and social prestige. Poor and working people are stuck in places that
society looks down on and that lack political clout. The well-off can enact policies whose negative consequences are borne primarily by geographically concentrated poor people who live distant from them. The development of "separate societies" for rich and poor not only directly increases income inequality by
affecting access to jobs and education; it also generates dangerous stereotypes
and tilts the political terrain.[68]

Cities as Engines of Prosperity

Because we emphasize the concentration of poverty in cities, readers may
get the impression that cities are basket cases—like sick people with so few
resources that they only serve to burden society. Nothing could be further
from the truth. In fact, cities are economic dynamos that provide extraordinary benefits to society as a whole. Cities are both reservations for the poor

(with all the burdens that entails) and centers of economic productivity and innovation. The contradictory nature of American cities is reflected in the fact that most cities have daytime working populations that are significantly higher than their nighttime residential populations. They export income to the suburbs. Ultimately, we argue, the residential concentration of poverty at the core undermines the entire regional economy's economic efficiency and ability to innovate. Greater regional cooperation, aimed at less economic segregation and sprawl, would benefit the entire society.

Over the last half century, suburbanization, deindustrialization, and the rise of new cities in the South and West have dramatically transformed the older cities of the Northeast and Midwest. In the process, metropolitan areas became far larger, encompassing four-fifths of the nation's population, but central cities became less dominant within them. A few old cities lost half their populations, and others remained roughly the same size but lost population relative to the surrounding suburbs. Some new cities such as Phoenix and San Diego, mainly in the Sun Belt, grew dramatically. Even in these new cities, however, much of the growth took place on the periphery, leading some observers to claim that cities are now "obsolete." In their eyes, the "old" industrial economy required dense cities with many factories and much face-to-face contact, whereas the "new" information economy is more comfortable in the suburbs, where computers, the Internet, and cell phones have made the dense face-to-face interactions of the older cities unnecessary.

This view profoundly misreads the key functions that most central cities continue to play in our national economy. Regional economies are integrated wholes, with different parts of the metropolitan area specializing in different economic functions. For routine goods production and distribution activities and even many corporate headquarters, suburban locations may be economically preferable; however, older central cities continue to provide large pools of private assets, accumulated knowledge, sophisticated skills, cultural resources, and social networks. Cities house most of the leading global, national, and regional corporate services firms, such as banks, law firms, and management consultants. They are still centers of innovation, skill, fashion, and market exchange.

Urban density enhances economic efficiency and innovation. What economists call "agglomeration economies" are still important in the global economy. The density of employment in cities reduces the costs of transportation and increases each business's access to skilled and specialized labor. The geographical clustering of industries in certain cities further enhances productivity. In many industries, understanding ambiguous information is the key to innovation. It cannot be communicated in an e-mail message or even a phone call; it requires the kind of face-to-face interaction that cities are good at fostering. The cultural production of these cities has been just as important as their economic role.

Some maintain that American central cities are making dramatic comebacks on their own.[69] Harvard Business School professor Michael Porter argues that inner cities have a "competitive advantage" and will prosper if city governments simply step out of the way and promote a favorable business climate.[70] What this view ignores is that the economic dynamism of cities persists alongside substantial poverty, social exclusion, and growing inequality. Indeed, the persistent vitality of many central cities has generated the vast disparities of wealth and poverty that are sometimes located only a few zip codes from each other. As we will show in chapter 3, concentrated poverty presents substantial barriers to market success. It is not simply a matter, as Porter implies, of government helping private-sector investors make the best of their opportunities. Moreover, as we demonstrate in chapter 5, cities cannot capture much of the wealth generated within their borders for use in reducing concentrated poverty. As productive investments have become more mobile, even large, prosperous cities have cut back on spending for the poor. Between 1970 and 1990, New York City, with a long tradition of helping the poor, cut its per capita expenditures on the poor from $537 to $285 (constant 1987 dollars).[71]

News coverage of our cities reinforces the tendency among Americans to associate "urban problems" such as crime and homelessness with cities. Images on the nightly TV news, the covers of newsweeklies, and the front pages of our daily newspapers present an unrelenting story of mounting crime, gangs, drug wars, racial tension, homelessness, teenage pregnancy, AIDS, school dropouts, and slum housing. They typically portray government programs to combat these problems as well-intentioned but misguided failures, plagued by mismanagement, inefficiency, and, in some cases, corruption. This drumbeat of negativism wrongly leads many Americans to conclude that urban problems are intractable.

Coverage of urban crime is a good example. The public's beliefs about crime are based primarily on what they see in the media, not on personal experience. This is particularly important for how suburbanites view the condition of nearby central cities. The media bombard their audiences with news about crime, especially violent crime. The phrase "if it bleeds, it leads" characterizes the disproportionate attention paid to crime, particularly on local television news. One study of news programming in fifty-six U.S. cities found that violent crime accounted for two-thirds of all local news.[72] This coverage typically has little to do with actual crime rates. Moreover, it overrepresents minorities as violent criminals.[73]

Despite the sensationalism, our cities and metropolitan areas do reflect widening national disparities in income and wealth, racial and economic segregation, and the fraying of the social safety net. But cities are only the site in which such problems arise, not their cause. It was not inevitable that these problems would manifest themselves mostly in central cities; as we will describe in some detail, these problems result from choices about our tax code, our housing policies, our transportation practices, our economic development programs, even our military spending priorities. Cities in Canada, Western Europe, and Australia do not have nearly the same levels of poverty, slums, economic segregation, city-suburb disparities, or even suburban sprawl as does the United States. The question is not whether we can ever solve urban problems but whether we can develop the political will to adopt solutions that can work.

THE PLAN OF THE BOOK

The chapters that follow are stages in developing this argument. We begin by documenting the problem of economic segregation and then go on to examine its causes in government policies that shape and reinforce market forces. We show that cities and regions cannot solve the problem by themselves as long as the playing field is tilted by federal and state policies. We end the book by proposing changes in the rules of the game and in the political strategies for implementing them. Throughout, we compare the United States with other developed countries to highlight the distinctive features of the American case.

Documenting the Problem

Chapter 2 establishes the factual premise of the book: that economic segregation is increasing both between and within regions. Not only are the rich living apart from the poor, but the distances are greater than ever as the mobile middle and upper classes flee to the edges of metropolitan areas, partly to escape deteriorating conditions in central cities and inner-ring suburbs. Chapter 3 documents the costs of economic segregation and sprawl. The contexts within which people live have important effects independent of the characteristics of the individuals who live there. The contextual effects examined in chapter 3 include jobs and income, health, consumer goods, and safety (crime). (The effect of economic segregation on access to public goods and services is covered in chapter 5.) One of the themes of the chapter is that although most of the costs of economic segregation fall on the poor, even the rich who live on the outskirts of metropolitan areas bear substantial costs caused by economic segregation and excessive sprawl.

Identifying the Sources of the Problem

Chapter 4 challenges the view that economic segregation and sprawl are simply the products of free markets. It shows that federal and state governments could have chosen different policies that would have encouraged less segregated and more compact metropolitan development patterns. Instead, government policies encouraged spatial inequalities and low-density suburban development. Chapters 5 and 6 examine the largely failed efforts to address the problems within the current rules of the game. Chapter 5 examines how central cities have tried to revitalize themselves and cope with the costs of economic segregation. Liberal, conservative, and progressive mayors have used different strategies for reversing deterioration and coping with fiscal stress. Without help from state and federal governments, however, these efforts have come up against the limits of localism. Chapter 6 documents halting efforts at regional cooperation, efforts that have been straitjacketed by the present rules of the game. There has been a revival of interest in regional cooperation in recent years, and many valuable experiments are under way in metropolitan areas such as Portland and Minneapolis–St. Paul. The new regionalism has had some success in promoting more efficient and environmentally sound development, but it has had less success addressing the problem of economic segregation and poverty.

Changing the Rules of the Game

Chapter 7 outlines the policies needed to level the playing field so that metropolitan areas can halt and even reverse the trend toward greater spatial inequalities. We support policies that improve the lot of the poor and working class, but we argue that federal and state policies must also directly address metropolitan inequalities. We advocate a range of reforms, including federal programs rewarding regions that cooperate on land-use planning, reduce the bidding wars between localities by subjecting local subsidies to federal taxation, supplement place-based community development efforts with mobility programs, and set up elected metropolitan councils through which each region can devise democratic and workable solutions to regional problems.

Chapter 8 addresses the difficult question of how a political coalition can be assembled to support metropolitan reform with equity. We argue that these coalitions must be formed "across city lines" in ways that unite central-city and suburban voters. For decades, politicians have successfully used "wedge" issues such as affirmative action and welfare to split suburbanites from central-city voters. But the suburbs are no longer lily-white and prosperous. The increasing racial and economic diversity of suburbia and the strains on inner-ring suburbs make it more difficult to pit suburbs against central cities. The tentative success of Bill Clinton in forging city-suburban coalitions can be a harbinger of a metropolitics for the twenty-first century. We argue that even outer-ring suburban voters ultimately have an interest in more equitable regional policies. Smart growth policies are the best way to address the congestion, pollution, and loss of green space that threaten even prosperous suburbs. Finally, we maintain that public opinion can be mobilized around the moral force of regional equity. A new metropolitics for the twenty-first century can break down the walls that divide us and achieve equal opportunity for all Americans, no matter where they live.

 The Facts of
Economic Segregation
and Sprawl

East of Seattle, across beautiful Lake Washington, lies the gated community of
Bear Creek. An exclusive community with home prices ranging from $300,000
to $600,000 in 1995, Bear Creek is a crime-free haven where salmon swim in
the local stream. Its 500 residents like it that way and preserve it with detailed
rules regulating house colors (nothing stronger than beige or gray), shrubbery
heights, and basketball hoops (prohibited). Four private security guards staff
the entrance gates twenty-four hours a day. The residents of Bear Creek enjoy their environmental amenities (paid for with steep fees) without sharing
them with the public because they own everything, even the streets and sewers.
Bear Creek's citizens like their private government and are not inclined to tax
themselves to help solve Seattle's problems. As one resident put it: "The citizens have moved ahead of government. The government has not kept up with
what people want."[1]

Bear Creek is not exceptional. Throughout American history, wealthy, high-
status families have developed exclusive enclaves, such as Scarsdale north of
New York City or Beverly Hills next to Los Angeles, to separate themselves from
the rest of society. Upper classes everywhere try to maintain social distance
from the "common people." Geography is one way to do so. Many people can
scrimp and save to afford a Mercedes or a $1,000 suit, but only a few can afford
to live in the most exclusive neighborhoods. In a society that eschews aristo-
cratic trappings, one shows that one has "made it" by moving into an exclusive
neighborhood. Indeed, a 1994 poll found that 60 percent of those making more
than $400,000 a year felt that it was important to live in an exclusive neighbor-
hood.[2]

The separation of the rich from the poor is a long-standing tradition in American society. Claiming to be a classless society, the United States is in fact acutely class conscious. Moving up the economic ladder has also meant moving away from the dust, grime, immigrants, and poor people crowded into the cities to high-status, sylvan suburbs. Geographical avoidance behavior does not apply only to the rich. More recent escapees from relative poverty, the working and lower middle classes, are especially anxious to put social (and physical) distance between themselves and the poor.

The right to distance oneself from others is upheld by private property and free markets. Where one lives is determined by a bidding process: the rich can bid on just about any location, while the poor are restricted to the few locations they can afford. (The homeless cannot even afford to participate in the auction.) In early-nineteenth-century cities, prior to the invention of the trolley and the automobile, the rich and poor were forced to live quite close to one another because everyone had to walk or ride a carriage or horse to work. (The rich often lived on the avenues and the poor on the side streets, a pattern still evident in cities such as New Orleans.) Technological improvements in transportation, from streetcars and subways to automobiles and freeways, have enabled people to live farther from where they work and, thus, to put more distance between themselves and people they consider inferior.

Economic segregation is not motivated just by status concerns; there are all sorts of other advantages to living in exclusive areas. Homes in wealthy neighborhoods appreciate more in price, and the schools are usually better. Wealthy neighborhoods often have cleaner air, lower property tax rates, and superior public services. Living in a homogeneously upper-class neighborhood eases social intercourse and makes for tighter communities. People generally prefer to live with others like themselves. The rich and poor will never live cheek to jowl. And the right to live where one wants to, subject to the limits of affordability, is a right that every American takes for granted.

Americans do not want the government to tell them where to live or to take away the right to move if they do not like their neighbors. The authors of this book are no exception. Our policy recommendations do not interfere with the right of Americans to live wherever they choose; instead, we seek to fulfill that right. The problem with our present residential housing markets is that they are neither free nor fair. As we show in chapter 3, economic segregation and sprawl produce extensive negative effects that cannot simply be viewed as by-products of free-market choices. Chapter 4 shows how government policies powerfully influenced the location of urban housing and jobs and accentuated economic segregation and suburban sprawl.

In this chapter, we focus on one simple question: what are the trends in the spatial separation of the classes? Economic segregation has been much less studied than racial segregation, partly because racial segregation is considered illegal and immoral, whereas economic segregation is not. Many different approaches can be taken to study economic segregation, and we use measures that were first developed to study racial segregation.[3] But economic segregation is different from racial segregation, because economic classes are in flux, and economic differences cannot be captured by racial categories. Economic class is a continuum from rich to poor. Because the Census Bureau defines a poverty level, we can study the degree to which the poor are segregated from the rest of the society (this is how most of the research on economic segregation has been done). But this captures only a small part of economic segregation. No one has agreed on a definition of "rich" or "middle class." Moreover, economic segregation occurs across the spectrum, with the working class separating from the poor, the upper middle class separating from the working class, and so on. Results also vary by the size of the geographical unit being considered: do we want to know if different economic classes live on the same block, or in the same neighborhood, city, or region? The following discussion starts by comparing regions, then looks at cities and suburbs, and finally considers economic segregation at the neighborhood level.

No matter what method or scale is used, however, research shows that economic segregation has increased since the 1970s. Sometime in that decade, something happened in the United States to drive different economic classes away from each other spatially, reversing the earlier trend of slow declines in economic segregation. The country has not been the same since.

INEQUALITY AMONG REGIONS

Whether listening to the radio, watching television, or reading the newspaper, we are bombarded with statistics on the national inflation rate, the growth rate, or the consumer confidence index. We have gotten so used to speaking of a national economy that we have almost forgotten that it is largely a fiction, because political boundaries are arbitrary. As Jane Jacobs observed, "Once we . . . try looking at the real economic world in its own right rather than as a dependent artifact of politics, we can't avoid seeing that most nations are composed of collections or grab bags of very different economies, rich regions and poor ones within the same nation."[4] Macroeconomic statistics hide tremendous variation. (A person can drown in a lake with an average depth of only one inch.) In 1999, for instance, commentators touted the lowest national unemployment rate in thirty years (4.2 percent), yet many cities had unemployment rates that were four times higher.

William Barnes and Larry Ledebur fault the "one-size-fits-all, 'rising tide lifts all boats,' nationalist economic framework" because it obscures the true nature of the economy. The American economy should be understood, they say, as a "common market of regional economies."[5] Each region has one or more urban centers surrounded by an outlying area that has job-commuting ties to the center. The Bureau of Economic Research has identified 172 economic areas in the United States with relatively unified labor and housing markets. Wages and house prices tend to track each other within each region. These regions are the real building blocks of the American economy. The United States competes in the global economy not so much as a nation but as a collection of regions with different levels of productive efficiency and abilities to innovate.[6] The metropolitan regions of the United States vary tremendously in economic prosperity and quality of life.

For the most part, inequality among regions has been viewed, like the weather, as a fact of life. Ironically, only during the administration of Republican Richard Nixon did the country flirt briefly with a national regional growth policy. In his 1970 State of the Union Message, President Nixon asserted:

> For the past 30 years our population has . . . been growing and shifting. The result is exemplified in the vast areas of rural America emptying out of people and of promise. . . . The violent and decayed central cities of our great metropolitan complexes are the most conspicuous failure in American life today. I propose that before these problems become insoluble, the Nation develop a national growth policy. . . . If we seize our growth as a challenge, we can make the 1970s an historic period when by conscious choice we transformed our land into what we want it to become.[7]

The main issue at the time was the emptying out of small towns and rural areas. Nixon's attempt to get the federal government more involved in planning where people live was attacked as centralized planning and zoning and, following the Watergate scandal, was killed in Congress.

Today, Nixon's support of national land-use policy sounds radical. Since Nixon, conservatives have attacked national land-use planning as an unwarranted interference in the marketplace. According to the free-market argument, inequalities between regions will tend to correct themselves over time. Booming regions, for example, will bid up wages, prompting investors to switch to lower-wage regions. In other words, free markets have a natural tendency toward balance, or equilibrium.

Through most of the twentieth century, trends supported this theory. At least since the Civil War, the South had been a backward region with a disproportionate share of the nation's poverty. But after the Great Depression of the 1930s, the South began to catch up to the rest of the country. Contrary to market theory, however, this had less to do with free markets and more to do with the federal government's infrastructure investments, such as highways, dams, and military spending in the South and West. In defending its decision to cut federal funding for needy regions, the Reagan administration's 1982 *National Urban Policy Report* observed with satisfaction that the gap in per capita income among regions had fallen dramatically between 1930 and 1977.[8]

The convergence of income trends across the different regions of the United States stopped sometime in the 1970s, and the gap is now widening again. Inequality among regions in the United States fell continuously up to 1975, reflecting primarily the rise to parity of the previously poor southern regions. Beginning in the 1980s, however, regional incomes began to diverge.[9] In general, during the past two decades, the richest states did better, and the poorest states began to fall further behind. The trend is similar whether one examines data for individual metropolitan areas or groups them into broad regions.

Although interregional inequalities remain smaller than they were earlier in the twentieth century, their reemergence is disturbing to those who care about equal opportunity. According to the census, median household incomes in 1989 varied by more than 100 percent across the seventy-eight largest metropolitan areas, from $24,442 in New Orleans to $49,891 in the Bridgeport-Stamford-Norwalk-Danbury, Connecticut, metropolitan area.[10] Secretaries living in San Francisco earned 46 percent more than their counterparts in Baton Rouge ($25,735 versus $17,577).[11] Although the cost of living also varied across these cities, it did not come close to wiping out the wage differentials. (The New York region stands out as an exception because it was 225 percent more expensive than average, primarily due to high housing prices.)[12]

The rising inequality among regions is partly a reflection of the bicoastal phenomenon: cities on the two coasts did better economically in the 1990s than cities in the interior. The coastal-interior gap is rapidly replacing the North-South gap as the primary regional divide. Between 1979 and 1989, median household incomes increased 40 percent in Boston but declined 20 percent in Detroit. Even after factoring in differences in the cost of living, a wide gap remained, with Boston up 33 percent and Detroit down 12 percent.[13]

Economic restructuring has produced significantly different proportions of low-wage jobs across metropolitan regions. Corporate service economies specializing in advanced producer services, such as law, finance, and accounting (Boston, San Francisco), do better than those areas that rely on manufacturing (Detroit, Milwaukee). Between 1970 and 1990, only 35.5 percent of the new jobs created in the Boston metropolitan area paid less than $20,000 (in constant 1990 dollars), compared with 77.4 percent in Milwaukee and 72.7 percent in metropolitan Detroit. At the top end, about one-quarter of the net new jobs in the Boston area paid more than $40,000, compared with only about 9 percent in Detroit and Milwaukee.[14] Place matters: a person with the same education, experience, and skills will earn a very different income depending on where he or she lives.

Regions that develop clusters of firms in cutting-edge industries also acquire an edge in the competition for economic growth. Clustering creates an economic dynamism because these firms, although competing in some ways, can also draw on a specialized labor force and share information on the best techniques and the latest innovations. A few years ago, DRI/McGraw-Hill identified 380 specialized geographical clusters that drive the U.S. economy.[15] New York City specializes in law, finance, and now the new media such as computerized graphics and Web pages (Silicon Alley); Minneapolis has Medical Alley, a center of innovation in medical instruments; Los Angeles is the worldwide center of the film industry; Portland, Oregon, has an innovative cluster in semiconductors; California's Silicon Valley and Boston's Route 128 are centers of the computer industry. The economic efficiency and innovation nurtured by clustering create what we call "sticky capital." Investors in many industries do not search for the cheapest site for production but for the richest soil in which to grow their firms, even if it is more expensive. Because regions that reach a critical mass in an industry take off, clustering compounds inequalities among regions.

Quality-of-life differences, such as clean air, a pleasant climate, excellent parks, and cultural attractions, also influence regional growth patterns.[16] Immigration appears to be another important factor. The Los Angeles and New York regions, whose economies grew strongly in the 1990s, also served as ports of entry for immigrants, with an astounding 1.9 million immigrants moving to those areas between 1990 and 1996.[17] Immigrants provide both skilled and unskilled labor and help link cities to the global economy. Hispanic immigration, for example, boosted Miami's economy by helping it become a major entrepôt for imports from and exports to Latin America.

Inequality among regions also affects inequality *within* regions. Other things being equal, prosperous regions can reduce their internal inequality by drawing previously unemployed workers into the labor market. Cities with rising average incomes, prosperous service-based economies, and tight labor markets enjoy declines in ghetto poverty.[18] The causal relationship also works in the other direction: growing inequality within a region hurts its regional economic performance. Regions with large spatial inequalities perform less well. Ledebur and Barnes found that metropolitan areas with higher central city–suburban income disparities had lower metropolitan employment growth between 1988 and 1991. Hank Savitch and colleagues found that per capita income in fifty-nine central cities was highly correlated (.59) with that of their suburbs, suggesting that central-city and suburban economic outcomes rise or fall together.[19] Inequality within a region may hurt regional growth if the burden of poverty deprives the central city of the resources it needs to invest in infrastructure. Seeking to avoid this burden, investors are forced to choose less convenient locations (or move out of the region), undermining regional efficiency and growth.[20] As employment disperses into suburban settings with lower job densities, the result can be lower productivity, because productivity is positively correlated with job density.[21]

In short, inequality among regions is increasing in the United States as the rich regions prosper and the poor regions fall behind. This troubling fact alone calls for new national policies. Regional divisions have torn apart many nations around the world. Although interstate wage differences are only a small cause of rising overall income inequality, it is important to address such differences.[22] If Mississippi eliminated all spending inequalities among the school districts in the state, its students would still receive inferior educations compared with those in other states that can spend more on education. Adjusted for cost-of-living differences, per pupil spending in 1997–98 varied from $4,000 in Mississippi to over $9,000 in New Jersey.[23] The larger inequalities, however, are within regions, not between them. As many analysts have observed, Third World conditions prevail in many urban American neighborhoods, even in the most prosperous metropolitan areas.

ECONOMIC SEGREGATION BETWEEN CITIES AND SUBURBS

In most advanced industrial countries, average income falls as one moves outward from the city center. Government planning ensured that this would be the case. Baron Haussmann's massive urban renewal of Paris in the 1850s cut wide, straight boulevards through the maze of narrow streets, partly to make it easier for the army to enter Paris to put down uprisings. In the process, Haussmann displaced thousands of low-income residents and replaced their crowded quarters with luxurious apartments lining the grand Parisian boulevards. A government-sponsored mortgage bank provided capital for building luxury apartment houses in central Paris. (The government still subsidizes central Paris as a place for the rich to live.)[24] In the late 1860s, Vienna followed suit with its Ringstrasse development, sponsoring luxury apartment houses that imitated Baroque palaces in the center of the city. The pattern spread from Paris and Vienna throughout central and eastern Europe and eventually to South America.

The opposite pattern holds in the United States: household incomes rise as one moves outward from the city center to inner-ring to outer-ring suburbs (see Table 2.1). In the Kansas City metropolitan area, for example, average home prices rise steadily as one moves outward, peaking in a ring fourteen to sixteen miles from downtown.[25] The tendency for the rich to live on the outskirts of American metropolitan areas and the poor to live near the center results primarily from the peculiar way that the United States has chosen to meet people's housing needs. (Chapter 4 shows how government policies heavily subsidized this system.) Middle- and upper-class households satisfy their housing needs not by rehabilitating older housing near the city center but by buying new housing on the urban periphery. Oliver Byrum, former director of city planning for Minneapolis, calls the American practice of housing the poor in deteriorating housing near the city center a "de facto national housing policy."[26] The practice was so well established by the 1920s that it served as the basis of the "concentric zone theory" of urban development, which projected a uniform pattern of development in which the working, middle, and upper classes lived separately in concentric rings moving progressively out from the city center.[27]

Another peculiar aspect of the American pattern is that one government runs the center of the metropolitan area, while many different suburban jurisdictions govern the wealthier periphery. Until the twentieth century, most central-city governments annexed adjacent territory as it was developed. Gradually, however, state legislatures passed incorporation laws enabling suburbanites to establish separate governments and avoid annexation by cities. By 1930, every state legislature had adopted such incorporation laws.[28] As a result, governance of every major metropolitan region is split between one or more central-city governments and many suburban governments (Table 2.2). Indeed, the 315 metropolitan areas in the United States in 1992 had an average of 104 general-purpose governments (not counting school districts and special authorities).[29] In *Cities Without Suburbs*, David Rusk explores the differences between "elas-

TABLE 2.1. Median Family Income, 1979–1989, in Distressed (Inner Ring) and Exclusive (Outer Ring) Suburbs in Three Metropolitan Areas (Constant 1982–1984 Dollars Adjusted by Consumer Price Index, All Cities)

Metro Area	Suburb	1979 Median Family Income	1989 Median Family Income	Percent Change 1979–1989
Kansas City inner	Independence	$30,376	$27,427	−9.7
	Raytown	$34,263	$30,479	−11.0
Kansas City outer	Leawood	$56,760	$63,904	12.5
	Overland Park	$40,220	$43,719	8.7
Detroit inner	Roseville	$31,918	$30,255	−5.2
	Hazel Park	$26,852	$24,882	−7.3
Detroit outer	Birmingham	$46,787	$56,894	21.6
	Troy	$47,096	$50,957	8.2
Minneapolis–St. Paul inner	Brooklyn Center	$34,341	$31,305	−8.8
	New Hope	$40,345	$36,149	−10.4
Minneapolis–St. Paul outer	Apple Valley	$39,854	$43,259	8.5
	Eden Prairie	$42,687	$47,969	12.4

Source: U.S. Bureau of the Census, *Census of Population and Housing*, 1980 and 1990, and consumer price index as reported in *Statistical Abstract of the United States*, various years.

tic" cities, which expanded to encompass their metropolitan populations, and "inelastic" cities, which did not.[30] In 1990, the central-city proportion of metropolitan area population varied from 15 percent in Atlanta to 80 percent in Albuquerque to 100 percent in Anchorage.[31]

Keeping in mind that the dividing line between the central cities and their suburbs is an accident of history and politics, we can trace the extent to which different economic classes have become concentrated in central cities or suburbs. Figure 2.1 shows that the gap between per capita income in the cities and suburbs in the eighty-five largest metropolitan areas grew continuously wider between 1960 and 1999. (Although we must await the 2000 census for definitive numbers, it appears that central cities gained slightly on their suburbs during the last decade.) Another study of 147 central cities found that median family income declined in 88 percent of them relative to their suburbs between 1960 and 1990.[32] Between 1970 and 1993, the urban poverty rate rose by half, from 14.2 to 21.5 percent, declining to 16.4 percent in 1999. During the same period, the suburban poverty rate rose a bit less, from 7.1 to 10.3 percent, falling back down to 8.3 percent by 1999.[33] These gaps between central cities and suburbs

TABLE 2.2. Governments in the Fifteen Largest Metropolitan Areas (Primary Metropolitan Statistical Areas, 1997)

Metropolitan Area	Governments	Governments/ 100,000 Residents	General Purpose Governments/ 100,000 Residents
Anaheim	147	6.1	1.3
Atlanta	261	8.8	4.3
Boston	1,000	17.9	7.0
Chicago	1,458	19.7	6.3
Dallas	326	12.2	5.8
Detroit	378	8.9	5.1
Houston	790	23.8	2.6
Los Angeles–Long Beach	354	4.0	1.0
Minneapolis–St. Paul	549	21.6	13.5
New York	213	2.5	1.0
Philadelphia	877	17.8	7.4
Riverside–San Bernardino	309	11.9	1.9
San Diego	181	7.2	0.8
St. Louis	789	31.7	12.5
Washington, D.C.	169	4.0	2.7
Average	520	11.9	4.4

Source: Alan Altshuler, William Morrill, Harold Wolman, and Faith Mitchell, eds., *Governance and Opportunity in Metropolitan America* (Washington, D.C.: National Academy Press, 1999), p. 23.

Note: Boston figures refer to Boston's New England Consolidated Metropolitan Area.

were created both by the downward mobility of existing city residents and by the out-migration of the better off.[34]

Notwithstanding talk of gentrification, the middle class, particularly parents with children, is still fleeing most central cities. Only a few cities improved the class composition of their in-migrants, and these improvements did not increase their median incomes.[35] During the 1980s, the suburban population grew 16.1 percent, triple the figure for central cities. Central-city populations declined in the Northeast and Midwest. In the 1990s, many central cities began to gain population again, after decades of continuous losses. After losing 20.7 percent of its population between 1970 and 1990, the city of Atlanta gained 5.7 percent from 1990 to 2000.[36] Figure 2.1 suggests that central-city average per capita income has also begun to gain ground on that of the suburbs, partly because central-city economies performed well during the economic expansion of this period, but also because poverty is becoming more prevalent in the inner suburbs.

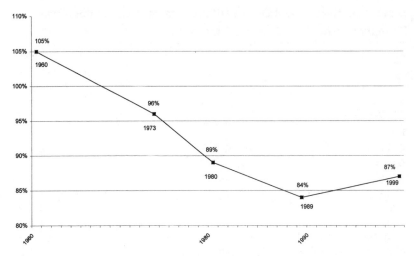

FIGURE 2.1. **Ratio of Central City–Suburban per Capita Income, 1960–1999**

Source: Larry C. Ledebur and William R. Barnes, "City Distress, Metropolitan Disparities, and Metropolitan Growth," comb. rev. ed., Research Report of the National League of Cities (Washington, D.C.: National League of Cities, September 1992), p. 2, and authors' calculation for 1999 from March 2000 Current Population Survey, not strictly comparable.

Cities became poorer relative to suburbs between 1960 and 1990, partly because two-parent households moved to the suburbs while single-parent, female-headed households stayed behind.[37] Even without this selective migration, however, the income gap between cities and suburbs would have grown, because more new jobs, especially entry-level jobs, were located in the suburbs. Manufacturing has continued to decline in central cities, and routine back-office service functions, as well as retail jobs, continue to relocate to suburbs.

The widening gap between cities and their suburbs imposes fiscal stress on central-city governments, which in turn causes taxpayer flight. David Rusk speculates that when city per capita income falls below 70 percent of the suburban average, the region reaches a "point of no return." "At this point," Rusk says, "economic disparities become so severe that the city, in a broad sense, no longer is a place to invest or create jobs (except in some fortress-type downtowns)."[38] Although there is nothing magical about the 70 percent cutoff, the twelve cities that reached this point in 1980 all suffered heavy population losses and fell further behind the suburbs by 1990. We must ask ourselves, at what point in the vicious circle of decline will society be forced to act?

ECONOMIC SEGREGATION AMONG SUBURBS

The positive stereotypes of suburbia have not caught up with the changing realities. Whether suburbia is viewed positively or negatively, the media portray it as uniformly white and middle class. At times, the stereotype depicts middle-class white suburbs as boring and bland, like homogenized milk. A few years ago, in the film *The Truman Show,* Jim Carrey played an insurance agent whose life was continuously filmed and broadcast to the world. He lived in a painfully perfect made-for-television suburb called Sea Haven, with others seemingly just like himself.

In fact, suburbs today are remarkably diverse, both racially and economically. The difference between cities and suburbs is that cities have considerable population diversity within them, whereas suburban economic diversity is mostly *between* suburbs, not within them. Every metropolitan area in the country has distressed, often inner-ring, suburbs that house working-class or even poor families and others that house the rich, usually on the suburban periphery. And the gap between the rich and the poor suburbs is widening. Table 2.2 shows distressed and exclusive suburbs in three metropolitan areas. Residents of distressed suburbs have more in common with their central cities than they do with the stereotypical middle-class suburbs. One of the most extreme examples of a distressed suburb is Harvey, Illinois, outside Chicago. Harvey's tax base is so depleted that the owner of a $100,000 house has to pay $5,000 in property taxes, three times what home owners in a nearby wealthy suburb pay.[39]

Ironically, many families who flee central cities to escape urban deterioration end up in suburbs that are *worse off* than the cities they fled. A nationwide study of 554 suburbs found the popular image of suburban prosperity to be a myth. Using a suburb's median family income compared with the regional median as a measure of prosperity, William Lucy and David Phillips found that 20 percent of the suburbs declined faster than their central cities between 1960 and 1990. The process of suburban decline speeded up after 1980, when almost one-third of the suburbs fared worse than their central cities. Between 1980 and 1990, over half (57 percent) of the suburbs lost population. Based on these trends, the authors call the period after 1980 the "post-suburban era," or the era of suburban decline.

This trend continued in the 1990s. Table 2.3 shows that, in the aggregate, the number of poor people living within metropolitan areas but outside the central cities held steady during this decade, even as the number of central-city poor declined by 14.3 percent. (The poverty population also dropped in non-metropolitan areas.) In a relative sense, poverty became more suburban.

TABLE 2.3. Poverty and Median Family Income, 1991–1999 (All Metropolitan Statistical Areas [MSAs])

	Central City	Balance of MSA	Non-MSA	Total
Poor persons 1991 (000)	15,314	11,513	8,881	35,708
Poor persons 1999 (000)	13,123	11,693	7,742	35,258
Percent change 1991–1999	−14.3	1.6	−12.8	−1.3
Total persons 1991 (000)	75,812	120,081	55,299	251,192
Total persons 1999 (000)	80,018	139,334	54,140	273,492
Percent change 1991–1999	5.5	16.0	−2.0	8.9
Poverty rate 1991	20.2	9.6	16.1	14.2
Poverty rate 1999	16.4	8.3	14.3	11.8
Median family income 1990	$32,546	$45,054	$29,554	$37,000
Median family income 1998	$43,918	$60,033	$40,724	$50,200
Percent change 1990–1998	34.9	33.2	37.8	35.7

Source: U.S. Bureau of the Census, Historical Poverty Tables, Table 8; 1991 and 1999 Current Population Surveys analyzed by authors; Metropolitan Area Population Estimates for July 1, 1999, October 20, 2000; and Joseph Dalaker and Bernadette Proctor, "Poverty in the United States: 1999" (U.S. Census Bureau, September 2000).

This table also helps explain why cities gained ground on the suburbs. Median incomes grew slightly faster in the central cities than in the suburbs, and their poverty rates declined more than those of the suburbs. If, in the wake of the 2000 census, the 1990s becomes known as the decade of rising suburban poverty — just as the 1970s and 1980s became known for concentrated urban poverty (a trend that abated in the 1990s) — it will amplify the common interests between central cities and inner suburbs.

Basically, rich suburbs have prospered while middle-income and poor suburbs have declined. As a result, the degree of income polarization among suburbs has increased rapidly. Census data for 554 suburbs show that the number of suburbs below 80 percent of the metropolitan median family income increased from 22 to 90 between 1960 and 1990, and the number above 120 percent of the metropolitan median fell only slightly (from 148 in 1960 to 142 in 1990). Just as the gap between rich and poor widened at the individual level, it widened tremendously between suburban places. The number of solid middle-income suburbs fell 40 percent, and the average ratio between the highest- and lowest-income suburbs increased from 2.1 to 1 in 1960 to 3.4 to 1 in 1990.[40]

Decline most affected not the oldest suburbs but those built between 1945 and 1970. The typical suburban tract home built during this period was quite small. The Levittown house of the late 1940s was 800 square feet; in 1954, the average size of a new house was only 1,140 square feet. By 2000, the average size of a new home had almost doubled to 2,260 square feet.[41] Older tract homes were often one-story bungalows reminiscent of Malvina Reynold's 1963 song about "Little boxes, little boxes, little boxes all the same." They also tended to lack amenities considered standard today, such as central air conditioning, two or more bathrooms, family rooms, and nine-foot ceilings. When these suburbs go downhill, they usually do so rapidly. Normally, all the housing was built about the same time. After twenty-five years, major systems such as roofs and furnaces need to be replaced. Those with money usually find that it makes more sense to purchase a new home on the suburban fringe, in exurbia, rather than to rehabilitate and expand older tract homes. Land prices are cheap there, and the latest construction technology gives buyers more bang for their buck. As Lucy and Phillips note, exurbanization is to the postwar suburbs what suburbanization was to central cities: it sucks the life out of older suburbs by siphoning off the most prosperous households.

Declining suburbs are usually quite depressing places. They lack the public spaces, universities, cultural institutions, nightlife, and downtowns that make central cities exciting places, even when they house many poor people. Following the suicide pact of four teens in suburban Bergenfield, New Jersey, journalist Donna Gaines explored what she called "suburbia's dead end kids" in Bergen County, New Jersey, and Long Island. She found suburban teenagers with bleak job prospects hanging out at 7-Elevens and immersing themselves in rebellious subcultures such as hip-hop, goth, and rave. Gaines interprets their cultural rebellions as understandable responses to a society that gives teenagers little respect and in many cases few opportunities.[42]

Exclusive suburbs, usually located at the outer edges of metropolitan areas or in the best-defended, best-located parts of the inner suburbs, are at the other extreme. Houses in these suburbs cost half a million dollars or more, and they are situated on large lots with winding roads and plenty of trees. There are usually few apartment buildings, and those that do exist are luxury apartments or condominium complexes with swimming pools and tennis courts. Instead of Chevy Novas and Hyundais, the residents drive Mercedes and Lexuses. Their kids do not hang out at the mall but are shepherded from one enrichment activity to another by harried soccer moms. Teenagers know that they are headed for college and good job prospects, and they are often obsessed with clothes, makeup, and SAT scores.

The poorest suburbs are not necessarily located closest to the central city. For that reason, the term "inner-ring suburb" is misleading. Many older suburbs built before 1940, like Philadelphia's mainline suburbs, have housing stock that was originally built to the highest standard and now has historic appeal. In most metropolitan areas, development proceeds in sectors or wedges that extend out from the city center, like pieces of pie. The ghetto spills over into inner-ring suburbs, which in turn causes second-tier suburbs to begin to decline. Suburban migration also follows highways, especially the interstates. Prosperous suburbs often emerge near the intersections of major interstate highways. In the Twin Cities, the most favored suburbs, locally known as the Fertile Crescent, stretch west and south of Minneapolis, following the Interstate 494 and Interstate 35 corridors. In Chicago, prosperous suburbs like Naperville are located west and north of the city, partly following Interstate 94, while the most distressed suburbs, like Harvey, border on Chicago's South Side ghetto.

The fragmentation of local government has powerfully influenced the pattern of economic segregation in American metropolitan areas. According to Table 2.1, the fifteen largest metropolitan areas had an average of 520 governments. (In 1961, Robert Wood, later secretary of Housing and Urban Development, published a book about the New York metropolitan area called *1400 Governments*.) Well-to-do families view their suburban governments as medieval fortresses protecting them from the dangers of crime and drugs that lie beyond the walls. Sometimes these fortresses are small and expensive. Countryside, a suburb of Kansas City, has only 134 homes, and property taxes are three times as high as in neighboring jurisdictions. "People like being separate and are willing to pay more for it," says Brian Smith, former mayor of Countryside.[43] Ensconced in exclusive enclaves protected by zoning regulations, the rich are far more isolated from other income groups than are the poor.

Suburban economic segregation is not just the result of exclusionary zoning regulations. Families choose suburbs based on their class and status aspirations. Gregory Weiher argues that suburban municipalities have become powerful sorting mechanisms for racial and class divisions. Lacking specific information about places, people use municipal boundaries and images to choose where to live. Increasingly, people buy into a suburb or a school system rather than a neighborhood. Over time, people are attracted by the identity of the suburb, thus making suburban municipalities more homogeneous and more distinct from one another. Using data from Cook County, Illinois, and Los Angeles County, California, Weiher found that between 1960 and 1980, municipalities became more homogeneous with respect to high-status occupational groups. Economic segregation was increasingly organized by municipal boundaries rather than by neighborhoods.[44]

St. Louis County, which includes ninety suburban governments, is a case study of how suburbs are becoming more economically distinct, with mass-produced suburbs built in the 1950s and 1960s increasingly having trouble maintaining their middle-class status. There are really two St. Louis Counties: Lindbergh Boulevard, a four-lane thoroughfare, is the generally accepted border between inner and outer St. Louis County. In the 1980s, median household income in outer St. Louis County jumped 4.6 percent after inflation to $48,433, while income fell 2.3 percent (to $32,745) in the inner areas.

Inner St. Louis County has stark class differences. A 92 percent black suburb that lost almost one-third of its population in the 1990s, Wellston is a place "where the streets are bleak and jarringly urban, lined with crumbling, long-abandoned auto repair shops, forlorn chop suey joints, houses with boarded up basement windows."[45] By contrast, Ladue is an upper-crust suburb of beautiful older homes on tree-lined streets with a 1989 median household income of $108,000. University City is perhaps the most interesting of the older suburbs. Located next to Washington University, University City is economically and racially diverse, with both stately older homes and modest apartments. "U City" has used its diversity as a selling point, attracting an eclectic mix of young professionals, college students, and senior citizens. The city enacted tough housing laws to maintain its substantial housing stock, but many people wonder whether even University City, with all its advantages, can stave off decline. It already has one of the highest tax rates in St. Louis County and a reputation for crime that makes outer suburbanites hesitate before shopping there.

ECONOMIC SEGREGATION AT THE NEIGHBORHOOD LEVEL

Over time, the neighborhood-level segregation of the rich and the poor has fluctuated. Pronounced spatial segregation by class did not emerge until the invention of the trolley. Olivier Zunz's careful study of Detroit shows that in 1880, people with different occupations (and therefore incomes) tended to live in the same neighborhoods. This tendency was reinforced by the tight ethnic and immigrant enclaves that thrived in the late nineteenth century. By 1920, however, Zunz found that occupational segregation was as high as ethnic segregation. Only in very tight-knit communities of Jews and blacks did a wide range of occupations live on the same block.[46] Using census tract data, Dudley and Beverly Duncan demonstrated that those at the top and bottom of the occupational rankings were highly segregated residentially in Chicago in 1950.[47] In the 1960s, segregation between high- and low-status workers declined. One study of ten urban areas found that residential distance between managers and laborers dropped by 23 percent in the 1960s, and between professionals and laborers it fell 19 percent.[48]

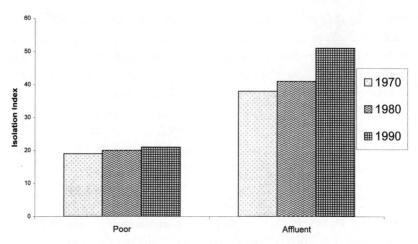

FIGURE 2.2. Concentration of Affluence and Poverty in the Ten Largest Metropolitan Areas in the United States, 1970–1990

Source: Douglas S. Massey, "The Age of Extremes: Concentrated Affluence and Poverty in the Twenty-first Century," *Demography* 33, no. 4 (November 1996): 399.

Since the 1970s, however, economic segregation has increased. Figure 2.2 shows the increases in economic segregation for the average poor household (below the poverty level) and the average affluent family (making four times the poverty level). The index is based on census tract data, areas defined by the Census Bureau with populations from 3,000 to 8,000. The first set of bars shows the proportion of poor people in the neighborhood of the average poor person. In 1970, the average poor person lived in a neighborhood that was 19 percent poor, with the average increasing steadily up to 1990. The second set of bars also shows that the affluent have become much more isolated from the rest of society than have the poor. In 1970, the typical affluent person lived in a neighborhood that was 39 percent affluent; by 1990, that had increased to 52 percent. Research on the 100 largest metropolitan areas in 1990 found that the geographic concentration of poverty and affluence varied tremendously across different regions.[49] But the overall trend is clear: households with more money have chosen to flee those who make less money and to cluster in affluent enclaves.

Little research has been done on concentrated affluence. By contrast, much attention has been paid to concentrated poverty. The most recent round of debate was stimulated by the publication of William Julius Wilson's *The Truly Disadvantaged* in 1987. Wilson's careful study of neighborhood change in Chicago documented the stunning rise in concentrated, largely black, poverty. He attributed the increasing concentration of poverty primarily to the loss of decent-paying industrial jobs for black men and the selective exodus of better-off blacks made possible by civil rights laws. The effect, he said, was to trap poor blacks in disadvantaged neighborhoods isolated from decent schools, jobs, and housing.

Researchers have applied techniques originally used to measure racial segregation to the study of the segregation and isolation of the poor. Regardless of method, they have found that the urban concentration of poverty increased markedly from 1970 to 1990. The index of dissimilarity measures how unevenly the poor are distributed, and the isolation index measures the extent to which the poor live with other poor people. From 1970 to 1990, the dissimilarity index increased 11 percent and the isolation index increased 9 percent in the 100 largest metropolitan areas.[50]

Wilson's original study of Chicago initiated the practice of identifying an area as underclass or ghetto poverty if its poverty rate exceeded 30 percent.[51] Subsequent researchers have generally used a 40 percent threshold. This approach is based on the idea that the spatial concentration of poor people magnifies the problems of poverty beyond the simple fact that people do not have enough money in their pockets. The 40 percent standard draws on the commonsensical notion that the negative effects of concentrated poverty multiply as the percentage of poor in a neighborhood rises. Living in a neighborhood that is 40 percent poor has many more negative effects than living in a neighborhood that is 20 percent poor. Wilson calls these the "concentration effects" of poverty.

Anyone who is familiar with big U.S. cities will immediately recognize neighborhoods with at least 40 percent poverty rates by their physical appearance. They have all the characteristics of what we call slums: abandoned houses and businesses, vacant lots, cars rotting in driveways, idle men standing on corners, and many liquor stores and pawnshops but few grocery stores or banks. Outsiders rarely venture into these areas, and surely not on foot or at night.

The most comprehensive national study of the concentration of poverty is Paul Jargowsky's *Poverty and Place*.[52] Using the 40 percent standard for census tracts, Jargowsky found that poverty areas, or ghettos, grew in almost every possible way between 1970 and 1990: in the number of tracts, in total population, as a percentage of the overall population, in the percentage of poor persons living in them, and in geographical size. The number of high-poverty census tracts in all metropolitan areas doubled, and their population increased from

TABLE 2.4. Persons in High Poverty Census Tracts, Top Ten Cities, 1990

1. New York	960,292
2. Detroit	418,947
3. Chicago	396,200
4. Los Angeles	267,666
5. McAllen, Texas*	234,467
6. New Orleans	165,571
7. Houston	162,487
8. Philadelphia	154,684
9. San Antonio	152,936
10. Miami	148,083
Total	3,061,333

Source: Paul A. Jargowsky, *Poverty and Place: Ghettos, Barrios, and the American Dream* (New York: Russell Sage Foundation, 1997), p. 78.

　*McAllen, Texas, located on the border with Mexico, has one of the highest rates of concentrated poverty in the nation. One reason is that the poverty line is not adjusted for the cost of living. McAllen is also one of the most economically depressed cities in the nation.

4.1 million to 8.0 million (while the national population grew only 28 percent). Although this was not a large fraction of the nation's 249 million residents in 1990, the trend is disturbing.

Between 1970 and 1990, the likelihood that a person would live in a slum or ghetto increased by 50 percent, from 3.0 to 4.5 percent. The percentage of poor persons living in high-poverty areas increased from 12.4 to 17.9 percent. Areas of urban blight, or high-poverty, expanded, more than doubling their land area between 1970 and 1990, with the average population of high-poverty tracts declining by 17 percent. To speak of concentrated poverty, Jargowsky observes, is misleading. Ghettos are no longer "teeming." Poor people increasingly live in areas with population densities that rival those of exclusive suburbs with one-acre zoning. Of course, the low density of the slums results from vacant land and abandoned houses, not large yards and parks.

The problem of concentrated poverty is mainly a metropolitan and central-city problem: 84.5 percent of all high-poverty census tracts were located in metropolitan areas in 1990; two-thirds of the people living in such tracts were located in the 100 largest central cities.[53] Indeed, more than one-third of all persons living in concentrated poverty tracts were located in just ten cities

(Table 2.4). Concentrated poverty is also clustered in older industrial cities of the Northeast and Midwest. It fell in the South in the 1970s but increased there in the 1980s, while the rate of increase fell dramatically in the Mid-Atlantic states in the 1980s. These surges and declines in concentrated poverty were closely related to the growth rates of the economies in these regions.[54]

As difficult as conditions are in concentrated poverty neighborhoods, most of their residents are hardworking and law abiding. Lurid media coverage and cynical politicians have fostered misleading stereotypes of people who live in ghetto areas. One is that they are simply lazy. Although workforce participation rates in high-poverty areas are lower than in other areas, still over half of all adults are working, looking for work, or in school.[55] When regional labor markets are tight, as in Boston during the "Massachusetts Miracle" of the 1980s, residents of poor neighborhoods enter the labor force in droves.[56] The big difference is that they can often find only part-time work and their wages are very low, averaging only $5.72 an hour in high-poverty areas in 1989. If a man with a wife and two children worked full-time at this wage, he would earn less than $12,000 — not enough to lift his family above the poverty line.

Another stereotype is that the residents of poor inner-city neighborhoods depend on government handouts. In fact, about three-quarters of the total income in high-poverty neighborhoods comes from wages and salaries, about the same percentage as in wealthy suburbs.[57] (Residents of wealthy suburbs are more likely to receive Social Security and Medicare, whereas residents of poor neighborhoods are more likely to receive welfare, although national welfare rolls have decreased by almost half since implementation of the work requirements of the 1996 welfare reform act.) The stereotype that women on welfare live good lives without having to work is false. A study of 214 women on welfare in Chicago, Boston, San Antonio, and Charleston found that 46 percent worked while receiving welfare, even though this was against the rules. The reason is simple: welfare does not pay enough to support a family.[58] These welfare recipients had a strong work ethic.

The burning issue in the study of concentrated poverty is whether it is caused mainly by economic factors or by racism. Wilson's initial formulation of the growth of concentrated poverty downplayed racial discrimination and focused instead on deindustrialization and the exodus of middle-class blacks. In contrast, Douglas Massey and his colleagues argue that racial discrimination is the main cause of concentrated poverty. Because blacks have been discriminated against in job markets (historically, blacks were excluded from unions and many skilled craft jobs), racial segregation in housing markets automatically means economic segregation. Massey and his colleagues argue that African Americans in poor neighborhoods could not follow jobs out to the suburbs, thus telescoping the negative effects of deindustrialization onto black communities. Even when blacks moved to the suburbs, they ended up in mostly black, poorer suburbs.[59]

Race is deeply implicated in concentrated poverty in the United States. In 1990, only 1.4 percent of all white persons lived in concentrated poverty tracts, compared with 17.4 percent of blacks and 10.5 percent of Hispanics. In other words, a black person was five times more likely than a white person to live in an area of concentrated poverty. Blacks composed about half the population of high-poverty census tracts in metropolitan areas in 1990, even though they were only 12.6 percent of the total population.[60] In short, racial segregation is clearly a major cause of economic segregation.

Racial segregation reinforces economic segregation by preventing poor blacks from moving out of ghettos, but it also decreases economic segregation among blacks by reducing the housing choices of middle-class blacks. Because of housing segregation, middle-income blacks live closer to poor blacks than middle-income whites live to poor whites. Blacks who move out of areas of concentrated poverty are more likely than whites to end up living close to poor neighborhoods. They also end up in suburbs with lower incomes and fewer fiscal resources than do whites. In the New York metropolitan area, for example, blacks located in places where the median income was $3,500 lower than in places where non-Hispanic whites with the same incomes moved.[61] Thus, blacks need higher incomes than whites to achieve comparable levels of social distance from the poor.

Racial segregation clearly increases economic segregation. But it is simply untrue that racial segregation caused the *increase* of economic segregation since the 1970s. For one thing, the concentration of white poor increased twice as fast as black or Hispanic concentrated poverty between 1970 and 1990. For another, racial segregation declined during this period, while economic segregation increased. Black poverty did not rise, but concentrated poverty did increase.[62] Given the declining population in areas of concentrated poverty, the movement of the nonpoor out of ghetto areas, including the flight of many middle-class blacks, clearly played a major role in the rising levels of concentrated poverty. In other words, the alarming increase in concentrated poverty is not just an artifact of race; it is being driven by class divisions. The isolation of the poor, not just the minority poor, is a growing problem in American society.

ECONOMIC SEGREGATION AND SPRAWL

Sprawl is different from economic segregation. Sprawl refers to a low-density pattern of land development in which residential units are spread out over a large area. Single-family homes built under three-acre minimum-lot zoning are a classic example of sprawl. Sprawl also encompasses the separation of residential from commercial land uses, the absence of clustered development or commercial centers, and widespread use of the automobile.[63] Although it is possible that a highly economically segregated metropolitan area might be compact and centralized, the fact is that American metropolitan areas have both high levels of economic segregation *and* high levels of sprawl. These two characteristics are connected.

Compared with other countries, metropolitan areas in the United States are remarkably sprawled out. European cities are three to four times denser than American cities. The claim that American cities are sprawled out because we have so much land is countered by the example of Canada, which has more land per person than the United States but whose cities are still twice as dense.[64] American cities have not always been this sprawled out. In the 1920s, they were twice as dense as they are now.[65] Suburbanization reduced central-city densities to a level approaching that of the older suburbs. American suburbs are also far less dense than they might have been. They could have been built following a clustered, mixed-use pattern surrounding commercial centers, as some suburbs built before 1940 were, such as University City outside St. Louis or Shaker Heights outside Cleveland. After World War II, however, large private developers concentrated on building huge tracts of single-family homes set apart from other uses. These homes were built in a short period and were often quite similar to one another.

Suburbanization is common in all wealthy nations. As incomes rise, households want bigger houses and more green space around them. Suburbs clearly have attractions—the "pull" factors in suburbanization. Scholars have debated over the years how much suburbanization can be attributed to pull factors as opposed to "push" factors, such as the desire to flee declining public services, rising crime, and concentrations of poor minorities.

The free-market explanation holds that the well-to-do naturally prefer to accept longer commutes as the price for cheaper land and larger houses in the suburbs, while the poor prefer to live in crowded conditions close to their jobs.[66] Both these assumptions are questionable. Most entry-level jobs are now located in the suburbs, where the vast majority of poor and working-class families would prefer to live. In other countries, the rich prefer to live near the center, where they have easier access to high-paying jobs and elite culture. Something else seems to be going on in the American context to make the middle and upper classes flee to the urban fringe.

That something else is the desire to escape the poor and minorities. Thomas Sugrue's history of postwar Detroit shows that race played a major role in white flight, but the statistical evidence about white flight is contradictory.[67] Some studies show that suburbanization occurred more rapidly in cities with large minority populations, but other studies show no significant effect. There is no doubt that households flee from high levels of crime and poor public services associated with concentrated poverty.[68]

Does concentrated poverty in the central city promote an exodus to the suburbs? In part, yes, but migration from other urban areas is a more important cause of suburban growth. Suburban population growth depends not so much on migration from central cities as on migration from other regions. In metropolitan areas with strong central cities, more migrants move to the area and settle in the suburbs. In other words, suburban well-being rests not primarily on siphoning middle-class residents from central cities but on attracting residents from other regions. People are less likely to move to an area, including its suburbs, if the central city is full of problems. Central cities and suburbs are complementary, rather than competitive.[69] Concentrated poverty in central cities therefore hurts the entire region, including suburbs.

Clearly, the deterioration of American central cities, itself closely related to concentrated poverty, has fostered suburbanization. Urban crime has promoted flight to the suburbs. One study estimated that moderate to large central cities lost more than one resident to the suburbs for each crime committed.[70] Many people moved to the suburbs to gain access to higher-quality schools with high test scores. As we discuss later, the poor performance of central-city schools stems both from lower expenditures and from special needs associated with concentrated poverty.

Suburbanization is partly a market-driven phenomenon. William Fischel estimated that income growth, transportation advances, and technological changes account for about 75 percent of suburbanization. This leaves 25 percent of suburbanization as being caused by nonmarket factors—negative factors that push people out of central cities. Mostly, these have to do with the problems associated with the growing concentration of poor people, such as crime and poor schools.[71] Households strive to escape the negative effects of concentrated poverty, exacerbating economic segregation.

Are concentrated poverty and urban sprawl related? On the one hand, the relationship is obvious, because as we have shown, suburban flight is partly motivated by a desire to escape concentrated poverty and its attendant problems; the emptying out of central cities is one major reason why America's metropolitan areas are so sprawled out. On the other hand, flight from cities is distinct from the question of where households settle once they make it out to the suburbs. Flight from central cities could have resulted in high-density suburbs, but it did not. Why?

Local zoning is the primary reason. Suburban zoning laws often exclude apartments, mandate large-lot single-family homes, and separate uses (thus requiring households to own at least one automobile). Even though concentrated poverty does not directly cause suburban sprawl, the two are indirectly related.[72] Exclusionary zoning regulations are motivated by the desire to avoid the negative effects of concentrated poverty. Suburbanites have a "fear of falling"—a fear that a sudden influx of poor people may cause the whole area to decline. They deal with this fear by banning apartments and requiring large lots for single-family homes. These regulations confine the poor to the urban core and foster leapfrog development that worsens sprawl. The fear of falling is not entirely unwarranted, at least in inner suburbs, because, as we have shown, poverty rates are rising in those areas. Policies to limit sprawl and promote "smart growth" would push development back toward the urban core, increasing the access of those who live in concentrated poverty areas to jobs, taxable resources, and retail services.[73]

IS THE UNITED STATES UNIQUE?

Economic segregation and sprawl are significant and increasing in the United States. But does this pattern differ from that in other advanced industrial countries? Yes. No other country has urbanized areas that are so sprawled out and economically segregated. But some predict that other countries will soon resemble the United States. There is growing discussion of the "Americanization" of urban development and poverty in Western Europe, often attributed to the effects of economic globalization. There, as here, the decline of industry and the growth of service employment have created a more polarized wage structure. As immigrants migrate to the developed nations, they are forced to take jobs in the low-wage service sector and end up crammed together in ghettos. In short, global economic forces are accentuating economic inequalities and economic segregation in all countries.[74] But predictions of the convergence of other countries with American development patterns are premature.

Among the most frequently cited examples of European ghettos are the large public housing estates, or *grands ensembles,* located on the outskirts of French cities, particularly the *banlieues,* or inner-ring suburbs, of Paris.[75] Many contain large concentrations of poor North African immigrants. In recognition of their similarity to American ghettos, they have been called "Little Chicagos." Like concentrated poverty areas in the United States, they are associated with poverty, crime, and social disorganization. Living in a Little Chicago stigmatizes a person as a loser; employers shun such residents, and mothers even warn their daughters against going out with boys who live there. The resurgence of the extreme right-wing Front National in the 1980s in France was based on hostility toward immigrants and their supposed threat to the French nation.

Although the French *banlieues* resemble American ghettos, the differences are also great. Most important, generous government benefits have generally lifted the incomes of those at the bottom in France over the past twenty years.[76] In France, most government benefits are nationally determined and do not depend on where you live, as they often do in the United States. France is one unified school district, for example. The poor in France are also less geographically separated from the rest of society than are the poor in the United States. Clearly, race is a major reason why ghettoization is more extreme in the United States than in Europe. European cities are economically segregated to a certain extent, especially when poverty status is correlated with ethnic or immigrant status, as in the case of the French *banlieue.* An important difference, however, is that the French *banlieues* are not as isolated from society, usually have excellent public transit, and do not suffer from greatly inferior public services, including schools. Even the poorest French *banlieue* lacks the social disorganization, violence, and sense of despair found in American ghettos.

Across Europe and even Canada, the experience of living in poor neighborhoods is qualitatively different from that in the United States. Walking through the worst neighborhoods of Amsterdam, for example, one is never in a world apart, like in the South Bronx. Even cities with high overall levels of poverty and unemployment lack such areas. "Italy's 12 major cities cannot be characterized by a very high degree of spatial segregation of social groups."[77] During the 1970s and 1980s, British Prime Minister Margaret Thatcher's policy of allowing public housing tenants to purchase their units meant that those who could not afford to do so concentrated in less attractive estates. But the level of ghettoization in British cities is still much less than that in the United States. Moreover, the public and private sectors have not abandoned the poverty areas in European cities. As one study of five poor neighborhoods in Birmingham, England, put it:

While the levels of deprivation and disadvantage prevailing in all five inner city wards indicate a concentration of economically weak populations (especially in pockets within each ward) including high levels of concentration of racial and ethnic minorities, these neighborhoods remain vibrant and heterogeneous. Their main streets are lined with shops, restaurants, banks, churches, neighborhood offices, community centers, as well as government job centers. In addition, they are connected to the commercial city center and other wards by a large network of buses.[78]

In European cities, the poor are much more integrated with the lives of the working and lower-middle classes than are the poor in American cities.[79] In the United States, members of the working class, regardless of race, are often trapped in distressed inner-ring suburbs. They shun the ghetto poor, whom they view as an economic threat because they absorb government funds and as a moral threat because they may spread their alleged culture of poverty.[80] European poor areas, by contrast, have fewer working poor and more unemployed. Even though the European poor rely more on government benefits than do the poor in the United States, there is relatively little hostility from those on the next rung up the ladder (who also benefit from these same policies). Generous European policies toward health, education, child care, and retirement make the quality of one's life less dependent on earnings and make the poor less frightening. By reducing inequalities, European social policies reduce resistance to economic integration.[81]

Probably the most disturbing difference is that residence appears to have little effect on social mobility in Europe. Education is funded nationally, so access to good schools is less dependent on living in a prosperous school district. Family assistance programs are also centralized, so the rich in Europe have far less fiscal incentive to move to a place with a separate government, where they can refuse to pay for programs that benefit the poor. Europe is less prone to a vicious circle in which economic segregation reinforces income inequality, which further fuels economic segregation.[82] In the United States, by contrast, the evidence shows that economic segregation has a momentum of its own. As we show in the next chapter, the accumulating negative effects of concentrated poverty cause households to flee these areas. This further accentuates concentrated poverty and makes it more difficult for those left behind to get ahead. In the final analysis, we argue, economic segregation and sprawl impose significant costs on all parts of the metropolitan area.

 The Costs of
Economic Segregation
and Sprawl

Every weekday, Cynthia Wiggins, a seventeen-year-old single mother, boarded the number 6 bus in her predominantly black Buffalo, New York, neighborhood. Engaged to be married, Wiggins was struggling to improve herself and dreamed of becoming a doctor. Her destination was the gleaming Walden Galleria Mall in the suburb of Cheektowaga, where she worked as a cashier at Arthur Treacher's Fish and Chips. Unfortunately, the owners of the mall refused to let city buses drive into the parking lot, and passengers had to walk 300 yards across a seven-lane highway with no sidewalks. On the morning of December 14, 1996, with mounds of snow lining the shoulder, a ten-ton dump truck struck Wiggins. She died of her injuries nineteen days later.[1]

Wiggins's tragic death highlights how place of residence can affect access to jobs and retail stores, as well as personal safety. In the Buffalo area, most job growth happens in suburban Erie County, which inner-city minorities have difficulty reaching because of poor public transit. Lacking cars, they can shop only in the inner city, where the number of retail outlets has fallen precipitously since the 1950s.[2] In Wiggins's case, she could get to her close-to-minimum-wage mall job only by public transit, which took her an hour and forty minutes, ending with a dangerous hike across a busy highway.

The lesson is clear: some people live in good neighborhoods that provide them with all sorts of advantages; others, like Cynthia Wiggins, live in not-so-good neighborhoods that impose numerous disadvantages on them. Many would say, however, that place is less important in people's lives than it used to be. According to this view, transportation and communication advances have freed us from the constraints of place. We have many more choices of where we can live. The more we earn, the wider our choices. Where we live reflects our economic success. It does not determine it.

We argue, on the contrary, that place has a powerful independent effect on people's lives. The automobile, jet travel, and the Internet have not enabled us to transcend the effects of place. Place is not only the result of our incomes and preferences; it also affects our ability to earn money, and it shapes our preferences. Specifically, the concentration of poverty in metropolitan areas undermines our prospects and damages the quality of our lives in myriad ways. Since it propels households to the metropolitan fringe, an exaggerated urban sprawl is the flip side of concentrated disadvantage. Though middle- and upper-class suburbanites benefit from economic segregation in many ways, they also bear substantial costs from economic segregation. Urban sprawl has hidden costs that undermine the reasons people moved to the suburbs in the first place.

Here, we document the impact of economic segregation and urban sprawl on four areas of life: jobs and income, health, access to private goods and services, and crime. (We address the crucial question of the effects of concentrated poverty on the cost and quality of local public services in chapter 5.) We examine each effect separately, but they are related to one another in myriad ways that compound the situation.[3]

JOBS AND INCOME

The Personal Responsibility and Work Opportunity Reconciliation Act of 1996 (better known as welfare reform) mandated that states cut their welfare caseloads in half by 2002, moving recipients into jobs or job-preparation activities. The law places a five-year lifetime limit on receipt of welfare and forbids able-bodied adults to receive welfare for more than two years in any one stretch. By the middle of 2000, the booming economy had already helped states cut the number of welfare recipients by more than 50 percent. We know little, however, about what happens to people after they leave welfare. Indications are that many families are worse off. An Urban Institute survey of former recipients found that two-thirds were working when interviewed in 1997, but they had alarmingly low wages averaging $6.60 an hour. Three-quarters lacked medical benefits.[4]

In the 1996 law, Congress addressed two obstacles facing welfare recipients seeking to get and keep jobs: job training and day care. Money was set aside for those purposes, though critics argued that it was not enough to meet the need. Implementation of welfare reform has revealed a third obstacle: job access, or the gap between where welfare recipients live and where the jobs are.

Although two-thirds of all new jobs are located in the suburbs, three-quarters of welfare recipients live in central cities or rural areas. Welfare rolls have fallen more slowly in cities than elsewhere.[5] Nationwide, just one in twenty welfare recipients owns a car. Moreover, if they purchase a decent car, welfare recipients are penalized with reduced benefits.[6]

Transportation is especially difficult for women with children. Zakiya Kyle, a former welfare recipient living in South Los Angeles, is a single mother who works at a nonprofit drug-abuse prevention program. She arrives at the bus stop at 6 A.M. with her two boys, fourteen-month-old Ishmael and five-year-old Mustafa. Two buses later, she drops Mustafa at his school in Inglewood; then she takes two more buses to get Ishmael to his baby-sitter in Watts. After two more buses, Kyle finally arrives at work at 9 A.M. In a masterful understatement, Kyle sums up the problem: "In L.A. County, it's very difficult to live without a car."[7] The fact is, a low-wage suburban job does not make sense for many former welfare recipients because commuting is so difficult and time-consuming. Women of all classes are much more likely than men to turn down a job because it is not accessible to home or their children's caregivers.[8]

This painful problem has been discussed for thirty years as the "spatial mismatch." In an influential article in 1968, Harvard economist John Kain launched research on the gap between where people live and where jobs are located. Using simple statistical techniques, he argued that housing segregation prevented Chicago's blacks from following jobs out to the suburbs, and as a result, they lost between 22,000 and 24,000 jobs.[9] Some argue that the spatial mismatch is primarily the result of "race," not "place,"[10] but a comprehensive review of research concluded that the evidence "consistently supports" the spatial mismatch hypothesis.[11]

The best way to test for a spatial mismatch effect would be to move people from concentrated poverty areas to mixed areas closer to jobs and see what happens. A "natural experiment" of this type ensued after a 1976 U.S. Supreme Court decision in the case of *Hills v. Gautreaux*. In *Gautreaux*, public housing residents had sued the Chicago Housing Authority and the U.S. Department of Housing and Urban Development for deliberately segregating public housing in poor minority neighborhoods. The Court ordered that public housing tenants be given the opportunity to move to middle-class white neighborhoods throughout the Chicago metropolitan area using housing vouchers. When the program ended in 1998, over 7,000 low-income black families had participated, with more than half moving to middle-income white suburbs and the rest moving to low-income black neighborhoods in Chicago. Gautreaux represents the closest thing we have to a rigorous experimental test of contextual effects.[12]

The results show that adults who moved to the suburbs enjoyed higher rates of employment, though not higher wages or better working hours. The results for children were more dramatic. "Compared with the children of city movers, the children who moved to the suburbs were more likely to be in school, in college-track classes, in four-year colleges, employed, and in jobs with benefits and better pay."[13]

The spatial mismatch literature has focused primarily on how racial segregation affects housing markets and job access. But economic segregation also causes spatial mismatches. The movement of jobs and people has perverse aspects, with jobs and the workers qualified for them moving in opposite directions.[14] Entry-level jobs with low to moderate education and skill requirements, such as routine manufacturing, retail, and data-entry positions, have been declining in central cities and growing on the urban fringe. Meanwhile, exclusionary zoning regulations prevent people who could take these jobs from moving nearer to them by limiting affordable housing in the suburbs. At the same time, the number of highly skilled professional jobs, such as lawyers and management consultants, has increased in central business districts, but those who hold them often live in the suburbs. A study of 101 metropolitan areas found that in 1997 average annual pay for central-city jobs averaged 10.5 percent higher than pay for suburban jobs.[15] It makes sense for companies to locate their most productive workers on the most expensive land and office space at the center of metropolitan areas. Downtowns, in contrast, are often surrounded by some of the poorest neighborhoods in the region, with few residents possessing the skills to qualify for professional jobs.

Suburbs used to be "bedroom communities" for workers commuting to jobs in the city. Now, many suburbs have more jobs than residents and, like central cities, import workers to fill them. Consider Westchester County, north of New York City. Between 1977 and 1997, Westchester County's job base increased by 21 percent, but its resident population actually fell slightly. In 1990, the Regional Plan Association calculated that there were 56,000 more jobs in Westchester than resident employees. Not surprisingly, the demand for housing is soaring in Westchester County. By 2000, desperate home buyers had pushed the average sales price for a single-family home to a record $552,700.[16]

Although supply is supposed to follow demand, housing supply has not kept pace with demand in Westchester County. The main reasons are the barriers to the building of new housing erected by local governments. In 1952, Westchester was zoned for 3.2 million residents. By the early 1960s, downzoning had reduced the county's population capacity to 1.8 million. The trend continues. Most towns in Westchester simply zone out apartments. In the 1980s, apartments were permitted on less than one-half of 1 percent of the developable land in the less intensely settled areas of the county, where most development could occur.[17] At the same time, minimum lot sizes for single-family homes are being changed from one acre to three or four acres. Richard Nicholson, a member of the Town Council in Somers, a small town in Westchester that enacted more restrictive zoning, put it this way in 1999: "[T]he days of one-acre zoning are over in northern Westchester."[18] Existing owners want to restrict newcomers from disturbing their lives by bringing more traffic and more children to educate in the public schools. Not coincidentally, restrictive zoning raises housing prices, handing present owners hefty profits when they sell. Those who rent do not have a place on the escalator of rising home values and inevitably fall further and further behind. In 1999, the average monthly rent for a two-bedroom apartment in Westchester was nearly $1,100.[19]

Well-to-do Westchester home owners strive to exclude lower-income people, but they do not want them too far away, because such people tend their gardens, watch their children, sell them groceries, and even police their streets. Many teachers, firefighters, and police officers cannot afford to live in the municipalities where they work. Most must look for houses or apartments in the older southern Westchester communities of Yonkers, Mount Vernon, and New Rochelle. Despite being the sixth richest of the nation's 3,147 counties in 1990 in per capita income, Westchester led the nation in per capita homelessness in 1989.[20] Many of its low-wage workers make under $20,000 a year. Hispanic immigrants work as gardeners, maids, and day laborers. To house them, some landlords simply crowd fifteen or more people into an apartment, charging them $100 to $150 each and making a windfall profit.[21] In suburban Long Island, where the housing market is as tight as Westchester, one enterprising businessman illegally converted cheap office space into housing, crowding fifteen people into seven tiny rooms and charging them $2,700 a month.[22] The demand for affordable housing pushes landlords to violate housing codes in ways that are dangerous and unhealthy.

Besides the physical problem of simply getting to jobs, place matters because neighborhoods link residents into networks that provide them with crucial information about jobs. More than half of all jobs are found through friends and relatives, not through the want ads.[23] These networks provide information not just to people looking for jobs but also to employers looking for good workers. More than 40 percent of Chicago firms reported that they did not advertise their entry-level openings in newspapers. Instead, they relied on informal means, such as referrals from present workers, which they felt ensured a better-quality worker with less likelihood of dishonesty or stealing. As one hospital personnel official put it, "If you are just a cold applicant, chances of you getting in are almost nil."[24] Unfortunately, if you live in a neighborhood with a high unemployment rate, your social network will be less valuable in finding a job, regardless of how skilled, honest, or hardworking you are. William Julius Wilson has shown that blacks in poor Chicago neighborhoods are less likely than others to have at least one employed friend.[25] In general, poor people, the less educated, and youths tend to have spatially confined social networks.[26] This is a problem if most entry-level jobs are located outside of central-city and inner-ring suburban neighborhoods, as is the case in most metropolitan areas. In short, where you live affects your chances of finding a job.

Concentrated poverty may also harm labor market success through the norms, values, and aspirations that are passed on in face-to-face interactions. Advocates of the controversial "culture of poverty" thesis argue that poor people adopt different values from mainstream middle-class society and, for this reason, do not respond to job opportunities even when offered. The question is not so much whether residents of concentrated poverty and minority areas differ from middle-class suburbanites, but why. For conservatives like Edward Banfield and Charles Murray, the culture of the poor causes their economic failure.[27] Employers fail to locate jobs in concentrated poverty areas, according to this view, because the residents lack a strong work ethic, engage in crimes, and suffer from drug addictions.

The evidence, however, is to the contrary. The results of the Gautreaux experiment in Chicago directly contradict the "culture of poverty" thesis, showing that former residents of low-income black neighborhoods responded to improved geographies of opportunity by working more and doing well in school. Even people who are stuck in the worst neighborhoods strive to enter the workforce. When Boston's economic boom produced tight labor markets in the 1980s, the ghetto unemployment rate plummeted.[28] During the sustained economic boom of the 1990s, more young black men with high school educations or less moved into the workforce and earned more and committed fewer crimes.[29] One study found that fourteen people applied for every available minimum-wage job at fast-food restaurants in central Harlem.[30] Even in neighborhoods with 40 percent poverty, most men are working or looking for work, and most household income comes from wages and salaries, not welfare or unemployment compensation.[31] These findings would not surprise William Julius Wilson. His survey of ghetto residents in Chicago found that fewer than 3 percent denied the importance of plain hard work for getting ahead in society. In short, some people in poor neighborhoods may not value work (as in any other neighborhood), but the vast majority want to work and do work. The main problem is that the only jobs they can get are poorly paid, unstable, and distant and have poor benefits.

Many residents of high-poverty ghettos behave differently from those of middle-income neighborhoods. For Wilson, however, the differences do not derive primarily from different values but represent ways people cope with having limited opportunities. Unable to attain respect through mainstream methods, ghetto youths compensate by joining a gang or acting in an aggressive manner in public. Wilson documents that black men are particularly likely to have attitudes and behaviors that make them less acceptable and successful in entry-level jobs, especially those that deal with the public. Wilson stresses, however, that these attitudes and behaviors are the *product* of restricted opportunities in ghetto poverty areas, not the primary cause.

Sprawl and Economic Success

Sprawl places a different set of costs on outer-ring suburbanites, including longer commutes, air pollution, and loss of green space. With regard to jobs and income, however, it seems that urban sprawl is beneficial to higher-income households. The reason is simple: high-income households can live pretty much anywhere they want to; if they choose to live in outer suburbs, it must be because of the advantages there. But even if the choice to live on the urban fringe maximizes their personal well-being, it also has substantial social costs that affect everyone, even the well-to-do.

Although outer-ring suburbs like Naperville (discussed in chapter 1) tend to be job rich, not everyone who moves there will find nearby job opportunities. To begin with, corporations move their headquarters out to the fringe for the convenience of top executives. Joel Garreau, author of *Edge City,* cites one rule of real estate development: "*Whenever a company moves its headquarters, the commute of the chief executive officer always becomes shorter.*"[32] For those down the corporate ladder, the outward movement of jobs often means longer commutes. For women with children, the sprawled-out character of the outer suburbs means longer shopping trips and more time transporting children to disparate destinations. The easy availability of retail jobs in the malls is useful for women seeking part-time, flexible employment, but long commutes are difficult for mothers and fathers with young children seeking to balance a professional career and child rearing. Most of the burden falls on women, who insist on easy access to the day-care center or school. As one author put it, "women put up with low-paying jobs to gain more flexible schedules or better commuting patterns in order to continue their unpaid labor of love [in the family]."[33]

The big question, however, is whether excessive sprawl undermines a region's economic competitiveness, in the long run harming income growth. Individual households moving out to the urban fringe may enjoy better housing and other advantages, but the overall impact of a thinned-out metropolis may be to reduce the size of the economic pie, hurting everyone in the long run. Exclusionary zoning can drive up housing costs, especially for rental housing, which in turn puts upward pressure on living costs. This forces employers to pay higher wages, making the region less attractive to investors. One study concluded that growth controls, including exclusionary zoning, caused housing prices in California localities to be 33 to 43 percent higher than they otherwise would have been.[34] Boston, San Francisco, and Los Angeles have clearly seen high housing prices drive up salaries. Awareness of this problem has led corporate leaders to support efforts to expand the supply of affordable housing.[35]

Whether sprawl and economic segregation hurt economic growth has been studied primarily by comparing different kinds of metropolitan areas, with a focus on the relationship between central cities and their suburbs. Such studies ask how the economic success of suburbs (or the metropolitan area) relates to the well-being of central cities and whether suburbs can prosper even when their central cities decay. A number of studies have documented a close association between the well-being of suburbanites and central-city dwellers.[36] The incomes of city residents and those of suburban residents are consistently highly correlated, for example, suggesting that the economic fates of cities and suburbs are intertwined.[37]

The argument about the interdependence of cities and suburbs boils down to the question of whether cities perform crucial functions in regional economies that are not performed as easily or as efficiently in suburbs. One argument against the city-suburban interdependence thesis is that advances in information technology render the dense face-to-face relations in cities obsolete, enabling anyone to gain the advantages of cities without having to live or work in them.[38] Most studies have found, however, that face-to-face relations are still necessary and desirable.[39]

The more compelling argument is that suburbs are now replicating all the place-based functions traditionally performed by central cities in regional economies. Places like Palo Alto and White Plains are becoming "mini-central cities" in the suburban realm. If all essential economic functions can move to the suburban fringe, then outer-ring suburbanites need not worry about the fate of cities or inner-ring suburbs. Joel Garreau argues that modern economies still require "urbanism," spatial concentration of diverse economic functions.

But he calls old downtowns "relics of the past" and argues that "edge cities . . . contain all the functions a city ever has." Garreau acknowledges that edge cities exclude the poor and minorities, but he argues that they are "astoundingly efficient," implying that they will sustain regional growth even if the old urban cores rot.[40]

The urbanization of the suburbs has clearly matured, as the multiplication of suburban office complexes and shopping centers bears out. But this has not come directly at the expense of central business districts, which have also continued to expand. As a result, suburban property values still depend on the availability of jobs in central cities. In 1989, 46 percent of all earnings in San Francisco suburbs came from residents who worked in the central city; the figure for Denver was 41 percent, for New Orleans 39 percent.[41] Suburban firms rely on the rich supply of corporate services, such as banking, law, and accounting, found in city centers. One study of 5,000 large firms found that 92 percent of the professional services purchased in the region were supplied by central-city firms. The author of the study concluded: "Suburbia does not yet comprise an economically autonomous 'outer city' or 'edge city.'"[42]

Why do so many high-paying jobs continue to locate in cities? The answer is that density nurtures economic dynamism and productivity. Employment density increases firms' productivity, regardless of workers' skills or companies' capital investments. Workers in the fifteen counties with the lowest employment densities produced an average of less than half of the output of New York City workers.[43] The concentration of economic functions in one area reduces the costs of transportation and exchange and increases each business's access to skilled and specialized labor. Companies in the downtowns of large cities can, for example, get easy access to highly specialized, highly productive lawyers. Even if they are highly compensated, their expertise makes them worth it. Thus, Wichita is second only to Seattle as a center of defense and aerospace manufacturing; Charlotte has become the nation's banking center; Miami specializes in Latin American trade and finance; and Cleveland excels in machine tooling and innovative think tanks.

Businesses that rely on exchanging sophisticated information that cannot be encapsulated in a formula or summed up in an e-mail message benefit from dense face-to-face relations. To be on the cutting edge of fashion, you need to be connected to New York (or Milan or Paris). Innovation has increasingly become the key to profitability, because the first stages of the product life cycle can convey monopoly-like advantages.[44] Innovation, in turn, often stems from informal collaboration between firms. In her study of Silicon Valley in California and Route 128 outside Boston, AnnaLee Saxenian showed how the superior dynamism of the former depended on face-to-face networks among employees of competing firms.[45]

Density also fosters production systems characterized by flexible specialization.[46] Old-style manufacturing based on low-skilled workers in continuous assembly lines that mass-produced identical products contrasts with flexible systems that produce small batches of customized goods to meet constantly changing consumer demands. Flexible specialization requires skilled, craft-type workers in smaller firms that cooperate with one another on marketing and have a network of suppliers providing just-on-time delivery of parts. The Los Angeles film industry relies on dense networks of independent contractors in cinematography, set design, computer graphics, script writing, and the like, which can be pulled together for the specialized production needs of each movie. Most film studios want to locate in Los Angeles. They are "sticky" rather than mobile.[47] Interest in "industrial clusters" as a tool of economic development has surged because it is clear that they foster a high-wage manufacturing economy. Mass production, by contrast, leads to the declining working conditions of labor as mobile capital seeks out the lowest-wage areas.

Although dynamic business clusters can exist in the suburbs, cities generally foster higher levels of density and dynamism. It is difficult to imagine cutting-edge clusters in fashion, theater, art, advertising, investment banking, or design prospering in low-density suburbs. Daniel Luria and Joel Rogers have argued that cities can nurture a "high road" to reindustrialization by competing not on low-cost, low-wage goods but on high-quality, well-designed, and better-serviced products. As they put it, "A high-road strategy must almost surely be a metro strategy because the high road generally requires the sheer density of people and firms found only in cities."[48]

In short, regional prosperity (and suburban well-being) still depends on good central-city performance. The issue is not whether suburbs depend on cities or vice versa, but how the various areas of high and low density and economic diversity function together. Cities have low-density neighborhoods, and suburbs have high-density clusters. Given the limited availability of urban land, many industrial and service employment clusters must be built in the suburbs. Garreau is right to talk about the need for suburban "edge cities," but he is wrong about their autonomy from a metropolitan economic network in which the central city still plays a vital role.

Ultimately, it makes as much sense to talk about suburban independence from the region as it does to talk about the independence of the head from the stomach. The parts of a region form an integral whole that is more than the sum of its components. These integrated metropolitan economies are the engines of

American prosperity.[49] The different parts relate to each other by specializing in different functions. In his famous description of a pin factory in *The Wealth of Nations,* Adam Smith pointed out that efficiency was maximized by getting workers to specialize in different phases of production. If the different parts of a region specialize in different economic activities that relate coherently to one another, greater efficiency and higher economic competitiveness result. Thinking about these specialized functions as somehow autonomous or unrelated is a fundamental mistake.

Cities perform essential functions for regional economies. They receive immigrants who provide badly needed workers and entrepreneurial energy, in addition to supplying crucial links to foreign markets. They house the low-wage workers required for retail, personal services, construction, manufacturing, and many other sectors. If these workers become more disconnected from the regional employment base, the costs of doing business will rise unnecessarily. Wages at a McDonald's in suburban Connecticut, for example, were found to be 19 percent higher than at a McDonald's 25 miles away in the Bronx.[50] Not surprisingly, the suburban McDonald's offers a free McShuttle from the central city for its workers. Could suburbs prosper independently of central cities? Probably. But would they prosper even more if they were part of a better-integrated metropolis? The answer is almost certainly yes.

HEALTH

In 1984, Dr. Arthur Jones and other urban missionaries founded the Lawndale Christian Health Center in one of the poorest neighborhoods in Chicago. The clinic provided decent and affordable health care for the neighborhood, but its doctors frequently complained that their patients did not follow simple directions to improve their health. In *Mama might be better off dead,* Laurie Abraham tells how Jones punctured a self-righteous doctor by describing the realities of the neighborhood: "Dr. Jones told of one woman who was suffering from a severe case of hives caused by an allergic reaction to her cat, yet repeatedly refused to get rid of the animal. 'I really got kind of angry,' Dr. Jones remembered, 'and then she told me that if she got rid of the cat, there was nothing to protect her kids against the rats.'"[51]

Epidemiologists have extensively documented a strong correlation between wealth and health at both the national and the individual level. Recently, however, epidemiologists have uncovered a troubling paradox. Although wealthy individuals live longer, on average, than the less affluent, the correlation between wealth and health disappears at the national level: among developed nations, wealthier nations are not necessarily healthier. This can be illustrated in various ways. Although the United States had the second highest gross national product (GNP) per capita (controlling for purchasing power) in 1997, it was tied for thirteenth in infant mortality and ranked seventeenth in expected life span at birth.[52] Similarly, poor areas sometimes succeed in achieving higher levels of health than richer nations as a whole. Despite having a lower per capita GNP than India, the state of Kerala achieved a life span exceeding seventy years, about the same as the much wealthier country of Saudi Arabia.[53] Black men in Harlem have a lower chance of reaching age sixty-five than do men in Bangladesh, even though average incomes in Harlem are many times higher.[54]

Trying to solve this paradox (that health is correlated with wealth at the individual level but not at the group or national level) has generated an outpouring of new research on the environmental causes of death and disease. Researchers have concluded that the explanation must be structural; that is, some social or economic factors prevent wealth from improving health. By far the most powerful explanation is that *economic inequality* negatively influences health, canceling out improvements from increasing GNP. Generally speaking, a society's income distribution matters as much as its overall standard of living. Economic inequality is correlated with lower life expectancy, regardless of the level of per capita income. One early study estimated that a highly unequal country had five to ten years less average life expectancy than a relatively egalitarian country, after controlling for overall wealth.[55] The country with the world's highest life expectancy, Japan, has one of the lowest levels of income inequality. The United States has one of the most unequal distributions of income among advanced industrial countries, and it has relatively low life expectancies, even though the United States spends more per capita on health care than any other country.

Most research has measured inequality at the individual level, not by place. But inequality is also clearly a trait of places. Accordingly, people in highly unequal societies experience more unhealthy conditions. So it is not surprising that a study of 282 U.S. metropolitan areas found a high correlation between regional inequality and an elevated death rate, after controlling for the overall level of income.[56] Another study of 369 local authorities in England found that the greater the inequality between their neighborhoods, the higher the mortality or death rate.[57] A study in Oakland, California, that followed individuals over a long period found that residing in a high-poverty area led to much higher chances of death, once again, controlling for individual characteristics. White males in poverty areas, for example, were 44 percent more likely to die than were white males in nonpoverty areas.[58]

The relationship between inequality and poor health is partly based on community characteristics. People living in concentrated poverty areas experience all sorts of detrimental conditions, in particular, poor access to health care, an unhealthy physical environment, and detrimental social relations and lifestyles. Moreover, even though these conditions are worst in poor central-city neighborhoods, economic segregation and sprawl also impose substantial health costs on middle-class suburbanites. Well-to-do people in highly unequal regions are more likely to have health problems than well-off people in areas characterized by more equality.

Access to Health Care

The United States is the only developed country in the world without universal health insurance. The government does provide the dependent poor and elderly with health insurance, through Medicaid and Medicare, but 42.6 million Americans, particularly the working poor and those in cities, lacked health insurance in 1999.[59] The quality of care received by the insured as well as the uninsured depends a great deal on where they live. Access to health care is not just a matter of money or insurance, but a question of supply.

Even though the supply of physicians in the United States has risen greatly in the past thirty years, it has not gone up in most low-income central-city neighborhoods. In New York City, Manhattan has the highest concentration of physicians, at 3.3 per 1,000 population, but some Brooklyn neighborhoods have only 0.3 physician per 1,000 population. Affluent northwestern Washington, D.C., and suburban Bethesda (Maryland) neighborhoods have one pediatrician for every 400 children, while the poor, mostly black neighborhoods of southeastern Washington have one pediatrician for every 3,700 children.[60] Even where doctors are present, many will not serve Medicaid patients. In the early 1990s, 67 percent of primary care physicians in large metropolitan areas limited the number of Medicaid patients they served, with the average practice having only 8 percent Medicaid patients.[61]

Most people believe that doctors shun Medicaid patients because of the program's relatively low payments and paperwork burden. The economics of the program are important, but doctors could cope by cross-subsidizing Medicaid patients with middle-income private payers. When many poor people are concentrated in an area of practice, however, this becomes difficult. Racial difference is also a problem. Nine out of ten doctors are white, and they prefer to practice in white areas. High crime and generally unpleasant conditions also discourage doctors from practicing in low-income areas, regardless of the doctor's or residents' race. Doctors serving high-poverty areas complain about language difficulties, missed appointments, lack of compliance with treatment, greater tendency to sue for malpractice, and frustration over the limited ability of medical interventions to improve health when patients live amidst homelessness, substance abuse, violence, unhealthy slums, and poverty. Those who do practice in concentrated poverty neighborhoods often run "Medicaid mills" that shuffle patients through as quickly as possible to collect fees. For many such doctors, this is the only place they can get a job. In the Mott Haven section of the South Bronx, described in chapter 1, fewer than 13 percent of primary care doctors were board certified.[62]

The United States spent over $177 billion a year on Medicaid by 1998.[63] Under present circumstances, it would take huge increases in Medicaid fees to entice doctors into the poorest areas, not just because these areas are poor, but because wealthier areas on the suburban fringe entice doctors to more profitable practices. Spatial inequality matters. Much Medicaid spending finances nursing care for the elderly, but much is also driven by health problems caused by poor living conditions. Even if we could provide excellent health care to people living in poor neighborhoods, it would not improve their overall health and longevity very much, because poor living conditions are an important part of the problem.

The Physical Environment

More than 100 years ago, Jacob Riis shocked the nation with the photographs in his book *How the Other Half Lives*. Like other nineteenth-century reformers, Riis thought that crowded tenements were breeding grounds for disease. Lacking light and ventilation, poor immigrants crowded on top of one another in filthy and degrading conditions that were perfect for spreading cholera, tuberculosis, typhus, and smallpox. Noting that half of all clothing was made in these tenements, Riis warned that the diseases could not be confined to poor immigrant areas: "It has happened more than once that a child recovering from small-pox, and in the most contagious stage of the disease, has been found crawling among heaps of half-finished clothing that the next day would be offered for sale on the counter of a Broadway store."[64] New York City has changed tremendously over the past century, but its slums still generate diseases from which middle-class people, even suburbanites, are not insulated.[65] The same is true in other metropolitan areas.

Many different aspects of low-income neighborhoods make them unhealthy places to live. Houses tend to be older, crowded, dark, and dangerous, with many health and safety code violations, resulting in more accidents and fires. Poor neighborhoods often lack parks and recreational facilities, forcing children to play in the streets, where traffic presents an ever-present danger.[66] Overcrowding is stressful and accelerates the transmission of infectious diseases. Tuberculosis was thought to have been controlled in the United States, but it has recently returned, nearing epidemic proportions in some inner-city neighborhoods. The emergence of multiple-drug-resistant strains of tuberculosis is an especially dangerous threat. As one author observed, treating it "requires proper follow-up and medical care, which is difficult for patients living in high-poverty areas. Too often they cannot afford the medicine, or follow-up appointments are impossible, as with the homeless." [67] Of the 20 percent of toddlers who are not immunized against preventable diseases such as measles, most are poor inner-city children.[68]

Lead paint was banned in 1973, but many older homes contain high levels of lead, either in paint or in lead pipes. Children in poor neighborhoods visit other homes and institutions likely to have lead paint and dust. At a certain age, children are apt to put anything in their mouths. In old houses with crumbling paint, they are prone to ingest large amounts of lead. Young children are especially vulnerable. Exposure to lead up to the age of six has been shown to impair children's IQs and their psychological and classroom performance. The damage is not reversible.[69]

Air quality in low-income neighborhoods is also often poor. Excessive traffic, especially truck traffic, pollutes the air. Inner-city neighborhoods often have hazardous industry or waste sites nearby. Black and low-income households are more likely to be exposed to environmental hazards, including toxic waste dumps, than are middle-class whites.[70] Polluting facilities such as garbage transfer stations and power plants are often located in low-income areas that lack the political clout to exclude them. A medical incinerator went to the South Bronx after residents of Manhattan's affluent East Side opposed it out of fear of cancer risks to their children. After eight years and 500 state violations, it was finally closed in May 1999.[71]

Polluted air is one cause of elevated asthma rates in poor neighborhoods. Asthma is a chronic, incurable disease that causes swelling and constriction in the lungs, making it difficult to breathe. Asthma attacks are triggered by allergic reactions to such things as dust, tobacco smoke, and cold air. For reasons that are not entirely clear, asthma has become much more common in recent years. Between 1980 and 1998, the number of asthma sufferers grew from 6.7 million to 17.3 million,[72] but it has reached epidemic proportions in concentrated poverty areas. In New York State, the rate of hospital admissions for asthma was 1.8 per 1,000, but it was more than three times higher in the Mott Haven area of the South Bronx.[73]

Cockroaches may explain the outbreak of asthma among inner-city children. One study of eight inner-city areas found that over 50 percent of the children slept in areas with high levels of cockroach allergen. Those who were exposed were hospitalized at a rate more than three times that among other children.[74] Controlling asthma is much more difficult in inner-city environments, where specialists are not available, patients are not educated about the illness, and families cannot afford expensive medicines and inhalers.

Social Integration and Lifestyles

At a certain stage, nations pass the "epidemiological transition." Diseases that used to be "rich men's diseases" begin to affect all classes as people live longer and enjoy better diets and sanitation. Degenerative diseases with multiple causes, such as cancer and heart disease, replace infectious diseases with a single cause as the most common cause of death. In such countries, health comes to depend crucially on developing a healthy lifestyle by eating a low-fat diet, exercising, abstaining from smoking, drinking alcohol in moderation, avoiding stress, having a satisfying social life, and developing a positive self-image.

One supposed implication of the epidemiological transition is that individuals now largely control their health prospects. Americans are obsessed with changing their diet or behavior in order to live longer, healthier lives. Whole racks of magazines and books are devoted to giving advice on healthy lifestyles. What they fail to note, however, is that the environments in which we live and work powerfully shape our ability to lead healthy lifestyles. Americans spend untold billions of dollars on diet advice and diet products, yet we are among the fattest people in the world. Environment can overwhelm personal willpower.

Socially connected people are healthier than socially isolated people, regardless of their individual characteristics. As one book notes, "The role of supportive social relationships in promoting health is one of the most thoroughly corroborated findings in social epidemiology."[75] Socially isolated people die at two to three times the rate of people with strong networks and emotional support. Social isolation is associated with cardiovascular disease, cancer, respiratory problems, and gastrointestinal disease, as well as with risk factors such as smoking and drinking.[76] Exactly why social ties promote good health is still the subject of study and debate, but the connection is not.

The quantity and quality of social relations are related to place. Residents of high-poverty neighborhoods have fewer social ties. Nearly half the residents of extreme-poverty areas in Chicago, for example, had no current partner, defined as being married to, living with, or steadily dating someone. One in five reported having no "best friend." Two-thirds did not belong to a formal organization, such as a block club or fraternal group. Residents of poor neighborhoods socialize with people who are likely to have their own problems with unemployment and debts.[77] Clearly, high levels of crime limit social relationships in poor neighborhoods. People are simply afraid to leave their apartments, especially at night. Limited social relations not only undermine health but also undermine a neighborhood's ability to organize politically to defend itself against unwanted land uses that create unhealthy environmental risks, such as a medical waste incinerator.

Residents of concentrated poverty areas are also more likely to engage in risky health behaviors, such as smoking, drinking, drug use, and unprotected sex.[78] Tobacco and alcohol companies target their advertising on central-city minority neighborhoods.[79] Where people live shapes their likelihood of smoking, consuming alcohol, eating fat, and failing to use seat belts. Because poor neighborhoods have fewer grocery stores charging higher prices for less healthy food, the people who live in these areas are more likely to suffer from obesity.[80] People in poor neighborhoods are more likely to practice risky behaviors. For example, people who live with high levels of stress are more likely to do things that may temporarily relieve stress, such as smoking. Risky behaviors are also infectious.[81] From the health viewpoint, such behaviors are clearly irrational. Low life expectancies, however, reduce the benefits of abstaining from these risky behaviors. Among seventy-seven community areas in Chicago, life expectancy at birth ranges from 54.3 to 77.4 years.[82] (The most important cause of the difference in life expectancy is the homicide rate, which ranges from 1.3 to 156 per 100,000 per year.) People who do not expect to live to a ripe old age discount the costs of risky behaviors, thus engaging in them more frequently.[83] Exposure to violence also stimulates risky behavior. Regardless of economic background, young people exposed to violence smoke more and feel less confident in their ability to affect their health.[84] Since risky behaviors reduce life expectancies, the result is a vicious circle of reduced life expectancies and risky behaviors.

Living in a concentrated poverty neighborhood also adversely affects people's emotional well-being. The neighborhood literally "gets under the skin" to affect health. Chronic stress leads to acute diseases, especially cardiovascular diseases, and premature death.[85] High-poverty neighborhoods experience stress from high crime rates, noise, overcrowding, unemployment, shortage of stores, and poor public services. Violent crime is probably the greatest stressor. Another is lack of control over one's living and working conditions. People in these neighborhoods, especially African Americans, usually have little choice about where to live.

Repeated stress can undermine the body's ability to protect itself from disease. It can result in allergic reactions to substances or conditions that were previously tolerated. (Stress is a well-known cause of asthma attacks.) The body may gradually fail to respond, reducing the body's immunity to various diseases. Stress heightens the severity of the common cold.[86] Chronic stress can accelerate the aging process.

Suburban Health

Most people agree that urban ghettos are unhealthy places and think that they can escape the ill effects by distancing themselves in remote suburbs. But the evidence suggests that this reasoning is wrong. The United States thought it had conquered tuberculosis and syphilis through antibiotics and public health measures. Instead, infectious diseases we thought we had left behind have returned with a vengeance.

The dynamic of economic segregation and suburban sprawl creates areas where disease thrives, as well as pathways for transmitting disease to the suburbs. The act of moving far away adds its own negative health effects. If exodus to suburbia is driven in part by flight from the problems of inner cities, and if excessive sprawl causes health problems, we must add this to the costs of economic segregation.

Concentrated poverty can incubate epidemics of infectious diseases that are then transmitted to suburban populations.[87] Between 1972 and 1976, for example, New York City cut back on fire service for the South Bronx, leading to an epidemic of fires that forced many people out of their homes. The resulting involuntary displacements disrupted people's social ties, harming the health of the community. It also drove intravenous drug users, the principal transmitters of the AIDS virus, out of a contained area and dispersed them throughout the South Bronx, spreading the disease. Overcrowding also contributed to an epidemic of tuberculosis. AIDS and tuberculosis, once they reached a certain level of concentration, spread first to Manhattan and then to other parts of the metropolitan area, following commuting patterns.

In the mid-1990s, Baltimore suffered an epidemic of sexually transmitted diseases, including syphilis, gonorrhea, chlamydia, herpes, and AIDS. This epidemic quickly moved from the inner city to inner-ring suburbs. A 1996 report by the National Academy of Sciences, *The Hidden Epidemic,* rang alarm bells about the fact that sexually transmitted diseases were not confined to the inner city.[88] Infectious disease rates in suburban counties of New York, Washington, D.C., and Detroit are driven by the rates of those same diseases in the central cities. One study concludes:

"Heterosexual" AIDS, multiple-drug-resistant TB, crime and violence, and the coming plagues of the 21st century, will not remain confined to poor inner-city ghettoes, but already reach out to threaten the vast, interconnected, urban and suburban system containing some three quarters of the US population. Without significant regional reform, even the rich will not be spared.[89]

To be sure, some outer-ring suburbs are healthful environments with little overcrowding and plenty of greenery, sunshine, and clean air. Middle-class suburbanites with private health insurance have access to the best health care in the world. But the spatial organization of suburbs also poses negative health risks.

The automobile is by far the greatest threat to suburban health. Although commuting times are not rising much, overall driving times and mileages are up significantly because of the spread-out nature of different activities in low-density suburbs. Women do most of the family errands, and they often engage in what transportation planners call "trip-chaining," long drives to do errands on the way home from work. Middle-class Americans now spend an average of thirty-two hours a month behind the wheel, with suburbanites driving three times as much as residents of a pedestrian neighborhood, where at least some activities can be reached on foot.[90] The increased vehicle miles traveled, caused in part by suburban sprawl, harms air quality. According to one study, vehicle-related air pollutants are responsible for 20,000 to 40,000 cases of chronic respiratory illness each year.[91]

People may move to the suburbs to escape urban dangers, but more than twice as many people die from traffic accidents as from homicide. In fact, traffic accidents are the leading cause of death for everyone aged one to twenty-four. Over 3 million people are injured in traffic accidents every year. Teens, whose crash rate is four times that of other drivers, suffer the most. Most murder victims are killed by their relatives or acquaintances, but traffic deaths are indiscriminate. Allen Durning estimated that it is actually safer, considering all sources of risk, to live in a central-city pedestrian neighborhood than to move to an outer-ring suburb.[92]

Time spent in traffic jams has other health effects. Commuting seems to elevate blood pressure, heart disease, back problems, lung cancer, and self-reported stress.[93] "Road rage" has now entered the American lexicon. Long commutes leave less time to relax with family and friends. The *Journal of the American Medical Association* editorialized that the American obesity epidemic stemmed partly from overreliance on the car and that the solution would require "substantial changes in community or regional design."[94] The spread-out nature of suburbs also undermines the sociability that is so directly connected to good health. As Robert Putnam noted, "each additional ten minutes in daily commuting time cuts involvement in community affairs by 10 percent."[95] The elderly and children under the age of sixteen who lack the ability to drive can be remarkably isolated in the suburbs. Those who drive are unlikely to have the kind of chance meetings made possible by the front stoop or sidewalk. As Jane Jacobs put it, "Lowly, unpurposeful and random as they may appear, sidewalk contacts are the small change from which a city's wealth of public life may grow."[96]

CONSUMER GOODS AND STANDARD OF LIVING

The shopping experience in a wealthy suburb is vastly different from that in a poor inner-city neighborhood. In the suburbs, people do not shop where they live; they meet day-to-day needs in stores strung out along commercial strips and make bigger purchases in big-box superstores or large shopping centers. Everything is oriented around the car, with shopping centers providing huge parking lots and many stores on commercial strips providing drive-in windows. The dominant chain stores are new and modern. The supermarkets are huge, use the latest technology, and offer specialized foods, such as sushi and live lobsters. Shopping centers include a dazzling array of stores specializing in everything from chocolate chip cookies to massage oils to athletic shoes.

Shopping in poor neighborhoods is very different. Stores are located along neighborhood commercial strips. They occupy the first floors of older buildings, with apartments or offices above. Most are small and locally owned, with the occasional exception of a chain drugstore, gas station, or fast-food outlet. Department stores and major appliance stores are rare. Residents of poor neighborhoods usually walk or take the bus to shop. The stores look old and are often run-down. Only a few use scanners for checkout, but many have cameras to prevent shoplifting.

It is easy to sum up the differences: areas of concentrated poverty have an undersupply of retail outlets, and areas of concentrated wealth have an oversupply. One study of retailing in 100 zip codes (averaging 15,000 in population) in seven Ohio cities found a consistent pattern: the number of stores per capita in ten retail categories fell as the poverty rate rose. Department stores disappeared entirely in the poorest zip codes. Even more revealing, the ratio of retail employees to the population in poor neighborhoods fell even more than the number of stores did.[97]

TABLE 3.1. Largest Retail Gaps in
Central Cities, 1998 Estimates
($ Billion)

New York City	$37.1
Chicago	$9.9
Los Angeles	$5.4
San Jose	$3.9
Long Beach	$2.8
Washington, D.C.	$2.8
San Francisco	$1.5
Detroit	$1.4
Baltimore	$1.3

Source: U.S. Department of Housing and Urban Development, *New Markets: The Untapped Retail Buying Power in America's Inner Cities* (Washington, D.C.: Government Printing Office, July 1999), p. 21.

Contrary to market theory, supply does not always meet consumer demand for retail purchases in metropolitan areas. Shopping in poor areas is less abundant not only because local customers spend less. Residents in concentrated poverty areas must often travel out of the neighborhood to make purchases. (We have already discussed the shortage of medical services.) By contrast, wealthy suburban areas enjoy such a surfeit of shopping opportunities that people travel from outside the area to shop there. In other words, poor central areas export shoppers, and rich outlying areas import shoppers.

This was not always the case. Cities used to be shopping magnets, attracting residents from miles around. Until the 1950s, most American cities drew people downtown to shop at department stores and central farmers' markets. The automobile freed shopping from its central location, however. Central-city shopping was "malled" to death. Now more city residents travel to the suburbs to shop than vice versa. As Table 3.1 shows, many central cities have a huge "retail gap" between their residents' purchasing power and total retail sales in the city. This study also uncovered a retail gap of $8.7 billion in forty-eight inner-city zip codes, with many suffering from unmet retail demand of 50 percent or more.[98]

The uneven distribution of shopping opportunities has unfortunate effects. As a pioneering book on this topic put it: *the poor pay more.*[99] Not only do residents of concentrated poverty areas pay more; they also have fewer choices and poorer quality and must travel farther to shop. The middle class often looks down on the poor for buying extravagant items like expensive sneakers and gold chains, and it is true that poor people often engage in what David Caplovitz labeled compensatory consumption: "Since many have small prospect of greatly improving their low social standing through occupational mobility, they are apt to turn to consumption as at least a sphere in which they can make some progress toward the American dream of success."[100]

The residents of wealthy suburban areas are equally prone, however, to engage in what Thorstein Veblen called "conspicuous consumption," or buying things to impress others. They are hardly a paragon of controlled consumption. Even though they have much more discretionary income, many middle-class families spend more than they can afford and fall into crippling debt. Aspects of the environment in outer-ring suburbs are partly responsible for this problem.

Groceries: The Poor Pay More

Food is obviously not a discretionary item. Poor people can cut their expenditures on food only so much. (Studies have shown, however, that poor families do spend considerably less on food than middle-class families do.) That is why food expenditures represent a high proportion of poor families' budgets. Poor families spend more than 30 percent of their income on food, compared with a national average of less than 13 percent.[101] One cause of the problem is price discrimination. Study after study has found that the poor pay higher prices for their groceries. Comparing a standard basket of food items in different parts of the metropolitan area, a 1991 study by the New York City Department of Consumer Affairs concluded that a family of four living in a poor zip code pays 8.6 percent more than a family in a middle-class area.[102] A 1988 study of 600 food items in 322 supermarkets in ten metropolitan areas concluded that prices were 4 percent higher in central cities than in suburban locations.[103]

Many city neighborhoods do not even have supermarkets, and residents purchase groceries at small convenience stores. Here the price differences can be huge. In testimony before Congress, Monsignor William J. Linder, director of the New Community Corporation (NCC) in Newark, New Jersey, reported that prices in the new Pathmark supermarket that the NCC helped attract were 35 percent lower than in local stores.[104] In addition, the small markets presented fewer choices, and their food was of inferior quality and freshness. Finally, shoppers who rely on mass transit or taxis to reach supermarkets outside their community have extra transportation costs of $400 to $1,000 a year.[105]

Why are food prices higher in poor, central-city neighborhoods? Is the difference due to the failure of grocery stores to serve these neighborhoods, or is it simply more costly to do business in poor neighborhoods? Michael Porter of the Harvard Business School argues that corporations have overlooked profitable opportunities in cities: "At a time when most other markets are saturated, inner city markets remain poorly served."[106] He implies that if governments simply educated entrepreneurs about the opportunities, the retail sector would blossom in the inner city. It is certainly true that profitable opportunities are being overlooked. The central Newark Pathmark is now one of the highest grossing in the nation, but Monsignor Linder's organization had to put together a complicated deal involving eight different public and foundation subsidies in order to get Pathmark to locate in this poor neighborhood.[107]

It would be wonderful if we could simply solve the problem by educating entrepreneurs. Unfortunately, the problem is more deeply rooted in the environment of concentrated poverty. Costs of doing business, including insurance, theft, parking, and land assembly, are higher in poor neighborhoods. But the main reason why the poor pay more is that different types of stores serve poor neighborhoods than serve well-to-do suburbs. Large, efficient supermarkets serve the suburbs. They are marvels of modern retailing, typically offering over 12,000 separate items and operating on a high volume that enables them to prosper with a profit margin of less than 1 percent of sales. They buy in bulk and apply the latest technology, including automated just-on-time inventory systems. Inefficient, low-volume grocery stores serving low-income neighborhoods must charge higher prices to remain in business.

Central cities are losing their large supermarkets. Between 1970 and 1992, Boston lost thirty-four out of fifty big-chain supermarkets. The number of supermarkets in Los Angeles County fell from 1,068 to 694 between 1970 and 1990. Chicago did worse, losing half of its supermarkets.[108] One study found that supermarkets with over fifty employees were nonexistent in the poorest zip codes: "Ghetto residents simply do not have access to chain supermarkets."[109]

The problem is not so much land acquisition, although this can be difficult. The problem is that population densities and rates of car ownership in low-income areas do not generate the desired volume of customers. As Adam Smith observed in *The Wealth of Nations,* the division of labor depends on the size of the market. Low-income, less mobile neighborhoods are not suited to the modern, high-volume supermarket. Therefore, they are serviced by small, technologically backward mom-and-pop stores that charge higher prices. The problem cannot be solved until the segregation of the poor is addressed.

Financial Services: The Rise of Fringe Banking

We think of pawnbrokers as relics of a bygone era, and pawnbroking did, indeed, decline from the 1930s to the 1970s. Since then, however, pawnshops have rebounded, almost doubling between 1985 and 1992. The 1980s also witnessed explosive growth in storefront outlets that cash people's payroll or government checks for a fee and sell money orders. Both pawnshops and check-cashing outlets are moving from poor urban neighborhoods to inner-ring suburbs, usually following well-traveled roads.[110] As with groceries, following the disappearance of conventional banks, a secondary market in financial services has sprung up to provide lower-quality services at higher prices to low-income areas.

Financial services are a necessity, not a luxury, in modern society. Almost all workers are paid by check, and most bills must be paid by check or money order. Access to credit is vital for participating in consumer culture. Few people could buy a house, go to college, or own a car without borrowing. Families need to buy expensive items when they are young and have relatively low incomes. Most families acquire their biggest asset by taking out a mortgage to buy a house. People rely on home equity and small business loans to start up businesses. For all these reasons, banks are essential to community stability. When they pull out, the neighborhood declines.

Traditional banks meet most people's financial needs, but those who live in concentrated poverty neighborhoods must often obtain financial services from more expensive alternative institutions that offer fewer services and may engage in predatory practices. Check-cashing outlets, for example, do not offer checking accounts, mortgages, or small business loans. They specialize in cashing checks, generally charging from 1.5 to 2.5 percent of the amount of the check. This costs a low-income person earning $20,000 a year about $400. (Check cashing is free to those with checking accounts.) Pawnshops offer consumer loans secured by property, such as a television or jewelry. Most states regulate pawnshops, but many pawnshops charge over 200 percent a year for a loan. Rent-to-own shops also are springing up in low-income neighborhoods to enable customers to rent furniture or appliances for low weekly payments and then take ownership at the end of, say, ninety weeks. A study in New Jersey found that they charged an average interest rate of 88 percent a year. No wonder they are called "rent-to-moan."[111]

Why do people in low-income central-city neighborhoods turn to these fringe banking institutions? According to Edward Banfield, poor people make poor choices because they are "radically improvident," that is, they buy things on impulse and do not save for the future.[112] Statistical studies, however, do not show that poor families are more wasteful in their spending habits.[113] Most poor people do not save or bank at conventional financial institutions because their incomes are too low and unstable. People who earn near the minimum wage constantly live hand-to-mouth. They cannot open up checking accounts, because they require minimum balances. The growth in the number of working poor who find it nearly impossible to save largely accounts for the growth of fringe banking.

Bank deregulation has also contributed to the growth of fringe banking. Increasing competition has forced banks to eliminate money-losing branches and services (such as low-cost or no-cost checking accounts) that were previously cross-subsidized by more lucrative services and locations.[114] Major banks have had to be ruthless about closing branches in neighborhoods where their customers are poor or even working class.

Fringe banking also has a clear spatial dimension. The problem of bank redlining has been well documented. Studies overwhelmingly show that, after controlling for other factors, banks discriminate against minorities and minority neighborhoods in mortgage lending.[115] Banks also discriminate against low-income neighborhoods, which is perfectly legal if they have good business reasons not to lend. Banks have closed many branches in low-income neighborhoods, as has been documented in New York and Atlanta.[116] As conventional lenders have declined and check-cashing outlets, pawnshops, and rent-to-own stores have proliferated in low-income areas, a two-tiered financial services marketplace has emerged. Children in poor neighborhoods grow up not even knowing what the inside of a bank looks like, reinforcing the isolation of low-income families from the economic mainstream.[117]

Suburban Overconsumption

At first blush, the surplus of retail outlets in the suburbs would seem to be nothing but a plus. The stores provide incredible choices, and competition brings low prices. So suburbanites benefit from a technologically advanced retail sector, paying less for groceries, financial services, insurance, and most consumer goods. But this outer-ring suburban advantage has subtle costs that we often overlook. Even though they have much more discretionary income, economic segregation and suburban sprawl contribute to the tendency of middle-class suburban families to spend themselves deeply into debt.

Approximately 40 percent of all American households spend more than their income each year, producing rising family debt.[118] In 1999, household debt totaled $6.8 trillion, up more than $3 trillion since 1990. From 1990 to 1999, personal savings as a percentage of disposable personal income fell from 7.8 to 2.4 percent, about the lowest personal savings rates of any developed country. By 1998, median debt payments had risen to 17.6 percent of income.[119] By 1999, household debt had reached an all-time peak.[120]

Going into debt can be rational at certain stages in the life cycle. For example, young families with steadily rising incomes should go into debt to make major purchases, such as a home, knowing they can pay the debt off as their income rises. The evidence is clear, however, that much household overspending in the United States is irrational, getting families in debt way over their heads and damaging their ability to achieve future goals. One indication is the phenomenal growth of high-interest credit card debt, which doubled between 1990 and 1996.[121] Another is the growth of nonbusiness bankruptcy petitions, which increased from 297,885 in 1985 to an astounding 1,391,964 in 1999, the ninth year of an economic expansion.[122]

Why are middle-class households overconsuming? Juliet Schor argues that it is driven by status concerns. The rich increasingly provide the reference group for middle-class consumers, who must overconsume, Schor argues, not so much to satisfy needs as to signal social status. People buy expensive cars and clothes to "keep up with the Joneses." The economic segregation of middle- and upper-class suburbs accentuates status anxieties. With fewer opportunities for families to compare their consumption patterns favorably with those of lower-income families, the need to overconsume becomes more powerful. To consume less is to be marked immediately as someone who does not fit in. Suburban teens even make subtle status distinctions about part-time jobs. Working at Starbucks or the Gap is cool; McDonald's or Burger King is considered lower class.[123]

To achieve and sustain high status, and to distance the family from urban problems, families must purchase expensive housing on the suburban fringe, taking on massive mortgage debt. Between 1980 and 1999, residential mortgage debt increased from $1.1 to $5 trillion.[124] Exactly how much of this represents flight from blight instead of rational consumer preferences is impossible to say, but part of this massive debt can clearly be attributed to the desire to escape from inner-city problems. Exclusionary zoning and growth controls, often designed to keep out the poor, also drive up the cost of suburban housing.

Once families are ensconced in an outer-ring suburb, they must also own a car or, more likely, two, since higher mortgage payments require both spouses to work. They can rarely take public transit to work or shopping, and bike paths and even sidewalks are usually absent. The average cost of owning and operating a car was 53 cents per mile in 1997.[125] A family with two cars that are each driven 10,000 miles a year must pay $10,600. Most cars are bought on credit. More than 50 percent of all families with car payments spent more than they earned in a given year, compared with the national average of 40 percent.[126] Urban households, in contrast, can often shed one or even two cars, saving thousands of dollars a year.[127]

With both parents working, families can produce fewer goods and services at home. Long hours at work and commuting put a premium on time, so spending on restaurants and fast food soars. Families hire baby-sitters, accountants, house cleaners, and gardeners to save them time. Expensive entertainment, massages, and vacations are needed to relieve stress. Finally, the need for more private consumption undermines suburban support for public goods.

Many years ago, John Kenneth Galbraith pointed out that our affluent society has an imbalance between booming private consumption and a starved public sector.[128] This imbalance is pronounced in many suburbs. Lacking a community pool or park, many suburban families feel the need for private pools, large backyards, and private clubs. (Public schools are the one crucial exception to the generally shrunken public sector in most suburbs.) Town-house and condominium housing developments are the ultimate expression of the pressure for privatization. Owners pay fees to an owners' association that privately provides a pool, security, and trash collection. Not surprisingly, residents of home-owner associations are reluctant to pay taxes for public services.[129]

The entire suburban environment, therefore, fuels overconsumption of private goods. In Orange County in southern California, one study noted, "The opportunity to consume permeates every aspect of life in Orange County, and few choose to ignore the chance to indulge since consuming less could lead to social marginalization."[130] Shopping is not just a way to satisfy needs; it provides entertainment and social identity. With no place to hang out except the mall, teenagers are especially vulnerable to the social pressures to consume. According to a Merck Family Fund poll, 86 percent of Americans agree that today's youth are too focused on consuming things.[131] Here, however, they are simply following the pattern set by their parents.

CRIME

The central action in Tom Wolfe's best-selling novel *The Bonfire of the Vanities* involves Sherman McCoy, a wealthy investment banker living in a $2.6 million apartment on Park Avenue in Manhattan. One night, he mistakenly drives his $48,000 Mercedes into the South Bronx and gets lost. The wealthy East Side and the South Bronx ghetto may be only a few miles apart, but Wolfe shows that they might as well be on different planets. Wolfe brilliantly conveys the cold fear that envelops Sherman and his companion, Maria, as they strain to extricate themselves from the chaotic streets of the Bronx. "Maria wasn't saying a word. The concerns of her luxurious life were now tightly focused. Human existence had but one purpose: to get out of the Bronx."[132] In a panic, they run over a young black man, setting in motion a plot that enables Wolfe to bring the separate societies of New York into crazy confrontations with each other.

Wolfe's novel assumes a well-established generalization in criminology— that crime rates vary significantly in different parts of the city. In the 1920s, University of Chicago sociologists found the highest juvenile delinquency rates in the "zone of transition" surrounding the downtown, with crime falling as one moved farther from the center. That pattern can still be found. For example, in the late 1980s in Minneapolis–St. Paul, Minnesota, the central-city violent crime rate was almost eight and a half times higher than the suburban rate.[133]

The dramatic drop in crime in the United States during the 1990s is good news for everyone, but the relationship between place and crime is still strong. Nationwide, between 1992 and 1999, the homicide and robbery rates fell by 36 percent.[134] The experts are still debating the reasons for the extraordinary drop in crime, but three common explanations are the booming economy, the decline of the crack trade, and the increased effectiveness of policing. The good news is that crime fell faster in central cities than in suburbs during this period. The bad news is that central-city crime rates are still about three times those of suburbs. Moreover, many inner-ring suburbs now suffer from higher crime rates than their central cities.

Crime deeply affects the quality of life. High rates of crime mean high crime victimization rates. In the United States as a whole, the property crime victimization rate was one-third higher in cities than in suburbs in 1996. The difference is greater for violent crime. Strangers commit only 40 percent of all violent crimes.[135] The criminal and the victim usually know each other, and most violent crimes occur near where they both live. Most violent crime involves people of the same race; so-called zebra crimes, black on white or white on black, are relatively uncommon. Living in a crime-prone neighborhood is associated with a higher risk of victimization.[136] No matter what you do, you run a higher risk of being hurt by crime if you live in a dangerous neighborhood.

The issue of race and crime is a volatile topic. Young black males commit a disproportionate share of violent crimes, causing many people to think that black communities harbor a subculture of crime.[137] Most of the association between black neighborhoods and crime, however, stems from the concentration of poverty, not the concentration of blacks. Blacks living in higher-income census tracts, like whites in such areas, experience low rates of homicide; only blacks living in concentrated poverty areas suffer from higher levels of homicide victimization.[138] The coincidence of race and crime is partly a by-product of whites' ability to flee high-crime areas; low incomes and housing discrimination prevent blacks from doing so.[139] The causes of high crime rates are rooted in the concentration of poverty, the social isolation of these areas from regional opportunity structures, and their ensuing social disorganization.

People living in poor neighborhoods also live in a floating consumer culture kept aloft by advertising and the mass media. They may be isolated from economic opportunities, but they are not isolated from the culture of consumption. The average American sees approximately 38,000 television commercials a year.[140] Since television is the cheapest form of entertainment, even poor single-parent households have one. Television ads and shows present the poor with an upper-middle-class, or even rich, reference group. Television stimulates consumption regardless of income. Research shows that each additional hour of television watched per week decreases savings by $208.[141]

Advertising seeks to sell commodities not for their material qualities or usefulness but because they will enhance the owner's status and satisfy his or her emotional needs. As Juliet Schor puts it: "For many low-income individuals, the lure of consumerism is hard to resist. When the money isn't there, however, feelings of deprivation, personal failure, and deep psychic pain result. In a culture where consuming means so much, not having money is a profound social disability." [142] What David Caplovitz noted almost forty years ago is still true today: "Americans in all walks of life are trained to consume in order to win the respect of others and to maintain their self-respect." [143] Advertisers never encourage modest consumption patterns that make sense for low-income households. Instead, they push extravagant consumption patterns that only the middle and upper middle classes can afford. In the 1980s, Nike conducted a sophisticated ad program using star athletes, such as Michael Jordan, to establish the desirability of expensive athletic shoes. The program was so successful that it triggered a rash of "sneaker murders" in major cities.[144] It is not surprising that President Clinton, among others, called for school uniforms as a way to get students' minds off of clothes and into books.

The primary source of frustration among low-income consumers is a lack of money. Deprivation in the midst of affluence encourages an obsession with money, leading people to turn to crime as a way to acquire possessions and respect.[145] Indeed, crime pays, at least in the short run. The 1989 Boston Youth Survey calculated that crime paid an average of $19 an hour. A survey of Washington drug dealers found an average pay of $30 for the hours worked, or the equivalent of $12 per hour full-time. Legitimate jobs paid less than half as much.[146] A life of crime poses long-term risks of imprisonment or bodily harm, but as we noted earlier, the shorter life expectancies of residents of high-poverty neighborhoods may lead them to discount such costs.

People engage in crime because the jobs available to them do not command respect or decent incomes, especially for men. Factories used to provide working-class men with jobs that valued physical strength and male bonding. Service-sector jobs, in contrast, value language skills over strength and often require men to take orders from women. Feeling inferior, many minority men respond with a cool pose and heightened sensitivity to signs of disrespect.[147] Anthropologist Philippe Bourgois lived for three and a half years in Spanish Harlem, listening to Hispanic youths talk about how their service-sector bosses disrespected their street culture. One man, Primo, ultimately turned to the crack trade, speaking bitterly about how his boss did not want him to answer the phone because of his Puerto Rican accent. His friend, Caesar, confirmed Primo's experiences: "I had a few jobs like that [referring to Primo's 'telephone diss'] where you gotta take a lot of shit from bitches and be a wimp. I didn't like it but I kept on working, because 'Fuck it!' you don't want to fuck up the relationship. So you just be punk [shrugging his shoulders dejectedly]."[148] Caesar later joined Primo in the crack trade.

Thwarted in achieving status through conventional channels, poor people can become obsessed with achieving respect any way they can. This includes walking with an exaggerated masculine swagger and wearing clothing that calls attention to themselves (behavior hardly confined to the poor). Whites often perceive this pose as threatening, but it is actually a defense against feelings of inferiority. In the words of psychologist Richard Majors, the cool pose "may be his only source of dignity and worth as a man, a mask that hides the sting of failure and frustration."[149] Sociologist Elijah Anderson describes how poor young males are hypersensitive to any signs of disrespect, or "dissing." They may respond violently to minor slights, such as failing to make room on the sidewalk or maintaining eye contact too long. Even those who are not provoked by minor slights must be prepared to use violence in order to survive.[150] As Douglas Massey puts it, "Asking residents of poor neighborhoods to choose a less violent path or to 'just say no' to the temptation of violence is absurd in view of the threatening character of the ecological niche that they inhabit."[151]

Social Ties and Crime

The high crime rate in poor neighborhoods may also reflect inadequate or uncertain police protection. The use of computer mapping to target police resources on high-crime locations certainly suggests that police services can make a difference. At the same time, soaring expenditures for police and prisons, and a dramatic increase in prison populations, have not prevented the crime rate from remaining remarkably high in some places. Many criminologists think that informal social ties are as important as formal law enforcement.

The link between poverty areas and crime is far from perfect. Some poor neighborhoods are much safer than others. These safe neighborhoods seem to possess higher levels of social organization, including strong families, friendship networks, and voluntary organizations such as churches and community groups. Residents of 343 neighborhoods in Chicago were asked a series of questions to learn their level of social ties. These questions included whether neighbors would intervene if they saw a crime being committed and whether they could be trusted. It found that areas with strong social ties had lower crime rates, regardless of the income of residents.[152]

Why do concentrated poverty neighborhoods have fewer social ties? The Chicago study found that poverty concentration, residential mobility, and the presence of immigrants accounted for 70 percent of the variation in social cohesion across neighborhoods. The turnover in high-poverty neighborhoods stemmed from sudden income loss, fires, and urban renewal. Scrambling to make a living, residents of poor neighborhoods lack the time and money to support a rich organizational life. William Julius Wilson argues that the shortage of "marriageable males" who make enough money to support a family drives up the percentage of female-headed households, weakening parental controls, especially over young males. Gangs replace ties to adults.[153] Crime itself also eats away at neighborhood social cohesion. People respond to crime by avoiding it, which also reduces their opportunities for social interaction. The result can be a reinforcing cycle of crime and social decay.[154]

The Effects on Suburbs

Many Americans responded to the soaring urban crime rates of the 1970s and 1980s by fleeing. Violent crime rates have a strong statistical association with increased moves from central-city neighborhoods to the suburbs, as well as with decreased willingness to move into high-crime areas.[155] Mobile households find such a strategy rational, at least in the short run. By moving away from where criminals live and altering daily routines to avoid high-crime areas, suburbanites can substantially reduce their chances of becoming crime victims.

The recent rash of highly publicized crimes in well-to-do suburbs has caused suburbanites to question whether they really are insulated from the problem. The growth of suburban gangs imitating the rituals, symbols, and criminal behaviors of inner-city gangs is well documented.[156] Plano, Texas, a wealthy Dallas suburb, had a serious heroin problem among its youth. Rockdale, a new, upper-middle-class suburb of Atlanta, was the subject of a PBS television documentary on a mysterious outbreak of syphilis and gonorrhea. Facilitated by the widespread abuse of alcohol and drugs, children as young as twelve practiced group sex in sumptuous suburban homes when overworked parents were away. The April 1999 rampage at Columbine High School in Littleton, Colorado, riveted national attention on the problem of suburban crime and violence. Two alienated teenagers killed twelve fellow students and a teacher before turning their guns on themselves. Less than a year later, two Columbine High sweethearts were shot to death in a sandwich shop.

Most people believe that suburban crime represents the "spread" of inner-city criminal subcultures to the suburbs. There is some truth to this. Suburbanites do go to the inner cities to purchase drugs or to buy sex, often bringing back sexually transmitted diseases to the suburbs. The social and economic factors that promote inner-city crime are spreading to inner-ring suburbs, some of which now suffer higher crime rates than poor inner-city neighborhoods. When a spate of carjackings erupted a few years ago, suburbanites felt vulnerable and responded by making carjackings a federal crime.[157]

Rising suburban crime rates did not stem primarily from poverty-stricken city neighborhoods, however. Suburban flight itself creates conditions that foster crime, especially teen delinquency. Scholars and the mass media seldom discuss this aspect of the suburban idyll, partly because crime remains generally lower in the suburbs than in central cities.[158] As we noted earlier, between 1992 and 1999, homicide and robbery rates fell more rapidly in cities than in suburbs, though the rates were still substantially higher in cities.[159] Crime rates also vary tremendously across suburbs.[160]

Teen delinquency is the major source of crime and violence in the suburbs. Annual surveys of a nationally representative sample of students show that crime and violence are spreading in the suburbs.[161] In the 1999 survey, 25 percent of central-city students reported the presence of gangs, but so did a surprising 16 percent of suburban students. Though 15 percent of central-city students said that they knew a student who brought a gun to school, so did 12.3 percent of suburban students. Almost as many suburban students (14.5 percent) reported that they were crime victims as did urban students (14.6 percent). This has led many suburban schools to ban gang insignia, install metal detectors, and issue ID cards to students. Wayne Doyle, a school superintendent in a Pittsburgh suburb, put it this way: "In some areas, people are saying, 'Well, that's happening in the city, but it won't happen here.' Others are being more realistic and realizing that it can happen anywhere."[162]

Suburban juvenile crime is probably far more prevalent than the official statistics indicate, because police have tremendous discretion when dealing with vandalism, graffiti, and drinking in public. Police may discriminate on the basis of race, but the evidence indicates that they also discriminate on the basis of place. Based on past experience, beat police view "all persons encountered in bad neighborhoods . . . as possessing the moral liability of the area itself."[163] In the Seattle Youth Survey, 43 percent of boys living in poor neighborhoods reported that they had not done what the police said they had done, compared with only 25 percent of the boys from high-income areas. Boys from poor neighborhoods were significantly more likely to get a police record than were boys from wealthy areas, even after controlling for the number of delinquent acts they committed. This may be because lower-class areas have limited private space and boys therefore drink or smoke marijuana on the street, where they are at a higher risk of police detection.[164]

Why do teens from privileged suburbs commit delinquent acts when they would seem to have everything, including good schools, healthy allowances, jobs, and an ample supply of material goods? It strikes many adults as odd that suburban teens imitate the clothes, speech, and mannerisms of ghetto youth. Boys in many suburban schools wear baggy pants slung down low on their hips, Tommy Hilfiger shirts, and expensive basketball shoes, and "Gansta" rap music enjoys huge popularity among suburban teens. Suburban "wannabes" seem determined to consternate their parents by bringing ghetto culture to the suburbs.

Many suburbanites view inner-city ghetto residents as hedonistic, incapable of controlling their desires, and coddled by a permissive welfare state. In fact, the image they project onto the poor accurately portrays many self-indulgent suburban teenagers. Suburban teenagers participate in a consumer culture that celebrates hedonism and self-indulgence. With generous parental support, they do not need to rein in their impulses or submit themselves to the discipline of work. They hang out at the mall and create their own teen subcultures that sometimes veer into self-destructive and violent acts.

Delinquent teen bonding is not the only cause of the problem. Adolescence is a time for separating from parents and seeking one's own identity. A study of suburban teen gangs concluded that middle-class children from two-parent families may join gangs as a way of learning about loyalty, identity, and courage. It becomes problematic when responsible adults withdraw completely from the teen culture and set no limits. Sustained attachment to competent and caring adults can limit this tendency.[165] This is what the poorest ghettos lack, and too often, so do many economically advantaged suburbs. Adults, usually men, are often absent from poor neighborhoods because they lack jobs that can support a family. Under incredible stress to make ends meet without strong community supports, single mothers struggle to control adolescent boys, often with little success. In wealthy suburbs, instead of too little work, parents have too much:

many parents are overworked and face intense time pressures; a smaller group, concentrated in cities, is underworked and often aimlessly idle.[166]

Between 1989 and 1998, the average middle-income married couple with children increased the amount of hours worked by 4.5 full-time weeks per year.[167] Women with children are working anywhere from sixty-five to eighty hours a week, including household duties. Long commutes are common in sprawled-out suburbs, and family errands are more time-consuming because everything is spread out. One Gallup poll reported that although only 13 percent of working mothers want to work full-time, 52 percent actually do.[168] They do so partly to afford mortgage payments for expensive houses in suburbs far from inner-city crime and social disorganization. The dad who leaves work at 5 P.M., typical of the 1950s, is rare today. "Thirty percent of men with children under fourteen report working fifty or more hours a week. . . . Thirty percent of them work Saturdays and/or Sundays at their regular employment. And many others use the weekends for taking a second job."[169] The Family Research Council reported that the "total contact time" between parents and children dropped 40 percent over a twenty-five-year span.[170] Most juvenile delinquency takes place between the time school ends and overworked parents get home, a period when children are left to fend for themselves.

Part of the time squeeze is clearly generated by the spatial arrangements that middle-class parents have chosen out of a desire to move far away from the perceived social pathology of the central city and inner-ring suburbs. Motivated by the best of intentions — removing their children from bad environments — parents may create the very conditions they were trying to escape.

Either way, suburbanites end up paying more for the costs of crime, either through problems facing their own children or through taxes paid to support a bloated criminal justice system that, including prisons, now costs $150 billion each year, an average of $545 per person. The National Institute of Justice estimated that the actual cost is three times larger, taking into account the value of human life, time lost on the job, legal expenses, and intangibles such as the emotional costs to a murder victim's family.[171]

Americans also spend lavishly on private security. By 1990, 2.6 percent of the U.S. workforce had private security jobs, double the percentage in 1970, and larger than the public security labor force.[172] Motivated largely by fear of crime, perhaps 8 million Americans live in gated communities.[173] Fear of crime also promotes gun ownership, and half of all American households possess firearms. Most juveniles who carry guns do so for self-protection.[174] Instead of making society safer, however, the spread of guns increases the number of accidental deaths, suicides, and homicides.

It is difficult to put a price tag on the ways in which fear of crime moves us to change our behavior and robs us of activities we would otherwise enjoy. That crime motivates many people to move to the suburbs is itself a substantial cost. The mobility caused by crime has an acidic effect, eating away at social ties in the old neighborhoods left behind. People also stay away from central cities and isolate themselves from cities' unique cultural and historical resources. Inner-city ghetto residents suffer even more, sometimes becoming prisoners in their own homes. The costs are especially great for women. Many of those who change their daily routines to avoid crime become more fearful rather than less so, once more setting a debilitating vicious circle in motion.[175]

As we noted in chapter 1, the media coverage of crime often generates a level of fear that exceeds actual crime levels. Watching television generates fear of crime in distant urban settings. People who watch a lot of television are afraid to go downtown, for example, but do not perceive more crime in their immediate neighborhoods.[176] Since local newscasts sensationalize crime, suburbanites have exaggerated fears of urban crime.[177]

THE VICIOUS CIRCLE

There has been a great deal of discussion of rising income inequality in the United States, but little discussion about how rising economic segregation both causes the problem and worsens its effects. Drawing on the scholarly literature, we can estimate those effects. One study of 11,000 male workers in Los Angeles County calculated that statistically "moving" a person with exactly the same education, skills, and demographic characteristics from a low-poverty to a high-poverty area lowered his or her wages by 15 percent (from $20,000 to $17,000).[178] Similar costs for living in a high-poverty area can be estimated for consumption. If that same person spent one-third of her income on groceries at prices that were 8 percent higher in the inner city, she would pay $453 more per year. Assuming further that she used a check-cashing outlet, she would be out another $340 (2 percent charge). And if she owned a modest home worth $50,000, it would cost $200 more to insure it in a low-income zip code than a high-income zip code.[179] Finally, she would pay about 50 percent higher property taxes in the central city than in the suburbs.

Although this presents only a hypothetical example and conditions vary from neighborhood to neighborhood, it is possible to use available research to estimate the economic costs of moving a person who would earn $20,000 a year in a low-poverty suburb to a high-poverty central-city neighborhood:

Loss of wages	$3,000
More expensive groceries	$453
Added cost of cashing payroll checks	$340
More expensive home owners' insurance	$200
Higher property taxes	$600
Total	$4,593

Such costs are devastating for low-income families, representing a 23 percent tax on their incomes. Moreover, this excludes many other costs that are difficult to quantify, such as exposure to crime, unhealthy environments, inferior public services, heightened stress, higher costs for retail goods besides groceries, and alienation from society and politics. Because these costs fall more directly on the poor, they widen inequalities. Those who live in suburban areas of concentrated wealth clearly enjoy many advantages, but they also indirectly bear many costs from concentrated poverty.

As high as these costs may be, our analysis has skirted around one crucial point. We have treated the dimensions of employment, health, retail services, and crime as if they were isolated from one another. In fact, they are part of a seamless web. Each is a *cause,* not just an effect, of economic segregation and suburban sprawl. In combination, they reinforce the vicious circle of regional inequality. Poor fire protection can lead to neighborhood instability, causing higher rates of disease and out-migration. With fewer customers, the retail sector declines, reducing job prospects in the area. With rising unemployment, the crime rate soars, which only encourages more families to move out. To speak of these spatial effects as "externalities," as economists do, wrongly implies that they are marginal and correctable with government interventions. In fact, they are ubiquitous, complexly intertwined, and difficult to change.

The Roads Not Taken
How Federal Policy Promoted Economic Segregation and Suburban Sprawl

Martin Wuest, an electrical engineer, gets up at 3:15 every morning so he can get to work at Pericom, a semiconductor company in San Jose, California. He lives in Los Banos, an old farm town eighty-six miles from San Jose. If he leaves his house at 3:50 A.M., he can usually make the drive in ninety minutes. If he leaves later, it takes a lot longer. He gets to his office by 5:30 A.M. More than one-third of the residents of Los Banos join Wuest in rising before dawn to fight their way through heavy freeway traffic to commute to Silicon Valley, the high-tech region around San Jose. Many of these families moved to Los Banos because they could not afford to live any closer. The median house price in Silicon Valley rose from $397,533 in October 1999 to $530,000 a year later, and the average monthly rent for an apartment is over $1,000. To accommodate them, Los Banos has allowed developers to build large tracts of single-family homes and apartments that cost less than half the price of those in Silicon Valley. Although the people living in Los Banos pay lower housing costs, they face long commuting times, less family time together, and more family stress.[1]

Few would dispute our contention that place matters in people's lives, but some would disagree with how we interpret this claim. Some would say, "Sure, some places are better than others, but this only reflects individual preferences and ability to consume. It has always been this way. If you make money, you can afford to live in a good neighborhood. If you are poor, you can't. It is only natural that people of different economic classes sort themselves out into different neighborhoods. It is a matter of personal preferences, market forces, and cultural values." In the case of Martin Wuest, the high-technology boom caused housing prices to soar in Silicon Valley. Given his income level, Wuest chose to trade longer commuting times for lower housing costs. Some would say that this was simply a rational decision, not the result of any plot to constrain his choices.

In this chapter, we dispute the contention that sprawl and segregation simply result from rational decisions made in the marketplace. Geographic sprawl and spatial inequalities were not the inevitable result of high-tech growth in the San Jose metropolitan area. Instead, these outcomes were shaped by a whole series of government actions, ranging from freeway construction and tax policies to local zoning policies, as well as inactions, particularly the failure to build adequate supplies of moderately priced rental housing, public transit, and socially integrated communities. Although Martin Wuest undoubtedly made the best choice from among the options available to him, previous political decisions had a lot to say about what these options would be.

In fact, government policies play a crucial role in producing and aggravating metropolitan inequalities. A recent survey asked 149 leading urban scholars to identify the most important influences on the American metropolitan areas since 1950. They identified "the overwhelming impact of the federal government on American metropolis, especially through policies that intentionally or unintentionally promoted suburbanization and sprawl."[2] Federal policies have had two major consequences. First, they have consistently favored investment in suburbs and disinvestment from central cities. These policies provided incentives for businesses and middle-class Americans to move to suburbs while deterring poor Americans from doing so. Government policies have also favored concentrating the poor in central cities. Second, federal (and state) policies encouraged economic competition and political fragmentation *within* metropolitan areas, primarily by allowing "local autonomy" over taxation, land use, housing, and education, but also by failing to provide incentives for regional governance or cooperation. The power of each suburb to set its own rules and the competition among local governments for tax-generating development have powerfully promoted economic segregation and suburban sprawl. Both federal policies and the jurisdictional ground rules have created an uneven playing field that fosters the conditions we have already described.

THE FREE MARKET PERSPECTIVE

The conservative conventional wisdom has it the other way around: government policies are biased in favor of cities, wasting huge amounts of money in a futile effort to stem urban decline driven by powerful market forces. This misperception is rooted in historical amnesia and fails to appreciate the influence of government and the power of place.

Although government policies have long been biased against central cities, these biases were especially pronounced from World War II through the 1960s. Once suburban sprawl and economic segregation had gained momentum, the federal government did enact a series of policies to stem urban decline, such as urban renewal and revenue sharing. But these policies were largely designed to protect central business districts, not reverse the dynamic of economic segregation and suburban sprawl. Only belatedly, and with few resources, did they even seek to address worsening conditions in central-city neighborhoods.

Many scholars have reinforced the conventional wisdom that suburbanization and economic segregation are the natural products of a free marketplace. They assume that people with similar incomes have similar preferences for government services, thus confirming the folk wisdom that "birds of a feather flock together." It is only natural that rich people choose to live in the same suburban areas with other rich people. This perspective represents the way many people think about metropolitan development. Only by challenging this conventional wisdom can we overcome the widespread cynicism that government can do little to counter economic and racial segregation and metropolitan sprawl.

Those who defend economic segregation generally view it as an expression of individual choices made in a free market. In a provocative article in the conservative journal *National Review,* Llewellyn Rockwell argued that "[t]he housing policy of a free society ought to be simple: people should be able to live where they want, using their own money and engaging in voluntary market exchanges." According to Rockwell, "markets mean choice, and with choice comes sorting. People tend to choose to work, socialize, and live with others in their own social, religious, cultural, and economic group. There's nothing wrong with that. In fact, it creates real diversity among neighborhoods." This has traditionally led to "neighborhoods centered on one group or another, whether WASP, Greek, Ukrainian, Italian, black, Chinese, or whatever."[3] Accordingly, society actually has less economic and racial segregation than is ideal, because government has interfered in this "natural system" by engaging in "social engineering" that imposes poor people and racial minorities on communities that would otherwise choose to be more homogeneous. Those who defend segregation from this perspective view the outcome not just as maximizing efficiency and free choice but as creating a superior moral climate. Rockwell, for example, calls segregation a "natural pattern, a product of rational choice," which "makes possible strong communities."[4] Fred Siegel adds that sprawl is "an expression of the upward mobility and growth in home-ownership generated by our past half-century of economic success." Larger incomes require bigger homes on more land, forcing our metro areas to stretch out. Sprawl is "part of the price we're paying for creating something new on the face of the earth: the first mass upper-middle class."[5]

These commentators believe that economic segregation is morally just. Howard Husock argues in a report for the conservative *Heritage Foundation* that "socioeconomic status is a universal sorting principle in American cities. People of like social rank tend to live together and apart from those of unlike rank." Moving to better neighborhoods is a mark of one's status, which, Husock argues, should be earned by hard work. Economic segregation reflects the rightful ability of those who have good values, whose hard work and saving are rewarded by the market, to move into good neighborhoods. Those who lack good middle-class values, who are lazy and live only in the present, do not deserve to live in such neighborhoods. If left to the free market, they would not be able to afford to. Programs like the Department of Housing and Urban Development's (HUD's) Moving to Opportunity, which provides vouchers to low-income families so that they can pay for private apartments in better-off suburbs, violate this moral order. Subsidized low-income housing developments in middle-class neighborhoods are equally bad because they "[rob] the poor of the will and even the means to climb the neighborhood ladder on their own." They are, Husock says, an "ill-gotten gain," a "reward not commensurate with accomplishment."[6]

In a *New Republic* article entitled "Suburban Myth: The Case for Sprawl," Gregg Easterbrook acknowledges that the desire of white people to "escape contact with blacks" promotes suburbanization, but he argues that their primary motivation is the preference for "[d]etached homes, verdant lawns [and] lower crime rates," which "represents a lifelong dream" to most Americans, regardless of race. People also move to suburbs to escape the "corruption and mismanagement" of urban governments, Easterbrook argues, especially "disastrous inner-city school systems." Acknowledging that suburban sprawl creates environmental problems, Easterbrook nevertheless believes that the benefits outweigh the costs. He associates cities with "high density tower housing" and "cramped quarters." In contrast, suburban housing tracts make widespread home ownership possible. Suburban shopping malls are a "furiously efficient means of retailing." Automobiles "promote economic efficiency and personal freedom" and, despite traffic congestion, typically get people to and from places more quickly than public transit would.[7] Freeways allow people to commute from homes in one suburb to jobs in another; subways and light railways, built along fixed corridors, do not offer nearly as much convenience and flexibility. Sprawl, he concludes, is "economically efficient."[8]

Some defenders of sprawl believe that central cities are becoming obsolete. *Washington Post* reporter Joel Garreau celebrated the emergence of "edge cities." The Gwinnett Place mall outside Atlanta, the Schaumburg area outside Chicago, the Bridgewater Mall area in central New Jersey, and Tysons Corner outside Washington, D.C., constitute the "hearths of civilization," according to Garreau. "Americans are individualists," he writes. "The automobile is the finest expression of transportation individualism ever devised."[9] Thanks to cheap land, highway access, and distance from central cities, farmland and open space on the urban periphery have become attractive for development. Edge cities are now practically self-sustaining. People can live, work, shop, visit their doctors, eat at nice restaurants, and attend plays and movies in the suburbs. They no longer need a big, central urban "hub." Moreover, Garreau says, none of this was planned by public officials or government bureaucrats. It came about because pioneering entrepreneurs recognized these exurban possibilities, invested in them, and attracted other entrepreneurs. What some view as ugly sprawl, sterile housing tracts, and congested highways, Garreau views as a symbol of entrepreneurial innovation.

In this view, government efforts to work against this logic of metropolitan growth and edge-city development are doomed to fail. Tamar Jacoby and Fred Siegel argue that government should instead seek to improve inner-city economic conditions by using tax breaks and loans to entice private businesses to locate in ghettos and by providing grants to community-based organizations to sponsor retail stores or provide social services. Regulating banks to lend in areas where they otherwise would not do so will inevitably backfire, they say, because government bureaucrats create too many rules and obstacles. They do not understand how the private market works or the flexibility that individual entrepreneurs require. Government programs just thwart the entrepreneurial spirit of inner-city businesspeople.[10] Instead, Harvard Business School professor Michael Porter tells us, government should get out of the way and allow the "competitive advantage of the inner city" to foster economic improvements in poor urban neighborhoods.[11]

Given the reality that most private choices—by individuals as well as businesses—about metropolitan location are shaped by local government taxes, infrastructure, services, and schools, scholars working from the free-market perspective have incorporated the local public sector into their analysis. This is called "public choice" theory. Its proponents view the multiplicity of local governments within metropolitan areas as creating an intergovernmental marketplace parallel to the private market. This promotes consumer choice. Just as shoppers can choose from among brands of towels, toothpastes, or television sets, households can choose where to live from an array of cities and suburbs.[12] Each jurisdiction represents a distinct bundle of amenities and services at a distinct price in taxation. Since people have different tastes in cities, just as they have different tastes in clothing, public choice scholars view this arrangement as the most efficient way to allocate public goods and services.

Charles Tiebout's 1956 classic essay "A Pure Theory of Local Expenditures" provided the first systematic statement of this view:

> The consumer-voter may be viewed as picking that community which best satisfies his preference pattern for public goods. . . . The greater the number of communities and the greater the variance among them, the closer the consumer will come to fully realizing his preference position.[13]

For public choice theorists, choosing a detergent and choosing a local government have much in common: "Individual choices differ for public goods and services as well as for private. Some consumers want more freeways; others want a rapid transit system instead. Some prefer local parks; others, larger private backyards."[14] Tiebout and those who embrace his argument, including Elinor and Vincent Ostrom, Paul Peterson, and Mark Schneider, view the competition among local jurisdictions as creating an efficient and responsive market for public services (although interference by government bureaucrats and other special interests distort the marketplace).[15]

Public choice theory justifies economic segregation on the grounds that people with similar tastes for public goods and a similar ability to pay for them will naturally settle in local government jurisdictions that provide those goods. According to Robert Warren, public choice theory "assumes that a metropolitan area is composed of diverse communities of interests which are territorially distinct from one another and which have different preferences for goods and services in the public sector."[16] While acknowledging that regional governments may be more efficient in providing air pollution control, transportation, and hospital services, the public choice perspective argues that most services are best provided by local governments, because, according to Werner Hirsch, proximity leads to more "effective citizen-consumer feedback into the government sector," better management, less corruption, and greater efficiency.[17] In other words, competition forces each government to be more efficient and more responsive to its citizens' concerns. If it does not meet their needs, people will move to a more responsive jurisdiction. Fragmented, competitive metropolitan areas provide a cornucopia of choices that maximize household satisfaction.

These critics believe that government plays a role in guiding metropolitan development, but they argue that government should adapt to market trends (or, following public choice theory, imitate the market). To be sure, they recognize that unregulated markets can generate environmental problems, racial separation, and urban ghettos, but they think that any attempt to "cure" these ills will only make things worse by violating human nature and introducing inefficiencies into the market. A metropolitan-wide government, for example, would only eliminate or reduce consumer choice.

THE MYTH OF THE "FREE" MARKET

The public choice perspective has two major flaws. The first is the assumption that markets are actually "free" of government influence. Although people do make real choices among alternatives in housing, business location, and other markets, government policies shape every aspect of how they make those choices and what they have to choose from. Indeed, government establishes the regulatory and legal framework that makes it possible to have functioning markets at all. Markets therefore cannot be isolated from government, public policy, and politics. The "free market" is an abstraction, not a reality. Garreau hardly acknowledges that edge cities have grown up around and depend entirely on publicly funded highways and, in some cases, airports and other government facilities. Local governments do compete for residents and investors, but the rules of the game under which they do so are neither free nor fair. They do not give all people and places an equal chance to succeed. In fact, they are strongly biased away from central cities and toward suburban jurisdictions.

Moreover, paths taken or not taken in the past frame current choices. Easterbrook may be right that cars are more efficient than public transit today, but he ignores what might have been if, earlier in the twentieth century, investment in public transit had been expanded rather than withdrawn. Likewise, the view that suburban home ownership reflects people's preferences ignores the reality that government programs and private lenders for many years refused to provide mortgages to members of many different racial and ethnic groups who would have been happy to remain in urban neighborhoods and strongly favored single-family dwellings over rental housing, cooperative apartments, and the like. Far from bowing to market forces, government policies have actually shaped them from the beginning.

The second major flaw is that public choice theory seems to work better for middle-class home owners than for the inner-city poor. It ignores all the other features of society that constrain or empower people's ability to choose. Most obviously, people with fewer means (or the wrong skin color) have a highly constricted range of choice. The market not only fails people who live in poverty; it punishes them through the negative effects of concentrated poverty. Let us now look in some detail at how government has shaped the construction of the current state of metropolitan America.

LOCAL GOVERNMENT FRAGMENTATION AND LAND-USE CONTROL

A fundamental force propelling economic segregation and suburban sprawl is the nature of local jurisdictional arrangements in the United States, specifically the fact that we grant wide latitude and autonomy to local governments. They regulate land use, provide crucial public services (such as education and infrastructure), and finance them with local taxes. As a result, local governments engage in a beggar-thy-neighbor competition with one another. In the competition for favored residents and investments, each jurisdiction has a strong incentive to adopt zoning and development policies that exclude potential residents with incomes below the median for their jurisdiction or who require more costly services. The better-off may view these people as "free riders" who do not pay enough taxes for the services they use. From the viewpoint of fiscal self-interest, this is a rational position. Widespread discriminatory practices in the rental, sales, and financing of housing reinforce this exclusion by price and income.[18] Similarly, each jurisdiction seeks new businesses that will pay more tax revenues than the costs of the services they will require. As the federal and state governments devolve responsibility for more programs to the local level, the fragmented nature of local government becomes even more important. This resulting dynamic strongly promotes economic segregation and suburban sprawl.

Out of this competition comes a pecking order of jurisdictions. Each tries to be more exclusive than the next. At the top end, exclusive and expensive suburbs provide their residents with excellent public services at a relatively small tax cost in relation to housing values and incomes. At the bottom, distressed suburbs and central cities provide housing of last resort for all those whom suburban jurisdictions can exclude by reason of low income, lack of mobility, or race. Over time, the loss of well-to-do residents can undermine the ability of a city to attract commercial investments. Suburbs are arrayed according to the incomes of their residents and their commercial tax bases. Inner-ring suburbs that house working-class families with school-age children and that have little commercial wealth are not in a good position to compete in this intergovernmental marketplace. Businesses have also sought out, and sometimes even created, suburban jurisdictions to provide them with tax havens and few regulations, thus siphoning off badly needed business investment from other municipalities.[19]

From the 1940s to the 1990s, this dynamic encouraged much of the mobile white middle class and, more recently, the black, Asian, and Hispanic middle class to move to suburbs. Those rendered immobile by discrimination and low incomes, especially the minority poor, were constrained to live in expanding urban, and sometimes suburban, ghettos. At some distance from them, yet still within city limits, are middle-income households that, depending on local circumstances, chose to remain in the city. These include gradually shrinking white ethnic neighborhoods (whose residents may have loyalties to the local church or the neighborhood ethnic stores and culture), emerging immigrant enclaves, zones where young people seek to start their careers, and defended enclaves (such as gated communities) of the urban elite. Despite the persistence of these groups in the city, the real median household income of city residents declined significantly compared with that in the surrounding suburbs.

These ground rules also encourage towns and regions to engage in "bidding wars" for manufacturing plants, "big-box" stores like Wal-Marts and Kmarts, shopping centers, industrial parks, luxury housing, and even sports franchises. For example, three adjacent cities in southern California (Oxnard, Ventura, and Camarillo) kept outbidding one another (with tax breaks) to attract large stores to their respective shopping centers. After several years of such maneuvering, one council member concluded, "this is not about creating new business. This is about spending $30 million to move two stores three miles."[20] The competition for business investment results in a "race to the bottom" in which the tax burden is gradually shifted from businesses to residents. The resulting development does little to help poor areas pull themselves up. After Detroit offered generous incentives for private companies to locate within the city, surrounding suburbs responded by offering the same incentives.[21] Whichever locality "wins" the bidding war ends up with fewer tax revenues to provide public services.

Every other major democracy in Europe and Canada exercises greater national control over land use than does the United States.[22] Here, local municipalities retain great power over land use (as well as local schools). This control enables them to determine what kind of businesses and housing get built and who can afford them.[23] Of course, suburbanization could have happened in the absence of metropolitan political fragmentation. Cities could have expanded their boundaries to encompass the spreading of population and jobs. With some exceptions, this did not happen.

In the United States, states charter local governments, which are not even mentioned in the U.S. Constitution. In the nineteenth century, state laws generally made it easy for growing central cities to annex new territory as their populations expanded. Early in the twentieth century, however, states revised their laws to make this more difficult and to enable residents of outlying areas to incorporate new suburban municipalities.[24] Although some cities (mostly in the South and West) retained the ability to annex adjacent suburban areas, most cities are trapped within their political boundaries.[25] States gave local governments the authority to tax, regulate land uses, and establish their own public school systems. Instead of promoting metropolitan government and consolidation, these laws encourage balkanization.

Local governments use zoning laws, which divide localities into districts, or zones, to segregate land uses and to limit access of potential unwanted new residents and land uses. (Although free-market conservatives decry government intervention, only a few have said anything about the restrictive nature of suburban zoning laws.) Racial zoning, such as South Africa's apartheid system, was struck down by the Supreme Court in 1917, but the federal courts have upheld zoning based on economic distinctions.[26] Los Angeles passed the first zoning ordinance in 1909, creating residential, light industry, and heavy industry zones. Later laws added zones for open space and retail shops. But later zoning laws went further, seeking to favor some kinds of housing over others. Some early planners described apartment buildings as "polluting" or "tainting" single-family residential areas.[27] In 1926, the U.S. Supreme Court (in *Euclid v. Ambler*) allowed the Cleveland suburb of Euclid to ban apartment buildings from neighborhoods with single-family housing. Zoning increasingly became a way to protect property values and to exclude "noxious" land uses, including apartment buildings.

States have the ultimate authority to regulate land use, but, encouraged by the federal government, they began to delegate that responsibility to local governments in the 1920s. Early state statutes were modeled on the 1924 *Standard State Zoning Enabling Act* and the 1928 *Standard City Planning Enabling Act* published by the U.S. Department of Commerce. By the late 1920s, 564 cities had zoning ordinances. The 1954 Housing Act provided federal funds for local, regional, and state planning and encouraged local zoning ordinances. By 1968, 65 percent of the 7,609 local governments in the nation's metropolitan areas had planning agencies that created and policed zoning laws.[28] Many federal task forces and commissions have recommended that Washington take a firmer stand on national land-use planning to promote efficient location of businesses and housing, to reduce geographic segregation based on income and race, and to protect the environment, but few of these recommendations have been accepted. In these and other ways, the federal government and the states have encouraged or condoned the nation's fragmented land-use practices and their social consequences.

Local zoning laws also allow municipalities to regulate the location and minimum lot size for various kinds of housing. Affluent suburbs have used "snob zoning" to limit housing for the poor. Many suburbs set minimum lot sizes (such as one-half acre per home) that increase the cost of housing and rule out the construction of dense housing—not just apartment buildings, but also bungalow-style single-family homes.[29] Intentionally or unintentionally (there is evidence of both), these zoning laws have the effect of excluding low-income and even middle-income families. They also restrict racial minorities, who generally have lower incomes than whites. Some suburbs that desire to limit school-age children, in order to avoid education costs, prohibit housing types favored by families with children.

Proponents of public choice theory believe that inequalities among local jurisdictions should balance themselves out over time as the market achieves "equilibrium." For the intergovernmental marketplace, this means that land prices should rise in successful areas, reducing their attractiveness to residents and investors, who will then be attracted to poor areas, where prices have fallen. But as the previous discussion has shown, spatial inequalities have become worse rather than better. The competition among fragmented local governments has led to a vicious circle of rising spatial inequality.

FEDERAL STEALTH URBAN POLICIES

Urban policies are normally understood as those that are targeted to cities or to poor people who mostly live in cities. Almost all federal policies have spatial impacts, however, that may harm or benefit cities. (Acknowledging this, the Carter administration during the 1970s experimented with an "Urban Impact Analysis," which would enable policy makers to anticipate the negative impacts of various policies on cities and thereby lessen them.)[30] Many federal policies with profound impacts on cities and metropolitan development are *implicit* or *indirect* urban policies. Because many are invisible to people's political radar, we call them "stealth urban policies."[31]

When the New Deal initiated a large public works program during the 1930s to lift the nation out of the depression, its primary goal was to create jobs. But a secondary effect was to lift up cities, where most of the unemployed were located. Similarly, when the Reagan administration adopted policies to reduce inflation in the early 1980s that brought on a deep national recession, it harmed inner cities far more than other areas.[32] Because cities have a disproportionate share of low-income people, federal efforts to help poor people, such as Medicaid, food stamps, welfare, and job training programs, generally benefit cities more than suburbs. And when these programs are cut, poor urban neighborhoods are hurt the most.[33]

Here we examine four stealth urban policies: transportation, military spending, federal programs to promote home ownership, and the federal failure to reduce racial discrimination in housing. None of these policies was intended primarily to shape urban development, but each had profound urban impacts. In reality, these federal policies subsidized America's postwar suburban exodus (and still do) by pushing people and businesses out of cities and pulling them into suburbs. The idea that this happened purely as a result of the free market is a myth.

Transportation Policy: An Arranged Marriage with the Automobile

America's marriage to the automobile began early in the twentieth century. But in many ways, it was an arranged marriage, not just a love affair. Each time the nation courted mass transportation, powerful interests intervened, objecting to the arrangement. The "highway lobby," composed of the automobile, trucking, oil, rubber, steel, and road-building industries, literally paved the way to suburbia by promoting public road building over public transit and by keeping gas taxes low (by European standards).[34] By the 1920s, cars and trucks began to outstrip trolleys and trains as the major form of personal and business transportation.[35] While government officials looked the other way, the major car, truck, and bus companies purchased and dismantled many of the electric trolley lines that urban Americans relied on.[36] State governments earmarked tolls and gas taxes for road construction instead of public transit and launched major road-building programs. In 1934, Congress required states receiving federal highway funds to dedicate state turnpike tolls to road building.[37] The highway lobby was gaining momentum.

The federal Interstate Highway and Defense Act of 1956 sounded the final death knell for alternatives to the car as a source of metropolitan mobility. Although the ostensible purpose was to promote mobility across the country and get Americans quickly out of crowded cities in time of war (this was the height of the cold war), it would also powerfully promote suburbanization by building radial and ring freeways around the major cities. It set up the Highway Trust Fund, which used federal gas tax revenues to pay 90 percent of the freeway construction costs. Trust fund expenditures grew from $79 million in 1946 to $429 million in 1950 to $2.9 billion in 1960. It "ensured that the freeways would be self-propagating, because more freeways encouraged more automobile travel, generating more gasoline revenue that could only be used to build more highways."[38] Ultimately, it built 41,000 miles of roads.[39] Urban scholars ranked this program as the most important influence in shaping America's urban areas in the past half century.[40]

By 1997, the United States was spending $20.5 billion a year through the Highway Trust Fund.[41] But gas taxes by then covered only 60 percent of the cost of maintaining the federal highway system, so federal and state governments made up the rest. (This cost does not include the negative health consequences of pollution or the loss of economic productivity from employees stuck in traffic.) Most other industrial nations fund highways out of general revenues (as they also fund national rail systems and often regional commuter railways), forcing roads to compete with other national priorities.

America's car culture is premised on the belief that automobiles provide a degree of personal freedom and flexibility that public transit cannot. We have shown that the car culture poses many costs for suburbanites, including environmental damage, long commutes, and personal injuries. Even if we discount these costs, the irony of millions of Americans simultaneously exercising their personal freedom by driving their cars only to end up in traffic jams has been parodied in such films as *Falling Down* (1993) with Michael Douglas and Jean Luc Godard's French film *Weekend* (1967). Drivers are spending significantly more time stuck in traffic. Since 1982, traffic gridlock has increased 700 percent in Indianapolis, 533 percent in Kansas City, 525 percent in Rochester, 480 percent in Colorado Springs, and 440 percent in Salt Lake City. These were the worst increases, but even areas with the smallest increases (Phoenix with 19 percent, Houston with 32 percent, Philadelphia with 40 percent, Honolulu with 63 percent, and San Francisco with 69 percent) experienced significantly more traffic congestion.[42] Americans now spend 8 billion hours a year stuck in traffic.[43] According to Jane Holtz Kay, "On the coasts that hold two-thirds of all Americans, the long-suffering 'BosWash' and the newer 'Los Diegos' freeways greet their share of the day's 80 million car commuters, and, with a screech of brakes, the love song of freedom and mobility goes flat."[44]

Throughout the twentieth century, advocates for public transit argued and battled for a more balanced federal transportation strategy. They won a number of victories. In the 1970s, neighborhood groups protested federal and state plans to build a highway through Boston's working-class neighborhoods and persuaded the U.S. Department of Transportation to halt the highway and divert funds to build a subway line. In recent decades, Atlanta, Miami, Baltimore, Buffalo, Detroit, Los Angeles, Washington, D.C., and San Francisco have all built new subway lines using federal funds shared from gas tax revenues. But federal policy had already cast the die in favor of roads and cars. Between 1975 and 1995, the United States spent $1.15 trillion for roads and highways, compared with $187 billion for mass transit and only $13 billion for Amtrak, the nation's interurban train system.[45] Highway construction continues to expand, exacerbating sprawl and undermining the economies of older cities and suburbs.[46] As a result, mass transit ridership is much lower in American cities than in Europe, Japan, and Canada, accounting for only 3 percent of all travel, one-fifth the Western European average.[47]

Our car-dominated transportation system was premised on individual choice, but it has reduced choice in many ways. Most Americans have no choice but to use the automobile. You need one to get to your job, buy groceries, or visit friends. In Canadian and European cities, households make great use of cars but can also live in pedestrian-friendly neighborhoods where they can rely on mass transit. Many live quite easily without using their cars often and can even do without them. The United States chose not to take this road.

Military Spending: More than Just Defense

Most Americans think that the search for cheaper land and lower taxes, along with the rise of truck transportation, inevitably shifted major manufacturing plants to suburban and outlying locations. Obviously, government transportation policies had an enormous impact on this trend, but so did the federal government's siting of military facilities and distribution of defense contracts. Throughout the post–World War II period, military spending has accounted for the largest part of the federal budget. Pentagon decisions about where to locate military facilities and where to grant defense contracts greatly influenced regional development patterns. They are America's de facto "industrial policy," a form of government planning that has dramatically shaped the location of businesses and jobs.

Before World War II, almost all manufacturing plants were located in the nation's central cities. When the war began, the federal government took control (though not ownership) of the nation's major manufacturing industries in order to mobilize resources for the war effort. Companies that built commercial airplanes were drafted to produce military aircraft; firms that produced clothing were conscripted to manufacture uniforms; firms that turned out automobiles and freighters began making tanks and battleships for military use. America's business leaders were wary of the potential implications of this government takeover, so President Roosevelt appointed corporate executives to run the War Production Board (WPB).

Rather than retool existing plants, many of which sat underutilized during the depression, the WPB executives decided to build new plants and to locate most of them (government funded but privately owned) in suburban areas. "In New York, Detroit, Baltimore, and Pittsburgh, for example, new investment was located outside the central cities twice or more as heavily as before the war. This pattern also held for such Sunbelt cities as Los Angeles, Dallas, Houston and San Diego." The leaders of the nation's largest industrial corporations used "government financing to reconstruct the private sector's capital base along new and more desirable lines." Suburban locations were desirable because they were "largely beyond the reach of the unions," which had a strong presence in the existing factories, and were not governed by big-city mayors, who were often sympathetic to unions.[48] These location decisions had a major impact on postwar America.

Mobilization for World War II also strongly affected the regional location of employment (with disproportionate shares of wartime investment being located outside the preexisting industrial base in the urban North) and population (prompting a northward flow of blacks and a westward and southward flow of whites). The Defense Department's support for the aerospace and electronics industries continued these shifts in the cold war era.[49] After World War II, key congressmen continued to utilize the "Pentagon pork barrel" to bring jobs to firms and workers in their districts, disproportionately in suburban areas. The ripple effects of Pentagon spending dramatically changed the population and employment map of the entire country.[50]

Even in the metropolitan areas that won the Pentagon sweepstakes, most Pentagon dollars went to the suburbs, not the central cities. One study compared the military contracts and salaries coming into each city with the amount of federal taxes drained out of each city to the Pentagon. In 1990 alone, eighteen of the twenty-five largest cities suffered a loss of $24 billion. New York City alone lost $8.4 billion a year; Los Angeles, $3.3 billion; Chicago, $3.1 billion; Houston, $1.7 billion; Dallas, $731 million; and Detroit, over $900 million. In Los Angeles, taxpayers sent $4.74 billion to the Pentagon and received $1.47 billion back, for a net loss of $3.27 billion, or $3,000 per family.[51] The employment impact of this drain-off of funds is equally dramatic.

Even those cities gaining dollars and jobs from the Pentagon have discovered that depending on military contracts makes them vulnerable to "downturns in the military spending cycle."[52] Both Seattle (dominated by Boeing, the nation's largest defense contractor) and St. Louis (where defense contractor McDonnell-Douglas is the largest employer) experienced severe economic hard times when the Pentagon reduced its funding for specific weapon systems or selected another contractor. Politics influences the rise and fall of regions and cities as a result of Pentagon spending.[53]

Federal Home Ownership Policies: A Suburban Bias

Federal home ownership policies have also had an enormous indirect impact on metropolitan development patterns. It is widely believed that home ownership benefits society as a whole by encouraging more stable families, higher savings rates, and greater civic participation. By their nature, home ownership policies are biased toward suburbs because, compared with cities, more suburban households own their own homes. But these programs were designed and implemented in ways that exaggerated the bias against cities and accentuated economic segregation and sprawl.

Early federal home ownership policies were shamefully racist. The federal government refused to insure loans for blacks, largely confining them to rental housing in cities and keeping them out of the great suburban migration. Although some minority families may want to live in predominantly minority neighborhoods, surveys consistently show that most minorities want to live in racially integrated neighborhoods; self-segregation is not the major factor in their residential isolation.[54] Federal policies in some respects initially created and then exacerbated the concentration of poor blacks and Hispanics in ghettos and barrios.[55] Racist behavior and racist policies directly contradict the free-market view of metropolitan development.

In the first half of the twentieth century, overt racial discrimination in housing was widespread. Whites often resorted to violence to keep blacks out of all-white neighborhoods, a practice that persisted into the 1960s, especially in northern metropolitan areas. Local governments enacted racial zoning laws and allowed "restrictive covenants" on deeds that forbade home owners to sell to Jews, blacks, and other groups. Real estate organizations promulgated codes of ethics that sanctioned members who helped blacks buy or rent housing in white neighborhoods. Real estate agents have routinely "steered" blacks and Latinos (regardless of income) to racially segregated neighborhoods, mortgage lenders and insurance firms redline urban minority neighborhoods and refuse to treat minority loan applicants equally, and landlords discriminate against minority tenants.[56] Racial segregation thus stems from the routine practices of the private real estate industry as well as from government policy. From the

1930s through the 1960s, however, the federal government generally ignored and in some cases endorsed these practices.[57]

Early in 1933, in the midst of the depression, Congress created the Home Owners Loan Corporation (HOLC) to provide low-interest loans to home owners who were in danger of losing their homes to foreclosure. The HOLC set up a rating system to evaluate the risks associated with loans in specific urban neighborhoods. Economically well-off and racially and ethnically homogeneous neighborhoods received the highest ratings. Neighborhoods that were mostly black or were located near black neighborhoods (which typically included Jewish neighborhoods) fell into the lowest categories, which led banks to undervalue these areas and limit loans to them.[58]

The HOLC did not invent these standards. It simply embraced the general practices of the real estate industry. But it put the federal government's stamp of approval on these practices, making racial discrimination part of government policy. Banks used HOLC's system in making their own loans, compounding the public and private disinvestment of black areas and urban neighborhoods by government and the private sector. Equally important, HOLC policy set a precedent for the later Federal Housing Administration (FHA) and Veterans Administration (VA) programs, which played a major role in changing postwar America, pumping billions of dollars into the housing industry.

The FHA was established in 1934 to promote home ownership and stimulate the construction industry, which had almost collapsed with the onset of the depression. The FHA provided government insurance to banks lending money for approved home mortgages. (Later, a similar program was established by the VA.) With the loan guaranteed in this fashion, lenders could confidently make long-term mortgages available, thereby reducing consumers' monthly payments and stimulating the housing market. The FHA carried out its mandate in ways that promoted suburbanization and racial segregation at the expense of rebuilding central cities and promoting racial integration.

During the FHA's early years, some housing experts and public officials pushed Congress to eliminate racial segregation in federal government housing programs, but they met enormous resistance.[59] In fact, it was official FHA policy to promote racial segregation and unofficial policy to promote suburbanization. Many FHA staff came from the private lending industry, which generally refused to make loans in integrated neighborhoods. In 1938, the official FHA underwriting manual discouraged loans to neighborhoods occupied by "inharmonious racial or nationality groups." It stated that "if a neighborhood is to retain stability, it is necessary that properties shall continue to be occupied by the same social and racial classes." [60] It noted that "a change in social or racial occupancy generally contributed to instability and a decline in values." FHA staff even advised housing developers to use restrictive covenants barring sales to nonwhites before seeking FHA financing as a way to promote neighborhood stability and property values.[61]

Pent up by the depression and World War II and then unleashed by postwar prosperity, demand for housing exploded in the 1950s and 1960s. Returning veterans sought to gravitate away from their immigrant parents' and grandparents' neighborhoods. As a practical matter, they would find the least costly new housing in the suburban periphery, which was also removed from the growing minority populations in many older central-city neighborhoods.

Much of this demand could have been satisfied within the existing city boundaries—for example, in the garden apartment complexes constructed on the outer boundaries of the prewar city. During the Truman administration, however, efforts to pass federal legislation to promote this type of middle-income rental housing in cities failed. The home-building lobby pressured Congress to make it easier to build in outlying areas.[62] So the FHA and VA home loan programs became the major vehicles for expanding housing construction, home ownership, and suburbanization. "[T]he power to award or withhold mortgage insurance gave the FHA the hidden leverage to shape the postwar metropolis."[63] The VA and FHA redlined the cities, speeding the migration of the white middle class out of the older central cities. When blacks wished to move to suburbs like Levittown and could afford to do so, they were not allowed.[64] Robert Fishman notes, "a white home buyer who wished to stay in his old neighborhood had to seek old-style conventional mortgages with high rates and short terms. The same purchaser who opted for a new suburban house could get an FHA-insured mortgage with lower interest rates, longer terms, a lower down payment, and a lower monthly payment."[65]

During the booming 1950s, one-third of all private housing was financed with FHA or VA help.[66] Almost all these homes were built in the suburbs. FHA policy favored the construction of new homes over the remodeling of existing homes, making it "easier and cheaper for a family to purchase a new home than to renovate an older one."[67] It also favored single-family homes over multifamily (apartment) buildings. Between 1941 and 1950, FHA-insured single-family starts exceeded FHA multifamily starts by four to one. In the 1950s, the ratio was over seven to one.[68] Suburban zoning laws guaranteed that most FHA-backed apartment buildings would be located in central cities.

The vast majority of FHA and VA mortgages went to white, middle-class families in suburbs. Few went to blacks, city residents, or even whites who wanted to purchase (or renovate) city homes. The FHA underwriting manual viewed mixed-use areas or high-density areas (i.e., cities) as bad credit risks. The FHA failed to make *any* loans in some cities. Between 1946 and 1959, blacks purchased less than 2 percent of all housing financed with VA and FHA help. In Miami, only one black family received FHA insurance between 1934 and 1949, and "there is evidence that he [the man who secured the loan] was not recognized as a black." [69] As late as 1966, the FHA had no mortgages in Paterson or Camden, New Jersey, older cities with declining white populations.[70] This treatment contrasts with that of Levittown, New Jersey, one of several planned suburban communities (all called "Levittown") in eastern states that featured thousands of similar single-family homes. When the development opened up in 1958, its homes were marketed and sold to whites only. The FHA went along with this practice. It took a lawsuit based on New Jersey's antidiscrimination law and seeking to prevent Levittown home buyers from getting FHA insurance to force the developer to relent. The first black family moved into Levittown in 1960. Starting in the 1970s, under pressure from Congress, the FHA began insuring more single-family home loans in central cities and to racial minorities. But by then, the suburban momentum was well under way.

Home Owner Tax Breaks: Subsidizing Suburbanization

The nation's tax code allows home owners to take mortgage interest and property tax deductions that are not available to renters. These tax breaks have been in the federal tax code since it was enacted in 1912, but they were initially intended to help family farmers, not wealthy home owners. By the 1960s, they were providing billions of dollars of tax subsidies, and by the 1980s, they had become by far the largest federal housing program. Most benefits go to well-off suburban home owners. In 1997, home owner tax breaks totaled more than $90 billion, including mortgage interest deductions ($53 billion), property tax deductions ($17 billion), deferral of capital gains on home sales ($15 billion), and exclusion of capital gains taxes on home sales for persons over 55 ($7 billion).[71] Between 1978 and 1997, the federal government spent $1.3 trillion (in 1997 dollars) on these breaks, compared with $461.8 billion on all HUD low-income housing subsidies.[72] The tax subsidies rose nearly fourfold, while HUD's budget authority declined by more than 80 percent.

Today, 30 million home owners, almost one-fifth of all taxpayers, receive one or more elements of the home owner deduction. But a highly disproportionate share of these federal tax breaks flows to the highest-income taxpayers with the largest houses and biggest mortgages. For example, more than 50 percent of the total mortgage deduction goes to the richest 7.8 percent of taxpayers, those with incomes over $100,000.[73] Local property tax deductions are similarly regressive.

These tax breaks have significant geographic and social consequences. They clearly encourage home buyers to buy larger homes in more outlying areas than they otherwise might. Moderate-income home owners, who generally do not get much advantage from this deduction, are concentrated in older suburbs and central cities. The property tax deduction helps both suburban and central-city governments raise revenues, but suburbs get a much greater boost because more of their taxpayers claim the deduction. Tax policy thus powerfully promotes suburbanization, metropolitan sprawl, and geographic segregation by social class and race.[74]

Since the 1960s, many tax and housing experts have recommended reducing this inequity in the tax code by reducing the amount that wealthy home owners can deduct and restricting deductions to only one home. The real estate industry has successfully fought these challenges, claiming that changing the tax law would undermine the American dream of home ownership. In 1984, President Reagan announced that he was planning to introduce a comprehensive tax reform plan that would simplify the tax system and reduce taxes on the well-off. One provision was to eliminate the mortgage interest deduction. The real estate industry quickly sprang into action, and when Reagan filed his bill in Congress (the Tax Reform Act of 1986), it retained the mortgage interest deduction.[75]

Federal Fair Housing Laws: Little Impact on Segregation

It was not inevitable that American metropolitan areas would become as segregated by race and class as they now are. As early as the 1940s, advocates for racial justice and housing reformers proposed laws to challenge racial discrimination and promote racial integration. During the debate over the 1949 Housing Act, progressive members of Congress sought to ban racial segregation in public housing, but their amendment was defeated.[76] Since the 1960s, new laws have been enacted to eliminate these practices, but federal enforcement has often been halfhearted or ineffective. Even if strongly enforced, laws to limit discrimination have little impact on the patterns of residential segregation.

In 1968, the Kerner Commission, appointed by President Johnson in the wake of ghetto riots, recommended enacting a national "open occupancy" law and changing federal housing policy to build more low- and moderate-income housing outside of ghetto areas.[77] Congress passed the Fair Housing Act of 1968 a week after the assassination of Martin Luther King, Jr., over the opposition of southern congressmen. It addressed the first Kerner Commission recommendation, but not the second. The act prohibited discrimination in housing, including racial steering, redlining, and blockbusting, but it did not promote racial integration in middle-income areas.[78]

The law remains an important symbol of the civil rights movement's success, but its enforcement mechanism was glaringly weak. It gave HUD, or state and local fair housing agencies (where they existed), the right to investigate complaints of housing discrimination by individuals. (State and local governments also began enacting parallel laws during this period.) But neither HUD nor the state and local agencies had the power to issue enforcement orders. They could only refer cases to the Department of Justice for prosecution. Hampered by filing deadlines for complaints, long delays in investigations, and infrequent prosecution, the law had little impact. Many complainants bypassed HUD and these other agencies and went directly to court. Civil rights lawyers won many cases, and courts fined landlords and real estate agents. Although they helped individual victims of discrimination, these time-consuming cases rarely changed housing industry practices. In 1988, the law was amended to give HUD the power to initiate complaints and allow administrative law judges to make rulings.[79]

In the three decades since the Fair Housing Act was passed, a network of private fair housing groups, attorneys with expertise in fair housing law, and state and local government agencies has emerged to utilize the law to promote racial justice. Much money and person power have been spent by these individuals, organizations, and agencies, but the overall impact of this activity is questionable. These federal, state, and local fair housing laws "have had little effect on the overall pattern of racial segregation in most suburban housing."[80]

Only a handful of suburbs have actively and voluntarily embraced racial integration by using reduced mortgages or campaigns against "panic" selling to encourage whites to live in racially mixed neighborhoods.[81] Fair housing and fair lending laws do not challenge the basic policies and practices that lead to racial segregation. Instead, they allow individuals or organizations to seek judicial redress for individual acts of discrimination by landlords, real estate agents, or banks. Legal victories may bring monetary rewards for victims and may deter overt discrimination by landlords, lenders, real estate agents, and insurance companies, but they have not significantly changed patterns of residential segregation. Few housing discrimination cases have been brought against municipalities or major developers for the practices that lead to racial segregation. The federal government has taken some aggressive enforcement actions, but only when such violations were overt and could be proved.

FEDERAL TARGETED URBAN PROGRAMS

It would be wrong to suggest that all federal programs have simply been designed to promote economic segregation and suburban sprawl. The federal government has responded to these problems in two ways: promoting regional approaches and targeting aid to cities. At various times, particularly the 1930s and 1960s, the federal government has recognized the connection between the problems of cities and the problems of suburbs and has tried to craft policies to address them both. Its halting efforts to encourage regional approaches are examined in chapter 6. Here, we review explicit urban policies targeted to cities.

Most federal policies exacerbated central-city decline and racial transition, but the federal government also adopted another (smaller and less powerful) set of policies to improve the economic and social conditions of central cities. In truth, federal aid to cities (whether to revitalize downtowns, attract private jobs to inner-city neighborhoods, stabilize poor and working-class neighborhoods, or provide fiscal assistance to local governments) has served, in effect, to "clean up the mess" it created with its larger subsidies for suburbanization and urban disinvestment.[82] In Alice O'Connor's phrase, federal urban policy has been "swimming against the tide" of most federal domestic policies.[83]

Many Americans think that the federal government coddled cities and that they are worse off despite the expenditure of billions of federal dollars. Steven Hayward of the conservative Heritage Foundation observed that the federal government spent $600 billion on cities between 1965 and 1990, yet older central cities continued to decline. Such federal policies are doomed to fail, he thinks, because they ignore the "logic of metropolitan development."[84] Although conservatives overlook the improvements in urban housing and the environment, as well as the creation of a black middle class, for the most part, they are correct that federal urban policies have failed. They are wrong about the reason, however. These policies did not fail because they violated the logic of the market but because other government policies had already set powerful antiurban forces in motion. Based on the false belief that minimal federal help would enable cities and urban neighborhoods to bootstrap themselves out of poverty, federal policy makers almost guaranteed that urban policy would fail, opening up these programs to political counterattack.

New Deal Urban Policy

The New Deal mounted the first serious urban policy initiatives during the depression. America's urban population had grown dramatically in the previous fifty years. The nation's key industries—steel and iron, meatpacking, textiles, and automobiles—were centered in big cities. European immigrants flooded into these cities between 1880 and 1920, providing cheap labor. Tenement slums grew around factories, leading to serious overcrowding and public health problems. The nation's labor wars were fought on urban battlefields.

Following World War I, a racist and nativist backlash led Congress to enact restrictive immigrant laws (such as the Emergency Quota Act of 1921 and the National Origins Act of 1924) and to attack immigrant culture by passing Prohibition in 1919. But America had already become an urban nation. By the late 1920s, urban voters wielded significant influence in state and national politics, symbolized by the Democratic Party's nomination of New York Governor Alfred Smith, an Irish Catholic, in 1928. Smith lost, and the 1929 depression, which devastated the nation's cities, became identified with Republican President Herbert Hoover. Many cities filed for bankruptcy. Cities were overwhelmed by the homeless (who constructed "Hoovervilles"), unemployed people stormed relief offices and city halls, tenants went on rent strikes, depositors rioted at bank closings, and workers organized a wave of strikes and protests.[85]

President Hoover personally opposed federal intervention but was forced politically to take some action. The Emergency Relief and Construction Act extended $300 million in loans to state and local governments so that they could provide relief to indigent people. In 1932, three years into the depression, voters rejected Hoover's approach. Urban voters played a key role in Democrat Franklin Roosevelt's landslide victory and the election of numerous Democratic congressmen, many representing urban Catholics, Jews, and blacks. Roosevelt had no coherent plan but promised to bring the power of the federal government to address the crisis. Americans were hopeful, but urban unrest continued after Roosevelt took office. Big-city mayors set up a new organization, the U.S. Conference of Mayors, to lobby Roosevelt for help. The first wave of federal urban policy soon followed.[86]

The New Deal significantly increased federal support for public works, social insurance, business regulation, and farm policy.[87] The Social Security Act created insurance for the elderly and cash assistance (Aid to Families with Dependent Children [AFDC], typically referred to later as "welfare") to women and children, many of whom lived in cities, but it was not specifically an "urban" policy. These two programs set the pattern for many later "people" programs such as food stamps and health insurance. New Deal public works projects put millions of unemployed people to work constructing urban parks, water and sewer systems, bridges, subways, airports, libraries, streets, schools, and other facilities. These programs bypassed state agencies and provided direct federal assistance to municipalities. These public works and infrastructure programs were later phased out because business groups viewed direct government involvement in job creation as an opening wedge to socialism, disappointing New Dealers who had hoped to create a permanent federal role in creating jobs for the unemployed.

The nation's mobilization for World War II drew millions more Americans into the cities to work in military installations and war production. More than half a million people moved to the San Francisco area between 1940 and 1945. The wartime migration included a substantial number of African Americans from the rural South, which led to competition with whites for housing and jobs and triggered racial tensions. This influx created serious housing shortages, especially for defense workers. During the war, the federal government funneled money for construction of public schools, playgrounds, child-care centers, and medical facilities and programs for public health and sanitation. In 1940, the Lanham Act authorized construction of 700,000 units of housing for defense workers.[88] In Oakland, California, "federal agencies built more than thirty thousand public housing units accommodating about ninety thousand war workers and their families."[89]

The unprecedented level of federal investment and planning in cities during the New Deal and World War II did not survive. These programs were all viewed as part of a wartime emergency; when the war ended, business groups pressured Congress to cancel them. The real estate industry successfully lobbied for a provision that all government-sponsored defense housing units had to be sold or demolished after the war, not converted into low-income public housing. Defense plants were sold to their operators for nominal amounts. The emerging efforts to build cross-class support for federal government intervention in urban development were all uprooted.

Low-Income Subsidized Housing

Alongside the home ownership programs described earlier, the New Deal launched a public housing program to improve housing conditions for the urban poor. The history of this program provides another example of a road not taken. Even though housing reformers played an important role in designing and implementing the initial program, it mainly served as a jobs and public works program during the depression. Today, HUD continues to support 1.3 million units of public housing managed by local public authorities, 1.4 million households receiving Section 8 certificates and vouchers to live in private rental housing, and 1 million households living in privately owned units constructed or rehabilitated by federal Section 8 funds.[90]

Until the depression, most Americans believed that the private market, perhaps with help from private philanthropy, could meet the nation's housing needs. Reformers who wanted government to play a major role in housing were a voice in the political wilderness. In the first decades of the twentieth century, a few unions and settlement house reformers built model housing developments for working-class families. Without government subsidies, however, poor families could not afford these apartments.[91] The depression provided reformers with the political opening to push their idea that the federal government should build "social housing" and create a noncommercial sector free from profit and speculation. Like their European counterparts, they envisioned that the middle class as well as the poor would want to live in this housing. The reformers believed in public enterprise and the positive effect of good architecture on people and communities. Beginning in 1933, their ideas and political activism inspired two federal programs that created well-designed housing, available to a mix of income groups, sponsored by labor unions and other nonprofit groups.[92]

The reformers hoped to turn these prototypes into a permanent government program, but the real estate industry, led by the National Association of Real Estate Boards, outmaneuvered them. Fearing competition from well-designed government-sponsored housing, the industry warned about the specter of socialism. With the enactment of the Wagner Public Housing Act in 1937, the industry successfully lobbied to limit public housing to the poor and to give local governments discretion over whether to participate and where to locate such housing. The progressive social housing programs were canceled.

Since then, public housing has been restricted to the very poor. These highly utilitarian, physically isolated projects became ugly warehouses for the poor, stigmatized as housing of last resort. Even today, American politicians use widely held (though often misleading) stereotypes about public housing to attack the idea of government activism. In a speech before the National Association of Realtors during his 1996 presidential campaign, Senator Bob Dole labeled public housing "one of the last bastions of socialism in the world" and said that local housing authorities have become "landlords of misery."

Public housing and other federally subsidized low-income housing have generally been racially and economically segregated. This outcome was not inevitable. It could have been created on a regional rather than a local basis. All communities, including suburbs, could have been required to participate. But opponents of public housing prevailed. So local participation is voluntary, localities determine where it will be situated, and state enabling laws make siting subject to local government approval and zoning laws. As a result, few suburbs participate in any federally assisted low-income housing program. In fact, a few suburban areas created their own public housing authorities specifically so that city housing agencies could *not* cross their boundaries. For example, DuPage County in Illinois created a public housing authority in 1942 that intentionally declined to build a single unit for thirty years. The Fulton County Housing Authority was established to prevent the Atlanta Housing Authority from building public housing in unincorporated parts of the county.[93]

The business and political leaders who served on local public housing authority boards from the 1940s through the 1960s sited public housing developments in segregated areas and adopted tenant selection policies that reinforced racial separation.[94] Since whites constituted the majority of public housing residents during those decades, the projects generally excluded minorities.[95] When the large-scale postwar migration of blacks to cities and the razing of black neighborhoods for federal urban renewal programs required local authorities to provide replacement housing, public housing developments became overwhelmingly black. Even then, local public housing authorities steered black and white residents to segregated developments.[96] Most black public housing residents live in black neighborhoods, and most white public housing residents live in white neighborhoods. Mostly black public housing projects are concentrated in high-poverty areas, and mostly white projects are likely to be in working-class areas. The siting of federally subsidized low-income housing has exacerbated the concentration of poverty among blacks, creating new ghettos.

From its inception, public housing was characterized by geographic, economic, and racial segregation. (Projects occupied exclusively by the elderly are less likely to be in high-poverty areas.)[97] For example, 61.4 percent of public housing units are located in central cities, 19.2 percent in suburbs, and 19.5 percent in nonmetropolitan areas; 68.7 percent are located in census tracts with median household incomes under $20,000, 53.6 percent in tracts with poverty rates of 30 percent or more, and 50.9 percent in tracts with a majority of minority residents. Subsequent programs, including the Section 8 new construction program and the Section 8 voucher program, are also disproportionately located in low-income areas, minority areas, areas that already have a concentration of subsidized housing, and cities.[98] Section 8 vouchers and certificates provide the potential for more mobility, but low-income renters still face a shortage of affordable apartments in the suburbs and landlord resistance to the program.[99]

Urban Renewal: Commercial Expansion at the Expense of Housing

In the postwar decades, the federal government's investment in highways, home ownership subsidies, and defense contracts heavily promoted suburbanization. This drew investment away from central-city business districts. In response, the federal government turned its attention to promoting private investment in urban downtowns. America's cities faced large-scale blight. As early as the 1950s, downtown department stores and other businesses worried about competition from suburban retailers. Manufacturing firms were relocating, and so were middle-class families. Hardly any private housing had been built or repaired in the cities during the depression and war years, leading to a severe housing shortage and widespread deterioration of existing housing. Business leaders and city officials believed that urban slums were causing property values and retail activity to decline.

Mayors, developers, business leaders, construction unions, and daily newspapers—the key components of an urban growth coalition—pressured Congress to address the worsening urban crisis.[100] Congress responded by enacting urban renewal, a key component of the 1949 Housing Act (which also reauthorized the federal public housing program, though it required one unit of slum housing to be torn down for every new public housing unit built). The Urban Land Institute, the urban real estate industry lobby group, drafted the urban renewal part of the legislation.[101] The goal was to revive downtown business districts by razing the slums, bringing new businesses into the core, and attracting middle-class residents back to the cities. Urban leaders also believed that the federal highway program would reduce traffic congestion and modernize the narrow and inadequate street systems of older urban areas, thus bringing suburbanites into cities to work, shop, and attend sports and cultural events. The goal of a "slumless city," in the words of New Haven Mayor Richard Lee, had much more to do with promoting a healthy business climate than addressing the needs of the urban poor.[102] Urban renewal began under Democratic President Harry Truman, expanded under Republican President Dwight Eisenhower, continued under Democratic Presidents John Kennedy and Lyndon Johnson, and was terminated under Republican President Richard Nixon in 1974.

Urban renewal's primary focus was to encourage private investment in central business districts and clear away neighboring "slums," which local elites and planners thought threatened central business districts and important institutions such as hospitals and universities. From the inception, commercial development took priority over low-cost housing. The program funded cities to use their eminent domain authority to purchase and assemble large tracts of land and sell them to developers at bargain-basement prices. Urban renewal projects were often coordinated with the construction of federally funded urban freeways. Cities often literally paved the way for private developers to build market-rate housing, commercial office buildings, and cultural complexes.

Between 1956 and 1972, urban renewal and urban freeway construction displaced an estimated 3.8 million persons from their homes.[103] In some cities, entire neighborhoods were razed or split down the middle by new highways and convention centers.[104] Some called the federal program "Negro removal" because of its focus on black neighborhoods. It pushed people out of their homes and businesses, destroyed social ties, and dispersed residents without adequate compensation for their economic and emotional losses. One-fifth of the entire population of New Haven was displaced by public projects over this period. City redevelopment agencies did a haphazard job of relocating the people and small businesses displaced by urban renewal. Public housing construction in the 1950s and 1960s was used to rehouse some of the victims of urban renewal, typically in isolated high-rise complexes.[105] Although the 1949 act authorized 810,000 units of public housing, only 320,000 units were built by 1960.[106] Freeway construction also destabilized blue-collar neighborhoods.[107] The interstate highway program damaged surrounding property, took land off city tax rolls, and created huge concrete walls separating neighborhoods from each other. The Cross-Bronx Expressway separated the South Bronx from the rest of the city, helping to turn it into one of the nation's worst ghettos. New federally funded highways cut downtown Boston and San Francisco off from their waterfronts.

The urban renewal program ignited controversy and opposition from liberals and conservatives alike. Conservatives opposed urban renewal as a misuse of "big government" social engineering. Martin Anderson described urban renewal as the "federal bulldozer."[108] Liberals viewed it as a giveaway to developers, who reaped huge profits, and as an attack on blue-collar neighborhoods and the urban poor. It soon became clear that "blight" was a term that could be used to destroy healthy neighborhoods.[109] The impact on black neighborhoods led many to view urban renewal as racially biased. Neighborhood groups protesting urban renewal and highway construction emerged across the country. Although few were immediately successful, they formed the basis for a growing movement of community organization and community development beginning in the late 1960s. They slowed down urban renewal projects, some of which took ten years to complete, undermining the program's credibility.

Even on its own terms, urban renewal had mixed results. It slowed down the deterioration of retail activity in some cities and may have helped a few, like Boston, to expand office space and tourist activity.[110] It certainly changed the skyline of some big cities by subsidizing the construction of large office buildings that housed corporate headquarters, law firms, and other corporate-oriented activity.[111] By razing slum housing, it may have removed some bad housing stock, but it destroyed far more low-cost housing than it built. Overall, urban renewal did little to stem the movement of people and businesses to the suburbs or to improve the economic and living conditions of inner-city neighborhoods. To the contrary, it destabilized many of them, promoting unmanaged racial transition and white flight.

Controversy led to the demise of urban renewal in the early 1970s. Likewise, resistance to the construction of public housing, often associated with urban renewal, grew significantly during the 1960s. The program had never had strong supporters, and Congress effectively ended new public housing construction by the mid-1970s, although it continued to fund existing developments. New public housing construction declined from 104,000 units in 1970 to 19,000 in 1974.[112]

Great Society Urban Programs

As urban renewal was winding down in the mid-1960s, it was replaced by another wave of federal urban policies designed more directly to improve social, economic, and physical conditions in poor neighborhoods and to aid city budgets. These programs were adopted in response to the civil rights movement, community protests against urban renewal, and political pressure from big-city mayors. Begun in 1964, President Lyndon Johnson's Great Society and War on Poverty initiatives continued the New Deal tradition of trying to lift the urban poor into the economic mainstream. Unlike the New Deal, Johnson's initiatives took place during a period in which rising affluence highlighted the persistence of urban poverty.

If rising affluence made a war on poverty possible, the civil rights movement and the urban unrest of the 1960s made it necessary. In the cold war battle between capitalism and communism, the conditions in America's ghettos and rural areas embarrassed the nation's political leaders as they espoused the advantages of the "American way of life." And for leaders in the Democratic Party, especially in the North and Midwest, the civil rights movement catalyzed a moral force and a voting bloc they could not ignore.

Representing the left wing of the Democratic Party, United Automobile Workers (UAW) president Walter Reuther had been making proposals since World War II to renew the New Deal and engage in national economic planning. He advised Presidents Kennedy and Johnson to champion a bold federal program for full employment that would include government-funded public works and the conversion of the nation's defense industry to production for civilian needs. This, he argued, would dramatically address the nation's poverty population, create job opportunities for African Americans, and rebuild the nation's troubled cities without being as politically divisive as a federal program identified primarily as serving poor blacks. Both presidents rejected Reuther's advice. Johnson's announcement of an "unconditional war on poverty" in his 1964 State of the Union Address pleased Reuther, but the details of the plan revealed its limitations. The War on Poverty was a patchwork of small initiatives that did not address the nation's basic inequalities. Testifying before Congress in April 1964, Reuther said that "while [the proposals] are good, [they] are not adequate, nor will they be successful in achieving their purposes, except as we begin to look at the broader problems [of the American economy]." He added that "poverty is a reflection of our failure to achieve a more rational, more responsible, more equitable distribution of the abundance that is within our grasp." [113]

Although Reuther threw the UAW's political weight behind Johnson's programs, his critique was correct. Since the 1960s, federal efforts to address poverty have consistently suffered from a failure to address the fundamental underlying issues.[114] With the exception of Social Security and Medicare (health insurance for the elderly), most programs targeted at individuals provide a "safety net" to keep people from physical suffering, not to lift them out of poverty. For example, even at its peak, welfare benefit levels, which vary dramatically among the states, never reached the official poverty threshold, even with food stamp benefits added. Medicaid was a means-tested health insurance entitlement for the poor, with benefits varying by state. Housing subsidies were not an entitlement at all and never reached more than one-third of the families who were eligible for them. The minimum wage has usually been far below the poverty threshold. Only the earned income tax credit (EITC) for the working poor, begun in the mid-1970s and expanded in the 1990s, has actually lifted some families above the poverty level.

Johnson and the Democratic Congress enacted a wide range of legislation to provide assistance to the poor, promote "equal opportunity" for the poor, improve conditions in poor neighborhoods, and give poor people greater access to local political influence. The programs targeted at individuals have lasted the longest, including Head Start (early childhood education), food stamps, Medicare, and Medicaid (health insurance for the elderly and the poor). In contrast, programs targeted at cities and states for job training, neighborhood revitalization, and subsidized housing have had a more complicated history. The number and size of federal grant programs targeted at cities and states increased dramatically for about a decade, peaking during the Nixon administration. In 1960, there were 44 grant-in-aid programs for city and state governments; by 1964, there were 115 programs and 216 separate authorizations for new spending; by 1966, 399 authorizations; by 1969, almost 500. Grant-in-aid funds grew from $2.2 billion in 1950 to $7 billion in 1960 and $24 billion in 1970.[115]

Programs designed to improve urban neighborhoods tended to be poorly funded, short-lived, or both. These included the Jobs Corps, Neighborhood Youth Corps, and VISTA (Volunteers in Service to America). The Model Cities program, enacted in 1966, targeted funds for both physical improvements and social services in these neighborhoods. The War on Poverty and Model Cities legislation required that residents participate in the planning and implementation of these programs. New local antipoverty agencies, called community action agencies, were set up. Churches, community development corporations, settlement houses, and other nonprofit organizations also received federal antipoverty funds. The federal government directly funded community-based agencies, often bypassing the local government. This angered many mayors, who viewed some of these agencies and their leaders as political opponents. Indeed, some community agencies mobilized people (often in black neighborhoods) to protest against local government, including urban renewal projects, public housing authorities, and county welfare systems.

In 1965, Johnson persuaded Congress to create a new cabinet-level agency, the Department of Housing and Urban Development, to focus attention on cities.[116] HUD assumed control of the public housing program, the urban renewal program, the FHA, and the Model Cities program. Even at the height of the War on Poverty, however, HUD lacked the power to coordinate other federal agencies involved in antipoverty efforts, such as the Office of Economic Opportunity, the Labor Department, and the Commerce Department. This fragmentation continues to hamper HUD's efforts to address the economic and social problems in cities. HUD has primarily been a housing agency, not an urban development agency. Federal funding for subsidized housing has seen dramatic swings in response to political pressures, but even at its peak, HUD served less than one-third of those low-income households eligible for housing subsidies.

In the 1960s, national housing policy began to shift from a reliance on public housing authorities to use of the private sector to produce and manage subsidized housing. HUD provided private developers with low-interest mortgages, tax breaks, and rental subsidies in exchange for their renting apartments to the poor. In 1974, during the Nixon administration, Congress created the Section 8 program. It had three components: constructing new buildings in which the units were reserved for the poor, rehabilitating substandard buildings, and providing tenants with rent certificates they could use to pay for market-rate rental units.

To win congressional approval, funds were spread widely across these housing, antipoverty, and community development programs. No one city or neighborhood received sufficient funds to make a large impact on housing conditions or employment. The Model Cities program was initially supposed to be targeted to a few cities, but it eventually spread to 150.[117] It was easy to view these relatively small antipoverty programs as mere symbolism and political co-optation. "We fought a war on poverty," it was often said, "and poverty won."

In fact, the nation's poverty rate was cut in half, from 22.2 percent in 1960 to an all-time low of 11.1 percent by 1973. National economic growth, fed by the military buildup for the Vietnam War, accounts for some of this success. But the various antipoverty programs, in combination with steady increases in the minimum wage, also contributed. Most dramatic was the decline of poverty among the elderly, from 35.2 percent in 1959 to 14.6 percent in 1974. Enactment of Medicare in 1965 and the indexing of Social Security to inflation in 1972 played a significant part in this trend. The poverty rate among blacks fell from 55.1 percent in 1959 (when most blacks still lived in the rural South) to 41.8 percent in 1966 (when blacks were an increasingly urban group) to 30.3 percent by 1974.

Frustrations among the urban poor, particularly those living in black ghettos, contributed to a wave of urban rioting between 1965 and 1968. Although each urban riot had its own precipitating incident, such as an altercation with police or the assassination of Martin Luther King, Jr., the underlying causes were high rates of unemployment, worsening neighborhood conditions, exclusion from national prosperity, and lack of political influence.[118] For a few years, Congress responded to the riots with increased funding for urban programs targeted at low-income neighborhoods. The riots also paved the way for the election of the first wave of black big-city mayors, starting with Richard Hatcher in Gary, Indiana, and Carl Stokes in Cleveland in 1967. But the riots also created a strong political backlash, accelerated the exodus of whites into suburbs, and created fertile ground for conservative politicians (including some big-city mayors such as Philadelphia's Frank Rizzo and Los Angeles's Sam Yorty) to use racial appeals and code words ("the silent majority") to get "tough" on urban crime while opposing funds to improve urban neighborhoods and provide assistance to the poor.

New Federalism

The postriot political climate led the Nixon administration and Congress to reduce and reshape federal assistance to cities under the guise of giving cities more control over federal funds. Nixon called his approach the "New Federalism."[119] It replaced hundreds of federal urban programs, each with strings attached and specific purposes, with general-purpose funding that gave cities much greater discretion over how the money was used. One version was "general revenue sharing," begun in 1972. Congress initially authorized $30 billion over a five-year period, with one-third going to state governments and two-thirds going to local governments. The funding formula was based on cities' population, per capita income, and tax base. Cities could use the money for law enforcement, public transportation, health, social services, and environmental protection, but not for education or cash payments to welfare recipients.[120]

The Nixon administration also consolidated the major urban programs into the Community Development Block Grant (CDBG). It combined urban renewal, Model Cities, water and sewer facilities grants, neighborhood facilities grants, public works loans, and grants for acquisition of open-space land into one grant. Here, too, cities had discretion over its use, so long as they helped low- and moderate-income neighborhoods or helped prevent or eliminate slums. A relatively small amount of funding ($4.75 billion in 1999) was spread over many more jurisdictions than had received funding under the predecessor programs.[121] Funds were allocated according to population, poverty rate, and housing conditions, with 1,000 cities and large urban counties given entitlement status; 30 percent was channeled through states to smaller towns. Cities could use the funds for housing, public facilities, business development, child care, and other purposes.[122]

Local officials liked the flexibility of these block grant programs (although local politicians shut out many community groups from funding). During the Nixon and Ford years, the overall level of federal funding to localities increased, and it continued to grow in the first half of Jimmy Carter's administration, reaching a peak in 1978. The amount going to cities with serious poverty problems actually declined, however. Although large cities received more funds than better-off suburbs (Detroit received $28 per capita, compared with less than $4 per capita for its wealthy neighbor, Grosse Point Farms), cities actually *lost* overall funding compared with what they had been getting. Not surprisingly, the revenue-sharing program shifted federal funds away from Democratic cities and toward Republican suburbs, away from the Democratic Northeast and Midwest and toward the Republican South and West. Governors and mayors often used the funds for their own pet projects rather than helping poor neighborhoods.[123] A 1973 Brookings Institution study noted that revenue sharing was "an inefficient means of dealing with the special plight of large cities because much of the money will be distributed among suburban governments that are not facing critical fiscal problems."[124]

During the 1970s, older cities faced a worsening fiscal crisis as middle-class residents and businesses moved; this was exacerbated by a wave of factory closings in these areas, symptoms of what came to be called "deindustrialization."[125] President Gerald Ford took a hard line against federal aid to New York City, which was facing bankruptcy, attributing the city's problems to mismanagement. (The *New York Daily News* dramatized the conflict with a large front-page headline, "Ford to City: Drop Dead.")[126]

After eight years of Republican control of the White House, big-city mayors, unions, and advocates for the poor hoped that electing Democrat Jimmy Carter and a Democratic majority in Congress in 1976 would produce a new round of federal urban programs. With a few small exceptions, however, Carter continued the urban policies of his Republican predecessors. His promise to develop a comprehensive urban initiative, and to coordinate the various federal agencies involved in urban matters, never materialized. His well-publicized visit to the South Bronx ghetto turned out to have little follow-through.[127] Carter set up a commission to recommend ways to improve urban neighborhoods and another commission to outline a comprehensive urban strategy, but their reports had no serious impact. Carter added several worthy programs for crime control, social services, and job training (the Comprehensive Employment and Training Act), which provided some support for community organizing.[128]

Carter initiated a competitive Urban Development Action Grant (UDAG) program to fund commercial, industrial, and housing development in older cities, a small-scale recreation of the urban renewal program. But fiscally strapped cities had to match the federal grants with their own dollars, and they could use the funds pretty much for their own priorities. In Boston, for example, Mayor Kevin White used UDAG funds to develop a downtown shopping mall with luxury stores such as Neiman Marcus and luxury housing. Even though most UDAG funds were used for commercial development, this failed to stem the decline of retail sales in most downtowns. President Carter and Congress increased funding for low-income housing during his first two years but began to cut HUD's budget in 1978, a trend that accelerated after Ronald Reagan took office in 1981.

The Carter administration revised the revenue-sharing formula to target needy communities in 1977, focusing more funds on big cities with high-poverty rates. The president also pushed an antirecession stimulus package through Congress that included fiscal relief, public service jobs, and public works that flowed to big cities. Under pressure from a national network of neighborhood activist groups, Congress enacted the Community Reinvestment Act (CRA) in 1977 to combat bank redlining in minority inner-city areas, a law that has had an important long-term legacy. Based on evidence generated by the Home Mortgage Disclosure Act of 1975, enforcement of the CRA has significantly increased bank lending in low-income and minority neighborhoods and boosted minority home ownership, but it appears to have had little impact on increasing racial integration.

In 1980, Carter's Commission on Urban Problems released a report that viewed the decline of older industrial cities and the population shift to the suburbs and the Sun Belt as "inevitable" and "ineluctable." It argued that a national policy for revitalizing older cities was "ill-advised," [129] providing a rationale for abandoning federal aid to such places. Rather, federal policy should focus on aiding poor individuals, wherever they happened to live, and encouraging them to move to areas with job opportunities.[130]

Reagan Retrenchment of Urban Programs

The Republican "Reagan Revolution" sought a wholesale shift in the federal government's approach to addressing domestic and urban problems. Ronald Reagan, a former actor and governor of California, came to office with what he (and the media) viewed as a mandate to reduce federal spending and involvement in state and local matters. Reagan owed little to big-city mayors, black or Hispanic leaders, unions, or any other Democratic constituency. He did receive support, however, from many once-Democratic blue-collar households living in older suburbs (so-called Reagan Democrats), giving the Reagan administration the political leeway to implement his conviction.[131]

During the Reagan and Bush eras (1981–1993), cities were under attack as symbols of the failure of activist government and well-intentioned but naive liberalism. Broad electoral support and the perceived poor performance of urban programs made it possible for the Reagan and Bush administrations to sharply cut federal assistance to cities while cutting taxes and significantly increasing military spending.[132]

Two Reagan administration task force reports released in 1982, the *Report of the President's Commission of Housing* and the *National Urban Policy Report*, explained the Reagan philosophy. Both said that the marketplace should determine social and economic conditions.[133] The developers, landlords, and bankers who dominated the housing task force called for "free and deregulated" markets and for reliance on vouchers instead of new construction when government help was needed.

The Reagan and Bush administrations slashed federal programs for local governments.[134] Reagan eliminated general revenue sharing, a $1.8 billion cut to the budgets of larger cities. He slashed funding for public service jobs and job training by 69 percent (in constant dollars) and the CDBG program by 54 percent. The social services block grant and funds for urban mass transit were reduced by 37 and 25 percent, respectively. The UDAG program was cut by 41 percent. Overall, federal assistance to local governments was cut 60 percent, from $43 billion to $17 billion (in constant 1990 dollars). The only program that survived cuts was federal aid for highways, which primarily benefited suburbs, not cities.

These cutbacks had a particularly devastating impact on cities with high levels of poverty and limited property tax bases, many of which depended on federal and state aid for half or more of their budgets. In 1980, federal dollars accounted for 22 percent of big-city (over 300,000 population) budgets; by 1989, federal aid was only 6 percent. State governments did not step in to fill the gap, as the president had said they would. State aid constituted 16 percent of city budgets in 1980 and remained the same nine years later.

The Democrats in Congress went along with these cuts but balked at Reagan's and Bush's efforts to sharply trim federal aid to needy individuals, who disproportionately lived in America's cities. Welfare funding increased 12 percent, to $12.2 billion in 1990, but because the size of the rolls also increased during this period, real benefits per family declined from $3,506 to $3,218 during the decade.[135] Likewise, the average food stamp benefit dropped from $719 to $690, although overall federal spending on food stamps remained the same.[136]

Federal funds for Medicaid grew 86 percent, reaching $41 billion in 1990, due primarily to increasing medical costs. The Reagan administration, which opposed government price controls, did nothing to stop the trend toward higher health care costs. Because states were required to match federal Medicaid funds, this put considerable strain on state budgets, leading them to cut aid to cities; this forced further local cuts in sanitation, police and fire protection, public libraries, and municipal hospitals and clinics.

The most dramatic cut in domestic spending during the Reagan and Bush years was for low-income housing subsidies. In his first year in office, Reagan halved the budget authority for public housing and Section 8 to about $17.5 billion. Each year thereafter, Reagan sought to eliminate federal housing assistance to the poor. Congress would not make such deep cuts, but it met Reagan more than halfway.[137] Federal housing assistance for the poor had never been an entitlement, but the proportion of the eligible poor who received federal housing subsidies declined during the 1980s, while urban homelessness rose dramatically. In 1970, there had been 300,000 more low-cost rental units (6.5 million) than low-income renter households (6.2 million). By 1985, the number of low-cost units had fallen to 5.6 million, and the number of low-income renter households had grown to 8.9 million, a disparity of 3.3 million units.[138] By the late 1980s, the number of homeless had swollen to 600,000 on any given night and 1.2 million over the course of a year.[139]

The nation's poverty rate increased from 11.7 percent in 1979 to 15.2 percent in 1983. The economic prosperity of the latter 1980s pushed it down to 12.8 percent in 1989, but the subsequent recession pushed it back up to 14.8 percent in 1992, when Bush left office.[140] The central-city poverty rate increased from 15.7 percent in 1979 to 21.5 percent in 1992.[141] The proportion of all poor living in central cities increased from 37 percent in 1983 to 42 percent in 1992.[142]

Clinton Urban Policy: Too Little, Too Late

Anticipating a Democratic victory in the 1992 presidential race, many think tanks, foundations, and advocacy groups began drafting new urban policy agendas. The explosion of the Los Angeles ghettos in April 1992 after the Rodney King verdict hastened this flood of new prescriptions and triggered growing interest in the condition of urban areas.[143] Urban activists and big-city officials hoped that Bill Clinton's victory would usher in a new era for the nation's cities. But Clinton was elected with only 43 percent of the overall vote. Almost half of all eligible voters (disproportionately the poor and minorities) stayed away from the polls. Clinton owed his victory to the fact that Texas billionaire Ross Perot, running as a third-party candidate, took 19 percent of the vote, mostly from George Bush, and to the support of middle-class suburban voters who had voted for Reagan and Bush in previous elections.

Although it captured a majority of Congress, Clinton's Democratic Party was deeply divided. Many members were closely linked to business interests that opposed progressive taxation, Keynesian pump-priming, and social spending. Clinton inherited the huge federal deficit produced by the Reagan-Bush tax cuts and defense spending, limiting his ability to address domestic concerns without significant tax increases or dramatic cuts in military spending.

President Clinton adopted a different symbolic approach to cities compared with his Republican predecessors. He visited inner-city churches and housing projects and gave stirring speeches about his personal commitment, and the nation's responsibility, to address poverty, racism, and urban blight. Presidents Reagan and Bush had refused to meet with the nation's big-city mayors, but Clinton met with them often to discuss their problems and agenda. He appointed two former big-city mayors (Federico Peña of Denver and Henry Cisneros of San Antonio) and a leading expert on urban social problems (former University of Wisconsin chancellor Donna Shalala) to his cabinet. His subcabinet included many of the nation's leading urban policy scholars and practitioners, people who had been waiting more than a decade to put their ideas into action.

Early in the Clinton administration, however, the Democratic Congress thwarted the president's efforts to enact a modest public investment plan, universal health insurance, and even a child immunization program, each of which would have significantly eased the problems facing cities and urban residents. After the November 1994 elections put a Republican majority in Congress, any significant progress on such matters was impossible. The Republican takeover exacerbated the political isolation of cities, symbolized by Clinton's proposal a month later to dramatically cut the HUD budget and his willingness to consider eliminating HUD altogether.

The Clinton administration did achieve three small-scale urban initiatives: the empowerment zone and enterprise zone (EZ) program, the crime bill, and stronger enforcement of antidiscrimination laws in housing and banking. The EZ program had almost been adopted during the Bush administration; it sought to induce private capital to invest in HUD-designated "empowerment zones" in eleven cities. Each empowerment zone city was eligible for $100 million in grants and tax breaks for businesses to create additional jobs. Another ninety-five cities received a scaled-down "enterprise zone" status. The crime bill funded 100,000 new police officers nationwide and stronger controls on the sale and ownership of handguns and assault weapons. Clinton also pressured federal bank regulators to strengthen their enforcement of the CRA, a move that led, in part, to additional mortgage loans in inner-city neighborhoods and to minority consumers.

Clinton also implemented two tiny but potentially significant pilot programs to promote mobility for the urban poor. The Moving to Opportunity program funded six cities to provide Section 8 vouchers to about 7,500 low-income renters to escape ghettos and move to better neighborhoods.[144] The equally small ($17 million) Bridges to Work program helped poor residents of ghetto neighborhoods in five cities get access to suburban jobs through improved transportation.[145] Clinton also revised several long-standing policies on public housing, permitting local authorities to tear down the most distressed projects and to change tenant selection policies to allow more working poor families to live in public housing.

By far, the most important Clinton antipoverty initiatives were not "urban" programs, even though most of those affected resided in cities. They were the expansion of the EITC, an increase in the minimum wage, and reform of AFDC (welfare reform). Using the rhetoric of "making work pay," the Clinton administration achieved a dramatic expansion of the EITC, which provides a tax credit of up to $3,800 to the working poor; families with incomes up to $30,500 are eligible. The EITC lifts many families out of poverty. In 1998, 19.3 million families and individuals claimed the EITC, with an average benefit of $1,523.[146]

Fulfilling his pledge to "end welfare as we know it," Clinton signed the Personal Responsibility and Work Opportunity Reconciliation Act in August 1996. It replaced AFDC (an entitlement with no time limits) with Temporary Assistance to Needy Families (TANF), a block grant to states that ends the federal entitlement to aid and sets time limits for receiving assistance.[147] During its first few years, TANF significantly reduced the number of people on the welfare rolls, although those concentrated in high-poverty, inner-city neighborhoods were least successful in leaving welfare.[148] It is not clear, however, whether the lot of former recipients has improved. Many simply went from the ranks of the "welfare poor" to the "working poor," with no betterment of their living standards.[149] It is also likely that when the economy takes a serious downturn and unemployment rises, former welfare recipients will be the first to be laid off.

During Clinton's final year in office, he sought to focus national attention on urban poverty.[150] He announced that the nation's strong economy had lifted more than 5.7 million poor Americans out of poverty between 1992 and 1999, and the poverty rate had fallen to its lowest level since 1979.[151] But despite the upbeat official statistics, poverty remained a serious problem. The U.S. poverty rate declined to 11.8 percent (32.3 million people), but it was still two to three times greater than the figures in most European countries, despite the United States' substantially lower unemployment level. The poverty rate in central cities was 16.4 percent. About 77 percent of the nation's poor lived in metropolitan areas, and 40.7 percent lived in central cities.[152] Despite the longest economic expansion in recent history and an unemployment rate below 5 percent, the gap between the rich and poor remained the widest of any democratic industrial nation.[153] In 1998, 44.3 million Americans (16.3 percent) lacked health insurance, an increase of 4.5 million since 1992. In 1999, the number declined slightly to 42.6 million (15.5 percent).[154]

In other words, Clinton sought to create and redefine an urban agenda, but the federal deficit, the Republican victory in 1994, the ensuing ideological attack on government activism, the identification of cities with people of color, and the relative weakness of urban constituencies inhibited the Clinton administration from promoting a bold urban policy. In particular, Clinton did not want his urban policies to threaten suburban interests that were central to his electoral victories. As a result, urban policies remained as separate targeted programs, with little effort to examine the stealth urban policies and regional dynamics that underlay the urban crisis.

SNOWBALL EFFECTS: ECONOMIC AND POLITICAL

The free-market view of urban decline and suburban sprawl is wrong. Federal policies toward metropolitan areas did not waste billions of dollars on programs targeted at cities in a futile effort to reshape powerful market forces. To the contrary, from a free-market perspective, federal policies toward metropolitan areas were an outstanding "success": they powerfully promoted economic segregation and suburban sprawl. (Of course, the social and economic costs of this "success" were extremely high.)

The political, economic, and social landscape that we take for granted is a product of federal and state policies that shaped individual and corporate decision making. Each major policy initiative began with serious debates about substantially different options. Powerful interest groups (such as the highway lobby and home-building industry) got exactly what they wanted—government support for suburbanization and metropolitan segregation. Had national policy makers been prompted to make different choices—for example, to support public transportation, to provide subsidies for mixed-income housing, to invest defense dollars and other public facilities in cities—our current metropolitan landscape would look substantially different.

Looking more narrowly at the policies and programs overtly targeted at central cities and poor neighborhoods, they partly failed. Despite billions of dollars spent on bolstering central-city business districts, central cities have lost population and jobs and become poorer relative to their suburbs. These targeted policies failed partly because far more governmental resources were devoted to promoting suburbanization. Spending on home owner subsidies was several magnitudes larger than spending on low-income housing programs; far more was spent on highways than on mass transit.

Even those urban programs most directly targeted to the urban poor were fundamentally flawed. They did not acknowledge that the problems facing poor people and poor neighborhoods are only one part of a larger dynamic of regional growth. Deeply propelled by decades of government support, this regional dynamic is hard to reshape. We have described the many ways in which it developed a self-reinforcing momentum. Compensatory programs, after the fact, are bound to have only marginal effects, especially when they do not recalibrate the institutional arrangements and incentive systems that promote economic segregation and suburban sprawl.

The federal government put its full weight behind suburbanization, refusing, for example, to insure loans in cities and integrated neighborhoods, thus encouraging redlining of cities. After governments and banks shunned economically and racially integrated neighborhoods, this decline became a self-fulfilling prophecy. Even if governments and banks no longer discriminate, spatial inequalities have a momentum of their own. The concentration of poverty leads to fewer jobs, higher crime, unhealthier environments, and fewer shopping opportunities. As a result, those who have the wherewithal flee to better neighborhoods, accentuating the economic and social decline of inner cities and distressed suburbs.

The three congressional districts discussed in chapter 1 illustrate these trends. The Thirteenth Congressional District in Illinois, a booming suburban area west of Chicago, was transformed by federal highway construction. Oak Brook, for example, is located near the nexus of three federally funded interstate highways (88, 294, and 290). The siting of one of the federal government's most prominent scientific facilities, the Argonne National Laboratory, with 4,500 employees, was another powerful factor in the district's growth. (Another federal facility, the Fermi National Accelerator Laboratory, is located in the adjacent district, but many of its employees reside in the Thirteenth.) New York's Sixteenth Congressional District also amply illustrates the powerful negative impact of federal policies on the urban and metropolitan fabric. Construction of the Cross-Bronx Expressway initiated the downward slump of the neighborhood, while suburban housing subsidies — and the absence of federal support for urban multifamily housing — drew off its population. Its numerous public housing projects tie poor people to concentrated poverty neighborhoods. Finally, in Ohio's Tenth Congressional District, local officials are even now battling the role of federal highway spending in sapping the vitality of inner suburbs.

This dynamic need not be perpetual and unalterable. The political dynamic will change as residents of outer suburbs recognize that current patterns have generated significant problems for them and that they cannot solve these problems by themselves — not without simultaneously addressing the problems of inner suburbs and central cities. As urban problems spread to thousands of suburbs, it will be more difficult to blame lazy urban poor people or incompetent and corrupt city governments for those problems. Better-off suburbs will discover that they cannot fix traffic gridlock, long commutes, environmental degradation, or skyrocketing housing costs without simultaneously addressing the interrelated problems of inner suburbs and central cities.

5 What Cities Can and Cannot Do to Address Poverty

Until recently, Jose Morales, a janitor at Los Angeles International Airport, slept on flattened cardboard boxes in a garage.[1] Every day at dawn, he commuted two hours by bus to his job, then another two hours back to his makeshift home in Compton, a decaying city adjacent to Los Angeles. His eight-hour-a-day job sweeping, dusting, and dumping trash paid Morales $5.45 an hour with no health insurance. He frequently scavenged in dumpsters for food, furniture, and other items. Then, in 1997, the "living wage" law enacted by the Los Angeles City Council boosted pay and benefits to employees of private companies with city contracts or subsidies. Morales got a raise to $7.25 an hour and health insurance. He still lives frugally because housing is so expensive in Los Angeles. But he was able to move with his sister and her family into a small two-bedroom house, which he rents for $615 a month. He began to buy furniture, including a dining room table, a comfortable bed, and a six-year-old used car. With his commute time cut in half, he can now sleep until 5:00 A.M.

The idea of a living wage law came from a coalition of unions, churches, and community groups trying to help the city's growing population of working poor. The coalition spent a year building support on the fifteen-member city council, spearheaded by councilwoman Jackie Goldberg. The Los Angeles business community fiercely opposed the law, claiming that it would damage the city's business climate. They lobbied Mayor Richard Riordan and city council members, wrote newspaper op-ed columns, and cried alarm. Responding to their pleas, Mayor Riordan, a moderate Republican, vetoed the law, but the city council overrode the veto.

The Los Angeles effort is one part of a national movement that brought labor unions together with community organizations. Baltimore passed the first living wage law in 1994, following a grassroots campaign organized by BUILD (a coalition of community groups affiliated with the Industrial Areas Foundation) and the Service Employees International Union (whose members work for local governments). This movement received a major impetus from efforts by city governments to contract public services to private firms paying lower wages and benefits than prevail in the public sector. Proponents are also motivated by the proliferation of low-wage jobs in urban areas. By the end of the 1990s, thirty-five cities and counties, including Milwaukee, St. Paul, Minneapolis, Boston, Miami, Portland (Oregon), San Jose, Detroit, San Antonio, and Oakland, had enacted living wage laws. Efforts were unsuccessful in some cities but are still under way in others.[2]

The living wage movement reflects both the potential and the limits of local efforts to address the problems of economic inequality and poverty. Living wage laws cover only a small proportion of a city's workforce (about 10,000 out of 1.7 million workers in the city of Los Angeles). Cities have no authority to enact minimum wage laws covering all private employees—only for those employers that do business with city government.[3] Everywhere that unions and community groups have proposed a living wage bill, business leaders have warned that it will hurt business and thwart private job creation. Like opponents of increasing the federal or state minimum wage, these foes argue that firms employing low-wage workers will be forced to close, hurting the very people the measure was designed to help.

Living wage laws have not in fact had such consequences, primarily because most covered businesses are immobile. Airport restaurants, private parking lots serving the city convention center, and sanitation companies under municipal contract to collect garbage are tied to the local economy. Equally important, low-wage workers tend to spend what they make, pumping money into the local economy (particularly in grocery stores and other retail outlets in low-income neighborhoods). Nevertheless, many local elected officials are reluctant to pass living wage laws for fear of costing their city jobs and themselves campaign contributions.

The clash over such measures reflects a larger debate over the degree to which cities can and should enact local measures to address the concentration of poor people within their borders. On the one hand, local officials want to improve conditions for the poor and near poor. On the other, local officials must make their cities attractive places to do business and retain middle-class residents. Living wage ordinances, housing "linkage" policies, business taxes, clean air laws, plant closing laws, rent control, and lower utility rates all confront this dilemma. It may be a bluff when corporations threaten to leave if they do not get tax relief, but it is hard for local officials, unions, and community groups to know for certain, especially when many cities have experienced substantial job losses. Business warnings are not always empty threats. Local officials are reluctant to judge which firms are more or less likely to leave and unwilling to see just how far they can push. Instead, they tend to err in favor of promoting local businesses.[4]

Of course, local elected officials cannot just throw up their hands in frustration at these problems. They typically promise more and better jobs, more affordable housing, safer streets, more (and more efficient) public services, and better schools. Even with the best of intentions, however, local political leaders, whatever their political orientation, face overwhelming obstacles in trying to reduce poverty within their boundaries. The realities of urban finance and economics limit even the most progressive city officials. They can reduce the incidence of poverty either by lifting up the poor people in the city or by enticing more affluent people to move in. (Cities typically lack the brazenness to kick poor people out.) But they cannot require the suburbs to build affordable housing for the central-city poor. Nor can they require suburban employers to hire poor city residents or force metropolitan transportation systems to reorganize their routes and schedules to help urban residents get to suburban jobs. And most of the incentives still favor suburbs in the competition to attract middle-class residents.

As a result, most cities focus on attracting new investments, in the hope that expanding tax revenues will fund programs to help lift up city residents. Instead of putting a high priority on antipoverty policies, they focus on attracting private investment and improving municipal services, even when the local business community is so poorly organized that it does not press them to do so.[5] As Mayor Kurt Schmoke, progressive mayor of Baltimore, said (in 1992, when one-quarter of his city lived in poverty), "I strongly believe that if cities are to be competitive in the twenty-first century, they need to be international . . . by creating an environment that will enable international companies to use Baltimore as a gateway to the United States."[6]

Conservative mayors have no qualms about attracting businesses by reducing government regulations and taxes and providing new subsidies. They expect a strong private sector to "trickle down" to the poor and near poor. Traditional liberal politicians have less sympathy for this approach and typically want businesses to hire local residents or minorities in exchange for regulatory and tax relief or for subsidies. The new progressive politicians resist reducing regulations and taxes or providing subsidies in the first place; they want companies to agree to pay decent wages, contribute to affordable housing funds, or provide other long-term benefits. In other words, local officials disagree over the degree to which they are willing to test the limits and call business's bluff.

Cities with high-skill economies that do not compete directly with low-skill and low-wage industries around the world usually have less of a problem with poverty and greater latitude in improving local economic and social conditions. Even in economically successful cities, however, local public officials compete on a playing field tilted toward their suburbs, with few mechanisms to promote city-suburb cooperation. Although both New York and Los Angeles experienced tremendous economic expansion in the latter 1990s, neither could marshal the political will to address growing inequality and persistent poverty. Most other cities have much less competitive advantage, and thus much less leverage, in addressing poverty, even if they wanted to. Most urban leaders, in short, are trapped in a fiscal straitjacket.

THE IRON CAGE OF MUNICIPAL FINANCE

City governments are often perched on the brink of fiscal distress. Central-city governments can tax only part of the economic rewards they generate, and these revenues fluctuate with local economic conditions. But while revenues are limited and variable, demands for services and expenditures are inexorable and often beyond municipal control (as in the case of the local share of Medicaid expenditures). As a result, even economically successful cities face chronic difficulty balancing their budgets. In 1996, local governments spent $794 billion, or 26 percent of all government spending in the United States.[7] They provide and finance most of the services that Americans use on a daily basis. As Robert Lineberry noted, they are "vital to the preservation of life (police, fire, sanitation, public health), liberty (police, courts, prosecutors), property (zoning, planning, taxing), and public enlightenment (schools, libraries)."[8] Cities cover most of the cost of providing these services through whatever they can raise from property, sales, and income taxes; fines; fees; and other sources. Education, public safety, and sanitation exhaust the lion's share of most municipal budgets. (Most cities also provide other services funded primarily by states or the federal government, such as welfare or public housing.) In comparing cities' fiscal capacities, Helen Ladd and John Yinger found some time ago that most had a significant gap between their ability to raise revenue and the amounts they needed to spend to provide average-quality basic services. The typical American city had poor "fiscal health."[9] Although some cities are better managed than others, and some suffer from corruption, these factors do not explain urban fiscal stress. As Ladd and Yinger explain, "[a]lthough the financial difficulties of these cities may be exacerbated by politics or management practices . . . the policy tools available to city officials are weak compared to the impact on city finances of national economic, social, and fiscal trends."[10]

As the nation's economy boomed in the late 1990s, cities' fiscal condition improved. Urban poverty began to decline, residents' incomes rose, and businesses prospered, which generated more revenue.[11] But cities still could not raise enough revenue to provide everyone with good schools, public safety, and rehabilitated infrastructure, or to grant raises to city employees that kept up with the rate of inflation, much less to lift the incomes of the poor. Their improved bond ratings masked the deeper reality that many cities had already tightened their belts and lowered residents' expectations during the downturns of the mid-1970s, early 1980s, and early 1990s. They closed public hospitals; reduced library hours; deferred maintenance on aging sewers, playgrounds, and parks; and reduced the numbers of public employees. If many cities were able to live within their means in the late 1990s, it is because they attempted to do less than they had in earlier years, especially in addressing the needs of the poor.

In addition to the competition across cities for investment, there are major fiscal disparities within metropolitan areas. Vast disparities of wealth and poverty are often located only a few zip codes from each other, even though they seem worlds apart. Not only do the well-off and the poor live apart from each other, but they receive strikingly unequal public services because the poor live in places that lack the fiscal capacity to provide decent public services at reasonable tax rates, while the rich live in places that can fund high-quality services at a relatively low tax rate.[12] In an extreme case, such as Camden, New Jersey, almost half of whose 85,000 residents live in poverty, the city cannot provide even minimal services despite punishingly high tax rates.[13] Residents of different communities in the same metropolitan area can pay the same tax rates but receive very different levels of public services, or pay different amounts of taxes for the same public services. In general, for obvious reasons, cities have worse fiscal conditions than suburbs.

We have already described how other factors reinforce this general dilemma. Cities no longer dominate their metropolitan areas as they did fifty years ago, when they housed half or two-thirds of the region's population and had higher per capita incomes than did the suburbs. Almost two-thirds of the nation's twenty-five largest cities lost population after 1950.[14] Even when they grew, they did so more slowly than their surrounding suburbs. Between 1993 and 1996, central cities' share of job growth continued to fall in most metropolitan areas; almost a quarter experienced an absolute loss of employment, and half increased jobs, but not as quickly as their suburbs.[15] Economic shifts and disinvestment left central-city per capita incomes considerably lower than those of suburbanites in almost every metropolitan area. They also lowered the tax base at a time when the average level of need among city residents was rising. "To compensate, the city must increase tax rates or reduce public spending—further convincing middle-class residents to leave."[16]

Most cities are still vital centers of culture, entertainment, and other key services within their metropolitan areas. Suburbanites and tourists flock to museums, sports complexes, concert halls, and convention centers, as well as hospitals and universities. But many of these institutions, as nonprofit organizations, do not directly generate tax revenue. One-third of New York City's property value is exempt from taxes, compared with 13 percent in suburban Nassau County and 22 percent in suburban Westchester County.[17] Public efforts to lure private professional sports teams by building stadiums usually backfire.[18]

Enormous amounts of private wealth also remain within many American cities. But city governments cannot tap much of it, in part because states restrict how cities can raise revenue. For example, only eight of the nation's twenty-four largest cities impose an income or wage tax on nonresident commuters, and at a very low rate at that.[19] In 1999, New York Governor George Pataki signed a law repealing a 0.45 percent tax on the New York City wages earned by suburban commuters. The repeal of the tax, first enacted in 1966, deprived the city of $360 million a year from the 800,000 people who work in the city but live elsewhere.[20] During the 1970s and 1980s, statewide referenda restricted the ability of municipalities to increase property taxes, such as Proposition 13 in California and Proposition 2½ in Massachusetts.

Cities also have broader service responsibilities than do most suburbs. The federal and state governments and courts have imposed many mandates on cities without providing the funds necessary to carry them out.[21] For example, the federal government requires cities to improve the water quality, remove asbestos from old school buildings and lead paint from public housing, and make municipal buses accessible to the physically disabled (under the Americans with Disabilities Act). In 1992, Chicago estimated that it would spend more than $95 million that year for capital improvements required by federal and state environmental mandates. Atlanta had to borrow $400 million in the early 1990s to comply with federal clean water mandates.[22]

Many of the new social problems of the 1980s, including homelessness, AIDS, crack cocaine use, and violent crime, were concentrated in cities. City governments did not create these problems, but they have to deal with them. In the 1960s and 1970s, federal and state laws "deinstitutionalized" mental hospital patients after the media exposed the inhumane treatment many of them received and new tranquilizers gave mental health professionals the ability to manage patients in "community" settings.[23] But the federal and state governments did not fund enough community mental health facilities, and neighborhood opposition made it hard to open those that were funded. The mental hospital patient population dropped from 558,922 in 1955 to 137,810 in 1980 and then to 118,647 in 1990. Younger schizophrenics, who previously would have been hospitalized, had no place to go for treatment.

The result was a dramatic increase in mentally ill persons on America's city streets. Many became homeless, often begging and sometimes committing crimes, triggering opposition from business and neighborhood groups. At the same time, federal funding for subsidized housing also declined. Many cities used police and other personnel to manage swelling homeless populations and responded by using public funds and charitable help to provide shelter, food, and medical treatment, but in many other cities, police harassed the homeless but provided few services. By 1988, partly in response to litigation, New York City had 30,500 shelter beds and was spending $375 million in local funds to shelter the homeless.[24]

Cities are also high-cost environments in which to provide services. Even when cities spend the same dollar amounts on public services as the suburbs, they cannot provide their residents with the same quality of services. As Anatole France bitingly observed, "The majestic egalitarianism of the law forbids rich and poor alike to sleep under the bridges, to beg in the streets, and to steal bread."[25] Treating unequals equally reinforces inequalities. The effectiveness of services provided to different neighborhoods varies tremendously because their needs vary tremendously.

Consider the world of eight-year-old Bernardo Rodriguez, who lived in the East Tremont section of the South Bronx. Bernardo was a quiet boy who did well in school. His grandmother did not let him play outside because it was too dangerous, but she thought that the hallway of their apartment building would be safe. Tragically, the elevator doors were defective, and Bernardo fell to his death. It is impossible to know whether better municipal inspection procedures would have saved his life, but it is a fact that many code enforcement inspectors refuse to go into buildings they regard as too dangerous. To protect themselves, they simply write on their report forms: "No access to building."[26]

Neighborhoods with older buildings require more frequent inspections and more rigorous enforcement. More resources may need to be committed to inspections in poor areas to achieve the level of safety expected in middle-class areas. In Los Angeles, where almost one out of six apartments is a substandard slum, the city has a huge backlog of inspections.[27] Similarly, police sometimes refuse to patrol dangerous public housing projects. Neighborhoods with many poor people need even more resources to achieve the same outcomes as better-off areas. If the goal is equal health and safety, poor neighborhoods need more housing inspectors and more police patrols and fire personnel. Their streets are more difficult to keep clean because people living in overcrowded apartments with inadequate parks use them for recreation. Poor areas also need public services that other neighborhoods do not. How many upper-middle-class suburban neighborhoods need lead paint monitoring or rat control programs?

This same logic holds for cities and metropolitan regions as currently organized. The differences *between* governments, not *within* governments, generate the most glaring inequalities. Central cities and inner-ring suburban municipalities often have to spend more to maintain service levels that are common in affluent suburbs, yet the median income of their taxpayers is lower. The fact that large central-city governments spend more per capita than do middle-class suburbs is often taken as a sign of their corruption or inefficiency or their spending on the undeserving poor.[28] In fact, it is largely a matter of greater need.

Not surprisingly, cities with many poor people spend more on antipoverty functions. But cities with high poverty rates also spend more on non-poverty-related services such as police, fire, courts, and general administrative functions. For every one-point increase in the poverty rate, cities spent $27.75 per capita more on non-poverty-related services.[29] This suggests that concentrated poverty carries a substantial fiscal burden. Moreover, these expenditures typically do not achieve the same results in public security or educational achievement as their suburban counterparts. To add insult to injury, these citizens are forced to pay more of their income in taxes.[30]

Suburbanization also drives up the cost of central-city services. Suburban commuters require central cities to provide police protection and road maintenance, but they rarely pay taxes to these cities.[31] Sprawl also reduces the efficiency of central-city public services. Urban decline has reduced the population density in most areas of concentrated poverty.[32] Cleveland's population fell from 915,000 people in 1950 to less than 500,000 today. Even though it has 400,000 fewer people, and they are poorer, the city has to maintain the same number of miles of streets, sewers, and water lines.

Many inner-ring suburbs also have problems providing local services, and they lack the downtown commercial properties that generate tax revenue. Myron Orfield notes that fifty-nine Chicago suburban municipalities had a lower tax base per household than did Chicago, which was itself considerably below the regional average.[33] If the average fiscal capacity of regional governments were scored 100, the city of Chicago (at 87) would be 13 percent below average, but the inner-ring suburb of Maywood would score 54, and North Chicago would score 60. At the other extreme, Winnetka would score 207 and Lake Forest 266.[34]

DIFFERENCES IN FISCAL CAPACITY

Cities differ a great deal in how much leeway they have in raising their own revenues. These differences are based in part on different demographic and economic characteristics. Cities with high poverty rates, large immigrant populations, and large proportions of school-age children have a harder time raising revenue and face greater expenditure needs. Cities that have been able to annex adjacent suburban areas and incorporate the middle class within their municipal boundaries and that face less competition from surrounding communities are often in a better fiscal position.[35] Those whose major employers are relatively immobile and relatively profitable can impose higher taxes with less risk of promoting a business exodus.

These fiscal differences are based more on the historical and current role a city plays in the regional, national, and global economies than on how well it is managed. The conventional wisdom about urban poverty rests on the experiences of old industrial cities such as Baltimore, Cleveland, Detroit, Gary, Newark, St. Louis, and Youngstown. As Table 5.1 shows, Detroit's poverty rate persistently exceeds the average for all cities and for the United States. The industrial cities rapidly gained population and employment between 1880 and 1930. After World War II, they gained large minority populations, suffered heavily from deindustrialization and the loss of corporate headquarters jobs, and became far worse off relative to their surrounding suburbs. Such cities have the least leverage over their internal problems.

A second group of old cities is better situated. They may have had a considerable amount of manufacturing, but they started out as port cities and transport nodes, and many were the first capital markets in their regions and provided the beginnings of advanced corporate services, such as corporate law firms. Typified by New York, Chicago, Boston, and San Francisco, these cities have been more prosperous than the first group. Although they lost a huge amount of blue-collar employment over the last half century, they experienced offsetting employment gains in corporate services, public services, and nonprofit services. These cities attracted black migration, but not to the extent of the first group, and they also received Hispanic and Asian newcomers, often from abroad. As a result, their minority populations are more diverse than those of

TABLE 5.1. Poverty Rates in Selected Central Cities, 1970–1995, and for All Metropolitan Areas, Central Cities, Suburbs, and the U.S., 1970–1999

	1970	1980	1990	1993 estimate	1995 estimate	1999
Atlanta	19.8	27.5	27.3	35.6	33.6	NA
Boston	15.5	20.2	18.7	19.9	18.2	NA
Chicago	14.4	20.3	21.6	27.1	22.8	NA
Detroit	14.7	21.9	32.4	39.6	33.1	NA
Indianapolis	09.2	11.5	12.5	15.6	13.3	NA
Los Angeles	13.0	16.2	18.6	29.9	28.6	NA
New York City	14.7	20.0	19.3	24.4	23.7	NA
Pittsburgh	15.0	16.5	21.4	23.3	20.2	NA
Metropolitan Areas	10.2	11.9	12.7	14.6	13.4	11.6
Central Cities	14.2	17.2	19.0	21.5	20.6	16.4
Suburbs	07.1	08.2	08.7	10.3	09.1	08.3
U.S.	12.6	13.0	13.5	15.1	13.8	11.8

Sources: Figures for metro areas, central cities, and suburbs from "Poverty of People, by Residence: 1959 to 1999," U.S. Census Bureau at: www.census.gov/income/histpov/histpov8.txt; National figure from "Poverty Status of People by Family Relationship, Race, and Hispanic Origins: 1959 to 1999," U.S. Census Bureau, at: www.census.gov/hhes/poverty/histpov/histpov2.txt; also from Joseph Dalaker and Bernadette Proctor, *Poverty in the United States: 1999* (Washington, D.C.: U.S. Census Bureau, September 2000). Decennial census figures for specific cities from "State of the Nation's Cities" database, Center for Urban Policy Research, Rutgers University, at supergenius.rutgers.edu/WylyWeb/Data/; 1990s estimates for specific cities from *Now Is The Time: Places Left Behind in the New Economy* (Washington, D.C.: U.S. Department of Housing and Urban Development, April 1999), Appendix Table 11, at: www.huduser.org. NA = Not yet available.

the first group of cities, and their Anglo elites remain far more committed to living in the central city. As Table 5.1 shows, their poverty rates have been lower than those of Detroit, an exemplar of the first group.

Finally, relatively new cities such as Los Angeles, Seattle, San Diego, Houston, Portland (Oregon), Phoenix, Minneapolis, St. Paul, and Columbus (Ohio) have metropolitan economies based on corporate and social services, high technology, the defense industry, energy, tourism, and, sometimes, state government. Most had low levels of black immigration, though those located near the Mexican border experienced high levels of Hispanic immigration.[36] The post-1965 wave of immigration into the United States clustered in the old port cities and the newer high-tech cities, while native whites and native blacks moved away from immigrant-receiving cities toward newer, faster-growing cities with high proportions of native-born populations.[37] Generally, their poverty rates have been lower than those in the other two groups of cities.

All three types of cities experienced the negative impacts of concentrated urban poverty, economic segregation, and suburban sprawl, however. Even the archetype "new city," Los Angeles, has come to experience historically high rates of poverty, as Table 5.1 shows. The number of high-poverty census tracts increased in almost every major U.S. city between 1970 and 1990.[38] Even such prosperous cities as San Jose, Seattle, Portland, Albuquerque, and San Diego have significant pockets of poverty amid the generally high family incomes surrounding them. But the negative impact was most pronounced in the declining old industrial cities and least pervasive in the new, growing, high-technology cities. All cities have experienced a declining share of metropolitan employment, but the geographic separation between concentrated urban poverty and suburban affluence is most pronounced in the older manufacturing cities confronted with severe industrial decline, racial transition, and white flight.[39]

THE CASE OF EDUCATION

Public education is probably the most important service that local governments provide. (It certainly absorbs the most resources.) In 1979, the hourly wages of college graduates were 57 percent higher than those of workers without high school diplomas. By 1999, they made 133 percent more ($20.58 an hour versus $8.83 an hour).[40] In an economy characterized by shrinking manufacturing employment, rising service employment, ubiquitous information technology, and low union membership, a strong back and willingness to work hard rarely provide a middle-class standard of living.

Public education in the United States is run by 13,726 independent school districts.[41] Their revenue capacities vary tremendously. In 1973, the Supreme Court ruled that the U.S. Constitution does not guarantee education as a fundamental right, and therefore it does not fall under the Fourteenth Amendment's equal protection clause (*San Antonio v. Rodriguez*). But eighteen state courts have ruled that fiscal inequalities across school districts violate state constitutions and have ordered action to reduce them. State equalization grants have lessened the gap in spending between the richest and poorest districts in many states, but expenditures per pupil still vary significantly. In 1997, in the New York metropolitan area, per pupil expenditures varied from $8,171 in New York City to $12,492 in suburban Nassau County and $12,760 in suburban Westchester County.[42]

Even if all school districts had the same resources, they would not produce equal educational outcomes because of social disadvantages in poor districts. Most state aid addresses fiscal disparities, not social disadvantages. Kenneth

Wong estimates that only 8 percent of state aid to local school districts is specifically targeted for the socially disadvantaged.[43] Many have concluded that schools simply reproduce the class inequalities that are present in American society.[44] Children from poor families typically have lower academic performance than do those from middle- and upper-class families. This has nothing to do with their intelligence but much to do with the social conditions that handicap their ability to learn, which are worst when they live in concentrated poverty neighborhoods.[45] Poor children are more likely to move frequently, and poor neighborhoods have less stability.[46] Of those children living in families with incomes below $10,000 a year, more than 30 percent have attended three or more different schools by the third grade.[47] These children lack a quiet place to study. Jonathan Kozol reports that one South Bronx boy used a flashlight to do his homework in the closet of his brother's bedroom.[48] Poor children are more likely to be malnourished and to come to school tired and are less likely to have books at home and parents who read with them. High crime levels in poor neighborhoods lead mothers to keep children inside for their safety and to send them to worse nearby schools rather than have them travel farther to magnet programs.

Many residents of poor neighborhoods have supportive social networks in their immediate neighborhood, but they lack connections to opportunities outside the neighborhood. Their social networks may help them to "get by" but not to "get ahead."[49] The payoff from education may not seem real to young people who do not know anybody who has graduated from college and has a good job. As a result, they often have low expectations of what they can accomplish.

Chicago's Gautreaux program, which provides housing vouchers to help the inner-city poor rent suburban apartments, provides clear evidence of the neighborhood effect on school performance. Dropout rates among poor urban students who moved to the suburbs were one-fourth the rate among those who moved to other areas within Chicago; the suburban youngsters were more likely to enroll in college-track courses, twice as likely to attend college, and more than twice as likely to attend four-year colleges as opposed to junior or community colleges.[50]

Equalizing the quality of all public services, not just education, within and across these different types of metropolitan regions, regardless of race or income, would have profound implications.[51] Confronted with the structural disparity between their revenue and their needs and unable to bridge the gap through regional tax sharing, cities have typically looked to the federal and state governments for fiscal help. All urban leaders, regardless of political party or ideology, want more state and federal resources for their cities. But, as the next chapter discusses, cities are in a weaker political position than they were even a few decades ago. When the federal government was at its most generous in the 1970s, it filled only part of the gap. Since then, federal aid to cities has dropped dramatically, from 15 percent of municipal revenue in 1978 to less than 3 percent today, and state aid did not make up the difference.[52] As a result, locally generated revenue now makes up 70 percent of city budgets.[53] "Fend-for-yourself federalism" has exacerbated cities' fiscal stress.[54]

WHO GOVERNS? URBAN POWER STRUCTURES AND URBAN REGIMES

If structural factors so tightly constrain cities, then what is urban politics all about? Is it all "sound and fury," as Shakespeare wrote, "signifying nothing?" Can candidates for city councilor or mayor really have significantly different programs, not just different personalities or characters? Within the overall constraints, liberal, progressive, and conservative city governments have in fact pursued substantively different local strategies for dealing with the effects of concentrated urban poverty. Three factors influence the choices local officials make about how to govern: their ideological perspective, the amount of resources the city can command, and the political coalitions that brought them into office. Public officials have different ideologies about the appropriate role of government in addressing such problems as housing, homelessness, AIDS, crime, and education. City officials are also influenced by those who helped get them into office and govern, including not only voters and campaign contributors but also business groups, the media, unions, neighborhood organizations, and other interest groups.

Urban politics followed some general patterns over the last fifty years. In the period after World War II, local pro-growth coalitions emerged to push for the physical redevelopment of the downtown areas. Typically, they were preceded by the formation of organizations such as the Coordinating Committee in Boston, the Committee of 25 in Los Angeles, the Bishops in Hartford, the Allegheny Conference on Community Development in Pittsburgh, the Metropolitan Fund and the New Detroit Committee in Detroit, and Central Atlanta Progress to bring together corporate leaders who could wield significant influence to smooth over differences, forge a consensus on public policy, marshal support for a pro-growth agenda, and promote local involvement in the federal urban renewal program.[55] These groups usually involved an "inner circle" of between 25 and 100 individuals with overlapping memberships on the boards of major corporations, universities, philanthropies, hospitals, museums, and social clubs.[56]

The breakthrough moment for these efforts came, however, with the election of mayoral candidates committed to a downtown redevelopment program, typically with support not only from real estate development interests but also from retailers, construction unions, the media, hospitals, and universities. The pro-growth coalitions they built carried out urban renewal and urban freeway projects that drastically reshaped the urban fabric, modernizing business districts and providing new facilities for many of the coalition partners, including nonprofit organizations such as universities and hospitals.

Ultimately, however, urban renewal generated tremendous conflict, provoking the protest movements of the 1960s and heightening racial tensions. Low-income and minority neighborhoods bore the brunt of the costs of urban renewal, which tore down many more units of housing than it built, disrupted neighborhoods, and divided parts of the city with new highways and upscale development projects.[57] Neighborhood activists increasingly challenged downtown-oriented development policies and advocated a shift toward rebuilding poor neighborhoods, paying attention to historical preservation, and improving economic opportunities for minority residents. Occasionally, they mobilized sufficient strength to win city council seats and even to elect sympathetic mayors. As black and Hispanic populations grew, minority electoral mobilization also catapulted black and Hispanic leaders onto city councils and into mayoral offices.

As neighborhood groups and minority activists challenged the downtown business coalition from one side, economic change was undermining it from the other. Starting in the 1970s, corporate mergers and downsizing eliminated many of the corporate headquarters that once dominated major cities, as well as the local family ownership that had controlled them.[58] Local executives were no longer the top decision makers. A small elite of civic-minded bankers, lawyers, and businesspeople was replaced by transient executives who were less willing to "give money for concert halls and museums, lend their names to fund-raising drives, work to build the critical mass necessary to get major projects off the ground."[59] These transformations opened up the political space for new political coalitions that put less emphasis on downtown development and more on building low- and moderate-income rental housing, enhancing neighborhood participation, and working with community-based organizations. Some cities began experimenting with new strategies to address concentrated poverty and fiscal stress.

Within the broad historical and structural outlines that constrain what cities can do about growing poverty, there has been a great deal of variety in what they have wanted to do and actually did. To explain why different cities followed different paths, scholars developed a new paradigm called "urban regime theory."[60] According to this approach, urban governance requires cooperation among an array of public and private actors. Politicians woo voters and contributors to win elections, but a majority *electoral* coalition may not be enough to ensure that they can carry out their programs once they are in office. For that, they need a *governing* coalition. Holding the formal reins of power is not enough. Public officials need active support not only from private-sector power centers but from other interests as well. Regime theory asks how different forms of cooperation emerge among economic, political, and civic interests. It argues that the nature of the regime depends on the makeup of the dominant political coalition, what resources each member brings to the coalition, and what position each holds relative to the other members, as well as on the political skills of those who put it together.[61]

Political regimes are not static and self-perpetuating. They can grow, decay, and be replaced by new alliances. Los Angeles had a liberal regime for much of the 1970s and early 1980s during the first half of Mayor Tom Bradley's twenty-year reign, but this evolved into a more conservative regime during the late 1980s and 1990s, especially after the election of Mayor Richard Riordan. By the late 1990s, it seemed that a progressive coalition might arise to challenge Riordan, based on the political forces that engineered the "living wage." These forces seriously contested for political power in the 2001 mayoral and city council elections.[62]

Although numerous typologies have been developed to describe local regimes,[63] here we discuss three different responses to the problems posed by the growing concentration of poor in central cities: traditional urban liberalism, urban progressivism, and urban conservatism.[64] Each type of regime is based on a different kind of coalition, each has a distinct philosophy about the appropriate role of government in addressing urban poverty, and each has fielded different approaches to that problem. Traditional urban liberalism tries to incorporate poor and working-class people, especially minorities, by expanding government services without challenging business influence over other aspects of the urban agenda, especially downtown development. Urban progressivism seeks to challenge business dominance of development issues, empower poor neighborhoods, and distribute more resources to poor and working-class people. Urban conservatism emphasizes reducing government regulation, promoting business growth, and "freeing" the marketplace to create "trickle-down" benefits for the poor. (Naturally, these are ideal types; actual regimes typically combine these elements and evolve, but one or another is usually predominant.)

Urban Liberal Regimes

In recent decades, urban liberalism has sought to target government benefits to ethnic and racial minorities who suffered past discrimination; more generally, it believes in expanding government services and government employment to improve the quality of life and to provide upward mobility for working-class residents of the city. Dating from the era of big-city political machines, it seeks not so much to empower minorities as a group as to provide individual benefits (jobs, job training, housing, and health care) to group members. Urban liberals do not see the populist distribution of benefits and services as antithetical to the interests or power of business. Indeed, private investment provides the tax base they use to finance services for the poor. As the focus of urban liberalism changed from assimilating immigrants in the early part of the twentieth century to managing racial succession in the 1960s and 1970s, its efforts were often underwritten by federal grant programs. As federal aid to the cities shrank in the 1980s, many urban liberals shifted their priorities toward downtown business development, linking it with set-aside programs for minority contractors. Opposition sometimes came both from white ethnics opposed to race-targeted programs and from neighborhood organizations opposed to the renewed focus on downtown development.

The urban political machines of the last century were an early manifestation of urban liberalism. They gained electoral majorities and held governing power by giving municipal jobs and other benefits to their ethnic supporters (Irish, Italians, Jews, and others) in return for votes and by giving contracts and other special benefits to favored businesses in return for money and political support. As one observer put it, "before social security, unemployment insurance, medicare, food stamps, and aid to families with dependent children . . . machines made meaningful attempts to distribute relief and welfare."[65] They promoted the employment of first- and second-generation immigrants by large public works projects, the municipal government, and private employers connected to the political establishment. Machines controlled as much as 20 percent of the job growth in their cities between 1900 and 1920.[66]

Urban liberalism fashioned the new immigrant groups into an organized electoral force. They made sure that immigrants could vote and mobilized reliable voters on election day, often on a block-by-block level. The regular party organizations sought to manage ethnic competition by spreading symbolic and material benefits and by recruiting candidates from different ethnic groups.

(They generally excluded blacks, however, from proportionate positions of power during the first half of the twentieth century, though they did create black "sub-machines.") [67]

In some turn-of-the-century cities, immigrant-based political machines vied with and even replaced business elites as the primary force in city politics. They enhanced their power by providing select businesses with tax breaks, construction contracts, and utility franchises. Business groups often criticized machines as a corrupt and inefficient "spoils" system and promoted various "reform" proposals to undermine their power, with limited success. At the same time, they benefited from the ability and willingness of political bosses to keep immigrant workers in line, undermine unions, and oppose labor-backed political parties.

Modern urban liberalism descends from its machine predecessor. After World War II, more forward-looking urban liberal politicians formed alliances with business elites to promote urban renewal, but they also took steps to bring African Americans and later Hispanics into the circle of beneficiaries and to manage and co-opt the levels of community protest and mobilization that occurred in the 1960s and 1970s. With help from the Great Society programs of that period, they expanded subsidized housing, job training, public employment, and other antipoverty programs that both served and employed these formerly excluded groups. As blacks gained access to well-paying government and nonprofit jobs, the black professional and middle classes expanded, but with little positive effect on the ghetto poor.[68] In fact, they suffered most from urban renewal.

The business leaders who joined with urban liberals in forming pro-growth coalitions viewed cleaning up the slums and improving central business districts as ways to bring shoppers back to the downtowns and retain new middle-class residents. Construction unions collaborated because these federal programs provided jobs for their members. Major employers viewed job training and school reform programs (such as Head Start) as a way to upgrade their potential labor pool. Private developers were eager to utilize federal funds to build low-income housing.

If one issue divided the more liberal from the more conservative variants of the pro-growth coalition, it was racial integration of public schools and neighborhoods. In theory, few business and civic leaders favored racial segregation. But as civil rights activists demanded that urban liberal regimes ban housing discrimination and integrate the public schools (through busing, if necessary), they saw that meeting these demands would trigger a serious white working-class and middle-class backlash. Similarly, demands for "community control"

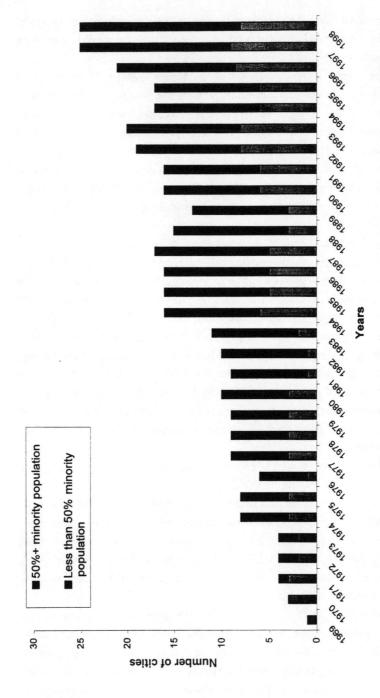

FIGURE 5.1. Black and Hispanic Mayors in the 76 Cities with Populations over 200,000 in 1990 (1969–1998)

Source: Dreier database on minority mayors.

Legend:
- 50%+ minority population
- Less than 50% minority population

X-axis: Years (1969, 1970, 1971, 1972, 1973, 1974, 1975, 1976, 1977, 1978, 1979, 1980, 1981, 1982, 1983, 1984, 1985, 1986, 1987, 1988, 1989, 1990, 1991, 1992, 1993, 1994, 1995, 1996, 1997, 1998)

Y-axis: Number of cities (0, 5, 10, 15, 20, 25, 30)

(which many whites perceived to mean African American control) of public schools upset white parents and teachers' unions. Controversies of this sort damaged the political careers of liberal mayors Kevin White in Boston and John Lindsay in New York.[69]

As their black and Hispanic populations grew rapidly in the 1950s and 1960s, urban liberal regimes clearly could not survive in many large cities without giving African Americans a greater foothold in school boards, city councils, and mayoralties. Some cities, such as Chicago under Mayor Richard Daley, clung to tokenism, but urban liberal coalition leaders actively recruited and promoted blacks in Atlanta, Los Angeles, and Cleveland.[70] In this way, a new genera-tion of African American (and later Latino) leaders won office (Figure 5.1). No major American city elected an African American mayor until 1967, when Gary, Indiana, elected Richard Hatcher and Cleveland elected Carl Stokes. By 1988, twenty-eight cities had African American mayors; by 1993, thirty-eight did.

When Baltimore finally elected Kurt Schmoke its first black mayor in 1987, every large city with a majority black population had done so. Civil rights activ-ism and the Voting Rights Act led to dramatic breakthroughs in the South, where black mayoral victories occurred in Atlanta, New Orleans, Richmond, Savannah, Memphis, Birmingham, and Charlotte. The nation's five largest cities all elected a black mayor at some point in the last two decades, including David Dinkins in New York City, Tom Bradley in Los Angeles, Harold Wash-ington in Chicago, Wilson Goode and John Street in Philadelphia, and Lee Brown in Houston. Though whites replaced blacks as mayors in some of these cities in the 1990s, leading some to argue that there was a backlash against mi-nority mayors,[71] minority mayors currently serve in one-third of the seventy-five largest American cities (many of which still have white majorities).[72] The total number of black local elected officials increased from 715 in 1970 to 5,210 by 1998. Likewise, Hispanic local officeholders increased from 1,304 in 1984 to 2,197 in 1994.[73]

Black and Latino mayoral candidates usually had to wait until their respec-tive racial groups were a near majority of the population before they won, and they still had to attract significant white support to win and to govern. Richard Hatcher could not have won in Gary, nor Tom Bradley in Los Angeles, with-out white liberal support. Although such mayors promised black and Latino voters that they would improve opportunities and conditions for minorities, to survive in office, they needed to build bridges to whites. They could not re-ward only their minority supporters. Such mayors thus had to navigate between actions that would favor African Americans but anger other groups and ac-tions that would broaden their political base but risk alienating core minority supporters, who could charge that they were watering down their campaign rhetoric or failing to deliver on their campaign promises. As a result, minority mayors had a hard time "delivering the goods" and building durable governing coalitions.[74]

Minority candidates developed "deracialized" campaigns and policy agendas to win "crossover" votes alongside their minority political bases in cities where whites remained a majority. Once elected, they too faced the challenge of forging a robust governing coalition that could deliver to specific constituencies without undermining support from white liberals and the business elite.[75] Their strategies typically included creating new public programs, awarding contracts to allies, reforming police practices, changing the racial makeup of the police force, building affordable housing, and appointing minority supporters to commissions, boards, and high-level jobs. They sought to improve snow removal, housing inspections, and police protection in previously neglected minority neighborhoods.[76] Typically, however, they failed at reforming public school systems, a major concern among minority voters.[77] They also had a hard time changing the strong organizational culture of police departments.[78] Above all, urban liberal mayors did not significantly decrease crime, which in high-poverty areas soared in the 1980s in almost every city.

Procurement programs requiring a percentage of city contracts to go to minority-owned firms offered urban liberal regimes one time-honored way to cement their position. Although increased minority representation in contracting and municipal employment is symbolically important, these mayors knew that public jobs and contracts go mostly to middle-income minorities, not the poor.[79] To address the poor's need for work, most minority mayors adopted the conventional pro-growth approach. Peter Eisinger observes:

> The black mayors operate on the basis of a simple equation: private economic development in the city produces jobs in the private sector and tax money that may be used for jobs and purchases in the public sector. Through the various affirmative action devices . . . a certain proportion of these jobs and purchases may be channeled to the black community.[80]

White and black urban liberal mayors often sought to accommodate business interests. Mayor Richard Hatcher discovered that U.S. Steel so dominated Gary's economy that he could do little that the company did not want.[81] Boston Mayor Kevin White first won office in 1967 with the slogan "When landlords raise rents, Kevin White raises hell," but he abandoned rent control in order to promote downtown development and neighborhood gentrification. As developer contributions filled his campaign treasury, he resisted neighbor-

hood demands for a "linkage" tax on downtown development to fund affordable housing.[82] In Atlanta, downtown business leaders exercised "preemptive
power" over the city's agenda because mayors needed their help to build a new
stadium and rebuild the airport. The day after being elected in 1981, Andrew
Young, once a top aide to Martin Luther King, Jr., told downtown business
leaders, "I didn't get elected with your help," but "I can't govern without you." [83]

As long as federal funds flowed, urban liberal regimes could deliver some
jobs, housing, and other benefits to the ghetto poor. Without them, urban liberal mayors felt that they had no choice but to promote development, even if
it led to rising rents and displacement of the poor. Some pushed for regional
housing integration, but others, fearing the dispersal of their voting bases, did
not.[84] Meanwhile, suburban governments, over which minority mayors had no
control, continued to maintain housing barriers to the poor, though they could
not keep out qualified minority buyers.

Tom Bradley provides one example of the dilemmas of urban liberalism.[85]
After losing to a white conservative, Sam Yorty, in the 1969 race for mayor of
Los Angeles, he won the 1973 election and held office until 1993. Though rising
black voter turnout and increased black activism played a key role in his early
campaigns, he maintained an electoral coalition of liberal whites, Jews, blacks,
and, increasingly, Latinos. He did not face serious opposition after his first victory. A liberal biracial coalition including three blacks also controlled the city
council. For much of his reign, the council did not have a Latino member, but
Richard Alatorre won a seat from the heavily Latino east side in 1985, and the
fifteen-member city council had three blacks and three Latinos when Bradley
left office in 1993.[86]

Bradley appointed many minorities and women to city boards and commissions, increasing their share from 16 percent in Yorty's last year to 31 percent
in Bradley's first year and to 49 percent in his last term. He also increased minority representation in the municipal workforce from 35.2 percent in 1973 to
49.8 percent in 1991. His modest efforts to rein in the police were hampered by
the city charter, which prevented him from dismissing Chief Daryl Gates, who
had served in that office for many years and whose practices angered the black
community.[87]

Bradley courted developers and promoted downtown renewal. He chan-
neled the tax revenue generated by new development (almost $750 million by
the late 1980s) back into downtown development projects instead of into poor
neighborhoods.[88] The city's changing skyline solidified Bradley's support from
business leaders and the construction unions. He largely ignored the flight of
manufacturing jobs, bank redlining in minority areas, and the shortage of low-

income housing.[89] Meanwhile, Table 5.1 shows that the poverty rate increased steadily, especially during the recession of the early 1990s, when it jumped dramatically. Poverty is more prevalent among blacks and Latinos than Anglos and Asians.

Atlanta provides another example of how urban liberalism failed to address concentrated urban poverty. During the 1970s and 1980s, the city had a prosperous regional economy, strong and continuous black leadership, and elite black colleges. Three liberal black mayors have led Atlanta since 1973: Maynard Jackson (1973–1981 and 1989–1993), Andrew Young (1981–1989), and William Campbell (1993–2001). Jackson was elected with strong support from black voters and black and white neighborhood activists. He entered office explicitly rejecting a "slavish, unquestioning adherence to downtown dicta."[90] Instead, he insisted that business leaders "come to City Hall to meet in his office and to ask for his support, rather than simply to inform him of their needs and assume his compliance."[91] But Jackson ultimately championed all the highly visible development projects that downtown business leaders wanted, including a light rail system that connected downtown to the Atlanta airport. Jackson's successor, civil rights activist Andrew Young, continued this record of support for downtown development.

Like Tom Bradley, Mayors Jackson, Young, and Campbell increased black public employment, gave government contracts to minority-owned firms, and put more African Americans on Atlanta's police force. Blacks already constituted a majority of the Atlanta population in 1973, but black-owned firms had received only a tiny fraction of the city's business. By 1988, preferential procurement had shifted 35 percent of the city's contracts to minority firms, including such major building projects as the Underground Atlanta shopping center. Jackson boasted that minority set-asides for Atlanta's airport expansion created twenty-one black millionaires. In 1996, under Mayor Bill Campbell, the corporation running the summer Olympic Games awarded one-third of its $387 million in contracts to companies owned by minorities and women.[92] But these preferential contract awards and affirmative action hiring practices benefited primarily higher-income minorities. No such equivalent benefits were targeted to low-income blacks. As vice mayor, Jackson had joined with picketing sanitation workers, but as mayor, he fired 2,000 striking sanitation workers, most of whom were black.[93]

Atlanta's booming downtown and suburbs did little to help blacks trapped in low-income inner-city neighborhoods. While the black professional middle class prospered, the black poor suffered from a one-third decline in manufacturing employment between 1970 and 1985, and Atlanta's poverty rate increased during most of the 1970s and 1980s.[94] Its housing and job markets remained highly segregated. When the *Atlanta Constitution* exposed widespread racial discrimination in mortgage lending in 1988, neither Young nor Jackson supported the community groups negotiating with banks.[95] As Table 5.1 shows, Atlanta's already high poverty rate climbed steadily through this period, peaking during the recession of the early 1990s.

If Atlanta typifies what urban liberals can do under good economic conditions, Detroit exemplifies what happens under bad conditions. Although some Detroit business and political leaders tried to carry out physical redevelopment, high levels of racial polarization and black poverty led most white businesses and middle-class home owners to abandon the city.[96] From the 1930s through the 1970s, top executives of General Motors, Chrysler, and Ford had "preemptive power" over the municipal agenda.[97] The United Auto Workers also played an important role, since many of its members lived in the city. As the UAW improved wages and benefits for auto industry employees, many of its members, particularly its white members, moved to Detroit's suburbs. The 1967 Detroit riots accelerated white flight and increased racial segregation in the Detroit metropolitan area.

The restructuring of the global auto industry badly hurt Detroit, which lost 40 percent of its jobs and its population after 1960.[98] Detroit's black population thus began to accumulate political influence just as its economy collapsed. A black mayoral candidate, Richard Austin, lost by only 1 percent of the vote in 1969. Four years later, Detroit elected Coleman Young, a onetime radical union activist, as its first black mayor. He was reelected four times, serving until 1994. Initially, he carried out the typical liberal policy agenda, reforming the police, employing more African Americans in government jobs, and pressuring private employers to hire more minorities. But as major downtown department stores closed and the middle class fled, he had an increasingly hard time pressuring employers to hire Detroit residents.

Like many of his counterparts, Young sought to bring jobs to Detroit, but he got little help from the city's corporate elite. After years of bashing business and the suburbs, he began to court business leaders in the 1980s, but most of them had little faith in the city's future or its business climate. As its suburbs boomed, the city became known as the "murder capital" of the country. Young invited General Motors to build a new plant in the white working-class neighborhood of Poletown, which triggered much neighborhood anger. His administration razed 3,600 dwellings and relocated fifty small businesses in order to expand the city airport, but to little avail in revitalizing the city's economy.

Young's confrontational style appealed to Detroit's black voters, but city council members and community organizations increasingly criticized him for ignoring the decay of residential neighborhoods. He alienated younger blacks, who had few memories of the civil rights and union struggles that had catapulted Young to political leadership. His victory margins became increasingly narrow, and after twenty years in office, he chose not to run for reelection in 1993.[99]

He was replaced by Dennis Archer, a black corporate lawyer and state supreme court judge. Archer won 57 percent of the vote, splitting the black vote with another African American candidate but winning 80 percent of the white vote.[100] Archer "aggressively courted the corporate community."[101] "I have to improve the image," he said. Under Young, business "didn't feel they had a partnership they could deal with."[102] Business Week called Archer "a politician who has won CEOs' trust, unlike his irascible predecessor."[103] He solicited involvement from the heads of the three auto companies, the local utilities, other major businesses, the UAW, and local foundations in his new Greater Downtown Partnership.[104]

Archer convinced some suburban firms to put operations into the city and assisted those already in the city to stay. He wanted suburbanites to attend cultural and sports events in the city. Rather than "demonizing the suburbs,"[105] Archer courted them. He pushed to merge the city and suburban bus systems. Though he failed to enact a regional tax on concert and sports tickets to provide $40 million a year for Detroit's cultural institutions, his strategy paid off politically.[106] Affluent suburbanites funded his campaigns.[107] He also earned respect from suburban business and political leaders.[108]

Archer was initially criticized for paying too little attention to poor neighborhoods, but he responded by bringing community groups together with businesses to revitalize poor neighborhoods and win a federal empowerment zone for Detroit. Developers began to build new single-family housing for middle-class families in the city.[109] He improved basic municipal services such as streetlights maintenance and trash pickup.[110] But he also reduced the municipal workforce, limiting his capacity to provide his supporters with public-sector jobs.[111] Detroit's two daily newspapers lauded Archer's boosterism, however, and he easily won reelection in 1997. Vital signs such as house prices, private investment, and crime rates improved, but one-third of Detroit's residents remained in poverty in 1995, and its infant mortality rate was among the highest in the nation. As Table 5.1 shows, Detroit's poverty rate, already moderately high by national standards in 1970, became acute during this period.

These examples show how urban liberal regimes distributed public benefits to their core electoral supporters but did not solve, and often did not even address, the problem of persistent, concentrated poverty. Faced with declining federal funds and severe fiscal constraints, they could not make bold policy changes. Instead, even those who entered office as activist liberals shifted toward a more moderate approach.[112] Their successors, a "new breed" of "post–civil rights" minority mayors, focused even more on downtown economic development and less on racial and economic equity.[113]

Urban Progressive Regimes

Urban progressive regimes differ from urban liberal regimes by seeking to empower previously excluded groups. They seek to challenge business domination of the urban development agenda, emphasizing "economic democracy" and "equity planning."[114] Such regimes grew out of the neighborhood revolt against urban renewal and the growing concern for historic preservation and neighborhood quality of life. They also drew political support from organized labor by supporting workers' rights and expanded municipal services for poor and working-class people.[115] The urban progressive movement originated outside the electoral arena in community organizing, protesting, and lobbying city hall to address neighborhood improvement and empowerment. In some cases, these movements built electoral coalitions that elected progressives to city councils, school boards, or other local bodies. In a few instances, they even elected mayors.

Historically, America's cities were the cradle of progressivism. In the first decades of the twentieth century, rapid industrialization, desperate poverty in immigrant neighborhoods, and growing inequality produced a variety of progressive reform movements. The trade union movement, housing reformers, women's rights reformers, and settlement houses all fought to uplift poor and working-class immigrants through collective organization and new public policies. Many upper-class people (primarily women) organized to investigate and publicize the problems of the poor, often joining with working-class activists through groups such as the Women's Trade Union League. Such muckraking journalism as Lincoln Steffens's articles in *McClure's* magazine, collected in *The Shame of the Cities* (1904); Upton Sinclair's *The Jungle* (1906), a novel about the harsh conditions among Chicago's meatpacking workers; and photographs by Lewis Hine exposed these conditions to a broad public. Religious reformers crusaded to eliminate child labor and unsafe factories, clean up slum housing, build decent homes for the poor, and create municipal sanitation agencies and public hospitals.

With votes from immigrants, workers, and a rising professional middle class, reformers won election in many cities. Mayors Tom Johnson of Cleveland

(1901–1909), Samuel "Golden Rule"Jones of Toledo (1897–1903), and Brand Whitlock of Toledo (1906–1913) fought against high streetcar and utility rates and for fair taxes and better social services. Reformers in Jersey City, Philadelphia, Cincinnati, Detroit, and many other cities sought to tax wealthy property owners, create municipal electricity and water utilities, and hold down transit fares. Detroit's progressive mayor Hazen Pingree (1890–1897) forged such a strong coalition of working-class Polish, German, and Irish immigrants and middle-class supporters that he was able to go on to two terms as Michigan's governor, where he continued the fight for progressive reform.[116]

Like the urban political machines, the progressives gave municipal jobs to immigrant and working-class voters. But they also took sides in the collective struggles of these constituents. They would not allow the police to protect strikebreaking "scabs" and pushed for laws to establish and enforce building codes. Socialists were a major component of the urban progressive movement. At its high point, about 1,200 party members held public office in 340 cities, including seventy-nine mayors in cities such as Milwaukee, Buffalo, Minneapolis, Reading, and Schenectady.[117] They pushed to create "public ownership of utilities and transportation facilities; increase social, recreational, and cultural services; and adopt a friendly attitude toward unions, especially in time of strikes."[118] They earned a reputation for clean government, leading some to claim that they were operating "sewer socialism."

The New Deal benefited from and nourished urban progressivism.[119] In Detroit, Frank Murphy won a surprise mayoral victory in 1930, a year after the depression began, by promising unemployment relief, despite opposition from the powerful auto companies. He invited twenty-nine mayors of major cities to a conference, stating: "We have done everything humanly possible to do, and it has not been enough. The hour is at hand for the federal government to cooperate." This meeting led to the formation of the U.S. Conference of Mayors (USCM).[120] An early USCM president, New York City Mayor Fiorello LaGuardia, spoke out strongly for urban progressive measures during the depression. New York's local public works program, slum clearance program, and low-rent public housing program became models for the New Deal's Works Progress Administration and public housing initiatives.[121]

Contemporary urban progressive regimes grew out of the neighborhood movements of the 1960s, 1970s, and 1980s. Many early community protests were sporadic and disorganized, but skilled organizers, often from the Industrial Areas Foundation (IAF; a national network founded by Saul Alinsky in 1940), helped neighborhood residents build strong grassroots organizations in many cities. Drawing on the experiences of the union movement, Alinsky's "people's organizations" used the threat of conflict to win concessions from local businesses and politicians.

Progressive and radical activists organized poor neighborhoods around housing, welfare, and other issues in the 1960s and 1970s. Leaders of the National Welfare Rights Organization turned in the mid-1970s to organizing low-income residents on housing and formed the Association of Community Organizations for Reform Now (ACORN) to push for local reforms. Community organizing forced government agencies to shift funds to affordable housing and community-based services, halted highway projects, and promoted mass transit. In response, President Lyndon Johnson's Great Society programs required community participation and shifted public funds to community-based organizations as a major vehicle for delivering public services.[122]

By the 1970s, the "neighborhood movement" had become a stronger voice on many policy fronts.[123] Middle-class neighborhoods joined in promoting "growth control" and historic preservation of neighborhoods threatened by market forces. Responding to these new constituencies, urban liberals sought to co-opt community organizations by turning them into housing development and social services agencies. Churches, social services agencies, tenant organizations, and civil rights groups began delivering Head Start, child care, job training, and housing development services in the neighborhoods they served. In 1970, 100 community development corporations (CDCs) existed; a decade later, there were more than 1,000. A 1989 survey of 133 cities found that 95 percent of them had active CDCs. By the 1990s, at least 2,000 CDCs operated.[124] They received support from private foundations, local and state governments, businesses, and religious institutions. Goaded by the Community Reinvestment Act, banks also began to help CDCs after 1977.[125]

The neighborhood movement was strongest in older northern cities, which had the biggest battles over urban renewal. The redevelopment bulldozer was less likely to threaten residents of newer southern and southwestern cities. A study of Houston called its neighborhood groups "largely invisible."[126] In San Antonio, however, the IAF-affiliated Communities Organized for Public Service helped elect the city's first Hispanic mayor, Henry Cisneros, who redirected city funds and public services toward poor Hispanic neighborhoods.[127] Portland, Seattle, and San Francisco all developed strong community-based organizations, but Los Angeles, San Diego, San Jose, and Phoenix, all with large Hispanic populations, had few community-based organizations and did not develop progressive-style politics through the 1980s. Although Atlanta, New

Orleans, and Birmingham elected black city councilors and mayors, they, too, had little grassroots mobilization challenging the business-oriented growth agenda.

Urban progressive regimes sought to give community groups a stronger voice in government decisions that affect neighborhoods. A 1990 survey of 161 cities found that 60 percent had neighborhood councils, some officially recognized by city hall.[128] Many cities reformed their charters to provide for the election of city council members from districts rather than at large. Many disbursed low-income-housing program money to CDCs. Some established affordable housing trust funds funded by revenue from commercial development.[129] Others adopted rent control, moratoria on condominium conversion of rental housing, and zoning ordinances requiring developers to include affordable units in their developments.[130]

Under the rubric of "growth control," neighborhood groups asserted that policies on economic development must be more aware of the costs in air pollution, traffic congestion, loss of open space, rising rents, and a less livable city. They sought to limit new downtown office construction and downzone commercial districts. In the early 1980s, they got San Francisco to place strict limits on downtown development and to enact a "linkage" law requiring developers to contribute to a low-income-housing trust fund.[131] Many cities required new buildings to be designed in ways that fit into the existing streetscape and protected historic buildings from being altered or torn down. As we have seen, community groups, unions, and churches began to push city governments to enact "living wage" ordinances in the 1990s.

By the mid-1970s, veterans of the civil rights movement, the New Left, and neighborhood organizing had helped elect sympathetic city council and school board members, and even a few mayors, in dozens of cities. The most successful progressive regimes took root in small, white, middle-class cities, often university towns such as Burlington (Vermont), Cambridge (Massachusetts), Madison (Wisconsin), Berkeley, and Santa Monica (California). Progressive regimes also took power in big cities, including Cleveland, San Francisco, Pittsburgh, Portland, Chicago, Hartford, and Boston. In most cases, organizers used concern over housing and community development issues to mobilize supporters and forge a governing regime.[132] Their coalitions sought to bring together neighborhood groups, labor unions, and poor and working-class residents, as well as residents and groups concerned about environmental and historic preservation issues. To carry out their program, however, they needed a broader base of support. Like urban liberals, progressives walked a political tightrope between the concerns of their core supporters and the constraints imposed by additional interests they needed to bring into their governing coalitions.

This tension made it difficult for urban progressive regimes to form stable and robust governing coalitions that could pursue their programs. Internal disagreement, business opposition, and economic recession undercut the perceived "antigrowth" stance of progressive activists. Racial and ethnic tensions plagued some progressive coalitions. Many progressive regimes emerged in cities with small minority populations, such as Burlington, Minneapolis, and Portland, but others faced a more complex terrain. In San Francisco, for example, activists from low-income minority communities wanted more attention paid to creating jobs for their constituents, while middle-class environmentalists sought to limit development.[133] Business leaders portrayed progressives as antibusiness zealots lacking a practical program for economic revitalization.[134] In Cleveland, banks pushed the city into default over progressive Mayor Dennis Kucinich's confrontational approach to downtown tax abatements and his opposition to the private takeover of the municipally owned utility, resulting in his defeat after only two years in office.

Pittsburgh, Chicago, and Boston each had sustained experiences with urban progressivism. Each demonstrates the potential and the limits of local reform. As Table 5.1 shows, all had poverty rates that were slightly above the national average for central cities in 1970, rose during the 1970s and (except Boston) 1980s, and peaked during the recession of the early 1990s but remained below the levels reached in Detroit, Atlanta, or Los Angeles. Pittsburgh's Mayor Tom Murphy experienced the tensions of maintaining business confidence while increasing services to the poor. A former community organizer, CDC director, and state legislator, Murphy lost a bid for mayor in 1989 but won in 1993. Community organizations played a key role in his victory, and he named several CDC leaders and community organizers, black as well as white, to high-level positions. His administration incorporated CDCs into decision making about community development funding. Even so, community leaders opposed Murphy's plans to demolish troubled public housing projects, redevelop downtown, and build middle-class housing to stem the city's population loss. Faulting some CDCs for not producing enough housing, Murphy turned to for-profit developers or required CDCs to form joint ventures with private developers. Progressivism in Pittsburgh thus gave neighborhood groups much more influence over neighborhood revitalization but did not challenge the priorities of downtown or regional development.[135]

Racial tension was the Achilles' heel of progressivism in Chicago. A coalition of organizations from black neighborhoods catapulted Congressman Harold Washington into the mayor's office in 1983. He represented many of the impulses of urban liberalism but was ultimately more of a progressive, because neighborhood empowerment and economic redistribution were key themes in his administration. Two weeks before the 1983 election, he issued a fifty-two-page document that called for balanced growth between downtown and neighborhoods, neighborhood planning, and fees on downtown development to support affordable housing. Washington battled the city council, the business community, and the Cook County Democratic machine to carry out his progressive agenda. Above all, his administration was limited by Chicago's racial divisions. White machine politicians held a majority of the city council seats until 1986 and did everything they could to thwart Washington's agenda.

Washington's neighborhood-oriented reforms were nonetheless popular, and he won reelection in 1987. With a more favorable majority on the city council, he seemed poised for new accomplishments, but unfortunately, he died a few months later from a heart attack. With him died the hope for urban progressivism in Chicago. His political coalition fragmented, many black elected officials reverted to supporting the political machine that Washington had sought to dismantle, and Richard M. Daley, son of the former mayor, defeated Washington's interim successor, a black Democratic regular. Reelected twice, the younger Mayor Daley has incorporated some neighborhood groups into his coalition but moved away from Washington's agenda, seeking a more traditional focus on the downtown business community, neighborhood businesses, and white ethnic voters. Blacks continue to hold countywide and statewide positions, and Hispanics have made significant inroads in public office, but Daley's regime has not sought to mobilize these groups to promote institutional change.[136]

Perhaps the most successful progressive mayor in recent years was Boston's Ray Flynn, who sustained a progressive regime for almost a decade after his election in 1983. Strong economic growth in Boston had sent rents and housing prices skyrocketing, owing to strong gains in income among the upper middle class. But poor and working-class residents did not think that they were sharing the benefits, which led to a surge in organizing among tenants, minorities, working-class neighborhood residents, and opponents of urban renewal. In 1981, these forces led to a charter revision increasing the city council from nine at-large members to thirteen members, nine elected from districts. In the 1983 elections, Flynn, who had been a councilman since 1978, built support among tenants' groups, neighborhood activists, and service worker unions by calling for the redistribution of downtown wealth to the neighborhoods.

In office, Flynn widened his base by including many minority leaders who had supported his opponent in the 1983 contest, black activist Mel King, and by co-opting parts of the business leadership. He appointed neighborhood activists to high-level positions within the city government while promoting "managed growth" and "balanced development." Despite opposition from the real estate industry, the city enacted a "linkage" fee on downtown development to fund affordable housing and required developers to set aside 10 percent of their units for low- and moderate-income families. The city also mandated that 50 percent of the workers on downtown construction projects must be city residents, 30 percent racial minorities, and 5 percent women. The administration strengthened the city's rent-control law and limited condominium conversions. Flynn also deposited city funds in banks with a good record of lending in poor and minority neighborhoods and walked picket lines to support workers in their disputes with management.

With help from local private foundations, the United Way, and major businesses, the city formed the Boston Housing Partnership to support housing development by CDCs. It also supported the Dudley Street Neighborhood Initiative (DSNI), an innovative, comprehensive neighborhood revitalization project based in the black ghetto of Roxbury. Although one-third of the area's land was vacant, it was owned by a jigsaw puzzle of interests that prevented DSNI from assembling land for housing, businesses, or parks. The city gave DSNI the power of eminent domain to purchase property from reluctant owners, an unprecedented move in urban development.[137]

These policies improved housing conditions for average Bostonians. By 1993, linkage had raised $70 million to fund 5,000 affordable housing units, mostly sponsored by CDCs. The inclusionary housing policy added another 400 units. Pushed by the city government and community activists, banks committed $400 million to a community reinvestment loan fund for low- and moderate-income neighborhoods. The Flynn administration gave neighborhoods more power over land-use decisions through neighborhood councils and other planning innovations.

The Flynn administration nevertheless reflected the limits of localism.[138] Its innovative efforts did not compensate for severe cuts in federal housing assistance, nor did they moderate the worsening income inequality produced by Boston's growing corporate service economy and the substantial number of families who remained outside the labor market. For a time, this boom began to reduce poverty and increase incomes at the bottom of the income distribution.[139] The advent of recession in 1989, however, led the media and other opinion leaders to question Flynn's progressive policies. By the time Flynn left office in 1993 to become U.S. ambassador to the Vatican, the community organizations in his political base had fallen on hard times, hurt by funding cutbacks, staff turnover, and complacency induced by years of city hall support. Flynn's successor, city council president Tom Menino, shifted to a conventional liberal pro-growth agenda.

These experiences show that even those cities with the most progressive local administrations cannot do much to correct economic segregation, concentrated poverty, and suburban sprawl. By the time urban progressivism emerged in the 1970s, the economic and demographic realities of cities had already changed dramatically. Cities had a weaker bargaining position toward business, had substantially lower median incomes than the suburbs, and were divided by racial and ethnic conflicts. It was good that neighborhoods played a larger role in development decisions and had more housing development resources, but these tools did not provide much leverage on concentrated poverty. In economic downturns, urban progressives become vulnerable to the charge that they are "antibusiness."

Urban Conservative Regimes

Urban conservatives think that urban problems are caused by the misguided actions of city government, not by the larger economic and political arrangements of society. They charge that urban liberal politicians cave in to minority, union, and neighborhood demands, resulting in profligate spending, mismanagement, and corruption. From this perspective, cities can blame only themselves for their fiscal crises. Government should be run like a business instead of trying to make social change by targeting spending on minorities or poor neighborhoods. The only real solution to the problem of concentrated poverty is to cut the size and scope of city government. This will free up the private sector to invest, so the benefits of private-sector growth will trickle down to the poor.

Historically, urban conservatism has its roots in the business-backed "reform" movements of the late nineteenth and early twentieth centuries. Business reformers wanted to weaken the political machines, labor unions, and radical and progressive urban reform movements supported by working-class immigrant voters. These mostly Protestant, middle-class conservatives viewed the mostly Catholic and Jewish immigrants as a cultural and economic threat.

In almost every city, business and professional reformers wished to reorganize local government along more "businesslike" lines, insulating it from political pressures and eliminating corruption. They wanted to keep taxes low and deliver public services efficiently. These local "good government" groups formed national organizations such as the National Municipal League to promote their views.[140] The vast majority of the individuals who spearheaded these changes were bankers, newspaper publishers, developers, lawyers, and corporate executives.[141]

These groups also pushed for at-large elections, the elimination of partisanship from local elections, and rules requiring people to register to vote.[142] They succeeded in many medium-sized cities during the first two decades of the twentieth century. By 1905, most states had voter registration laws; by 1920, one-fifth of all cities had a commission form of government. Nonpartisan, at-large elections were instituted in Los Angeles (1908), Boston (1909), Akron, Ohio (1915), and Detroit (1918). By 1929, more than half of all cities had adopted nonpartisan elections.[143] Where cities adopted nonpartisan elections, secret ballots, and voter registration requirements, voter turnout declined among immigrants and the poor, shifting the balance of power back into business hands.[144]

Conservatives also lobbied to shift power from elected officials to professional administrators, who, they believed, would run cities through "expertise" rather than political favoritism. They revised municipal charters so that city managers would replace strong mayors and appointive commissions would oversee departments. By the 1950s, many cities took it for granted that this was how municipal governments should work.

In addition to support from business interests, modern urban conservatism drew popular strength from the backlash of white voters against the urban liberal and progressive movements of the late 1960s. Urban conservatives have often used racial code words to solidify white support.[145] As early as Richard Nixon's appeal to the "silent majority" in 1968, urban conservatism has resonated with voters who resented "favoritism" toward blacks and other minorities. It also drew on fears of rising crime and the increasing disillusion with "big government" common in the late 1980s and early 1990s. Its rhetoric stressed reducing government regulations and taxes and providing "public order" and "keeping the peace." These slogans reflected real concerns about crime rates but also acted as code words indicating opposition to minority advancement.[146]

Urban conservatism was aided by a vibrant intellectual attack on the liberal and progressive record on the urban crisis. With ample funding from corporate-sponsored foundations and think tanks such as the Manhattan Institute, Cato Institute, and Reason Foundation, conservative public intellectuals blamed cities' fiscal problems on the liberal policies of the 1960s.[147] According to them, public employee unions had too much influence with local politicians, leading to bloated municipal budgets, excessively high salaries, and inefficient management.[148] They argued that the "civil rights generation" of black elected officials had simply rewarded their constituents with government jobs or contracts for which they were unqualified, subverting government efficiency and undermining the confidence of business leaders and white middle-class voters. Liberals had, in their view, created an "entitlement mentality" that was indulgent of absenteeism, tardiness, poor language skills, poor work habits, and incompetence among city workers.[149]

Edward Banfield's book *The Unheavenly City*, published in 1970, was perhaps the most influential early statement of these positions. One chapter, "Rioting for Fun and Profit," blamed liberal policies for encouraging irresponsible, even illegal, behavior among the poor. Twenty-five years later, Fred Siegel's *The Future Once Happened Here* echoed and updated Banfield's themes. He blamed the urban crisis on the "riot ideology." Banfield, Siegel, and other conservative pundits also claimed that many big-city mayors and other public officials pressured the federal government in the 1960s to expand welfare and other antipoverty programs (such as food stamps and public housing). As cities became "magnets" for the unemployed and the "undeserving" poor, the social fabric of urban neighborhoods unraveled, cities spent too much on serving the poor, and alarmed businesses and middle-class residents voted with their feet by moving to suburbia.[150]

These conservative critics also charged that liberal politicians tolerated criminal behavior and drug use and argued that low-level public nuisances (and other visible signs of neglect) encouraged more serious crimes. "We now believe that we can reduce crime through good policing," said Myron Magnet of the Manhattan Institute, a conservative think tank admired by New York Mayor Rudy Giuliani. "The root causes of crime are not poverty and racism. They're criminals." [151] Instead of carrying out basic "civic housekeeping" functions that would retain middle-class residents, they blamed liberal and progressive officials for frightening private investors away with rent control, public housing, and high business taxes.[152]

In office, urban conservatives typically seek to reduce taxes and regulations on business and to alter the social services practices that they think reward bad behavior by the poor and repel middle-class residents. They prescribe the unfettered promotion of private investment. Conservative regimes oppose height limits, zoning guidelines, hiring set-asides, rent control, environmental standards, and linked development fees.[153] They claim to address poverty by promoting private investment in the hope that benefits will trickle down. Conservatives are against protecting the poor from rising rents and displacement on the grounds that gentrification is a free-market process. Conservatives address fiscal strains by attempting to close public hospitals, increasing tuition for municipal colleges, raising fees for public transportation and other public services, and privatizing public education.[154] This has occasioned conflict with municipal unions and attacks on long-standing civil service protections.[155]

Most centrally, urban conservatives have embraced tougher police operations and crackdowns on "deviant" behavior such as public begging.[156] These measures often have a strong racial component, allowing police to stop or arrest people based on their demeanor or clothing rather than on hard evidence of criminal activity. They reject civilian police monitoring boards or community involvement in crime prevention strategies, while supporting more jails and tougher sentences. How such regimes operate in practice may be seen in Los Angeles and New York, where white Republicans succeeded black urban liberal mayors in 1993, and in the Republican bastion of Indianapolis, where Steven Goldsmith vigorously advocated downsizing government as a proponent of the new urban conservatism.[157]

Racial tensions had festered in Los Angeles for many years. By 1990, whites were only 37 percent of the city's nearly 3.5 million people. Latinos represented 40 percent, and blacks had fallen to 14 percent.[158] Unemployment rose to more than 10 percent during the recession of the early 1990s but was much higher in black and Latino areas. Localized conflict had been building for years between blacks and Korean store owners, between blacks and Latino immigrants for construction and other jobs, and between whites and other racial groups over the public schools. In April 1992, a major riot broke out in a predominantly black and Latino area after police officers were acquitted of the beating of a black man named Rodney King. Tensions over immigration surfaced in 1994, when the state's voters approved the anti-immigrant Proposition 187; tensions over affirmative action came to a head a year later with the statewide success of Proposition 209, the initiative against affirmative action.

The 1993 mayoral race was a pivotal moment in these developments. Prior to the election, Michael Woo, a liberal Democratic city council member, had been considered the likely heir to Mayor Tom Bradley. He had strong ties within the black, Latino, and Asian communities. Richard Riordan, a multimillionaire Republican businessman and attorney, proved to be a wild card in the nonpartisan primary, however. Little known to the public, he had made large campaign contributions and philanthropic donations to black and Latino community leaders and could personally finance a campaign. In the runoff, Woo portrayed himself as a "multicultural" racial healer, while Riordan campaigned on the slogan "tough enough to turn LA around" and promised to make government more efficient, hire 3,000 additional police, and shake the city out of its economic doldrums. Riordan decisively defeated Woo, despite the fact that voter registration was two-thirds Democratic, most of the population was nonwhite, and white voters had previously strongly supported Bradley. Not only did Riordan get strong support from white conservatives, but many moderate and even liberal whites gave him their votes.[159]

Riordan reversed Bradley's practice and appointed people from affluent white areas to the city's top jobs. Even his minority appointments came from well-off neighborhoods, leading H. Eric Schockman to call his base a "neo-rainbow coalition, based on class, not on race."[160] He sought to privatize city agencies and add 3,000 police officers while holding the line on taxes. He did not embrace the recommendation of the Christopher Commission, formed in the wake of the riots, that the city move toward community policing.

As we have already seen, Riordan opposed the "living wage" law on the grounds that it would undermine the city's business climate. Riordan and business leaders also lobbied the federal Environmental Protection Agency to relax its enforcement of the Clear Air Act on the dubious grounds that it put Los Angeles businesses at a competitive disadvantage.[161] Because Los Angeles's city council was considerably more liberal than the mayor, it stymied him on these and other issues.

Riordan continued Bradley's focus on downtown development but paid little attention to neighborhood development and affordable housing. He pushed for a new sports complex and supported a $75 million tax break for the Dream-Works film studio. As a key member of the Metropolitan Transportation Authority, a major source of public contracts for politically connected businesses, Riordan backed the building of new subway lines over improvement of the bus system on which poor and minority riders rely. He did not oppose cutbacks at Los Angeles County's public health clinics and hospitals, which serve the poor. His fiscal priorities included expanding commuter rail lines, increasing the number of police, bailing out the county public health system, and repairing the damage from the 1994 earthquake.[162] None of these measures did anything to address concentrated urban poverty. As Table 5.1 reveals, poverty reached a high point in Los Angeles during the early 1990s and has subsided only slightly in response to the long national expansion.

Republican Mayor Rudolph W. Giuliani's victory in New York City also introduced a much more conservative administration to what has long been considered the quintessential liberal city. A long tradition of multiracial political coalitions and a strong trade union movement, especially among blue-collar and lower-middle-class Jews, have been central to the city's liberal political culture.[163] The city's two previous Republican mayors, Fiorello LaGuardia in the 1930s and John Lindsay in the 1960s, had been among the most liberal in the nation.

In the wake of the fiscal crisis of the mid-1970s, Democratic Mayor Ed Koch (1977–1989) responded by cutting municipal services, especially those that served the poor. Although he came into politics as a liberal Democrat, Koch, a former congressman, began to shed his liberalism as he positioned himself to win the mayoralty. He backed the death penalty and criticized racial preferences. He initially won office with black and Latino political support, but his electoral coalition became increasingly focused on white voters.[164]

Municipal scandals involving close allies, Koch's narrowing electoral support, and a series of violent, racially charged incidents enabled Manhattan Borough President David Dinkins to defeat Koch in the 1989 Democratic primary and, in a narrow victory over Republican former U.S. Attorney Rudolph Giuliani, to become New York's first African American mayor.[165] Dinkins governed as a liberal but could not build a durable governing coalition or widen his electoral base. A severe economic recession, fiscal tensions, the perception that crime was rampant, and his handling of black-Korean and black-Jewish conflicts undermined his administration.

Giuliani narrowly won his 1993 rematch with Dinkins. Giuliani received relatively few black or Latino votes but strengthened his position among whites compared with 1989. Black turnout declined, as did that of Latinos and white liberals. Jews, who had been solidly liberal from the 1930s through the 1960s, continued their steady shift toward more conservative candidates; exit polls indicated that Jewish support for Dinkins declined from 33.8 to 31.3 percent. Once in office, Giuliani "terminated affirmative action programs, cut social spending, increased the size of the police department, and cracked down on 'quality of life' problems like homeless people and panhandling."[166]

It is not accurate to call Giuliani an archconservative. Compared with national conservatives such as Pat Buchanan, Newt Gingrich, or Trent Lott, urban conservatives are much more liberal on social issues and questions of diversity. Giuliani avoided being trapped into advocating socially conservative positions on abortion or gay rights that might have pushed white liberals back toward a multiracial coalition.[167] He spoke out in favor of federal and state aid to New York City, strongly defended immigrants' contributions to the city, and even endorsed Democratic Governor Mario Cuomo for reelection in 1994. In 1997, when the Republican state senate threatened to allow the state's rent-control law to expire, Giuliani offered lukewarm support of rent regulation. He bolstered the city's system of monitoring child abuse and providing foster care and unsuccessfully fought Republican Governor George Pataki's move to eliminate the city's payroll tax on suburban commuters.

But Mayor Giuliani's top priorities have been expanding the city's police force, lowering the crime rate, reducing the welfare rolls, requiring welfare recipients to work off their benefits, cutting business taxes, and privatizing municipal hospitals. He did not address the growing crisis in the city's low-income-housing production system until 2001, nor did he acknowledge middle-class decline and growing income inequalities as major problems facing the city.[168] Here too, as Table 5.1 shows, poverty rates climbed in recent decades and remain stubbornly high. The mayor's policies have been far more successful in reducing welfare receipt than in reducing poverty.

Our final example, Steven Goldsmith of Indianapolis, took office in a far more conservative environment than Los Angeles or New York. Since 1970, Indianapolis has been a consolidated city-county government in which minority and low-income voters constitute a small fraction of the electorate and Republicans continuously win the mayoralty.[169] Though perhaps the most ideologically conservative mayor of a major city, Goldsmith created a policy agenda designed to include low-income and minority residents in his governing coalition.[170]

Goldsmith's predecessor, William Hudnut, had pursued a typical growth coalition focused on making Indianapolis a center for amateur and professional sports. Running in 1991, Goldsmith argued that the condition of the low-income neighborhoods surrounding downtown had undermined the city's economic health, causing firms to relocate outside the city's expanded boundary. He sought to "reduce government intervention in order to open up opportunity."[171] Once in office, he quickly reduced the municipal workforce, lowered property taxes, allowed private firms to compete with city agencies to provide municipal services such as garbage collection, and privatized some functions.

Unlike some GOP soulmates, Goldsmith gave neighborhood groups a strong voice in municipal management. His administration targeted seven low-income neighborhoods, diverted municipal funds to neighborhood organizations, and relied on community-based organizations as the primary vehicles for neighborhood improvement efforts. City government stepped up enforcement of housing codes and took over troubled properties. Stephen McGovern argues that Goldsmith's conservative populist regime "contradicts his immediate political interests; after all, suburban neighborhoods have the heaviest concentration of GOP voters while inner-city neighborhoods continue to vote Democrat."[172] Overall, however, Goldsmith's policies made no serious impact on reducing concentrated poverty in Indianapolis. Table 5.1 shows that Indianapolis has been a relatively low-poverty city, but its poverty rate climbed gradually between 1970 and 1990, tracking the national and urban trend.

THE LIMITS OF LOCALISM

Urban liberals, progressives, and conservatives have all formulated approaches to local government that have lasting value. Almost every city mirrors some aspect of urban liberalism's attempt to assimilate racial minorities through public employment and contracts with community-based organizations. Even conservative mayors now include blacks, Hispanics, and Asians among their top-level appointments. Similarly, many cities have been attracted to the community-based approaches to economic development and the "living wage" laws advocated by urban progressives. Urban progressives also helped shift the urban political debate away from appeals to racial identity and toward a narrowing of the economic divide between races.[173] Urban conservatism can take credit for gaining wider acceptance of the idea that agencies must meet performance targets and be accountable for their results.

Whatever the real improvements to urban governance, however, none of these three approaches has made much progress on growing inequality, persistent poverty, and racial and economic segregation. Even the most well-managed and progressive cities failed to lift the incomes of their poorest residents or substantially reduce the class separations within them. All three types of urban regimes developed symbolic responses to these problems, but none can claim significant success.

It may be odd to say that localism has such stark limits when so many observers are talking about the revival of central cities in the first year of the twenty-first century. Mayors Giuliani of New York and Riordan of Los Angeles are joining the leaders of many other cities in taking credit for renewed job growth, falling crime rates, a higher quality of life, and even some improvement in urban poverty rates. This revival is real, but it stems mostly from the long economic expansion of the 1990s, which pulled even some badly off cities into its wake. Of course, we must remember that cities with strong, advanced corporate service economies did the best and that the benefits flowed disproportionately to those at the top.

This urban revival has had little positive effect on economic segregation and concentrated poverty. Even as New York City's economy revived in the mid-1990s, the percentage of its residents classified as middle class fell from 35 to 29 percent.[174] Income growth for jobs in the bottom half of the earnings distribution was too sluggish to pull many families out of poverty. Most entry-level job growth is located far from areas of concentrated central-city poverty. So long as national policy heavily subsidizes new homes on the urban fringe, cities will find it difficult to reverse the trend toward increased poverty concentration.[175]

The problem is even worse for distressed, inner-ring suburbs, where, as we have shown, urban problems are migrating. Inner-ring suburbs have had to cope with rising poverty rates.[176] They are often in worse shape than central cities are. They lack the commercial and industrial investment that provides cities with much of their tax base. Nor do they have nonprofit institutions to address their social problems or amenities to attract new residents. Regional elites are concerned about central-city decline because they have substantial investments in downtown businesses, hospitals, universities, and museums. They have no such commitments to distressed suburbs. And by themselves, there is little these suburbs can do to arrest their decline.

Regionalisms
Old and New

As the previous chapter showed, it is difficult for central cities by themselves to solve the problems generated by economic segregation and urban sprawl. It is only natural, therefore, for cities to reach out to suburban municipalities and attempt to forge regional solutions to their problems. Regional approaches face their own obstacles, however. Consider the efforts of Hartford, Connecticut, and Memphis, Tennessee.

Hartford is the capital city of the richest state in the nation, but for a long time, it has had one of the country's highest poverty rates and large areas of concentrated poverty. In 1969, Hartford's major employers formed a new organization, the Greater Hartford Process (GHP), to solve the region's problems.[1] Three years later, this elite group unveiled a plan to rebuild the city's low-income areas, create an entire new town in the suburbs, and develop new regional approaches to housing, transportation, health care, education, and social services. The plan would affect 670,000 persons in twenty-nine communities in a 750-square-mile area.

The most dramatic impact was on the town of Coventry, fifteen miles from the city. GHP had quietly begun buying land in the all-white town of 8,500 residents in order to create, from scratch, a new town of 20,000; 15 percent of the housing units were to be set aside for low-income families. Coventry officials refused to cooperate with the plan, which was ultimately shelved. One suburban official noted, "I don't see the problems of the central city as my responsibility." Within a few years, GHP had ceased to exist. Although most Hartford residents had responded positively, "some leaders of Hartford's black community claimed that the new-town idea was an attempt to dilute their power in the city, and others objected to the lack of citizen input into Hartford Process plans."[2]

Two decades later, Hartford's newly hired city manager, Raymond Shipman, proposed another regional plan. It required suburbs to join a regional government, provided some public services, enacted a tax on suburban commuters to Hartford, and would raze three public housing projects and relocate their residents to the suburbs.[3] Shipman was soon gone as Hartford's city manager. Then, in 1996, the city council took a different approach to the problem, placing a moratorium on new social service agencies that serve the poor, such as soup kitchens, homeless shelters, and drug treatment centers. Within its 18.4 square miles, the city (with a population of 140,000) had 150 social service agencies, which, city officials said, attracted poor people to the city.[4] Hartford city council members claimed that these programs were "ruining the climate for urban revitalization, hurting business, shrinking the tax base, and scaring away the middle class." They also argued that the suburbs were not doing their share to address the needs of the poor — certainly an accurate statement.[5] It was almost as if Hartford officials had decided that if the suburbs refused to cooperate, the city would stop accommodating the region's poor, potentially forcing them out to the suburbs.

Memphis is another central city with many poor, minority citizens that has attempted regional solutions. In 1971, suburban residents in Shelby County, Tennessee, voted two to one against merging with Memphis.[6] In 1990, an attempt to merge the largely black Memphis school system with the predominantly white county school system also failed, due to suburban opposition. In 1993, Mayor W. W. Herenton, the city's first African American mayor and former school superintendent, took a politically courageous stand and again proposed merging the city with suburban Shelby County. The reason Herenton's proposal was courageous was that if it had been successful, it would have diluted the black electoral power so recently gained with his election.

Between 1940 and 1980, Memphis captured 54 percent of all population growth in the region by annexing suburbs. After 1980, suburban opposition ended Memphis's expansion, and during the 1980s, Memphis lost 6 percent of its population, while that of the surrounding Shelby County suburbs more than doubled. Many African American political leaders, who had recently gained six of thirteen seats on the city council and five on the nine-member school board, argued that the merger would dilute black voting strength and cost blacks "some of the political control we have fought for so long." Herenton, who had been elected mayor in a highly racially polarized election, countered that "blacks gain little by controlling a city that is broke."[7] Herenton garnered support from Memphis business leaders, who predicted that the merger would lessen their tax burden, but many suburbanites opposed the merger, fearing that suburban Shelby County (median household income $43,784) would face additional tax burdens when merged with Memphis (median household income $22,674). The proposal failed at the polls.

These two examples show the difficulty of implementing regional solutions to the problems of concentrated poverty and suburban sprawl. They are not the only examples — we will also point to more positive ones — but they are instructive. In this chapter, we examine regional initiatives over the past 100 years, looking especially closely at the "new regionalism" that has emerged since the early 1990s. We applaud these efforts but argue that under the present state and federal rules of the game most regional initiatives are limited and difficult to sustain.

THE PROBLEM

The competition among metropolitan jurisdictions to attract higher-income residents and exclude the less well-off has been a powerful factor promoting the concentration of poor people in central cities. In the typical metropolitan area, dozens, even hundreds, of suburban towns seek to establish their places within the metropolitan pecking order. A "favored quarter" houses upper-income people and businesses that pay taxes but do not demand many services and do not lessen the quality of life.[8] These places use zoning regulations, high prices, and even racial prejudice to keep out the unwanted, or at least the less privileged. Elsewhere, less exclusive residential suburbs, suburban commercial and industrial areas, and aging inner-ring suburbs seek to carve out their own places in the hierarchy of municipalities. Even those aging, economically stagnating working-class suburbs on the city's edge often try to keep out inner-city residents. For those with limited means, living in the central city may be their only choice.

A similar but less keen competition takes place among central-city neighborhoods. Here, neighborhoods do not have their own formal authority to exclude some residents and attract others, but factors such as housing quality and price, neighborhood amenities (particularly a good neighborhood primary school), and city zoning and land-use regulations can serve the same purpose. Unlike exclusive suburban towns, however, even well-off central-city residents pay into the city's common budget. As a result, higher-income central-city residents who do not want to pay for services for the less fortunate, or who do not use the central-city services for which they are paying (such as schools, public transit, and parks), have a strong incentive to move to a more exclusive suburban jurisdiction.

Federal policies heightened this competition and made the suburbs attractive by building freeways, fostering suburban home ownership, and encouraging central cities to specialize in social services for needy constituents. Many suburbs reinforce this arrangement by regulating land uses to maximize property values and tax revenues, by customizing their services for middle-class professionals, and by declining to build subsidized housing or sometimes even any kind of rental housing. Central-city public officials have also contributed to this state of affairs by relying on the growth of social services to enhance their budgets, provide jobs for constituents, and build political support. They are no more willing to give up responsibility for, and control over, these activities than exclusive suburbs are to embrace them. Defenders of this system draw on widely held beliefs that localism, private property, and homogeneous communities are sacred parts of the American way of metropolitan living. As Gerald Frug observed, "current law not only has fragmented the metropolitan area, but is perpetuated by the kind of person this fragmentation has nurtured."[9]

Although this deeply embedded system may seem rational to suburban residents and public officials, it has produced dysfunctional consequences for the larger society. Metropolitan political fragmentation has encouraged unplanned, costly sprawl on the urban fringe. It has imposed longer journeys to work on commuters, allowing them less time for family life. It has undermined the quality of life in older suburbs, hardened conflicts between suburbs and their central cities, hampered financing for regional public facilities such as mass transit, and encouraged disinvestment from central cities. Countries with strong national land-use regulation and regional governments have avoided many of these problems. Indeed, the United States could have avoided them if we had chosen a more intelligent path for metropolitan growth over the last fifty years.

As these problems became increasingly evident, they drew criticism from scholars, planners, and good-government groups. These critics have focused on how metropolitan political fragmentation undermines administrative efficiency, environmental quality, economic competitiveness, and social equity. As early as the 1930s, administrative experts promoted regional solutions as ways to address the overlap, duplication, lack of coordination, and waste in the provision of public services. Concern today is becoming widespread. Even longtime suburban residents have expressed concern over the environmental costs of sprawl as they see their countryside being gobbled up by new development and find themselves in traffic jams even while doing their Saturday morning shopping. They have made "smart growth" a hot-button issue across the country. Executives of large firms, transportation planners, and economic development officials most often express concern that fragmented metropolitan areas undermine the economic competitiveness of urban regions.

Finally, those who crusade for civil rights and racial desegregation, who care about the plight of the inner-city poor, and who champion greater civic participation have criticized the ways in which metropolitan fragmentation has hurt the social and economic fabric of our communities. They argue in favor of fair housing and housing mobility programs, metropolitan administration of economic opportunity programs, tax-base sharing, and metropolitan school districts. Indeed, metropolitan fragmentation, sprawl, and inequality are major causes of the decline in community and civic participation, as is convincingly documented in Robert Putnam's *Bowling Alone*.[10] In the words of Harvard law professor Gerald Frug: "The suspicion and fear that infest our metropolitan areas threaten to generate a self-reinforcing cycle of alienation: the more people withdraw from each other, the higher percentage of strangers that cause them anxiety, thereby producing further withdrawal."[11]

ORIGINS OF THE NEW REGIONALISM

The current debate over regionalism echoes earlier concerns. At the end of the nineteenth century, New York, Chicago, and many other cities moved to annex or consolidate most of the adjacent territory likely to be developed in the next fifty years. The formation of Greater New York from New York City, Brooklyn, the hamlets of Queens County, the Bronx, and Staten Island in 1898 was a grand and highly successful experiment in metropolitan government. Indeed, much of the current vitality of cities such as Chicago and New York stems from these early actions. By the 1920s, however, middle-class urbanites, dismayed by the rapidly increasing density and inequality of their industrial cities, and frustrated by their inability to continue to dominate their politics, increasingly fled to the suburbs. Once they established themselves as suburbanites, they persuaded state legislatures to pass laws hindering cities from further annexation. Metropolitan growth would henceforth take place largely outside the jurisdiction of the cental city.

Responding to such trends, an early group of regionalists foresaw, as early as the 1920s, the need for new forms of metropolitan planning and cooperation. Echoing the "garden city" idea first promulgated by Ebenezer Howard in England, Lewis Mumford and his colleagues in the Regional Planning Association of America, formed in 1923, hoped that coherent regions would gradually emerge to dissolve the problems of the industrial city. "The hope of the city," Mumford wrote in 1925, "lies outside itself." [12] Other radical (though less utopian) thinkers called for regional land-use planning as an antidote to fragmentation. In 1927, the Regional Plan Association's magisterial plan for metropolitan New York called for knitting the region together with a comprehensive system of highways and rail transit that would concentrate economic growth in Manhattan and in a few suburban centers. In 1937, the New Deal's National Resources Committee called for federal efforts to foster regional planning, including the establishment of multistate metropolitan planning agencies. [13] In the face of resistance from those who saw such measures as abrogating private property and local democracy, however, none of these visionary blueprints had much impact on the post–World War II evolution of American cities. As a result, many of the problems they anticipated did indeed come to pass.

Efficiency Arguments for Regionalism

The negative consequences of unplanned metropolitan growth triggered new strains of regionalist thinking and new political constituencies that favored the creation of new regional institutions. Public administrators, city planners, and municipal reformers viewed regional planning as the best way to promote regional economic efficiency and maintain a sound environment. Writing for the National Municipal League in 1930, Paul Studentski criticized metropolitan fragmentation and called for a framework that would support "real, democratic, comprehensive, and permanent organization of the metropolitan community." [14] Prominent academics and planners such as Charles Merriam, Victor Jones, and Luther Gulick elaborated on these themes in the postwar period. [15] Robert Wood's 1961 classic *1400 Governments* argued that postwar suburbanization in metropolitan New York was irrational, inefficient, and unaccountable. The federal Advisory Commission on Intergovernmental Relations, created by Congress in 1947 and eliminated in 1996, recommended ways to broaden the urban tax base and improve the regional distribution of services.

A common theme was that fragmented metropolitan governments promoted wasteful duplication, uneven standards of public service, and wasteful competition between local governments. These trenchant critiques were no more effective than the work of earlier metropolitan visionaries had been in restraining the construction of freeways, suburban shopping malls, and tract housing in the 1950s and 1960s. It nevertheless remained a key doctrine of public administration that regions required some level of metropolitan planning in order to function well. The 1960s saw the creation of many regional councils of government (often called COGs) and single-purpose regional agencies for functions such as water and sewer systems, garbage disposal, and transportation. City-county consolidation took place in Miami, Nashville, Jacksonville, and Indianapolis, but voters in many other areas rejected proposals to merge city and suburban governments into regional governments. Bucking this trend, in the November 2000 election, voters in Louisville, Kentucky, and its suburbs approved (by a 54 to 46 percent margin) the consolidation of the city of Louisville with Richmond County. This is the first major city-county merger to win approval in thirty years.[16] Fast-growing cities of the South and Southwest, such as Phoenix and Albuquerque, also annexed surrounding territory long after that practice ended elsewhere in the country. Finally, voters and public officials sought to streamline and modernize the governance of suburban areas in the postwar period by enhancing county government and consolidating school districts. All these efforts, however, fell short of the goals espoused by the first and second generations of regionalists.

Environmental Arguments for Regionalism

Concern for administrative efficiency motivated the early advocates of metropolitan governance. Beginning in the 1960s, a new generation of regionalists emerged, concerned about environmental protection, sustainable development, and "smart growth." Development rapidly swallowed the metropolitan countryside after World War II, and the freeway construction of the 1960s and 1970s increased traffic congestion to new, more disturbing levels. Confronting these realities, suburban residents and those who represented them became less enthusiastic about unbridled metropolitan growth.

In 1974, the Council on Environmental Quality issued a report titled *The Costs of Sprawl*, calling for greater regulation of suburban development.[17] Today, several national environmental organizations, including the Sierra Club, are campaigning against sprawl, Oregon and Maryland have adopted state legislation for "smart growth," and many other states are actively discussing similar measures. Some approaches call for the establishment of regional growth boundaries monitored by the state; others merely provide incentives to channel new investment toward already developed areas while attempting to preserve agricultural land uses or otherwise protect undeveloped areas. Regional groups are active in the San Francisco Bay Area, Washington, D.C., Pittsburgh, and Suffolk County, New York. A movement for "new urbanism" has emerged among architects and city planners who favor denser, more pedestrian- and transit-oriented forms of neighborhood development.[18] Despite naysayers who see an adverse impact on housing affordability and consumer choice, a growing consensus has emerged in many places on behalf of rethinking older growth policies.[19] Residents of Cook County, Illinois (an old urban area), and Santa Clara County, California (the high-tech Silicon Valley), both showed overwhelming support for regional approaches to solving urban problems.[20] Voters across the country have approved ballot measures to limit suburban sprawl and preserve open spaces.[21] Responding to such sentiments, Vice President Al Gore made smart growth a central theme in the Clinton-Gore administration's "livability agenda," which focused on preserving open spaces, redeveloping brownfield areas, mitigating congestion, and improving urban air quality.[22]

Economic Competitiveness Arguments for Regionalism

Contemporary regionalists have also argued that metropolitan areas divided against themselves cannot compete successfully in the new global economy. In particular, business leaders and regional planning organizations have recognized that regionally oriented planning and development policies could make metropolitan economies more competitive. Although business-supported regional planning groups have existed at least since the Regional Plan Association was established in New York in 1923, groups like San Francisco's Bay Area Council and Pittsburgh's Allegheny Council for Community Development became more common after World War II. The radical changes in technology, business organization, and global competition since the 1980s gave this perspective new force. The high-technology companies of Silicon Valley took the lead in supporting regional approaches to the South Bay's housing, transportation, and development issues. One scholar, Annalee Saxenian, found that Silicon Valley entrepreneurs' ability to collaborate in this way made that region more successful, over the long haul, than the similar technology complex along Route 128 around Boston.[23]

As we discussed in chapter 3, social scientists who examine the interrelationships between central-city and suburban economies find a high correlation between the two, though in some cases, substantial central-city decline has not prevented the surrounding suburbs from prospering. Nevertheless, there are obvious linkages in the economic conditions and income growth rates of central cities and their suburbs. Central cities continue to perform functions and provide services that are critical to regional growth. The evidence suggests that cooperative regions are more likely to prosper than are more competitive, divided regions.[24]

These realities have given impetus to new efforts to form regional public-private partnerships to promote regional growth. Syndicated columnist Neal Peirce, who has given visibility to all forms of new regionalism, and his colleague Curtis Johnson have been particularly active in inspiring and advising a new generation of such organizations. They have not promoted any particular organizational forms, stressing instead the general need for collaboration, trust, dialogue, and leadership.[25] These collaborations have produced many Web sites and a journal, *The Regionalist*.[26]

Closely associated with this perspective is the growing focus on industrial clusters as a basis for urban and regional economic development. Advanced by Michael Porter's *The Competitive Advantage of Nations*, this perspective argues that a region's competitiveness is based on the quality of networks and interactions among related and often physically close firms. Even though they may compete against one another in some ways, they share technical knowledge, a skilled labor pool, and support services and spur one another to rapid technological innovation. This has led some policy makers to promote clusters as a way to address such regional needs as better-paid jobs, more rapid innovation, and a better quality of life for industrial workers. This perspective was given national prominence in the 1996 report *America's New Economy and the Challenge of the Cities*.[27]

Many state and local agencies hoping to emulate Silicon Valley's success have embraced this way of thinking about economic development, such as the Regional Technology Alliance organized by the San Diego Association of Governments. San Diego has also surveyed employers in these clusters to understand their workforce needs and has developed programs to address them.[28]

Equity Arguments for Regionalism

The spatial concentration of urban poverty is another concern motivating many new regionalists. As Michael Schill observed, "although segregating themselves in the suburbs may serve the interests of large numbers of Americans today, the long term costs of doing nothing to alleviate concentrated ghetto poverty are likely to be tremendous."[29] Distinguished public intellectuals, including Anthony Downs of the Brookings Institution, former Albuquerque mayor David Rusk, Minnesota state legislator Myron Orfield, and Harvard professor Gary Orfield, among others, have concluded that regional approaches are the only way that the problem of inner-city poverty can be solved.[30] Increasingly, they have been joined by officials representing the inner-ring suburbs who are facing the growth of "urban" problems that they cannot solve within the limits of their own jurisdictions. With foundation funding, Orfield and his associates have launched initiatives to document and remedy "growing social and economic polarization" in twenty-two metropolitan areas.[31]

Increasingly, planners are arguing that there need not be a trade-off between equality and efficiency, or growth. Indeed, regional strategies that lift up the central city can make regions more competitive. The Center on Wisconsin Strategy at the University of Wisconsin has advocated that workforce developers and regional employers cooperate to train central-city residents for high-wage jobs in technologically innovative firms. This "high road" approach to regional economic development would simultaneously enhance wages, upward mobility, and employer competitiveness.[32]

THE PRACTICE OF METROPOLITAN COOPERATION

Although support for new, regional approaches to metropolitan problems has grown steadily stronger over the last several decades, the actual practice of metropolitan government has made less progress. Most regions have some elements of cooperation, but they vary considerably in terms of their institutional arrangements, the political constituencies they bring into play, and their capacity to address their region's social and economic challenges. A variety of constituencies has supported regional cooperation — business leaders seeking to enhance regional economic competitiveness, program administrators concerned with better coordination, community groups seeking regional equity, and suburban advocates of slowing growth. Their aims and interests obviously diverge on many points. In contrast to this diversity, the local interest in autonomy, particularly among suburban jurisdictions, is quite consistent. This has hindered the growth of metropolitan cooperation but may not prevent it in the long run.

What experiences has the United States had with metropolitan cooperation, why have they been so ineffective, and what forms would a more effective regionalism take? In formal terms, regional cooperation ranges from limited, single-purpose activities (such as a regional sewer or transportation authority or a reverse commuting program) through multipurpose cooperative arrangements to full-fledged regional governments. What follows is a brief review of the history and experience of metropolitan cooperation. First, we review the weak efforts that the federal government has historically made to promote regional cooperation. Then we turn to the local experience. We discuss three patterns: the typical state of affairs, which H. V. Savitch and Ronald Vogel termed "avoidance and conflict";[33] the more ambitious forms of metropolitan governance attempted by Portland, Oregon, and Minneapolis–St. Paul; and approaches specifically designed to reduce the spatial concentration of the poor in central cities.

Halting Federal Efforts at Promoting Metropolitan Cooperation

During the depression of the 1930s, President Franklin D. Roosevelt appointed a National Resources Committee, composed of federal administrators and academic experts, to recommend federal actions to lift the nation out of its economic crisis. In its 1937 report, *Our Cities: Their Role in the National Economy,* the committee asserted that slums and urban blight threatened economic recovery and recommended federal policies to improve the economic performance of cities. Among the key challenges it identified were real estate speculation and "uncontrolled subdivision" on the urban fringe. The "greatest obstacle," the committee said, was the "great number of conflicting and overlapping political and administrative units into which [metropolitan areas are] divided."[34] To tame these forces, the committee urged the federal government to promote metropolitan planning, limit metropolitan political fragmentation, and restrict local governments' authority to adopt their own zoning laws. Had Roosevelt and Congress taken this advice, metropolitan America would have evolved differently, but business, real estate, and suburban and rural local government interests prevailed. Even the committee's modest proposal to select nine cities for an experiment in comprehensive long-range planning was scuttled, and the National Resources Committee was eliminated in 1943.[35]

In 1961, the American Society of Planning Officials and the Ford Foundation sponsored a report by zoning lawyer Richard Babcock, *The Zoning Game,* which criticized the fragmented control of land use by local governments. "Land use planning is in chaos," he wrote. "I doubt that even the most intransigent disciple of anarchy ever wished for or intended the litter that prevails in the area of land-use regulation."[36] President John Kennedy warned that "bold programs in individual jurisdictions are no longer enough. Increasingly, community development must be a cooperative venture toward the common goals of the new metropolitan region as a whole." In 1962, Kennedy proposed a new Department of Urban Affairs, arguing, "There must be expansion, but orderly and planned expansion, not explosion and sprawl."[37] (HUD was established in 1965, under President Lyndon Johnson, but it has always lacked the authority to deal with local zoning laws.)

President Johnson, too, took up the cause of metropolitan-wide planning. Unplanned growth, he said, caused "the decay of the urban centers and the despoiling of the suburbs."[38] The urban riots of the 1960s gave even greater impetus to concerns over racial and economic segregation in metropolitan areas. In 1968, the report of the National Advisory Commission on Civil Disorders (the *Kerner Report*) blamed suburban zoning practices for "restricting the area open to a growing population" and giving landlords incentives "to break up ghetto apartments for denser occupancy, hastening housing deterioration." It called for federal action to challenge suburban zoning practices that excluded the poor and racial minorities.[39] In 1969, the National Commission on Urban Problems made recommendations similar to those of the National Resources Committee thirty years earlier. It noted that "problems of air and water pollution, transportation, open space, solid waste disposal, housing, and employment do not end at municipal borders. At the same time, land-use controls, which are important factors in the creation and solution of such problems, are lodged in local governments with virtually no supervision by metropolitan or State agencies."[40]

In 1970, Senator Henry Jackson (a moderate Democrat from Washington) introduced a National Land Use Policy bill to establish uniform guidelines for state laws. Republican President Richard Nixon supported the bill, arguing that "the time has come when we must accept the idea that society as a whole has a legitimate interest in property land-use."[41] The legislation was backed by many business groups frustrated by local zoning laws that made it difficult for corporations and developers to develop office parks, manufacturing facilities, and housing developments.[42]

None of these proposals for a federal land-use policy made any headway. Despite the backing of major national political figures and business leaders, strong local opposition, which saw these proposals as infringing on "local control," proved too powerful. Congress consistently failed to adopt any federal plan that would significantly trespass on local authority.

In the 1960s, the federal government did use the carrot of federal funding to encourage regional planning. Federal requirements stimulated the creation of regional COGs. There are about 500 COGs in the United States today, but for the most part, they focus on limited functions and do not address overall land-use planning. The 1962 Federal Highway Act provided matching funds to states for highways but required applicants to show that their projects were consistent with a regional plan. Especially noteworthy was the 1991 Intermodal Surface Transportation Efficiency Act (ISTEA — called "iced tea"), which required that governments in each region designate a Metropolitan Planning Organization to plan transportation improvements, including mass transit and bicycle and foot paths.

In recent decades, several reports, some sponsored by the federal government, identified exclusionary zoning practices as obstacles to creating affordable housing, particularly in affluent suburbs.[43] For the most part, however, the federal and state governments have been reluctant to systematically challenge local zoning laws that have the effect, if not the intent, of excluding minorities and the poor. The closest HUD came was during the Carter administration in the 1970s. HUD set up metropolitan Areawide Housing Opportunity Plans (AHOPs) and created the Regional Housing Mobility Program to plan for the dispersal of Section 8 housing certificates throughout metropolitan areas, with the help of regional planning agencies and cooperating suburbs. Before these programs could be carried out, the Reagan administration took office in 1981 and canceled them. Not until the early 1990s did the federal government try this approach again, through its Moving to Opportunity program. This was a small-scale but apparently quite successful effort to replicate Chicago's Gautreaux program, which provides vouchers and housing counseling to low-income renters to help them find apartments in the suburbs on a voluntary basis.[44]

A few states have passed laws challenging exclusionary zoning. New York, New Jersey, California, and Massachusetts adopted "inclusionary zoning" laws to make it easier for developers to build affordable housing in suburban jurisdictions.[45] New Jersey's law emerged from its famous *Mt. Laurel* court cases; California and Massachusetts enacted legislation on their own.[46] These state laws have had only modest success in expanding low-income housing opportunities in suburbs. Starting in the 1980s, in response to federal housing cutbacks, a few local governments also adopted inclusionary zoning ordinances requiring developers of market-rate housing to set aside some units for low- and moderate-income residents or to pay fees to support affordable housing, schools, or infrastructure.[47] But neither the federal government nor these states has used the carrot-and-stick approach of withholding funds for transportation, school, infrastructure, or other programs to localities that have not complied with the law.

The Local Experience: Avoidance and Conflict

In the typical metropolitan area, a region's constituent towns and cities may realize that they belong to a common region, but they seek to retain their autonomy and continue to act independently or compete with one another for economic resources. Savitch and Vogel and their colleagues found that New York, Los Angeles, and St. Louis epitomize this pattern.[48] It is common in older industrial areas with long histories of central city–suburban tension and long-standing racial, class, and social differences. David Rusk has shown that these "inelastic" central cities also have the worst race and class segregation and weak regional economic performance.[49]

The New York City consolidated metropolitan statistical area includes thirty-one counties in New York, New Jersey, Connecticut, and Pennsylvania and houses more than 21 million residents.[50] It contains some 1,787 county, municipal, town, school district, and special district governments. The nonprofit, business-backed Regional Plan Association has advocated three regional plans since 1923, most recently calling for a new emphasis on concentrated development around regional transit nodes and greater emphasis on workforce development.[51] These plans, however, have had more effect on thinking among academics and policy elites than on actual development patterns.

Efforts to create a true regional planning agency with significant authority have failed. The two public agencies that could undertake this mission have not done so. The Port Authority of New York and New Jersey, created in 1921, operates the region's seaport, its three airports, the Hudson River bridges and tunnels, a commuter railroad, and the World Trade Center office complex. In recent decades, it has responded to the development agendas of the governor, who appoints its board, rather than acting as an agent for the region's municipalities. Mayor Rudolph Giuliani of New York City has campaigned to dissolve the Port Authority, or at least to return the New York airports to city control, and the agency suffers from the need to balance any benefit to one state with an equivalent benefit to the other. On the New York side of the river, the Metropolitan Transit Authority operates the city's subway and bus systems, bridges and tunnels, and a commuter rail system. It, too, is a creature of compromise between the governor and mayor, the city of New York and the adjacent counties it serves. It has had difficulty achieving agreement on new initiatives, such as providing rail service to the airports, although it has substantially upgraded the rolling stock and performance of its constituent properties.

Although New York City dominates the region and the borough of Manhattan draws more than 41 percent of daily commuters, it does not dominate the region's highly fragmented politics. The surrounding states and municipalities compete vigorously to attract business investment away from the city. Since the 1970s, Westchester County and Stamford, Connecticut, have lured away many large corporate headquarters; New Jersey enticed the New York Giants and Jets football teams to the Meadowlands complex, and Jersey City has attracted many back-office operations. In response to "predatory moves" by other jurisdictions, New York City has granted large tax abatements and other concessions to attract corporations to Manhattan or to retain them.

Concerned about these bidding wars, the governors of New York, New Jersey, and Connecticut and New York City's mayor signed a "nonaggression" pact in 1991. They vowed to avoid negative advertising and the use of tax breaks and other incentives to steal investment from one another and agreed to cooperate on a regional development strategy. Within a year, however, the economic rivalry accelerated, all three states launched new business incentive and tax reduction programs, and the "job wars" continued as before. For example, New Jersey induced First Chicago Trust Company to move 1,000 jobs from lower Manhattan by subsidizing the company's office space. Bruce Berg and Paul Kantor note, "The economic competition for jobs among states and localities in the tristate region goes unregulated, to the disadvantage of almost everyone except the corporations that are the objects of subsidies."[52]

Similarly, the St. Louis region comprises twelve counties in Missouri and Illinois with a 2000 population of 2.6 million, divided by the Mississippi and Missouri Rivers.[53] In 1992, it had 771 local jurisdictions, primarily special districts (140 more than in 1972). The central cities of St. Louis (in Missouri) and East St. Louis (in Illinois) suffered massive depopulation, while the suburban parts of the region grew. The region's poor and black residents are concentrated in these two cities. Per capita taxable property among the region's municipalities ranged from $2,178 to $143,285.

The St. Louis region created a regional agency responsible for sewers, junior colleges, zoos, museums, and a regional medical center. However, these serve only St. Louis County and the city of St. Louis, not the remainder of the region. In 1949, the two states created a seven-county Bi-State Development Agency, but it lacks taxing authority and focuses almost exclusively on transportation matters. Efforts to promote broader regional cooperation failed in 1926, 1955, and 1959. In 1992, voters rejected ballot measures to create a metropolitan economic development commission (funded by a 2 percent tax on nonresidential utility service) and a metropolitan park commission (to be funded by property taxes).

Los Angeles is the quintessential "fragmented metropolis."[54] The five-county region (Los Angeles, Ventura, Riverside, Orange, and San Bernardino Counties) contains 16 million people, a land area almost the size of Ohio, and an economy that would rank twelfth largest in the world if it were a separate country.[55] It includes more than 200 cities (33 with more than 100,000 residents) and hundreds of special district governments. The city of Los Angeles, with 3.7 million residents, holds one-fifth of the region's population, but no one center dominates this decentered region. Much of Los Angeles, including the central city, has a "suburban" character, reflecting the area's reliance on the automobile. Its region's population grew 25 percent during the 1980s, most dramatically among Latino and Asian immigrants, and grew another 13 percent in the 1990s. Although black ghettos and Latino barrios are disproportionately located in the city of Los Angeles, the region's minority population is dispersed throughout the region, and high-poverty census tracts have also spread across the metropolitan area.[56] During the 1980s, the poverty rate increased in each county; it is significantly higher in San Bernardino County than in Los Angeles County.

The region's many municipalities compete for private investment. After the passage of Proposition 13 in 1978, which drastically limited property taxes and forced localities to try to increase the collection of local sales taxes to expand their revenue base, this competition accelerated. Cities such as Glendale, Ventura, Pasadena, Anaheim, and Cerritos utilized redevelopment projects to reinvent themselves as office, sports, tourist, and retail centers. This competition has made efforts at regional cooperation more problematic.

The splintering of the region's media market also hampers the emergence of a regional identity. In most metropolitan areas, one daily newspaper and a few local broadcast stations constitute a single media market. Although the *Los Angeles Times* is the region's largest and most influential newspaper, most cities in the region have their own daily papers. Los Angeles television stations dominate the market, but outlying cities such as San Bernardino, Santa Ana, Ventura, and others have their own network-affiliated stations.

Los Angeles once mounted bold regional public works initiatives designed to expand the area's economy. The regional water system required complex land purchases, canals, and aqueducts that diverted water from the Owens Valley and the Colorado River. The Metropolitan Water District, a regional special district, now oversees this activity. Regional leaders also developed a port to foster regional economic growth.[57] Los Angeles and Long Beach now have separate and competing ports, however, and many smaller airports compete with Los Angeles Airport.

Business, environmental, and planning groups have frequently sought to promote regional governance. Business leaders believed that traffic congestion, polluted air, and water shortages hurt their competitive position and funded studies to encourage stronger regional coordination. In 1988, Mayor Tom Bradley appointed a Los Angeles 2000 Committee, which called for a regional planning agency to manage land use, housing, and transportation and a regional environmental agency that would consolidate the regional antipollution agency with its water control and solid waste agencies. It also proposed to strengthen the region's airport authority. Despite much debate and the filing of the necessary bills in the state legislature, municipal leaders intensified their competition during the economic downturn of the early 1990s, and support for regional approaches fell apart.

Like many areas, the region has a council of governments, the Southern California Association of Governments (SCAG). An unwieldy body, SCAG has representation from seventy elected officials (sixty-three selected by municipal elected officials, and seven by county supervisors). The city of Los Angeles has only two members. Membership is voluntary, and SCAG has no authority over its member governments. It can recommend approval or rejection of projects proposed by cities under the federal ISTEA (now TEA-21), which allocates over $1 billion annually for transportation in the region. It can also withhold funds for local road improvements unless cities and counties develop plans to reduce auto usage. To comply, the various county-level transportation agencies embarked on such projects as a subway in Los Angeles, the imposition of tolls in Orange and Riverside Counties, and a high-speed train project.

This is one of the most polluted metropolitan areas in the nation, and the most powerful regional body is the South Coast Air Quality Management District. It has set tough standards for industry and automobile emissions, required construction of new public transportation facilities, caused county government to implement measures such as car-pool lanes, and influenced local land-use decisions. As a result, air quality has significantly improved: exposure to unhealthful ozone levels fell by half, despite population growth and constant business opposition.[58]

This improvement occurred only because federal law required it and the agency was able to set timetables and threaten sanctions. Otherwise, the region's cities still compete for investment. In 1994, for example, Los Angeles granted DreamWorks, a new film company, a $75 million tax abatement to build its headquarters in the city, even though it was unlikely to locate anywhere else. The Los Angeles region has so many separate local governments and special districts that no one local constituency, even the region's major employers, could induce all of them to cooperate or collaborate on a voluntary basis.

New York, St. Louis, and Los Angeles typify the experience of most metropolitan regions, especially the older ones. Regional cooperation is restricted to a few specific functions, parts of the region still compete for investment and advantage, and regional rivalries hamper regional planning for public improvements that would spur economic growth. Indeed, these regions have difficulty coordinating even simple functions, such as meshing the schedules of regional mass transit systems. Myriad local jurisdictions take their own approaches to federally funded activities such as the construction and management of subsidized housing, the distribution of housing vouchers, the creation of job training programs, and the like, all of which might be more effective if carried out on a regional basis.

Experiments in Metropolitan Governance

Advocates of regional approaches consistently point to two places that have most fully developed the promise of regional government: the Twin Cities of Minneapolis and St. Paul, Minnesota, where an appointed metropolitan council carries out a number of functions and a regional tax-sharing scheme redistributes revenues from high-growth to low-growth areas; and Portland, Oregon, where an elected metropolitan government regulates suburban land development within a regional growth boundary.

The Twin Cities have a 2000 population of 669,769 in a metropolitan area of 2.9 million people.[59] In 1967, the state legislature created a seven-county Metropolitan Council responsible for land use, housing, transit, sewage, and other metropolitan issues. The governor appoints its members, who set policies that local governments then carry out. In its first decade, the council solved a crisis in wastewater treatment. In the 1960s, the Federal Housing Administration threatened to stop insuring mortgages in burgeoning suburbs that lacked sewage treatment. In response, the Metropolitan Council created a Metropolitan Water Control Commission to finance and run treatment plants and build trunk sewer lines.

By the late 1970s, the Metropolitan Council had created or absorbed regional agencies for transportation, housing, and redevelopment. It had its own tax base and a substantial capital budget, and it received federal grants, which allowed it to provide regional infrastructure, encourage affluent suburbs such as Golden Valley to develop low- and moderate-income housing, and create regional parks where shopping centers might otherwise have been developed. In 1971, the state adopted the Fiscal Disparities Act, which required all metropolitan jurisdictions to pool 40 percent of the growth in their commercial industrial tax bases and to allocate the proceeds according to population and level of tax capacity, thus dampening competition for new development and reallocating resources from affluent, fast-growing suburbs to older, more urban parts of the region. The council also created a regional development framework to contain suburban sprawl and limit the cost of extending public services to outlying areas.

Despite these considerable successes, the Metropolitan Council has disappointed many of its early supporters. It did not provide leadership on the major development issues of the 1980s, including the building of several sports complexes and the world's largest shopping mall. It lacks an independent political base. When its views clash with those of the governor, influential state legislators, or even some local officials, it has difficulty mobilizing support for its agenda. Moreover, the existence of the Metropolitan Council and regional tax sharing has not prevented the Twin Cities from becoming one of the most sprawled-out metropolitan areas in the United States. Minneapolis has actually fared poorly under tax-base sharing because the formula stresses revenue-raising capacity, which counts the city's booming downtown but ignores the spending needs generated by its relatively large poor population.

The council also did not address neighborhood decay in the central cities or restrain the growth of central city–suburban disparities. During the 1980s, the two cities' population remained stable, but the metro area increased by 15 percent. By 1990, median family income in the Twin Cities was $33,364, compared with $43,252 in the metro area; the poverty rate was 18.5 percent, compared with 8 percent in the metro area. Poverty had become markedly greater and more concentrated since 1970. Racial minorities constituted less than 10 percent of the metro area population, but almost 20 percent of the two cities' residents. Most job growth took place in the affluent southern and western suburbs, but many central-city residents (including almost half of black households) lacked cars or public transit access to these areas.

Since 1993, state legislator Myron Orfield of Minneapolis has sought to give the Metropolitan Council the tools to address these disparities. He introduced bills to elect the members of the Metropolitan Council, to mandate low- and moderate-income housing development goals for each suburb, to empower the council to deny sewer and highway funds to suburbs that failed to comply, and to create a council-administered affordable housing trust fund from taxes on the value of residential construction in excess of $150,000 per home. Orfield calculated that three-quarters of the region's suburbs would benefit from the fund and only one-quarter (including the wealthiest suburbs) would contribute. He used color maps to convince legislators from Minneapolis, St. Paul, and the inner suburbs that they had more in common than they thought, especially in terms of social problems and the distribution of state and regional funds.[60]

The legislature passed Orfield's housing bills, but the Republican governor vetoed them; the bill to elect the council failed by one vote in the state house and five in the senate. But Orfield's efforts drew public attention to the council's potential and its weaknesses and shifted the political climate toward reform. In 1994, the legislature abolished single-issue commissions (such as the Waste Control Commission) and gave their powers to the council. A growing number of business, civic, and political leaders, including the daily newspapers, acknowledged the need to address the region's social disparities along the lines suggested by Orfield. With the election of a new governor in 1998, Reform Party candidate Jesse Ventura, it appears more likely that these issues will come back onto the political agenda.

Portland, Oregon, has the nation's only directly elected regional governing body, the Metro Council.[61] It serves twenty-four cities and three counties. Its seven nonpartisan members are elected for four-year terms from districts that each contain about 200,000 constituents; its executive officer, elected at large, is responsible for daily management. The Metro Council formulates and implements policy on solid waste, tourism, transportation, land use, and growth management. The state legislature authorized it in 1977, and the voters of Clackamas, Multnomah, and Washington Counties approved it the following year. Metro's revenue base comes from a variety of taxes and fees; it has the authority, which it has not yet exercised, to seek voter approval for regional income and sales taxes.

In 1970, Portland was a city of 382,619 in a three-county region of 878,676. By 2000, the city had grown to 529,121 and the region to 1.9 million. The region's economy is dominated by shipping, electronics, and manufacturing. In contrast to many cities, Portland's employment base has grown significantly, even though job growth has been greater in the surrounding suburbs. Many believe that the region's planning efforts have been a major factor in this outcome.[62]

Until the 1970s, Portland seemed headed for decline. It lost its ability to annex suburban localities in 1906. By 1956, the three-county area had 176 governmental units, including many special districts. In 1960, the League of Women Voters published *A Tale of Three Counties*, which criticized uncoordinated services and wasteful spending and called for a new, more efficient, more accountable government structure. During the 1960s and 1970s, the legislature and voters approved regional agencies for transportation, the zoo, and solid waste. In 1983, a large budget deficit in Multnomah County (which includes Portland) and the need for services in the unincorporated suburban areas east of Portland led the County Board of Supervisors to encourage Portland to annex some unincorporated areas, provide services to some suburbs, and create a sewer construction program for the county. These reforms created support for a metropolitan-wide governance structure. Nevertheless, heavily dependent on such troubled industries as paper and pulp, timber exports, shipbuilding, fishing, and metalworking, the Portland economy did not appear especially well positioned for future growth.

Following several blue-ribbon study commissions, the voters of the three counties approved the creation of an elected metropolitan government in May 1978. Its first task was to designate a metropolitan urban growth boundary under Oregon's land-use legislation, the nation's strongest. Under it, Metro can compel local governments and counties to coordinate their land-use and development plans. As baby boomers moved to Portland to enjoy its environment, as basic resource exports recovered from their slump in the 1980s, and as employment surged in new industries (including Intel, Tektronix, and Nike), the demand for new development grew steadily, as did the political base for managing this growth. A political alliance between Portland's business interests and residents of older neighborhoods also sought to strengthen the downtown area against competition from suburban shopping malls while saving abandoned housing from the threat of large-scale land clearance and redevelopment. When Neal Goldschmidt was elected mayor in 1972, he incorporated neighborhood activists into his administration (1972–1979) and continued that policy after becoming governor (1987–1990).

This coalition largely achieved its goals for coordinating land-use planning and transportation policy, emphasizing public transit, revitalizing older neighborhoods, and strengthening the downtown business district. These efforts were bolstered by state land-use planning laws that preserved farmland and forests around Portland and directed urban growth into Portland and its neighboring areas. Although more office and retail development has taken place outside the city of Portland than within it, the downtown still accounts for 60 percent of the region's office space and half its upscale retail space. Several highway projects were abandoned in favor of buses and light-rail connections between the central city, outlying neighborhoods, and nearby suburbs. By the 1990s, the region's bus and rail system carried 43 percent of downtown commuters, compared with 20 percent in Phoenix, 17 percent in Salt Lake City, and 11 percent in Sacramento. Portland shows that metropolitan government can succeed. As Orfield observed, its "regional government has been more willing than the Twin Cities' appointed Metropolitan Council to exercise its powers vis-à-vis competing authorities."[63]

Even so, Metro is not all-powerful. It does not provide water, sewer, police, airport, parks (other than the zoo), transportation, subsidized housing, cable television, or many other services for the region. Local school districts remain distinct, eighty single-purpose special districts still have the ability to tax, and twenty cities and three counties provide a broad range of services. Key activities that might help promote mobility of the poor out of the central city — subsidized housing construction and the administration of Section 8 vouchers — are administered by the Portland city housing authority and do not operate on a metrowide basis. Two metrowide agencies with appointed boards, Tri-Met (which runs the transit system) and the Port of Portland (which runs the port, industrial parks, and the airports), operate independently of Metro. Metro's most important function is to set ground rules for development and growth. For example, it selected the site for the region's $65 million convention center.

It has enhanced the region's ability to resist costly and inefficient sprawl, but it is not a full-service government.

Portland suffers less from the spatial concentration of the poor in the central city than do most other places. Portland's 1990 poverty rate of 14.5 percent was below that of most other large central cities, and the area's low-income residents were spread out, not highly segregated, concentrated, and isolated. The income gap between the central city and the suburbs remains one of the smallest in the nation.[64] Since Portland has a small minority population (7.7 percent African American, 3.2 percent Hispanic, and 5.3 percent Asian), the relationship between the city and its suburbs has not been racially charged. The state's "fair share" housing and land-use mandates, along with Metro's planning efforts, have encouraged suburbs to develop more low-income housing than in other metropolitan areas. The region's housing prices increased more than the national average during the 1990s, although not as much as in booming cities such as Denver or Salt Lake City, which lack Portland's strict growth management.[65] The heritage of cooperation between advocates for the housing needs of the inner-city poor and the region's real estate industry, together with the institutional strength of regional government, has led to discussions about taxing regional real estate transfers to fund subsidized housing production on a regional basis. If this does occur, it could put Portland in the forefront of regional equity, as well as regional environmental planning. At the same time, dispersing the inner-city minority poor to the surrounding area has not been a priority for Portland's metropolitan government, nor has subsidized housing been administered on a regional basis.

Efforts to Promote Regional Equity

As Scott Bollens observed, even at its best, "the current state of regional governance in the United States does not effectively address issues of concentrated poverty and social equity" because it tends to focus on infrastructure rather than people and because, lacking a broad political base, it takes a narrow, technical approach to its work.[66] Recognizing the difficulty of changing this situation and the likelihood that it would not soon reduce the embedded patterns of regional inequity and constrained opportunities for the inner-city poor, many advocates have sought more direct regional solutions to the problems of concentrated urban poverty. Because the courts have generally upheld suburban jurisdictions' right to impose restrictive zoning and have found that federal law on housing discrimination does not apply to low-income households but applies only to "particular groups such as racial minorities,"[67] these advocates have generally attacked the racial dimension of exclusion. They have, for example, sought to induce suburbs to take on their "fair share" of housing for lower-income residents and designed programs to connect the inner-city poor with suburban job opportunities, such as reverse commuting, portable Section 8 vouchers, and new institutions that train inner-city residents and place them in suburban job openings.[68]

Since a "spatial mismatch" often prevents inner-city poor people from taking advantage of suburban job opportunities, advocates of regional equity have long sought to increase access to suburban housing. Because many urban poor are also members of federally protected minority groups, vigorous enforcement of federal fair housing and affirmative mortgage lending regulations seems to be an obvious way to provide better access. As Michael Schill has pointed out, however, this legal framework does not provide a way to roll back the over-all framework of exclusionary zoning practices in the suburbs. Instead, it is most effective where least needed: for middle-class minority individuals who are obviously victims of discriminatory practices such as "steering" by real estate agents. Even in New Jersey, where the *Mt. Laurel* cases mandated sub-urban jurisdictions to do more to house the state's low-income residents, they can (and do) meet this obligation by financially supporting the construction of subsidized housing elsewhere.[69] Shifting the financing of local schools away from the property tax and toward state budgets may reduce suburbanites' fiscal incentive to exclude the less well-off, but it is not likely to lessen the propen-sity of middle-class whites to flee districts when the percentage of minorities in their children's classrooms begins to rise significantly.[70] Recent efforts to help central-city residents use Section 8 vouchers for suburban rental housing have shown promising results. But because these programs run up against exclusion-ary suburban zoning laws, it is difficult for them to help significant numbers of families.[71]

A number of metropolitan regions have adopted "fair-share" housing poli-cies to provide some affordable housing in otherwise expensive housing mar-kets that exclude low- and even moderate-income residents. One of the oldest and most successful programs is in Montgomery County, Maryland, an afflu-ent and fast-growing area of 497 square miles adjacent to Washington, D.C., with a 2000 population of 873,341 divided among fourteen incorporated mu-nicipalities.[72] During the 1970s and 1980s, Montgomery County changed from a bedroom community of Washington to a large employment center. The popu-lation boomed, and housing costs spiraled. In the early 1970s, housing advocacy groups such as Suburban Maryland Fair Housing and the League of Women Voters began pushing to increase the supply of affordable housing. The elected county council responded by adopting an inclusionary zoning law. Since 1974,

Montgomery County has required that all new housing developments with fifty or more units include a percentage (now 12.5 to 15 percent) of moderate-priced units. In exchange, it provides developers with a "density bonus," permitting them to increase a project's density by 20 percent. The first units were built in 1976.[73] To maintain the supply of affordable housing, the county limits the resale price for ten years and the rent for twenty years. The county's Housing Opportunity Commission (HOC) or nonprofit agencies can purchase up to 40 percent of these affordable units and, with federal subsidies, provide housing for very-low-income families.[74]

By the end of 1999, the program had created 10,595 units, 72 percent of them for sale. About 16 percent of the units were purchased by either the HOC (1,600 units) or nonprofit groups (another 70 units) for very-low-income families. The county requires developers to integrate these affordable units within market-rate housing rather than isolate them and create mini ghettos. The county insists on high standards of design and construction for these developments. They do not look like the stereotype of government-subsidized "projects." The program is limited to people who live or work in Montgomery County. Although there has been some opposition to particular developments, "the programs have been generally well-accepted by developers and by neighbors."[75] Montgomery's program is a successful effort to address the problem of economic segregation, but it is a drop in the bucket. Indeed, because the program has a long waiting list, the families are chosen by lottery.

Recognizing the difficulties of a frontal attack on exclusion of the urban poor from suburban housing markets and school districts, proponents of greater metropolitan equity have turned to a variety of other strategies.

"Reverse commuting" programs help low-income residents of central cities get to jobs in suburban areas. They address both the spatial mismatch dilemma and the reality that many poor workers cannot afford cars and that most public transit systems do not connect the areas where poor people live and where a growing number of entry-level jobs are located.[76] Chicago's Suburban JobLink was founded in 1971 to enhance employment opportunities among low-income residents of the city's poverty neighborhoods, particularly on the West Side.[77] It had close ties to suburban employers. By the early 1990s, it operated a fleet of six buses and a car-pool service and provided rides to employees who worked for about 150 different companies. The buses operated on multiple shifts. The program served 400 to 600 workers per day.[78] It also created a job training and job search facility to help inner-city residents find and apply for jobs and, in the process, "provides an island of cultural, ethnic and racial familiarity in an unfamiliar world."[79]

Philadelphia, Baltimore, Detroit, and other metropolitan areas created similar programs in the 1980s and early 1990s.[80] But the number of reverse commuting efforts mushroomed in the early 1990s after the Clinton administration set up federal pilot programs modeled on these local initiatives. The U.S. Department of Transportation (DOT) created JobLinks projects in sixteen sites, including urban and rural areas; the DOT and HUD created the Bridges to Work demonstration program in Baltimore, Chicago, Denver, Milwaukee, and St. Louis. These programs give localities considerable flexibility in designing projects to help connect people to jobs: van service, jitneys (taxis), even counseling and child care.[81]

Despite these innovative reverse commuting initiatives, Margy Waller and Mark Alan Hughes warn that they will never serve more than a small fraction of the poor who need transportation from urban ghettos to suburban jobs. "In most cases," they write, "the shortest distance between a poor person and a job is along a line driven in a car."[82] They argue that the most efficient way to help the poor is to provide them with subsidies to buy cars.[83] Typically, however, state welfare and food stamp programs deny benefits to anyone with a car worth more than $1,500.[84] Now, however, five states exclude the value of at least one car from the eligibility standards to receive welfare.

Even when the poor are able to get from home to work, the jobs they go to are often inadequate to support a family. Although upgrading the job skills of the workforce will not, on its own, directly address the increasing proportion of jobs that pay poverty-level wages, it can address the immediate needs of poor people who are currently separated from decent jobs. The goal of job training programs should be to "redistribute jobs, earnings, work experience, and dignity to the residents of low-income communities."[85] Most employment training programs, however, offer poor people little more than low-wage and dead-end jobs.[86] A major obstacle to successful job training is the disconnect between training programs and employers, especially those that provide decent-paying jobs in growing industries and thus offer employees a career ladder.

Innovative employment training programs in a number of metropolitan areas have sought to overcome these hurdles by linking community-based organizations, key businesses, and educational institutions on a regional level. One of the most successful is Project Quest in San Antonio, Texas, which has utilized the tools of community organizing to connect residents of low-income neighborhoods not only with effective job training but also with good jobs in a metropolitan-wide context.[87] Two community organizations affiliated with the Industrial Areas Foundation—Communities Organized for Public Service (COPS), based primarily in Catholic congregations in the Mexican American neighborhoods, and Metro Alliance, based primarily in Protestant churches in African American neighborhoods—founded Project Quest following a wave of layoffs in their communities. The San Antonio area had added as many as 19,000 good jobs in such fields as health care, office work, education, and mechanical repair, but "these new jobs were out of reach for most of the folks who worked or hoped to work at places like Levi's." [88] Project Quest created a new "workforce development intermediary" to package resources from a wide variety of sources and institutions. It pressured elected politicians to provide more than $6 million in local, state, and federal funds. Local businesses, particularly large firms, helped Project Quest identify occupations and sectors with growth potential and career ladders and helped design the training curricula. Between its inception in 1993 and the end of 1995, Project Quest enrolled more than 800 trainees in a "comprehensive, expensive package of supports, including child care, transportation assistance, medical care, tutoring, modest cash assistance for incidentals, and tuition to community colleges." [89] Programs such as Project Quest that make connections between the limited social networks of the inner-city poor and dynamic centers of growth in the regional economy are promising.[90] Economic segregation and suburban sprawl, however, place huge obstacles in the way of successful implementation.

So far, these experiments have produced modest but promising results. Several lessons can be drawn from them. First, they have been tried only on a pilot basis. Substantial additional investments will have to be made to bring them to full scale. It appears that with sufficient counseling of tenants and careful handling of landlords and suburban communities, the central-city poor can find better suburban housing opportunities without bringing on the social calamities and political opposition that defenders of suburban exclusion predict. It appears, therefore, that deconcentrating the central-city poor is feasible at a reasonable cost and will produce desirable results. Second, it is unlikely that physical juxtaposition or spatial mobility alone will dramatically improve the access of the urban poor to suburban job opportunities. Instead, the central-city poor require not only better skills (both "soft" and "hard") but also incorporation into networks of contact, reciprocity, and support with potential employers. In short, new labor market intermediaries may be needed. Finally, it is clear that the vast bulk of social programs are administered in a way that hinders them from functioning on a regional basis. That is, programs for subsidized housing, education, job training, and the like are typically administered by units of central-city governments that operate within those restricted jurisdictions. Even if they have the authority to operate outside central-city boundaries (as in the case of county public housing authorities), they generally do not. Suburban jurisdictions simply, unobtrusively, opt out. For such programs to take a regional approach to their work, they must be reorganized into a metropolitan-wide jurisdiction.

THE POLITICS OF REGIONALISM IN THE NEW MILLENNIUM

Historically, many forces have worked against a regional perspective in urban governance. Suburbs have been happy to benefit from being located in a large metropolitan area while excluding the less well-off and avoiding the payment of taxes to support services required by the urban poor. Central cities, for their part, have made a virtue of necessity by increasing spending on social services as a way of expanding the employment of central-city constituents. This spending has become an increasingly substantial part of municipal budgets and an important form of "new patronage" in city politics. As federal benefits have increasingly flowed to needy people, as opposed to needy places, it has helped to expand these functions. Legislators elected to represent areas where the minority poor are concentrated develop a stake in this state of affairs.

As we will see in chapter 8, this dynamic is gradually but steadily shifting. The first wave of inner, working-class suburbs has long since been built out, their populations have aged, and their residents' incomes have stagnated since the early 1970s. These suburbs have developed increasingly "urban" problems that they cannot solve on their own. Black and Hispanic central-city residents have increasingly moved to the suburbs. Although minority suburbs have significantly better conditions than inner-city minority neighborhoods, they still have higher rates of poverty and disadvantage than white suburbs and may face some of the same forces of decline that operate on inner cities. Even as metropolitan economic segregation has increased, metropolitan racial segregation has declined and suburban diversity has increased. As Orfield has pointed out, these inner suburbs are coming to realize that they share significant interests with their central cities. And as Juliet Gainsborough has shown, voters residing in more diverse suburbs are substantially more likely to vote like their urban neighbors.

The November 2000 vote in favor of consolidation between the city of Louisville and surrounding Jefferson County shows that elite consensus can be a powerful force in promoting regionalism. After previous defeats in 1982 and 1983, the proposal was backed by the current mayor and county executive, former Louisville mayor Jerry Abraham, the business community, and the local newspaper. The main opposition came from the local chapter of the NAACP, the gay community, and city and county legislators (whose offices would be abolished in favor of a twenty-six-seat county assembly); all worried that the new form of government would dilute gains they had made in the city of Louisville. A group of African American professionals and the local black newspaper, however, argued in favor of consolidation. The final vote was 54 percent in favor, 46 percent opposed. Part of the appeal was to position Louisville more favorably in its competition with Lexington, which was about to overtake it in size.[91] The Louisville case will be an interesting experiment in how the various forces favoring regionalism will play out.

It has thus become clear that many powerful players, including corporations, foundations, unions, political leaders, and community organizations, think that regional collaboration offers the surest route to competitive advantage in the new global economy. Regions divided against themselves are least likely to be able to undertake the necessary investments in physical, human, and social capital. Emerging metropolitan governance institutions should carry out functions that make the most sense from economic, environmental, and equity viewpoints. These include regional capital investments, transportation, land-use planning, economic development, job training, education, and tax-base sharing. This form of cooperation can generate more widely distributed benefits if they follow a high-productivity, high-wage "high road" instead of engaging in a "race to the bottom" that competes for low-wage, low-value-added jobs in highly mobile industries.

To be truly effective, metropolitan cooperation must develop a broad, democratic base and the organizational capacity to articulate the common good, not merely to sum up the aims of the individual parts of the metropolis. Cooperation of the region's constituent elements must be secured through consent, not through unwanted mandates imposed on resistant local jurisdictions. To achieve this consent, the new regional form must provide tangible benefits to its constituent jurisdictions, and its actions cannot be subject to the veto of an exclusive "favored quarter."

Metropolicies for the Twenty-first Century

The arguments we have made about place in this book are frequently attacked by critics from both the Left and the Right. Many of these positions have taken the form of "conventional wisdom," ideas so familiar that no one questions them anymore. Because these critics dominate the mass media and most policy discussions, we need to demonstrate why these views are wrong. Subjecting the conventional wisdom on place to rigorous debate, we believe, exposes its unexamined assumptions and questionable values. Throughout the book we have attempted to state our opponents' arguments in their strongest form before developing our own arguments. At this point, it is useful to sum up the views of our critics and how we have attempted to rebut them.

"Free markets are the answer."[1] Many people agree with us that place matters, but they think that its effects stem from the operations of the free market. According to this view, some places succeed in attracting jobs and investment because they do a better job of offering investors what they want. They are more efficient places for production. Free markets ensure that every parcel of land is utilized for its "highest and best use," resulting in "the greatest good for the greatest number." Free marketers argue that if governments interfere, they only mess up the fairness and efficiency of markets. They go so far as to say that local governments should be run according to free-market principles. Local government fragmentation creates a marketplace of governments in which mobile citizen-consumers can choose which bundle of taxes and services they prefer by moving into that jurisdiction. Competition between local governments ensures that the local public sector will respond to consumer preferences.

According to free-market theory, where one lives may make a big difference in the quality of one's life, but where one lives reflects market success—it does not cause it. Good neighborhoods with low crime rates and good schools are more expensive. If you work hard, get a good job, and save, then you will be able to afford a house in a good neighborhood. If you don't, you won't. Place does not determine economic success; economic success determines place.

Our rejoinder. Throughout the book we have argued that the effects of place are not just reflections of free-market exchanges. To use the language of social science, place is an independent variable. Place has power. In chapter 3 we documented the contextual effects of place, and in chapter 4 we argued that they are not just the result of free markets. The United States has never had a free market in land. Land markets are highly regulated and highly influenced by federal and state policies and local political arrangements that tilt the playing field in favor of sprawl and economic segregation. The rules of this game prevent central cities and inner-ring suburbs from solving their problems themselves (chapter 5). Local governments cannot give citizens what they want because they must compete for taxable investment. It is impossible for cities and even whole regions (chapter 6) to reverse economic segregation and sprawl unless state and federal governments change the rules of metropolitan governance.

"A 'culture of poverty' causes the problem."[2] For many advocates of the free market, free markets in housing not only are efficient and responsive but also reinforce moral order. Certain moral or cultural values, such as the Protestant work ethic and family values, undergird economic success. People who possess these values succeed in job markets and congregate in more expensive neighborhoods. Their choices reflect cultural affinities as well as individual preferences. Families lacking these values generally cannot afford to rent or buy houses in such neighborhoods. The market thus protects good neighborhoods from disruptions in their cultural consensus. Disadvantaged neighborhoods suffer not because of their structural position but because the values of their residents deviate from middle-class norms. Unable to defer gratification in order to save, learn, work, and invest, the residents of disadvantaged neighborhoods live only for the moment. Those who do work hard, save, and invest are able to leave these neighborhoods. If government helps people from bad neighborhoods move into good neighborhoods, it will upset the present moral order, spreading the culture of poverty and making good neighborhoods bad.

Our rejoinder. The organization of space does not represent an underlying moral order. On the contrary, it represents a violation of core American values of equal opportunity and democratic governance. As we noted in chapter 3, most residents of so-called bad neighborhoods are hardworking and law-abiding citizens, preyed upon by a few of their neighbors who engage in anti-social behaviors such as crime and drug use. We do not propose to expand the housing choices of able-bodied people who refuse to work, use illegal drugs, or break the law. The vast majority of lower-income people who live in central cities and inner-ring suburbs hold to mainstream values but are held back by structural disadvantages, including the disadvantages of place. People with lower incomes do not have bad values, nor do rich people necessarily have good values. The culture of poverty argument is a red herring that distracts attention from the true sources of our problems.

"If the problem is poverty, the solution is jobs." [3] Moving people around is nonsense, because the fundamental causes of inequality are economic. Economic restructuring has meant a loss of well-paying industrial jobs and the rise of a service economy with a dual wage structure (high- and low-wage jobs). People in disadvantaged neighborhoods lack the education to qualify for high-wage jobs. The solution is to help people wherever they live by stimulating full employment through macroeconomic policies, investing more in education and job training, and increasing income supports such as the minimum wage and the earned income tax credit.

Our rejoinder. We support government policies to reduce economic inequality and enhance life chances for the poor, wherever they live. Raising the quality of life for the poor through stronger social welfare policies, like those of Canada and Western Europe, would reduce people's fear of the poor and make economic integration easier. But inequality is not just a matter of incomes but of people's unequal abilities to function effectively in American society. Place-based inequalities remain a key source of the problem. Broad social policies do not address the spatial basis of social, economic, and political inequality. As we noted at the end of chapter 2, economic segregation varies tremendously across advanced economies, suggesting that national policies and institutional practices, not the level of economic development, have the most bearing on it. The United States has significantly narrowed the educational gaps between different groups in society over the past thirty years, and the economy is now performing better than it has in many decades; yet many places in the United States are still being left behind. Place-based inequalities, we argue, make it more difficult for society to recognize and deal with inequalities of all kinds. Addressing place-based inequalities will not solve the problem of inequality on its own, but it is a crucial component of any solution.

"If the problem is poverty, the answer is community development where people live." [4] The predominant view among social policy analysts, practitioners, and philanthropists is that neighborhood disadvantage should be solved through neighborhood economic development. This approach brings jobs to people, rather than people to jobs. One method is enterprise zones: reduce taxes and regulatory burdens, and markets will flourish in disadvantaged neighborhoods. Another approach is community development corporations (CDCs), which are touted as expressions of American grassroots democracy with the best ability to identify the needs of neighborhoods. Bringing together the public, private, and nonprofit sectors into neighborhood partnerships, CDCs can revitalize the worst neighborhoods and make them attractive places to live again.

Our rejoinder. The problems of low-income neighborhoods are not caused by too much regulation or too few government programs. Enterprise zones provide inequitable and inefficient subsidies that, for the most part, simply move economic activities from one place to another. CDCs do great work, but the evidence shows that they cannot revitalize neighborhoods by themselves. The reason is simple: the main source of the problem lies outside the neighborhood, within broader regional dynamics. Until the regional dynamics that continually pull higher-income households and jobs out of the central cities and toward the urban fringe are dealt with, CDCs will be struggling to go up the down escalator. Regional issues must be addressed at the same time.

"The real issue is race, not class or place." [5] Talk about economic segregation distracts attention from the most important issue: racial discrimination and segregation. Even though the law forbids racial discrimination in housing, the level of racial segregation has not improved much in American metropolitan areas. Economic segregation is caused, in large part, by racial discrimination. Because blacks tend to be poorer than whites (because of historical discrimination), when blacks are restricted in their housing choices, the result is economic segregation. The white poor are far less segregated from middle-class society than are the black and Hispanic poor. Since racism is the primary obstacle to more economically integrated metropolitan areas, enforcing laws against discrimination is the answer.

Our rejoinder. Racial segregation is clearly an important issue and an important cause of place-based inequality. Nevertheless, as we argued in chapter 2, there is an important class dimension to the problem that transcends its important racial aspect. We must therefore focus directly on economic segregation as well as on combating racial discrimination. Racial segregation is declining slowly, but economic segregation is increasing rapidly. Racial discrimination is illegal, but the courts have upheld the right of local governments to discriminate on the basis of income (poverty is not a constitutionally protected "suspect classification"). Indeed, economic segregation has become a crucial prop for racial segregation. Racial segregation is a problem not so much because it forces blacks to live with other blacks, but because it forces them to live in disadvantaged, concentrated poverty neighborhoods. Although we freely admit that reducing place-based inequalities will not make racism go away, it will undermine one of the pillars of black economic deprivation.

WHERE DO WE GO FROM HERE?

If you accept our argument that place—specifically, the way metropolitan areas are organized—has independent negative effects not just on the inner-city poor but on whole regions, the next question is obvious: what can we do about it? The answer is not easy.

Metropolitan sprawl remains out of control in the United States. Our metropolitan areas are much more spread out than necessary to serve population growth, income growth, and housing needs.[6] In the absence of comprehensive land-use planning, metropolitan political fragmentation has encouraged suburban sprawl and economic segregation. Housing developers, businesses, upper-middle-class families, and some local politicians have a short-term stake in maintaining this system. They can benefit from regional advantages while escaping regional costs. Meanwhile, the older, lower-quality, lower-cost public housing of the central cities makes them repositories of the poor, a position increasingly shared by older inner suburbs. Suburban sprawl and concentrated urban poverty are thus two sides of a single metropolitan dynamic. It provides many residents with a range of choices, but it also imposes increasing costs on many, perhaps most, participants.

This arrangement has been marked by a downward spiral in urban influence. As middle-class families grew less likely to live in cities, cities became more politically isolated and less able to win support in state legislatures or Congress. Even those with sizable middle-class populations and strong economies faced growing conflict over whether they could afford to spend more on services to the poor, as well as growing skepticism about whether these services in fact reduced poverty. Increasingly, they came to feel that they might disadvantage themselves by trying to swim alone against national tides.

We have shown that this is not a "natural" phenomenon: federal, state, and local political institutions and policy have actively promoted these outcomes during the twentieth century. Now, as we begin the twenty-first century, new approaches to public policy must play a central role in addressing these problems. We cannot, of course, turn back the clock. The United States is a suburban nation with a car-centered culture, but we can begin to address the problems that plague urbanites and suburbanites alike. Fortunately, a growing number of Americans are recognizing the perils of economic segregation, concentrated poverty, and metropolitan sprawl. The rise of poverty in inner-ring suburbs has made them more sympathetic to the situation of the central cities. Many suburbanites are angry about having less time for their families or leisure because they spend more time gridlocked on their way to work or even while running household errands. New "leapfrog" development consumes the countryside, lowering the quality of life for exurban residents.

We have also seen that other advanced industrial countries, including Canada, do far better than the United States on many of these issues. Their large cities also experience spatial segregation and social exclusion, but not nearly to the extent typical in the United States.[7] They have lower levels of class and racial segregation and more compact metropolitan development. They have narrower gaps between the rich and poor and lower overall levels of poverty, including much lower levels of child poverty. They have fewer slums and much less urban crime. Urban residents have better access to health insurance and child care, regardless of income.[8] The Netherlands made the reduction of spatial segregation and the promotion of regional integration a central part of its economic adjustment policies in the 1990s.[9]

Cities in the United States have difficulty following the European path because they are trapped in an "iron cage" of jurisdictional competition. Especially in light of the way federal policies favor suburbs over cities, elected officials in central cities and inner suburbs simply cannot redistribute income from the well-off to the poor or provide adequate public services within their jurisdictions without triggering a series of difficulties.

Only cities with strong economic advantages and large, politically well-organized social service establishments, of which New York City is the paradigm, have attempted substantial local efforts at redistributing resources. Even in these cities, most of this redistribution flows to service providers, not the poor. Although such efforts produced some tangible, positive results, they also subjected these cities to chronic fiscal strain and often ended up tethering the poor to concentrated poverty neighborhoods. As a result, even cities with the most economic advantages cannot solve the problem of concentrated urban poverty. Indeed, their efforts to do so risk provoking the flight of those with assets and income subject to local taxation.

This is an uncomfortable conclusion for urban liberals and progressives.

When Jay Forrester asserted, in his 1969 book *Urban Dynamics,* that helping the poor would only undermine urban economic growth, urban liberals and progressives countered that cities could and should provide subsidized housing, income transfers, social services, public hospitals and health clinics, and economic opportunity to needy residents. To do otherwise, they reasoned, would not only be heartless and inhumane but would renege on the cities' historic promise to help lower-income residents achieve upward mobility. When Forrester's argument was reclothed in more liberal terms, as in the 1980 report *Urban American in the Eighties,* urban liberals and progressives countered that cities *could* fight poverty on their own.[10]

Notwithstanding the fact that cities enjoyed greater economic leverage three decades ago than they do now, the evidence is now in. Absent national policies to constrain local fiscal competition and to narrow differences in local fiscal capacity, central cities that engage in local income redistribution put their economic position at risk. The parameters of this risk are not known, because the mobility of people and businesses is not everywhere the same, but the mere perception that large local public sectors and tax burdens contribute to economic deterioration in big cities makes such policies harder to sustain.

This does not mean that we should stop trying to reduce the concentration of the poor. Besides being morally imperative, it will bolster the future of American democracy. Metropolitan polarization is more than a troubling statistical trend. It violates basic American values. The spatial and political isolation of the central-city and inner-suburban poor prevents them from forging the cross-class coalitions necessary to make their influence felt and makes blatant class legislation against the poor more likely. It threatens to dissolve the bonds of solidarity that join us as Americans. As a former president of the Federal Reserve Bank of New York observed, it forces us to ask "whether we will be able to go forward together as a unified society with a confident outlook or as a society of diverse economic groups suspicious of both the future and each other."[11] Indeed, Henry Richmond argues that the political fragmentation of metropolitan areas represents "the most important community-building challenge to face America since the adoption of the Constitution."[12]

Acting alone, cities or even metropolitan areas can make only limited progress on reducing and deconcentrating poverty. In the long run, only the nation as a whole can limit, and ultimately reverse, the factors that created the current situation. It remains a sound article of faith among public finance economists that income redistribution should be left to the federal government. Since wealthy individuals subject to taxation can usually quit any local jurisdiction that engages in redistribution, only the federal government can prevent flight from obligation. (Even this scale may not be wide enough. Many observers fear that the current global economic system encourages capital to flow from more egalitarian, social democratic nations to more unequal, neoliberal nations.)

In thinking about what new policies must be adopted, we can draw on the considerable efforts made by thoughtful observers to determine the measures that are needed to deconcentrate urban poverty, diminish urban sprawl, and promote regional cooperation. These observers have called for breaking up existing concentrations of urban poverty; creating new metropolitan forms of tax sharing, land-use regulation, and cooperation; and reforming the underlying mechanisms that promote concentrated poverty and suburban sprawl.[13] Such goals require action at the national, state, regional, and local levels.

We urgently need a federal *metropolitan policy agenda* that will improve economic, social, and environmental conditions in our urban areas and can marshal sufficient political support from voters in a majority of congressional districts. We recognize that this is not an easy task. Place-oriented policies alone will not improve the lives of a majority of Americans. The United States also needs to deal with its widening overall economic divide and the persistence of high rates of poverty. This will require national policies to achieve full employment and to provide social insurance against ill health, market failures, and business cycle swings. These, in turn, will require reducing the influence of money in American politics and increasing the power of mobilized people in our political system. We recognize, however, that our political culture does not favor a large, intrusive central government. Moreover, national policies adopted to moderate our national trend toward greater income inequality will not, on their own, be sufficient to end metropolitan fragmentation and concentrated urban poverty.

Specific new steps are needed to redress the spatial dimensions of severe income inequality. To do so, we must overcome what Harold Wolman called "an ominous lack of consensus [about] how to create a viable political strategy to persuade the majority of Americans who are not poor and do not reside in cities to respond to the needs of these areas."[14] Here, we outline a metropolitan policy agenda to address the place-oriented problems discussed in this book. The next chapter addresses the political dimensions of this agenda, suggesting the kind of political appeals that could knit together a majority coalition in support of metropolitan reform.

LEVEL THE METROPOLITAN PLAYING FIELD

Federal policy makers must reverse those policies that exacerbate the economic gaps between and within metropolitan areas. As we showed in chapter 2, inequality across and within the metropolitan regions of the country has grown since the 1970s. Entire metropolitan areas have lagged far behind, even during periods of national economic prosperity. Since effective metropolitan cooperation depends partly on regional wealth, tax-base sharing alone will not help poor metropolitan areas, for example, achieve the level of per student school spending typical of more wealthy metropolitan areas.

The disparities among metropolitan regions do not stem entirely from natural advantages. In the past, federal policies have both widened and narrowed such regional differences. The Tennessee Valley Authority, rural electrification, and the creation of national parks improved economic conditions in poor rural areas. Since World War II, military spending has advanced the economic well-being of southern California and Seattle while drawing resources out of the industrial Northeast and Midwest.[15] Given the variation across regions and the uneven impact of federal policies, Washington should distribute federal resources in ways that provide more help to less well-off regions.

The wide economic disparities *within* metropolitan areas, however, are far more pressing. As we showed in chapter 4, they are clearly influenced by the myriad federal and state policies that promote economic and racial segregation, encourage better-off people and businesses to depart the central cities for the suburbs, and tie the poor to the central cities. A first step in strengthening the capacity of metropolitan areas to address such problems would be to remove the perverse incentives that currently promote spatial inequality.[16] In short, we need to level the metropolitan playing field.

The federal government can take many steps to foster balance and promote cooperation within and across our metropolitan regions. Although we have noted that competition among local jurisdictions produces some real benefits, more balanced competition achieved through a new regionalism would *increase* the ability of local jurisdictions to realize their goals. As conservative urbanist Peter Salins has written:

> Federal, state, and local politics should focus on creating a level metropolitan playing field. No longer should the well-being and service capabilities of metropolitan localities, central city or suburban, be hostage to their economic, social, or demographic profiles, nor should they be harmed by the beggar-thy-neighbor scramble of their sister municipalities for regional economic advantage.[17]

Limit Bidding Wars

The federal government should repeal features of the tax code that work against cities and in favor of suburbanization, enact new provisions to dampen interjurisdictional competition, and pay more attention to equalizing its outlays within and across metropolitan regions. In particular, the federal government should prevent localities from using tax abatements and other incentives in "bidding wars" for private investment. Such incentives are extremely inefficient and damaging.[18] One option, embodied in a bill (H.R. 1060) introduced in Congress in 1999 by David Minge of Minnesota, would impose a heavy tax on local economic development subsidies and remove the tax exemption of local development bonds.[19] This "Distorting Subsidies Limitation Act" deserves passage. (Although some forms of federal assistance to localities, such as the Community Development Block Grant [CDBG] program, have antipiracy provisions, a general ban of the sort proposed by Martin Meehan of Massachusetts in 1995, in H.R. 1842, should also be passed.) If the federal government can use its muscle to get states to raise the blood alcohol level for drunken driving from 0.08 to 0.10, it should also be able to dampen other state practices that promote destructive forms of local economic competition. Here again, the European Union is far ahead of the United States in requiring local governments to disclose substantial local subsidies and gain EU approval for them.[20]

The federal government should also substantially reform the preferential home mortgage deduction on the personal income tax. As we noted, this deduction promotes sprawl and the exodus of better-off families from central cities and inner suburbs.[21] It should be capped at a fairly high level, with any resulting new revenue devoted to expanding federal housing and home ownership subsidies for families of modest means, such as a progressive tax credit to help working families purchase homes.

The federal government should also encourage jurisdictions in metropolitan areas to participate in regional tax-base sharing, as Myron Orfield has advocated. It makes no sense for a few suburbs to gain the tax benefits of a new shopping mall, amusement park, office complex, or other development while their neighbors have to live with additional traffic and air pollution. Some metropolitan areas have agreed to tax themselves to support regional sports stadiums, airports, or other facilities because the whole region clearly benefits. Only a handful have broad tax-sharing plans that distribute portions of increased property tax revenues created by new business development throughout the entire metropolitan area.[22] Instituting metropolitan-wide tax-base sharing would not only limit inefficient bidding wars but would also create the potential for more equitable distribution of tax revenues, especially for public schools.

Implement Programs on a Metropolitan Basis

The federal government should restructure all its domestic programs so that they are carried out on a metropolitan basis. Housing markets, labor markets, transportation systems, and the interorganizational networks of modern production all operate at a regional scale. This should be (but is not) the natural unit for domestic social and economic development policies.

Federally funded programs that ought to be administered on a metropolitan basis include housing (particularly the Section 8 program), workforce development (training and job placement), welfare (job search for employable recipients), and transportation and other infrastructure investments (regulating development on the urban fringe and creating a cohesive regional transportation system). The fragmented administration of these programs currently constitutes a major obstacle to mobility out of inner-city poverty neighborhoods. Local governments administer HUD funds, local and regional Private Industry Councils (now called Workforce Investment Boards [WIBs]) allocate federal job training programs, and county social service agencies carry out welfare programs.[23] There is hardly any coordination among these agencies, although some WIBs work with regional social service agencies to administer the new welfare-to-work program.

For example, some 3,400 local housing agencies administer HUD's public housing and Section 8 housing vouchers and certificates, while separate local housing or community development departments administer the CDBG and Home Investment Partnership (HOME) programs.[24] This makes it difficult to promote "mobility" across city lines or to get suburbs to develop their fair share of low-income housing. At a minimum, all HUD programs should be administered by regional agencies. All local jurisdictions should be required to permit a minimum level of low-income housing, but these should not be built as 100 percent low-income developments. Rather, HUD should support only mixed-income housing developments, with no more than one-quarter or one-third of the units (for sale or for rent) targeted to low-income families. It should require suburban jurisdictions to approve the development of market-rate rental housing as well and should make some of those units available to low- and moderate-income families with Section 8 vouchers. The Section 8 vouchers should be easily portable within (and across) metropolitan areas. Shifting federal housing subsidies from specific units toward eligible families is sound, but federal, state, and local policy makers need to pay more attention to expanding the range of choices that these families can make.[25] Moreover, Congress should expand the Section 8 voucher program to reach all eligible families.[26] (Currently only one-quarter of eligible low-income households receive any federal housing assistance.) Finally, new federal legislation should ensure that federal housing programs are coordinated with federal welfare, job training, and transportation programs on a regional basis. For example, we should build more low- and moderate-income housing where entry-level jobs are growing.

Federal guidelines now require that federal transportation funds be administered by regional agencies, with planning and allocation by metropolitan planning organizations. Recent federal legislation also requires regional agencies to consider all transportation options (not just highways) and to consider the links between traffic congestion, air pollution, and urban sprawl. Under these laws (ISTEA and the Transportation Equity Act for the Twenty-first Century [TEA-21]), "if a suburban community wants to build a new highway interchange to alleviate congestion, before proceeding, it must demonstrate that the interchange will not increase traffic and worsen air quality." [27]

Because these provisions affect only transportation funds, regional transportation planning agencies are limited in their ability to carry out this directive. Some regional agencies are single-purpose transportation organizations; others are multipurpose organizations. The latter have been innovative and flexible in linking transportation funding with other initiatives, such as the federal government's "reverse commuting" Bridges to Work program, so that residents of high-poverty neighborhoods can find jobs in outlying areas. [28] Similarly, the Clean Air Act of 1990 requires regional agencies to determine whether metropolitan areas meet federal air pollution standards. In many areas, different regional bodies implement the Clean Air Act and TEA-21. These responsibilities should be combined.

In short, the federal government should require the planning, resource allocation, reporting, and evaluation functions of all federal domestic grant programs to be undertaken on a metropolitan basis. It should condition the provision of both direct funding and indirect assistance (such as FHA insurance) on regions' adopting a fair-share approach to housing (in the form of mixed-income developments or acceptance of housing vouchers), sharing the regional tax base, and balancing spending on different transportation modes, not just on new road-building projects that promote sprawl. [29]

Promote Metropolitan Cooperation and Governance

Metropolitan regions generally lack the institutional framework to carry out these functions. Federal policy should therefore help them create the necessary governance infrastructure. This infrastructure would help metropolitan regions work in a cooperative manner while leaving plenty of space for local jurisdictions to remain innovative and responsive and to debate and decide how best to utilize federal and local resources. This effort should build on the experiences of Portland, Oregon, and the Twin Cities described in chapter 6. They exemplify how strong regional land-use planning can promote a more livable metropolitan environment and how regional tax sharing can spread the benefits of suburban growth.

By helping metropolitan regions build an institutional base that empowers localities to join in defining mutual problems, debating how to solve them, and crafting coalitions to implement these solutions, the federal government can, over the long haul, have a major impact on the perverse dynamics we have outlined. During the Clinton administration, senior officials at the Office of Management and Budget and a working group involving many different departments crafted proposals to set aside funds from federal grant programs for a bonus pool that would reward regions that fashioned new metropolitan solutions to urban problems.[30] Although such a fund would be a good beginning, it is far too modest. The federal government should take the initiative by crafting model legislation for metropolitan councils, requiring that federal domestic programs be administered under their aegis and providing matching funds for modestly sized regional support staffs.

The ad hoc metropolitan bodies now carrying out specific functions within metropolitan areas are not a good starting point. They have not led to broad-based regional cooperation, much less to a regional focus on the problem of concentrated urban poverty. They are typically undemocratic, with each jurisdiction, regardless of population, having one seat on their boards. Others include a corporatist mix of government and business leaders, with little involvement of unions or community groups.[31] To encourage a vital metropolitan voice to emerge, to enable individual jurisdictions to understand what they have in common with others, and to fairly represent each part of the metropolis, the nation must create a new level of political deliberation. Note that this is not the same as creating a new level of government, for the new regional bodies could still deliver many services through existing city and county arrangements.

Portland's Metro is the only democratically elected, multifunction regional body in the United States. Its citizens seem quite happy with how it is performing, with the main complaint being that development controls may have driven up housing costs.[32] The federal government should help other regions replicate this experience. Metropolitan council members should be elected from single districts, balancing the desire to represent all parts of the metropolis with the need for a manageably sized council. Different-sized metropolitan areas would have to make this trade-off in different ways. The recent consolidation of Louisville and Jefferson County in Kentucky created a new council with twenty-six seats, each representing about 25,000 voters. In this way, both central-city neighborhoods and unincorporated areas outside the city achieved representation. In the New York and Los Angeles consolidated metropolitan areas, with populations approaching 18 million and 16 million, respectively, districts would have to be far larger, perhaps 250,000 inhabitants, to preserve this balance.

Historically, the federal government has had an enormous impact on the evolution of state and local governmental institutions and practices. Most existing regional councils of government were created in response to Section 701 of the Housing Act of 1954, which provided federal aid for them.[33] During the Great Society programs of the 1960s, the federal government stimulated the creation of CDCs and new patterns of neighborhood participation. Long after its demise, localities continue to embrace citizen participation, CDCs, and decentralized program administration. Title 23, Section 134 of the U.S. Code, which established metropolitan planning organizations for transportation under TEA-21, shows that the federal government can stimulate the creation of new regional institutions.[34] The federal government should amend this legislation to cover other federal domestic programs, including economic development, housing, public assistance, and workforce development programs.

In addition to overseeing federal domestic programs, many of which local governments would still carry out on a day-to-day basis, metropolitan councils should be charged with identifying regional problems, debating alternative solutions, and advocating desired solutions to local and state officials. In this way, they would create new regional identities and enable parts of metropolitan regions to coalesce in new ways. In particular, they would foster coalitions among central cities and inner suburbs and between regional elites (who understand the importance of regional platforms in the global economy) and the working population of the region.

LINK COMMUNITY DEVELOPMENT TO THE REGIONAL ECONOMY

Over the last three decades, the hard truth is that neither central-city government programs nor nonprofit neighborhood-based interventions have prevented the emergence of concentrated poverty neighborhoods or substantially improved the life conditions of their residents.[35] Cities with a shrinking job base, such as Detroit, Camden, or St. Louis, face the most difficulty in lifting people up where they live.[36] Such people would be more likely to find jobs and be able to send their children to decent schools if they lived in the suburbs or moved to another metropolitan area. Harsh as it may sound, it would best serve them (and the nonpoor residents of such declining cities) to help them move to places with more opportunities.

Even though neighborhood revitalization efforts have yielded only limited results, cities should continue to support them. Overall urban vitality depends on healthy neighborhoods that attract people who have choices about where to live. Neighborhood revitalization encourages a common purpose among residents from different racial, cultural, and economic backgrounds. This bond encourages them to invest in their surroundings rather than flee or retreat into individual coping strategies. Healthy neighborhoods provide access to employment, attractive retail services, parks, playgrounds, and other amenities, as well as decent, affordable housing. Washington can help promote such neighborhoods by replacing the current top-down, functionally fragmented urban service delivery system with more holistic neighborhood- and family-based approaches that will build a sense of common purpose.

Various community-based organizations seek to lift low-income people out of poverty by helping them get decent-paying jobs, but it does not really matter if those jobs are located within the neighborhood. Instead, people should be helped to learn about good jobs, wherever they are, and to develop the skills and get access to the transportation necessary to obtain them. If they continue to live in the neighborhood, their higher incomes will contribute to neighborhood vitality. If they move, it will probably be to make life easier and better. As well as promoting mobility of the poor out of concentrated poverty neighborhoods, central-city development officials should seek to attract working families back into poor neighborhoods, thereby diversifying them.[37] The added clout that these working families exert on behalf of neighborhood schools and services will benefit the remaining poor. Building affordable housing, investing in housing rehabilitation, improving local schools, and providing local amenities all work toward this end.

The problem, of course, is that such strategies have had uneven results among neighborhoods. They work best in neighborhoods that already have the most going for them. They work least well in the poorest, most socially disorganized areas, whose better-off residents may be drawn to more attractive neighborhoods nearby. As a result, the current round of "comprehensive community development initiatives" is unlikely to alter the prevailing spatial concentration of the poor unless they can link the poor to wider opportunities in the regional economy.[38] The same can be said for "empowerment zones," which shift some jobs to places where poor people live instead of improving their access to job opportunities throughout the metropolitan area. However valid within their own terms, such efforts will have little impact on the matrix of forces that promote concentrated urban poverty. Much the same can be said about the other federal community development programs operating through community-based organizations and public-private partnerships.

If the overall planning, resource allocation, and program objectives are determined on a regional basis, the perspective of local community-based partners might change in a fundamental way. The community development movement has spent thirty years developing alliances and partnerships with the political and business actors who can provide the necessary resources. They have forged links with institutions outside poor neighborhoods, even outside the city limits. Some CDCs have established networks (or business alliances) with employers and community colleges at the regional level. Community developers that focus only on the neighborhood level risk becoming, in Jeremy Nowak's words, "managers of decline." In the new institutional context, they would be encouraged to develop a regional perspective on housing, business development, job training, and transportation, thus maximizing the benefit to their constituents.[39]

STRENGTHEN PUBLIC SCHOOLS

If educational attainment is a key determinant of individual upward mobility, greater federal support is needed for improving the public primary, secondary, and postsecondary educational systems serving the urban poor and near poor. The decreasing impact of a person's parents' background and the increasing importance of educational attainment on a person's life chances led Daniel McMurrer and Isabel Sawhill to conclude that federal policy makers should make decent local schooling a federal entitlement independent of local fiscal capacity, set national standards for inner-city school performance, and expand funding for early childhood education.[40]

In the long run, promoting economic mobility for the poor means promoting far better educational outcomes than currently prevail, especially with respect to getting a college degree. The political isolation of central cities, the resegregation of their schools, and the poor quality of the schools in concentrated poverty neighborhoods have had devastating consequences for poor neighborhoods. Many urban schools are not doing as badly as some think, especially in light of the lack of funding and the difficult situations their students come from.[41] Even so, dropout rates remain persistently high, achievement levels persistently low, and conflict and alienation pervasive. As currently configured, urban school systems systematically reinforce initial disadvantage. The problems of urban school systems not only derive from concentrated urban poverty; they also contribute to it.

As Richard Rothstein notes, most public schools do a good job at educating young people.[42] But many schools with students from low-income families do not meet basic educational goals. Student performance clearly varies tremendously across metropolitan-area school districts. In general, more money (and higher family income) makes a big difference in educational outcomes in public schools.[43] For example, smaller class sizes (better teacher-student ratios) improve student performance.[44] Schools that are in physical disrepair or lack adequate books and equipment are also less likely to reach standard educational outcomes. Students with poorly trained or poorly paid teachers do not perform as well as those with well-trained and well-paid teachers.

Simply "equalizing" per student expenditures will not solve this problem. For one thing, much of the increase in public school spending in recent decades has gone toward students with physical and mental "special needs" or toward transportation, school meals, and other functions.[45] Comparisons of school district spending should focus on class size, teacher pay, books and equipment, and similar expenses. Because students from poor families come to school with more educational and psychological disadvantages, they need more than "equalized" spending on these items.[46] We need to spend *more* on the schools that teach poor students in order to provide them with a level educational playing field.

Metropolitan-wide tax-base sharing would help reduce the gap in school spending between poor and wealthy jurisdictions within the same urban area. But the wide disparities among metropolitan areas mean that geography still determines the kind of education students receive. The same holds true, to a lesser degree, with states. Legal action by parents in poorly funded central-city school districts has led to many efforts to equalize fiscal capacity for school spending within states and to break the link between the local tax base and local school expenditures. But even if every state equalized educational spending per student, students in Connecticut would still receive a far better education than those in Mississippi. This is an obvious area where the federal government can level the playing field, first by requiring states to equalize spending, and second by supplementing educational spending in those states with below-average fiscal capacities.

Breaking this vicious circle must be an urgent priority in the battle against concentrated poverty. Great controversy has swirled around local school reform, and radical measures are clearly in order. Creating metropolitan school districts, increasing the financial resources flowing into them, making individual schools more accountable to students and their parents, closing failing schools, giving parents more choice among public schools, and improving the connection between schooling and employment opportunities will all broaden political support for urban schools. Increasing parental involvement is also critical to revitalizing urban schools. The work of Industrial Areas Foundation in Texas in organizing parents to improve local schools and in pushing corporations to forge alliances with community groups to help the poor get access to jobs is a good example of the importance of grassroots mobilization.[47]

Gary Orfield has argued that the resegregation and political isolation of inner-city schools have materially contributed to their poor performance and that metropolitan school districts offer important benefits.[48] Creating metropolitan school districts would help the larger society restore its stake in improving inner-city schools. Ending balkanization and equalizing metropolitan school financing would also dramatically reduce the incentives for suburban jurisdictions to exclude the relatively less well-off.

Improving public primary and secondary education is only a first step. More young people from poor families must be helped to attend and graduate from college. The urban campuses of public state college and university systems will inevitably educate the vast majority of them. Over the last several decades, most states have shifted resources away from public higher education toward prison building and shifted the burden of financing college educations onto the families of college students. States provide less tuition assistance to poor and working-class families (who are more likely to attend community colleges and second-tier state universities) than to upper-middle-class students (who are more likely to attend the more expensive and prestigious state universities).[49] Parents who can afford higher tuition at public institutions should pay it. States should offset tuition increases with more financial aid to poor and working-class families and provide more core support for urban public higher education. Typically, they have failed to do either of these things. (With higher levels of funding for these institutions should come responsibility for higher levels of performance.) The public colleges and universities that educate central-city and inner-suburban residents should also seek to build new relationships with metropolitan labor markets. Political leaders of our metropolitan areas should rally local employers to hire the graduates of these institutions. In this way, and probably only in this way, can our cities provide upward mobility to the urban poor and grow their middle-class populations.

MAKE WORK PAY

Education alone is not enough to offset the basis of concentrated urban poverty. The educational level of low-wage workers has increased substantially in the last two decades. As Jared Bernstein noted, "we now have a more skilled (at least in terms of years of education) yet lower-paid low-wage worker."[50] Regardless of how much we improve our educational system, society's "dirty work" always needs to get done. As the labor market increasingly polarizes wages and salaries, many people who work full-time can barely make ends meet.[51] Most of them live in America's central cities and inner suburbs.

There are as many different views about how the federal government might reduce poverty as there are diagnoses of the problem. Some even dismiss the idea that poverty is a problem. When the *New York Times* ran a seven-part series on the downsizing of America in March 1996, conservative economists and commentators lauded the overall rate of job growth, praised American flexibility in laying off workers, and dismissed the lifetime job as "more nostalgic myth than historic reality."[52] One commentator even argued that Americans' expectation that they should enjoy continuous economic betterment was a dangerous illusion.[53]

We are sympathetic with those who say that we cannot fully redress the growing spatial concentration of poverty in America without making it into a more egalitarian, social democratic society. Those developed countries that have centralized wage setting, strong labor unions, and unitary welfare states (especially those that support working women) also have lower rates of poverty and inequality. The United States is at the wrong end of each of these scales. It has highly decentralized wage-setting mechanisms, weak and declining labor unions, a patchwork of labor regulation, and highly decentralized and variable social welfare policies.[54] We clearly need national legislation to address these problems. As we have already noted, however, efforts to achieve these ends face enormous opposition from politically entrenched forces.

In the absence of such measures, efforts to increase labor force participation and to make work pay, even low-wage work, are vital. Although national welfare reform has substantially cut the rolls, the states have not done enough to ensure that former welfare recipients find and hold decent jobs. Many have used their fiscal windfall from welfare reform for tax relief.[55] More emphasis needs to be placed on providing support for working mothers, matching them with decent jobs and ensuring that these jobs turn into careers, not just sources of poverty wages. Much progress has been made in the last decade by increasing the earned income tax credit (EITC) and the minimum wage, but much more needs to be done.

Further Expand the Earned Income Tax Credit

The EITC, begun in 1975, is a refundable tax credit that subsidizes low-wage workers, especially those with children, raising household income above the poverty line. It is tied to family income and household size, so it is clearly progressive. The maximum annual benefit is $3,888 for a family with two or more children and an income of $9,720 or less. It is phased out altogether at an annual income of $31,152. Even families that owe no federal income tax can receive a check from the IRS. President Clinton expanded the EITC, increasing benefit levels and expanding the number of eligible households. In 1997, 18.5 million persons claimed the EITC, costing the federal government $30.6 billion.[56] The EITC has definitely helped raise the incomes of the nation's poorest workers. In 1999, the EITC lifted 4.8 million people, including 2.6 million children, out of poverty.[57] Even though the average income of the bottom 40 percent of households fell by 3 percent before taxes between 1989 and 1999, after-tax income was unchanged, mostly because of the EITC.[58] The National Bureau of Economic Research found that the percentage of single mothers who worked jumped from 74 percent in 1992 to 87 percent in 1998 and concluded that the EITC had a greater effect on workforce participation than did changes in welfare law.[59]

There are several ways to make the EITC more effective. One is to expand outreach through labor unions, churches, and community-based organizations to increase the participation rate of eligible workers. The federal government could also require employers to inform employees about the EITC, as Illinois currently does.[60] Congress could increase the maximum credit by $500 or more for workers with large families and slow down the pace at which the EITC is phased out for families with two or more children. This would help millions of hard-pressed working families, most of whom live in central cities and inner suburbs.[61] The Economic Policy Institute recommends converting the dependent exemption into a child credit and combining it with the EITC into a "universal unified child credit," which would be available to most taxpayers with children, helping many working-class families.[62]

Raise the Minimum Wage Above the Poverty Level

About one-quarter of employees eligible for the EITC do not take it. Some friendly critics argue that the EITC subsidizes low-wage employers, perhaps lowering wage rates across the board.[63] Expanding the EITC should thus go hand in hand with raising the minimum wage, which helps the poorest workers and has an upward ripple effect on wages. The inflation-adjusted minimum wage declined substantially during the 1980s; its nominal value remained $3.35 an hour from 1981 until April 1990. Despite increases in 1991 and 1997, it is still worth 25 percent less than it was in 1978.[64]

In the 1960s and 1970s, the minimum wage (for a worker who worked full-time, year-round) was roughly equal to, and occasionally above, the federal poverty threshold. Today, a full-time worker earning the minimum wage earns $10,712, only three-quarters of the poverty level of $14,150 for a family of three.[65] (As noted, even this level does not guarantee that a family can meet basic necessities.)[66] This has prompted some states to enact their own higher minimum wages and more than thirty-five cities to enact "living wage" laws targeted to employees of firms with city contracts or subsidies.

Critics argue that the minimum wage primarily benefits teenagers (including those from wealthy families) who work part-time, as well as persons whose other family members make good incomes. In fact, the vast majority of minimum wage earners are adults; 40 percent are the sole breadwinners in their families. Most teenagers who earn the minimum wage are from low-income families. Others argue that raising the minimum wage will cause substantial job loss, but considerable evidence indicates that this is not so. States that have raised the minimum wage above the federal level have experienced no employment decline.[67]

Expand Health Insurance and Child Care

The United States is the only industrial country without universal health insurance. More than 42.6 million individuals, including 10 million children under age eighteen, lack health insurance. The number of Americans without health insurance increased by 4.5 million between 1993 and 1998; then declined slightly in 1999.[68] Those without health insurance are concentrated in urban areas, which helps explain their high rates of infant mortality and disease.

In recent years, some employers have cut health benefits for employees or their dependents; others require employees to pay more, which many low-wage employees cannot afford. The private-sector jobs created in the last decade are less likely to offer insurance.[69] Also, many parents and children who were pushed off welfare have lost their Medicaid coverage and cannot afford to replace it out-of-pocket, leaving them worse off. Many private health maintenance organizations are dropping elderly Medicare recipients as patients.[70] The decline of union membership from the 1970s to the mid-1990s also contributed to these trends, since workers with union contracts are more likely than others to have health insurance.

Minimally, the federal government should respond to this situation by assuming the cost of a basic health plan for children, even those who are covered by employers. This would immediately have a dramatic impact on the well-being of the poor and near poor, reduce their out-of-pocket spending for health care, and increase their income available for other basic necessities, especially housing. Extending Medicaid-like health insurance to all 10 million children under eighteen without insurance would cost about $12 billion.[71] Of course, publicly subsidized preventive health care saves money in the long run by reducing the need for costly crisis medical care.

Child care is also critical. Sixty-four percent of mothers with children under age six, and 78 percent of mothers with children ages six to thirteen, are in the labor force. As more women work, the shortage of affordable child care imposes a severe economic and emotional burden on American families. Other industrial nations provide child care as a basic right.[72] In the United States, it is a privilege for those who can afford it. Quality child care also should prepare children for school. A 1999 study found that low-income children who received comprehensive, quality early educational intervention score higher on cognitive, reading, and math tests than a comparison group of children who did not receive the intervention. Moreover, these effects persisted into their twenties. In the long term, each dollar invested in such quality programs saved over $7, because these children were more likely to attend college and be employed and less likely to be school dropouts, dependent on welfare, or arrested for criminal activity. Nationally, only one in ten eligible children now gets assistance because funds are so limited.[73]

Affordable child care should be available to all families. This should primarily be the federal government's responsibility. Barbara Bergmann recently designed a "Help for Working Parents" program that would provide $60 billion for child care and $30 billion for health insurance.[74] It would enable all parents working at the minimum wage to reach a "basic needs budget" and would drastically reduce the child poverty that has become epidemic in recent years.[75]

DECONCENTRATE POVERTY

These general measures to lift the standard of living for the urban poor will not, by themselves, significantly reduce the spatial concentration of the less well-off in our central cities. They will continue to be hampered by the negative "neighborhood effects" associated with living in high-poverty areas unless we attack the spatial dimension of the problem head-on. We must therefore adopt measures specifically aimed at deconcentrating urban poverty within metropolitan areas. Though hard to achieve, such policies are consistent with the American political tradition of decentralized federalism and are well within our reach. In place of the vicious circles that now operate, we must, as Margaret Weir has written, create "virtuous circles" in metropolitan America.[76]

Logically, there are only two ways to deconcentrate the urban poor. Either we must help the poor move out of concentrated poverty neighborhoods to more promising areas, or we must attract more opportunities and resources, and more economically diverse residents, into poor central-city neighborhoods. In practice, we must do both, since the two strategies work best together. The "people versus place" debate is a false dichotomy.

We have already discussed the importance of linking community development to the regional economy. Ironically, community development will also be aided by greater mobility. If families have greater choices, they will feel more loyalty to their neighborhoods and be more willing to engage in community-building activities. We approach the task of opening up the suburbs to poor and working people with a realistic understanding of its magnitude. Although certainly not simple, neither is it unmanageable. Alan Abramson and colleagues concluded that 5.7 million of the nation's 33.6 million poor persons in 1990, or about 1.4 million households, would have to move to new neighborhoods in the same metropolitan area to achieve an even distribution of the poverty population within the 100 largest metropolitan areas.[77] Over a ten-year period, that would involve only 140,000 households per year. Abramson also calculated how many poor people would have to move in each metropolitan area. In metropolitan Houston, for example, 156,523 poor persons (in an area with a population of 3.7 million), or about 39,130 households, would need to move to spread the poor evenly throughout the metropolitan area.[78] If we devoted ten years to this task (and assuming that those who left were not replaced by new poor people), only about 3,900 poor families a year would have to move to non-poor neighborhoods — certainly not a magnitude that would prove disruptive or administratively difficult.

A less dramatic approach would dismantle urban ghettos rather than spread the poor randomly throughout metropolitan areas. In 1990, 17.1 million poor persons lived in the nation's 100 largest metropolitan areas.[79] Less than one-quarter — only 3.9 million persons, or 1 million households — lived in neighborhoods with more than 40 percent poverty. Providing each of these families with a Section 8 voucher would cost $6 billion more a year.[80] Phasing in a program over ten years would involve about 100,000 families a year. If we enable, say, 60 percent to move to nonghetto areas, that would mean 60,000 families a year nationwide. This is a serious task, but hardly overwhelming either politically or fiscally. And if these poor families are moved closer to jobs, in a few years, many might no longer need housing assistance.

These goals cannot be achieved solely by local measures. Promoting this kind of mobility requires federal, state, and local policies to be harmonized in ways that help poor people relocate and assist them in getting and commuting to jobs in the suburbs, enforce fair housing regulations, and redistribute federal housing subsidies away from current areas of poverty concentration. Federal housing "mobility" programs such as Moving to Opportunity offer one model for achieving these ends. "Reverse commuting" programs, such as the federal Bridges to Work program, should also be expanded. More vigorous enforcement of antidiscrimination laws and continued implementation of affirmative action would also help promote this type of mobility. Finally, training programs run by community colleges based in the central cities should be better linked with their regional labor markets.[81] It is not enough simply to overlay a new set of mobility programs on top of the existing administrative structure for social programs. Providing low-income central-city residents with better information about and access to suburban opportunities will require workforce development and housing programs, among others, to be reorganized along metropolitan lines.

We recognize that there is likely to be political resistance to these mobility efforts. When HUD announced its pilot Moving to Opportunity (MTO) program in 1994, conservative politicians in Baltimore's working-class suburbs, fueled by right-wing radio talk-show hosts, raised the specter of masses of poor black families invading their neighborhoods. The truth is that the MTO rules prevented participating families from moving into the white working-class areas because the poverty rate was already too high there. Although the resulting clamor killed the program's expansion, it has proceeded quite successfully below the political radar screen in all five MTO pilot cities, including Los Angeles, New York, Chicago, and Boston. Like the Gautreaux program, MTO was invisible because it was small, tenants and potential landlords were both counseled, and no single suburban community got more than a few MTO families.[82]

We should recognize, however, that middle-class families resist having the poor live nearby because the income gap between them is much wider in the United States than in other advanced societies.[83] The poor in the United States are, relatively, much poorer than their counterparts in Canada and Western Europe and are thus more likely to be viewed by the middle class as "them" rather than "us." Helping to lift the poor closer to, or even slightly above, the poverty line would reduce this gap and make economic integration more acceptable and likely. That is why "making work pay" is central to our overall approach.

We do not discount the racial factors that lead middle-class whites to resist programs to deconcentrate poverty. Poor whites are much more likely to live in nonpoor neighborhoods than are poor blacks and Hispanics.[84] Of the 3.9 million poor individuals who live in high-poverty urban neighborhoods, 2.2 million are black, 1 million are Hispanic, and only 712,000 are white.[85] Many white (and even some black, Asian, and Latino) middle-class families fear that if "too many" people of color move into their communities, crime and other indicators of neighborhood deterioration will increase. People clearly believe that there is a "tipping point." But studies indicate that most middle-class whites would not feel uncomfortable if fewer than 15 percent of their neighbors were black.[86] Thus, efforts to deconcentrate poor families currently living in high-poverty neighborhoods—a majority of whom are black—must limit the proportion of the poor in any given neighborhood to avoid resegregation.

METROPOLITAN APPROACHES TO MOBILIZING CIVIC ENGAGEMENT

Many of the problems we have discussed stem from the imbalance of political power between well-off individuals and business, on the one hand, and the poor and the working class, on the other hand. This imbalance will not change unless we change our political rules to increase popular influence and access. Reforming our voting rights and labor laws will increase the voice of urban constituencies in national political life.

Voting Rights

The civil rights movement removed many barriers to political participation. The Voting Rights Act of 1965 eliminated the poll tax, literacy tests, and other arbitrary obstacles used to deny African Americans basic rights of citizenship. Its enforcement and expansion have been instrumental in increasing the number of black elected officials, particularly in the South.[87] But serious barriers to voting remain, particularly in the poor minority and immigrant neighborhoods of urban areas. Because the poor move more frequently than others, they must constantly reregister. Registration sites, such as city hall, are often inconvenient for individuals without an automobile or those who cannot take time off from work to register during business hours.[88]

The National Voter Registration Act of 1993 (often called the "motor voter" law) removed some of these barriers, but others remain. Laws that require voters to register far in advance of election day depress voter turnout, because many voters do not pay attention to campaigns until close to election day, "as media coverage, advertising, direct mail, and face-to-face electioneering reach their peak. The pace of registration quickens as the election approaches."[89] But since most states close registration a month before the election, many motivated voters are denied the opportunity to register.[90] Studies of presidential campaigns reveal that the closing date for registration has a major impact on the turnout rate.[91] Political analysts have also recommended adopting proportional representation to give marginalized voters a stronger voice.[92] Although some say that simply easing registration rules, without intensifying mobilization of voters by unions, community organizations, and other groups, would have little impact on voter turnout, a strong case can be made that same-day voter registration would increase turnout.[93]

Redistricting also has significant place-based consequences. As we note in the next chapter, the number of central-city congressional districts has declined significantly in recent decades. This is due not only to the suburbanization of the population but also to the way state legislatures and courts draw district boundaries. Since the 1965 Voting Rights Act, civil rights groups have adopted a political and legal strategy of pushing for congressional (as well as state legislative, city council, and school board) districts that will increase the odds of electing African Americans and Latinos to public office. As a result of their legal victories in the 1970s and 1980s, the number of black and Latino elected officials increased dramatically, due in great measure to the creation of more districts where African Americans and Latinos made up more than half of eligible voters. Although these districts have yielded more minority elected officials, they have also created relatively "safe" seats for minority candidates, which has engendered less political competition and therefore lower voter turnout. This undermines the chances of progressive candidates at the state and national levels, who rely on high turnout in low-income and minority areas. Carving out these safe minority districts also may have made other districts more white and middle class and therefore more likely to elect conservatives and Republicans. Lacking an urban constituency, these representatives have had little concern for urban problems. This undermines potential coalition building between urban and working-class suburban constituencies in Congress.[94]

A series of landmark U.S. Supreme Court decisions, beginning with *Shaw v. Reno* in 1993, nullified some of these majority minority districts on the grounds that they were so contorted as to represent an illegal form of racial segregation. Legislators were forced to redraw them, and in most cases, the districts continued to send African Americans to Congress, often with crossover support from white voters.

This experience suggests that in the future, urban progressives should seek to create congressional districts that straddle central cities and inner-ring suburbs, so that representatives have a stake in building bridges between poor and working-class constituents. Consider, for example, two adjacent congressional districts in California. The Thirteenth Congressional District comprises predominantly low-income neighborhoods in Los Angeles, where 60 percent of residents are Latino and 21 percent are Asian. It is among the safest Democratic seats in the country. The seat is held by a liberal Democrat, Xavier Becerra, who won in 1998 with 81 percent of the vote. Contiguous to the Thirteenth is the Twenty-seventh Congressional District, represented from 1996 to 2000 by the far-right Republican James Rogan. The district comprises the economically and racially diverse urbanized suburbs of Pasadena, Glendale, and Burbank and the more affluent suburbs of San Marino, La Canada, and La Crescenta. In 1998, Rogan was elected with only 51 percent of the vote in a suburban district in which registered Democrats have a slight edge. Rogan won because Democratic voters were less likely than Republicans to vote. In 2000, Rogan was defeated by moderate Democrat Adam Schiff. The Twenty-seventh Congressional District is still considered one of the most volatile "swing" districts in the country.

Since the 2000 census is likely to show a significant population increase in the neighborhoods of the Thirteenth Congressional District, urban progressives should push to shift some of Becerra's heavily Democratic precincts into the Twenty-seventh. Becerra's seat would still be safe, but the Twenty-seventh Congressional District would become an urban-suburban district with a higher proportion of low-income and Democratic voters, who, motivated by a more competitive race, would be more likely to turn out to vote, especially if mobilized by community and labor organizations.

Reform Labor Law

Union strength reached a peak of 35 percent in the mid-1950s, enabling blue-collar Americans to share in the postwar prosperity and join the middle class. Union pay scales even boosted the wages of nonunion workers. Unionized workers continue to have higher wages, better pensions, longer vacations and maternity leaves, and better health insurance than their nonunion counterparts. In unionized firms, the wage gap between black and white workers is narrower than elsewhere. Whites and blacks earn roughly the same wages, and they both earn more than workers without union representation. Unionized black males earn 15.1 percent more than blacks in comparable nonunion jobs; for whites, the union "wage premium" is 14.9 percent. It is 18.7 percent for Latinos.

The erosion of America's labor movement contributed to declining wages and living standards and the nation's widening economic disparities. Most new service-sector and light manufacturing jobs are not unionized. During the last several decades, the federal government's cold war against labor unions has made unionization more difficult to achieve. Since the 1970s, union density has declined precipitously. In 2000, only 13.5 percent of the workforce belonged to unions, with less than 10 percent of the private workforce unionized.[95] AFL-CIO president John Sweeney has pledged to expand union organizing, and union membership has increased modestly in recent years. But successful organizing is difficult without labor law reform. Union growth would reinvigorate what has historically been the single strongest source of political support for progressive urban policies.

Union elections supervised by the National Labor Relations Board are biased in favor of management. Any employer with a clever labor attorney can stall union elections, allowing management time to intimidate potential union recruits. According to one study, one in ten workers involved in an organizing drive is fired. Employers can require workers to attend meetings where company managers and consultants give antiunion speeches, show antiunion films, and distribute antiunion literature. Unions have no equivalent right of access to employees. To reach them, organizers frequently must visit their homes or hold secret meetings. At least 40 percent of employees want union representation, but they will not vote for a union if they feel that their jobs are at stake. Reforming our nation's cumbersome labor laws will give workers elementary rights of free speech and assembly, provide a democratic voice in the workplace, and change the balance of national political influence.[96]

Our perspective is at once radical and incremental. It is radical because we propose a series of institutional innovations and policy approaches that actually address the root causes of growing spatial inequality and metropolitan political fragmentation. We can never adequately solve our national problem of growing inequality until we specifically confront its spatial dimension. Neither national policies aimed at equalizing incomes nor local efforts to reduce concentrated poverty can succeed unless this basic dynamic is confronted. National economic prosperity, for example, has increased incomes at the lower end of the distribution and reduced poverty in the last few years, but it has left the geography of inequality largely intact. In the absence of a comprehensive approach, local measures are also bound to fail.

Our perspective is also incremental because we recognize that the present arrangements have evolved over more than half a century and that many interests have developed a stake in them. It will take many decades to undo these arrangements. We call for renewed federal efforts to reduce poverty by making work pay, improving schools, assisting in the provision of housing, and helping to provide basic health and child-care services. But the centerpiece of our program is not huge tax increases, massive new spending programs, or even significant redistribution to the central cities. The missing piece in the puzzle of poverty and inequality is the need for the federal and state governments to level the playing field, encourage regional cooperation, and foster closer relationships between working families and opportunities. By reframing the institutions of local federalism, we can nurture regions that are more livable, fair, and economically successful. These measures are all worthy and laudable. Without a majority political coalition, however, they will not see the light of day. How such a political coalition can be assembled is the subject of the next chapter.

Crossing the City Line
A Metropolitics for the Twenty-first Century

Most observers would probably agree with our diagnosis that metropolitan sprawl and the growing concentration of poverty in central cities lie at the heart of our urban problem and that the urban problem, in turn, keeps America from being the country it would like to be. Although some might quibble about which factor is most responsible, most would probably also agree that federal, state, and local public policies have interacted with metropolitan political fragmentation to make the urban problem worse, not better. Finally, many would sympathize with our contention that the nation must move forcefully to increase the levels of cooperation, inclusion, and spatial mobility within our metropolitan areas. The rub comes not with whether we need to pursue these ends but with how to accomplish them. The most potent criticism of our proposals is that they are politically impossible to achieve.

We have already highlighted the factors that would support such a conclusion. Many powerful interests have helped to create the existing dynamic of sprawl and poverty concentration, which in turn has reinforced the desire to maintain the status quo.[1] Residents of better-off suburbs clearly enjoy the benefits of strong metropolitan economies, still driven by central cities, while they avoid the cost of providing public services for the central city. Those who reside in less exclusive suburbs have more ambiguous interests, but as William Schneider has argued, blue-collar suburban home owners may also seek to separate themselves — politically and socially — from the urban poor.[2] Certainly, the high degree of polarization in some metropolitan areas encourages many such residents to identify more with wealthier people in outer suburbs than with the central-city poor. Finally, we cannot overlook the fact that many central-city political leaders are also heavily invested in these arrangements. They, too, show little interest in policy approaches that might dissipate their population base or dilute their authority over the place-based programs under their jurisdiction.

Suburban resistance is most stubborn with regard to policies that would gradually reduce the concentration of poverty in central cities by spreading poor people more evenly across the broader metropolitan area. This leads a wide range of observers to be skeptical of the chances for achieving greater metropolitan equity. For example, even progressive individuals who are highly sympathetic to the urban poor demurred from Yale law professor Owen Fiss's recent proposal for a large-scale program to assist urban ghetto residents to move to the suburbs (or wherever else they wanted). As Columbia political scientist J. Phillip Thompson says,

> white suburbia has already shown in practice where it stands on racial integration and poverty deconcentration. . . . Trying to legally force white Americans to integrate against their will, in a country where they are a voting majority, has not worked and it will not. In this context, in place strategies such as [William Julius] Wilson's public works jobs proposal are a lot more politically realistic than housing and school integration.[3]

Famed child psychologist Robert Coles doubts the desirability of "bureaucratically assisted realignment of neighborhood populations," while Jennifer Hochschild, a gifted observer of race relations in America, worries that "absent a revolution in most Americans' preferences with regard to the race and class of their neighbors, Fiss's proposal is politically hopeless." Even Gary Orfield, perhaps the most articulate and thoughtful advocate of metropolitan school integration, doubts that massive efforts to provide more housing vouchers, build affordable housing, and change local land-use controls can be mounted "when both political parties are responding to suburban majorities who are hostile to such policies."[4]

We harbor no illusions about the difficulty of developing a sufficiently broad political coalition to enact the proposals outlined in the previous chapter. We also understand that elected officials and legislators will not embrace measures designed to promote greater equality across metropolitan areas unless they are well managed, not highly intrusive, and part of a policy package that serves, and is seen to serve, the interests of a substantial majority of their constituents. Our political system is too prone to stalemate, and suburban opposition would be too strong, to allow the adoption of measures that suburbanites viewed as major threats, even if a large majority of everybody else favored them. Our program can be adopted only after a great deal of dialogue, consensus building, and agreement that it truly serves a diverse set of interests. This said, we are far more optimistic about assembling such a political coalition than our previously quoted friends.

We base this optimism on several grounds. Most crucially, the perception that suburbs are a homogeneous constituency lacking any similarities or shared interests with central cities is simply wrong. In fact, suburbs are highly varied. Many suburbs, perhaps a third of them, are actually doing worse than central cities on such indicators as poverty rates and the incidence of female-headed families.[5] The evidence shows that where suburbs are experiencing decline, suburbanites are more likely to vote like urban dwellers, except where that decline is perceived to emanate from adjacent central-city neighborhoods.[6] More generally, the immediate economic interest of many suburbanites remains tied to the central city because many earn their incomes there. Suburban residents will also support our proposed reforms when their towns have lost out in the beggar-thy-neighbor game of metropolitan development and thus would benefit directly from many of the measures proposed. Myron Orfield's efforts in metropolitan Minneapolis–St. Paul show that coalitions can be fashioned between central cities and inner suburbs.

Even better-off suburbs are not what they used to be. As John Logan, William Frey, and a number of other observers have noted, the demographic trajectories of our major metropolitan areas are no longer dominated by the dynamic of whites fleeing to the suburbs as central cities become increasingly populated by blacks.[7] In many respects, we are moving beyond the paradigm of "politics in black and white." Although most large central cities, such as New York and Los Angeles, are becoming less white, they are also becoming less black, as African Americans suburbanize and immigrants and their children take the place of the native born. Most suburbs are also becoming more heterogeneous in racial and ethnic terms. Unlike in the 1960s and 1970s, these transitions are not pitting whites against blacks, but rather are creating more complex patterns.

The political implications of this shift have yet to play out fully, but the black-white racial cleavage that drove urban politics in the postwar period is now being overlaid with new forms of ethnic expression, and, in some cases, cooperation. The emerging politics of interethnic relations is not going to be easy, but at least it is less likely to be locked in racial polarization. More complex forms of interracial coalition formation will arise. As Gary Orfield has observed, these trends surely offer "new possibilities for successful diversity."[8]

With the right leadership, sufficient dialogue, and new institutional settings, even many privileged suburbanites will come to believe that our proposals are in their self-interest "rightly understood" (as de Tocqueville put it). Many of us like to drive faster than the speed limit on occasion or smoke cigarettes, yet we support the government's efforts to enforce speed limits and limit smoking. Although the present rules of the game encourage many suburban jurisdictions to act selfishly by excluding the poor or even preventing multifamily rental housing from being built, upon reflection, residents of these areas may realize that the resulting high levels of economic segregation and sprawl harm the overall competitiveness and success of their metropolitan areas. They certainly understand that the resulting traffic congestion, lack of planning, and pollution undermine their quality of life.

The present institutional arrangements do not provide an incentive for anyone to protect the regional commons, that is, the shared interests of all members of the region. Changing the rules of the game in the ways proposed in the previous chapter would create an institutional framework that would encourage the articulation of such interests. Even though narrower interests would persist, they would at least encounter claims on behalf of achieving greater regional efficiency, environmental soundness, and equality of opportunity. Indeed, in the nascent movements for "smart growth," the "new regionalism," and "taking the regional high road to economic growth," one can begin to see the practical realization of this "self-interest rightly understood."

In making the case for the political possibilities of metropolitan reform, we begin, as we have done throughout the book, by forcefully stating the counterargument. In a nutshell, the counterargument is that a majority of the electorate now living in the suburbs is naturally conservative and opposed to aiding central cities or forming political coalitions with them. Indeed, Republicans have successfully used opposition to urban policies as a wedge to pry working- and middle-class voters away from the Democratic Party. At first glance, this argument is persuasive, but we will show in the succeeding sections that under Bill Clinton, the Democrats, in defiance of the conventional wisdom, successfully united central-city and suburban voters in two presidential elections. (Although less successful, Al Gore did the same thing in 2000.) This coalition did not push the kinds of metropolitan reforms that we advocate in this book, but its existence demonstrates that central-city and suburban electorates are not irrevocably divided. In fact, as we have shown throughout the book, suburbs are no longer lily-white enclaves for the middle class. Instead, they are incredibly diverse and suffer in their own ways from the problems of economic segregation and sprawl. We will show how our reform agenda could win support in the three very different congressional districts we profiled in chapter 1. We end by identifying the political actors who are already pushing for a new metropolitics and identify the stakes for the future of American democracy.

THE DIVIDED METROPOLIS: SUBURBS VERSUS CENTRAL CITIES

Postwar suburbanization and rising metropolitan spatial segregation have had dramatic political consequences. Since the late 1940s, the suburban component of the active voting population has steadily increased. By the early 1990s, national exit polls suggested that suburbanites represented more than half of all voters in presidential elections. The proportion of suburban seats in Congress and state legislatures has increased as well. This change, along with the move away from parties and toward a candidate-centered, media-driven national politics heavily dependent on corporate contributions, has dramatically shifted the balance of political power away from central cities. Suburban voters and congressional districts now not only outnumber their urban counterparts; suburbanites also provide a disproportionate share of campaign contributions. All this has translated into less political influence, and indeed a degree of political isolation, for American cities. As a result, any effort to promote the agenda described in the previous chapter must rest on a coalition between central cities and a substantial component of the suburban electorate.

In the eyes of some observers, this shift drew a new fault line through American politics. Thomas and Mary Edsall argue in their 1991 book *Chain Reaction* that "[s]uburbanization has permitted whites to satisfy liberal ideals revolving around activist government, while keeping to a minimum the number of blacks and the poor who share in government largess," leading toward "a national politics that will be dominated by the suburban vote."[9] CNN commentator and American Enterprise Institute analyst William Schneider argued that the 1992 election was the first in which a majority of the voters lived in the suburbs. As the center of gravity shifted to the suburbs, he argued, the concerns of the typical voter would also shift in a private, familial direction. In this "suburban century," said Schneider, presidential candidates and congressional majorities could ignore urban America without paying a political price.[10]

Unquestionably, postwar suburbanization altered the metropolitan political terrain. In 1944, thirty-two major central cities cast 27 percent of the national vote in presidential elections. By 1992, their share had declined to only 14 percent. Similarly, a study of twelve large central cities found that they cast 21.8 percent of the national vote in 1948 but only 6.3 percent in 2000 (up from 5.9 percent in 1996), even as they became more distinctly Democratic and less likely to turn out compared with national voting patterns.[11] Residents of cities with populations over 500,000 cast only 9 percent of the vote in 2000.[12] Clearly, big-city electoral clout has shrunk tremendously in the postwar years, especially in large, old cities of the Northeast and Midwest.

Much of this change derived from the changing location of the eligible electorate. But the political demobilization of central cities relative to the suburbs is also noteworthy. During the depression and the New Deal, urban political machines and labor unions mobilized urban voters, enabling large cities to match the national rate of turnout. Their propensity to vote peaked in 1944 at 113 percent of the national average and remained above it through 1952. Subsequently, urban voter turnout declined relative to that of the rest of the nation. In 1960, voter turnout was 62 percent in the thirty-two major central cities, compared with 64 percent in the nation. Urban turnout exceeded the national average in only two subsequent presidential years, 1976 and 1984. In all others, it fell well below the national level; it was 47 percent in 1992, compared with an overall rate of 55 percent.[13] According to Peter Nardulli, Jon Dalager, and Donald Greco: "This drop in the relative propensity to vote accounts for almost 40 percent of the loss in voting power experienced by these cities between 1944 and 1992. Based on a drop in the cities' share of the national electorate, they should have dropped only 8 points (from 27 percent to 19 percent) rather than 13 points."[14] Although a rising rate of noncitizenship in big cities accounts for some of this relative drop, the demobilization of potential urban voters clearly compounded the overall population trends.

This shift had a major impact on state politics as well as national politics. As the share of the large central-city vote fell in the major states, the attention of presidential candidates, governors, and state legislators shifted away from the interests of those cities. In 1948, for example, New York City cast 50 percent of the votes in New York State, Chicago cast 46.5 percent of Illinois' ballots, Baltimore had 42.3 percent of the Maryland vote, and Detroit had 31.8 percent of Michigan's. Los Angeles and San Francisco combined for 51.3 percent of the California vote, while Philadelphia and Pittsburgh formed 30.7 percent of Pennsylvania's electorate. Since these were key states in the electoral college, the relative mobilization of their big-city vote could be decisive in national elections. By 2000, New York City cast only 31.6 percent of the presidential votes in New York State. The shares of Chicago (20.2 percent), Baltimore (9.6 percent), Detroit (6.5 percent), Los Angeles and San Francisco (10.6 percent), and Philadelphia and Pittsburgh (13.9 percent) fell precipitously.[15]

Similar trends have affected the urban delegation in Congress. Harold Wolman and Lisa Marckini found that central-city districts in the U.S. House of

Representatives declined 23 percent between the 1960s and the 1990s, from 121 to 93, while suburban districts rose 96 percent, from 122 to 239.[16] Excluding the relatively conservative central cities of the South and West, urban House districts fell even more sharply, from 62 to 40. Wolman and Marckini concluded that "Congress has changed from an institution that largely reflected nonmetropolitan interests to one that is now thoroughly dominated by suburban representatives."[17] The same trends have also weakened cities' influence in state governments, where suburban politicians now dominate state legislatures.[18] As a result, the road to the political and legislative majorities necessary for enacting the programs we have proposed runs squarely through the suburbs. But which way will suburban voters lean? Will they side with the more conservative, white, middle-class Republican countryside, or with the more liberal, white, ethnic, minority, Catholic, working-class, Democratic cityside? The answer depends a great deal on how parties, leaders, and the media frame the issues.

Republicans gained a good deal of political ground since 1968 by activating suburban sentiments founded on the class and racial divide between suburbs and central cities. Between 1965 and 1992, Republican presidential candidates practiced "subtractive" politics designed to peel white suburbanites away from the Democrats to win every presidential election except for Jimmy Carter's 1976 post-Watergate victory. (For their part, Democrats found it difficult to forge an "additive" politics that bridged the differences between the central cities and inner suburbs.) Republican candidates had long found their most supportive base in rural constituencies and white, well-to-do, predominantly Protestant suburbs. They also gained steadily in the South as whites left the Democratic Party over its commitment to civil rights and activist government. But to make this base into a majority in the electoral college, Republicans had to improve their position among traditional Democrats residing in the suburbs, especially blue-collar and middle-class white Catholics. Republican presidential candidates used urban unrest, welfare dependency, and crime as major wedge issues to push voters to their side.

Until 1994, however, Republicans could not defeat enough Democratic incumbents in suburban and southern House districts to win a majority in that body. Suburban voters perceived these incumbents, unlike the Democratic presidential candidates, as responsive to their needs. To win more support in these suburban House districts, Republican congressional leaders sought to capitalize on suburban resentment over paying federal taxes for programs that benefited urban constituencies. Unlike Democrats, whose national majorities always rested on an urban base, they could appeal to white suburbanites without fear of alienating large numbers of nonwhite voters. Republicans worked to convince white Catholic suburbanites that they were socially and ideologically closer to the white, rural and small-town, Protestant Republican core than they were to the increasingly black and Latino central cities. Republicans could seek the moral high ground on the racial divide by asserting that the liberal Democratic welfare state was causing, or at least perpetuating, poverty, not curing it. Certainly, as we described earlier, cities got poorer relative to their suburbs over the last three decades, and poverty became more spatially concentrated within them, although the cause was hardly too generous welfare payments. Nevertheless, Republican conservatives found a receptive audience for their calls to terminate failing welfare programs and get the government out of taxpayers' wallets, while Republican moderates could stress the superiority of using targeted tax credits and deregulation to encourage private investment in central cities. Republicans finally won this political battle in 1994, ending six decades of Democratic control of Congress.

CROSSING THE LINE: CENTRAL CITY–SUBURBAN COALITIONS

In 1994, the prospects for central city–suburban coalitions seemed dim indeed. The politics of subtraction, pitting suburbs against central cities, appeared to be working to perfection. There was a fly in the ointment, however: in 1992, Clinton had won more suburban congressional districts than his Republican opponent, George Bush. As Table 8.1 shows, Clinton won 88 of 152 suburban districts in 1992 and increased the number of his suburban victories to 100 in 1996. How Clinton won back the "Reagan Democrats" — white, ethnic, often Catholic, blue-collar and middle-class voters — provides important lessons, we believe, about how to unite central-city and suburban voters behind a metropolitan agenda.

Clinton's 1992 campaign pollster, Stanley Greenberg, spent the 1980s studying this population and argued that the Democratic Party's focus on urban blacks had "crowded out" this "forgotten middle class." These descendants of New Deal supporters told Greenberg that they believed that the urban poor lacked basic work and family values and received an unwarranted share of federal aid, themes played on by Republican candidates. Given the gradual and perhaps permanent loss of southern whites to the Republicans, Greenberg argued that suburban defection was a key ingredient of Republican national presidential majorities.[19] To reach that vote while holding on to the Democrats' urban base, candidate Clinton developed a "common ground" message. While the embers of the Los Angeles riot smoldered in May 1992, he campaigned in

TABLE 8.1. Voting Trends by Congressional District Type, 1990–2000

	Central City	Suburban	Rural	Mixed	Total
1990 citizen voting-age population	31,164,126	60,847,890	30,835,882	51,784,685	174,632,583
1992 vote	17,485,402	37,669,244	17,770,011	31,357,616	104,279,273
1992 turnout	56.11%	61.91%	57.62%	60.55%	59.71%
Clinton vote (1992)	55.48%	41.13%	40.80%	38.98%	42.84%
Bush vote (1992)	29.43%	38.93%	43.37%	39.31%	37.60%
Clinton districts (1992)	66/82	88/152	38/74	62/127	254/435
1994 House vote	10,562,896	23,759,116	11,710,294	20,325,285	66,357,591
1994 turnout	33.89%	39.05%	37.98%	39.25%	38.00%
House Democratic vote (1994)	60.50%	44.14%	43.36%	43.74%	46.84%
House Republican vote (1994)	37.65%	53.52%	53.25%	54.20%	51.15%
Democratic districts (1994)	62/82	60/152	33/74	46/127	201/435
1996 vote	15,378,067	34,730,013	16,391,509	29,191,004	95,690,893
1996 turnout	49.35%	57.08%	53.16%	56.37%	54.80%
Clinton vote (1996)	62.18%	49.17%	45.42%	45.19%	49.40%
Dole vote (1996)	30.63%	41.47%	43.88%	44.48%	41.04%
Clinton districts (1996)	70/82	100/152	44/74	65/127	279/435
1998 House vote	9,545,946	20,722,413	10,987,871	18,796,764	60,052,994
1998 turnout	30.63%	34.06%	35.63%	36.30%	34.66%
House Democratic vote (1998)	64.30%	46.23%	44.43%	43.69%	47.98%
House Republican vote (1996)	32.02%	50.54%	52.53%	53.27%	48.82%
Democratic districts (1996)	64/82	71/152	29/74	48/172	212/435
2000 vote	16,589,906	38,404,673	17,886,981	32,187,837	105,069,392
2000 turnout	53.32%	63.12%	58.00%	62.16%	60.17%
Gore vote (2000)	62.85%	49.55%	42.06%	42.95%	48.36%
Bush vote (2000)	33.21%	46.75%	55.01%	53.19%	47.99%
Gore districts (2000)	68/82	91/152	14/74	34/127	207/435

Sources: 1992–1998 election results from Barone and Ujifusa, *Almanac of American Politics 1998* and *2000;* 2000 results from POLIDATA, a private demographic and political research firm located outside Washington, D.C., compiled from state and local election authorities (www.polidata.org). Citizen voting-age population from U.S. Census Bureau, 1990 Census of Population, Summary Tape File 3D. Districts are classified by the proportion of their population living in central cities with 30,000 or more, urbanized areas not in central cities, or rural areas. Mixed districts had no majority population type. One Independent House member from Vermont was reclassified a Democrat; another from Virginia, a Republican. Turnout is expressed as a proportion of 1990 citizen voting-age population.

the suburbs of nearby Orange and San Diego Counties, linking the problems of suburbanites with those of the inner cities.[20]

In the 1992 election, the constituencies that were most likely to favor Clinton — blacks, Hispanics, Jews, white liberals, union households, and senior citizens — were also disproportionately located in the cities.[21] As a southern Democratic governor who had won office with the support of a biracial coalition, Clinton knew that he needed black votes to win and was comfortable campaigning in black churches and neighborhoods. Big-city party organizations and public employee unions also provided the bulk of the Clinton campaign's field operations. But he needed to stretch far beyond this base across city lines to achieve an electoral majority. He had to do this in ways that would not antagonize his urban base but would signal to suburban voters that he spoke to their needs as well. He developed campaign themes that spoke about defending the middle-class standard of living (for example, health care reform), promoting middle-class values (for example, "ending welfare as we know it"), and achieving economic competitiveness (for example, balancing the budget and adopting the North American Free Trade Agreement). He was not above distancing himself from urban blacks, as happened when he publicly criticized the lyrics sung by black rap singer Sister Souljah. Table 8.1 shows that central-city voters gave Clinton a significant advantage in both 1992 and 1996, enabling him to emerge with margins of 4.5 million votes in 1992 and 4.9 million votes in 1996 over his Republican competitors. But he got the bulk of his votes in predominantly suburban congressional districts, winning 800,000 more votes than Bush in 1992 and extending this margin to 2.7 million over Dole in 1996.

Clinton's ability to gain ground in both the suburbs and the central city between 1992 and 1996 owed much to the Republican takeover of Congress in 1994 and its pursuit of the "Contract with America" under Speaker Newt Gingrich. Many voters perceived Republican efforts to cut spending as threatening not only programs for the inner-city poor but those benefiting the middle class. The budget conflicts of the 104th Congress swung public sentiment in Clinton's direction. As Table 8.1 shows, between 1992 and 1996, his support in central-city districts surged from 55 to 62 percent (although turnout declined there more than it did overall), but it also strengthened from 41 to 49 percent in the suburbs, substantially widening his previous margin. In the 2000 election, Al Gore held this vote share in the central cities and suburban congressional districts, but won fewer districts than Clinton had taken in 1996.

On the presidential front, therefore, Democrats can clearly construct a central city–suburban alliance around a program of actively promoting the middle-class (read suburban) quality of life. This is not to say, however, that the Clinton administration cemented such an electoral coalition any more effectively than previous Republican presidents had consolidated a rural–small town–suburban alliance. The Clinton administration's approach relied on an ad hoc collection of policies designed to appeal to specific urban and suburban constituencies, not on synthesizing the interests of urban and suburban voters through the sort of policy agenda recommended here. Instead of working on ways to reduce the cleavages between these constituencies or build commonalities between them, he attempted to shift political attention away from racially charged issues and toward specific differences with the Republicans around which he could engage in symbolic populism. Although some within his administration sought to develop a metropolitan approach to domestic policy, these efforts were abandoned after the 1994 congressional elections. In the 2000 Democratic presidential primaries, candidates Al Gore and Bill Bradley walked the political tightrope between urban and suburban supporters by favoring federal social policies flowing to urban constituencies while appealing to suburbanites on limiting suburban sprawl.[22] In 2000, according to exit polls, Gore beat George W. Bush by 71 percent to 26 percent in big cities, by 57 percent to 40 percent in smaller cities, and took 47 percent of the suburban vote to Bush's 49 percent.

If forging a political and programmatic coalition between urban and suburban voters requires (but will not be guaranteed by) the election of a Democratic president, more is needed: electing a substantial Democratic majority in Congress. Only when Democrats from outside the South, together with black southern Democrats, have outnumbered Republicans and white southern Democrats has Congress been willing to enact major changes in federal urban policy.[23] Such a Democratic majority is hardly sufficient to guarantee that the measures we propose will be adopted. Many Democratic representatives are so heavily invested in existing place-based programs that they are reluctant to consider metropolitan alternatives. They, too, are heavily influenced by the role of big money in politics. At the same time, doubts about place-based urban programs, together with the reality of the shifting demographic terrain, have prompted Democrats to become more receptive to new thinking. Since the Democratic Party's future prospects for Congress as well as the presidency depend on its ability to bridge the gaps between the cities and the suburbs, its members will be increasingly likely to focus beyond the boundaries of their present districts. Whatever the obstacles, only when the party creates synergies between central-city and inner-suburban constituencies will it be able to build a durable electoral majority.

If Table 8.1 shows that Democratic candidates can win presidential elections by combining urban and suburban votes, it is less encouraging on whether Democrats can reclaim a congressional majority, though it is not entirely discouraging. Prior to 1994, Democrats controlled Congress, but southern Democrats, the more conservative northern nonurban Democrats, and Republicans often joined to form a conservative majority that was sufficiently large to block or restrain avowedly pro-urban legislation.[24] Gradually, as the Democrats lost southern House seats to the Republicans, the potential for a Republican House majority rose, and in 1994, Republican House candidates, united behind the explicitly antiurban "Contract with America," scored a stunning victory, winning 234 seats, including 92 of the 152 majority suburban congressional districts, where they amassed almost ten percentage points more of the vote than did the Democrats.

House Republicans were not able to consolidate and extend this stunning victory in the 1998 congressional elections, however. Their attacks on welfare, urban programs, and other measures perceived as benefiting the urban poor; on more broad-based programs such as Social Security and Medicare; and on the president himself clearly did not go down well with the suburban constituencies that had put them in power in 1994. In the 1998 House elections, the Republicans lost a net of fifteen seats to the Democrats, including eleven suburban seats. (They won twenty-seven others, including seven suburban and four central-city seats, by less than 20,000 votes in 1998.) The decline in turnout, which had been disproportionately urban between the 1992 and 1996 presidential elections, was disproportionately suburban between 1994 and 1998. Although Republicans still won more votes than Democrats did in suburban districts, the margin narrowed considerably. Still, Republicans hung on to eighty-nine House seats where Clinton had won a plurality in 1996, thirty-one of which were predominantly suburban. Although Democrats were not able to regain a majority in the House, neither did Republicans forge a solid suburban-rural coalition based on opposition to the cities, tax cuts, and reducing the size of the federal government.[25] The 2000 presidential election further narrowed the Republican lead, with Democrats gaining three more House seats compared to 1998.

Table 8.1 reveals another crucial feature of the metropolitan political terrain. Turnout in central-city congressional districts (relative to voting-age citizens in 1990) persistently lagged behind turnout in suburban, rural, and mixed districts (often geographically large districts containing small central cities as well as rural areas, where no one type of population is a majority). In every election, it was below the national average and below every other type of district, usually by significant margins. The central city–suburban difference was 5.8 percentage points in the 1992 presidential election, 10.7 points in the 1996 presidential election, and 9.8 points in the 2000 presidential election, as well as 6.3 points in the 1994 congressional election, and 4.6 points in the 1998 congressional election. Overcoming this disadvantage is crucial to building the large urban pluralities Democratic presidential candidates need to offset the Republican advantage in nonmetropolitan and mixed areas, which also have high turnout rates.

There are many obvious reasons why eligible urban residents turn out to vote less often than their suburban and rural counterparts. We have already described many of them in our discussion of the negative effects of concentrated poverty. But the negative relationship between population density and turnout remains statistically strong even after controlling for (white) race, income, educational attainment, and home ownership (all of which promote turnout and Republican advantage). One reason why the relative demobilization of urban areas is so persistent is that general elections in these areas are so predominantly Democratic that they are rarely contested. This has two effects: voters do not turn out because the Democratic primary has already determined the outcome, and the Democratic votes that are cast are "wasted" because Democratic candidates pile up many more votes than needed to win office. For example, in 1998, Democrats in central-city districts piled up almost a million more votes than they needed to comfortably win their districts. If these voters were transferred to suburban districts, they would have made the races in these areas a dead heat. As the example in the previous chapter concerning the adjacent House districts in the Los Angeles–Pasadena area shows, expanding central-city districts to include more suburban voters would result in more competitive races in both central cities and suburbs, which would produce higher levels of central-city turnout as well as improve the prospects for Democratic victories in suburban districts.[26]

The 152 mostly suburban congressional districts are characterized by a wide diversity of conditions. As a group, their residents are more likely to be white, middle class, home owners, in families with children, and employed than are residents in central-city districts. But the average suburban district is definitely not "lily white," and there is variation along racial, ethnic, and class lines. On average, they are 76 percent white, 9 percent black, 10 percent Hispanic, and 4 percent Asian, but the black percentage can range up to 64, the Hispanic percentage up to 84 percent, and the Asian percentage up to 64 percent. Home ownership rates also vary, with as many as 54 percent living in apartments.

Suburban congressional districts averaged 12.3 percent residents with British ancestry in 1990, but they also averaged 9.9 percent Irish ancestry and 6.8 percent Italian ancestry, suggesting substantial Catholic populations. On average, 6 percent of the households received public assistance, 9.3 percent of the people were poor, 10.6 percent of the young people were high school dropouts, 21 percent of the adults lacked a high school diploma, 28 percent have only a high school degree, 23 percent of the adults were in blue-collar occupations, and 25 percent of the households received Social Security benefits (above the national median). The median 1990 household income of the median suburban congressional district was $36,224, but thirty of them (19 percent of all suburban districts) were below the national median of $28,905.

In short, suburban congressional districts are not socially and economically homogeneous, nor are they uniformly well-off. Their populations differ by race, ethnicity, class, and political outlook. In 44 of the 152 districts, the minority percentage was 20 percent or more. These districts cast about 24 percent of the suburban vote for president in 1996 and 27 percent of the 1998 House vote; they gave both Bill Clinton and the Democratic House candidate about 53 percent of their votes in these elections. Clinton got 48 percent of the vote and the House Democrats got 47 percent, even in the predominantly white suburban districts. So although some suburban residents are certainly open to joining a conservative, antiurban coalition with rural and small-town voters, a great many can also be involved in an urban-suburban coalition based on middle- and working-class interests.[27]

This is especially true where suburbanites remain tied to the central city. On average, 35 percent of employed suburbanites work in central cities, and the share of a suburban congressional district's workers who have city jobs is significantly correlated with the rate at which the district votes for Democrats, particularly Democratic candidates for Congress.[28] In addition, residential density and union membership, independent of other demographic characteristics, powerfully promote Democratic voting in suburban districts. A one percentage point increase in unionized workers produced three-quarters of a percentage point increase in the 1998 vote for the Democratic House candidate.[29] Efforts to promote union membership and to foster clustered suburban development will thus have a positive long-term impact on support for the policies we proposed.

In politics, as in the rest of life, place counts. Most political pundits do not focus on this factor as much as they should. For them, place is only one factor influencing political orientations. They lean more heavily on sociocultural distinctions such as race, ethnicity, religion, gender, and differential exposure to the stresses of social change, not to mention different values and ideological leanings. How people fit into these various categories clearly affects how they line up on the liberal-conservative and Democratic-Republican scales. Since these social groups tend to be concentrated in some places and not in others, this explains some of the differences in the way urban, suburban, and rural voters behave.

In fact, local context has a big impact on how people behave politically, over and above their individual characteristics. Controlling for basic racial and ethnoreligious categories and for family characteristics, urban dwellers give stronger support to Democrats and to liberal positions than do their suburban counterparts, who in turn are more supportive than rural dwellers. In the 1994 congressional elections, for example, the exit polls showed that among married white Protestants with children, 61 percent of big-city residents voted for Democratic House candidates, compared with 35 percent of small-city dwellers and only 31 percent of suburbanites. White married Catholics with children supported Democrats by 46 percent in big cities, 52 percent in small cities, and 31 percent in suburbs. The 1996 exit polls showed urban whites giving President Clinton 56 percent of their votes, suburban whites 47 percent, and rural whites 40 percent. Similar patterns hold for other racial groups. Despite what pollsters routinely do, people cannot simply be randomly plucked out of their context. Their political attitudes and actions are shaped by the webs of political, social, and economic relations they share with their neighbors. Many aspects of the urban context promote support for Democrats, and as suburbs become more urbanized, the Republican advantage will become more contested. This may be most pronounced in the "mini-central cities" that have emerged in the suburban realm, such as the Pasadena and Silicon Valley cases described earlier.

America's first-by-the-gate-takes-the-prize election system also makes place important. A national majority does not require just 50 percent plus one of the national vote. Instead, as the 2000 election vividly demonstrated, a presidential candidate must win pluralities in a sufficient number of states to compose a majority of the electoral college. Likewise, control of the U.S. Senate is based on winning states, not a national majority. For the House, electoral majorities in 218 of the 435 districts are required. Many votes do not count in a presidential election, including all votes above a comfortable majority in states where a presidential candidate gets more than a majority, as well as all votes from states where he or she cannot get close to a majority. Quite reasonably, this shifts the attention of campaigns away from noncompetitive areas to competitive areas. The downside, of course, is that national presidential campaigns will spend relatively little time on local races in noncompetitive states, and local elected officials representing noncompetitive (and often uncontested) seats have little incentive to mobilize voters to increase the statewide chances for their party and its candidates for the House, Senate, or governor.

TOWARD A METROPOLITAN POLITICAL STRATEGY

How should those who advocate an urban-suburban alliance think about winning suburban majorities? We must begin by recognizing that the suburbs, despite being varied, do differ from central cities. If we array suburban House districts along several key dimensions, we find that the middle district was 82 percent non-Hispanic white in 1990, that 81 percent of the households were married-couple families, that 36 percent of the households had children under age eighteen, that 67 percent owned their homes and lived in single-family dwellings, and that 23 percent of the adults had at least a college degree. At the same time, 67 percent of all women, including 67 percent of all mothers with children under age eighteen, worked, 49 percent of all children had two working parents, 70 percent of white adults lacked a college degree, 33 percent worked in the central city, 23 percent worked in blue-collar occupations, 13 percent worked for government, about 10 percent belonged to unions, and 25 percent of the households relied on Social Security. These hardworking, middle-income families, most of which do not include highly educated managers or professionals, are the critical terrain where the balance of power in American politics will be fought out.[30]

Second, in the wake of the 2000 census, advocates of a metropolitan strategy should attempt to convince those responsible for redistricting to make congressional races more competitive by shifting population from the overwhelmingly Democratic, often uncontested, central-city House seats toward suburban House districts. As Table 8.2 shows, fourteen of the fifteen uncontested central-city House seats were held by Democrats in 1998, while Republicans held twenty-six of the thirty-five uncontested suburban House seats. Moreover, the margin of Democratic votes over Republican votes in central-city districts (more than 3 million) was far larger than the Republican margin in the suburbs (only 89,000 votes). If one considers only House seats contested by both major parties, this imbalance was even more obvious (Democrats piled up 2.4 million more votes in the central cities, compared with only 34,000 for the Republicans in the suburbs). Moving some of the heavily Democratic precincts over to suburban congressional districts would make all districts more competitive and help forge central city–inner suburban political coalitions.

Finally, those who wish to mobilize political support for a new metropolitan

TABLE 8.2. Competition for House Seats by Incumbent Party and Geography, 1998

Congressional District Type	1998 Incumbent	Contested	Uncontested	Total
Central	Democrat	50	14	64
		78.1%	21.9%	100.0
	Republican	17	1	18
		94.4%	5.6%	100.0
	Central-city total	67	15	82
		81.7%	18.3%	100.0
Suburban	Democrat	62	9	71
		87.3%	12.7%	100.0
	Republican	55	26	81
		67.9%	32.1%	100.0
	Suburban total	117	35	152
		77.0%	23.0%	100.0
Rural	Democrat	23	6	29
		79.3%	20.7%	100.0
	Republican	34	11	45
		75.6%	24.4%	100.0
	Rural total	57	17	74
		77.0%	23.0%	100.0
Mixed	Democrat	38	10	48
		79.2%	20.8%	100.0
	Republican	62	17	79
		78.5%	21.5%	100.0
	Mixed total	100	27	127
		78.7%	21.3%	100.0

Sources: Same as Table 8.1.
  Note: Contested seats are those in which both major parties fielded candidates.

majority must develop a new political rhetoric. The task of bridging the divisions between suburban and central-city voters will not be easy, given the way political elites have played on them in the past (and not only on the Republican side). The following steps can help a new metropolitan coalition overcome these divisions:

- Make clear, effective, substantive policy appeals to white, Catholic, blue-collar suburbanites, whose once strong familial attachment to progressive positions has weakened, by addressing their actual needs, which revolve around the reality that they are working harder but not gaining a higher standard of living or achieving a more family-friendly workplace.
- Communicate with and mobilize emerging black and Hispanic suburban populations with nonracial appeals that speak to the same kinds of needs.
- Emphasize issues that cut across groups and move them toward coopera-

tion, rather than heightening intergroup polarization. The most potent policies would support working mothers, promote fathers' involvement in family life, improve schooling, and create new work opportunities for their children as they come of working age.

- Use existing county Democratic Party organizations, or develop new multi-county metropolitan party organizations, to strengthen working relationships between central-city political activists and suburban Democratic candidates for the House.
- Encourage all other groups mobilized in city politics, be they trade unions, church groups, or community organizations, to develop a metropolitan perspective on their work, following the example set by the Texas Industrial Areas Foundation and the Los Angeles County Federation of Labor.
- Follow Myron Orfield's lead in building regional coalitions of central cities and older, working-class suburbs in favor of tax-sharing schemes that would share the benefits of regional growth taking place in "favored quarter" suburbs.
- Rally around existing efforts and help establish new regional efforts at collaborative planning for regional economic development, economic competitiveness, infrastructure investment, housing, labor force development, and regional environmental quality, making sure that equity remains high on the regional agenda.
- Encourage corporations with a regional perspective (through their site locations, supplier networks, employee residence base, and logistical needs) to take the lead in addressing these issues.
- Form regional legislative caucuses at the local, state, and federal levels.

We now turn to the ways in which such strategies can be pursued.

CROSSING THE CITY LINE

The urban ghetto underclass has been used as a kind of bogeyman to frighten white working-class suburbanites into supporting conservative Republicans and opposing domestic policies associated with central-city constituencies, but the negative effects of racial and economic segregation extend across the entire metropolitan area. These negative effects provide the basis for mobilizing a new suburban-urban majority. The policies proposed in the previous chapter can appeal to both suburban and urban constituencies. In particular, they will increase the quality of life in suburban areas by limiting sprawl, bringing housing and work closer together, improving metropolitan transportation, promoting regional cooperation, and ending destructive bidding wars for private investment. Smart growth policies save money by using infrastructure that is already in place instead of building expensive new roads, sewers, and water lines, by diversifying inner-city poverty concentrations, and by attracting jobs and residents back to central cities and declining suburbs.

To illustrate the appeal of this program, consider the arguments that could be made to members of Congress representing the districts highlighted in the first chapter: New York's Sixteenth District in the South Bronx, Illinois' Thirteenth District in suburban Chicago, and Ohio's Tenth District spanning the city and suburbs on Cleveland's West Side. Federal policies have profoundly shaped each of these districts, producing local outcomes that exemplify the broader trends described in earlier chapters.

Federal policy has had a devastating impact on New York's Sixteenth Congressional District.[31] Urban renewal, freeway construction, and FHA mortgages not only drained away much of its middle class to the suburbs but also directly assaulted its neighborhoods. For example, the construction of the Cross-Bronx Expressway "displaced five thousand households and demolished the heart of the neighborhood," while making the South Bronx a corridor for those commuting into the city from suburbs in Westchester County, New Jersey, and elsewhere. Construction of many public housing projects concentrated poor families, primarily African Americans and then Puerto Ricans, in the area, with all the negative effects we examined in chapter 3.[32] In the 1970s, an epidemic of arson-for-profit, bank redlining, and housing abandonment left the area increasingly depopulated.

Congressman Jose Serrano has represented the district since 1990, when he replaced the previous incumbent who had been indicted for corruption. He was reelected in 2000 by 95 percent of the vote, but only 132,061 voters went to the polls, one of the lowest turnouts for a contested seat in the election. Since his district had the lowest per capita income of all 435 House districts in the 1990 census, he naturally supports federal programs that bring jobs and benefits to the inner-city poor. Serrano has one of the most liberal voting records in Congress, overwhelmingly favorable toward unions, environmental groups, senior citizens, and other liberal constituencies.[33]

After the spiral of decline in the 1970s and 1980s, the South Bronx experienced a significant rebound in the 1990s. Although a Clinton-era federal empowerment zone covers a small part of the district, most of this improvement can be attributed to the city's Ten-Year Housing Program, begun by Mayor Koch and continued by Mayor Dinkins. It rebuilt a significant part of the rental housing that private owners had abandoned, often with the involvement of local CDCs, churches, and tenant groups. In addition, the substantial reduction in crime rates achieved during Mayor Giuliani's administration has been pivotal in encouraging reinvestment in local housing and businesses.

Relatively few of the working-age adults of the South Bronx benefited from the city's economic growth in the 1990s, however. The most important problem facing Serrano's constituents is clearly the lack of employment. (Only one other district, in Detroit, had a lower percentage of working-age men employed as of the 1990 census.) Although the hospitals and government agencies of the Bronx employ many of his constituents, and parts of the private sector continue to function (for example, the city's wholesale produce market), it is unlikely that, the empowerment zone and Yankee Stadium notwithstanding, many more big private employers will move into the South Bronx.

Midtown Manhattan is only a subway ride away, but most residents of the South Bronx do not have the credentials to work in the corporate services economy. The employment centers of suburban Westchester County are also close by and might afford employment opportunities to lower-skilled people, but they are inaccessible by public transportation. It would be strongly in the interest of Serrano's constituents to be able to move closer to these opportunities, or at least to have better transportation links to them. Serrano might oppose mobility policies if they led the working-class Hispanics who are the backbone of his political support to migrate away from his district, but he would surely favor opening up more job opportunities for them. He would also applaud policies that would lead other towns in the northern part of the New York metropolitan area to take his constituents into consideration in their housing, labor market, and transportation policies.

In the long run, Congressman Serrano might realize that increased residential choices would benefit not just those who move but also those who remain in the area. People should not feel that they are trapped in the South Bronx. If they were helped to move to suburbs or better-off parts of the city, they would probably benefit from better access to jobs and other opportunities. Those who chose to stay in the Sixteenth District would do so out of a strong sense of attachment, not because it was a last resort. Further investment in the housing, economic development, and infrastructure of the South Bronx would encourage middle-class people to move in. No longer would a negative stereotype of the South Bronx as a zone of concentrated poverty be used to drive a wedge between, say, the residents of that neighborhood and the residents of Westchester.

Illinois' Thirteenth Congressional District lies at the other end of the economic spectrum from the South Bronx.[34] It includes the southern part of DuPage County, the southwest corner of Cook County, and the northern section of

Will County, comprising mostly upper-middle-class suburbs of Chicago. The population of DuPage County, west of Chicago, surged from 103,000 residents in 1940 to 904,000 in 2000. Its small towns morphed into edge-city suburbs like Downers Grove, Naperville, and Oak Brook, featuring new housing subdivisions and newly built headquarters for many national corporations. Federal highway and housing programs played a key role in this transformation. Growth was also spurred by one of the federal government's most prominent scientific facilities, the Argonne National Laboratory, with 4,500 employees. It has sparked the creation of many private research firms nearby.

The many business executives and well-paid professionals of the district vote consistently for Republican candidates and hold moderate to conservative positions in the political spectrum. The district can be counted on for high voter turnout. In 2000, 312,000 voters went to the polls. In 2000, Republican Judy Biggert was reelected to Congress with 66 percent of the vote. She replaced seven-term Congressman Harris Fawell, the Republican who replaced John Erlenborn, who himself had served in Congress for twenty years. In 1988, George Bush garnered 69 percent of the district's vote against Democrat Michael Dukakis, but the district gave 21 percent of its vote to the Reform Party's Ross Perot in 1992, leaving Bush with 47 percent and Clinton with 32 percent. Four years later, 50 percent voted for Bob Dole, while Clinton got 41 percent and Perot 9 percent. In 2000, the Republican share climbed to 55 percent.

Fawell had a consistently conservative record on economic and fiscal issues, which he looked at from a businessman's point of view. He was a firm opponent of organized labor, receiving low rankings from groups concerned about economic justice but somewhat higher ratings from pro-choice and environmental groups. He was a cofounder of the "Porkbusters Coalition," a mostly GOP organization that opposes wasteful government spending, but nevertheless remained a big supporter of the Argonne lab.

Congresswoman Biggert appears to have little reason to support metropolitan governance reforms that would address economic segregation and sprawl. After all, her district is part of the favored quarter of the Chicago area, and her constituents benefit from their insulation from the concentrated poverty in the city and the tax effort required to fund city services. To be sure, it will be difficult to sell parts of our program to the residents and leaders of such places, but the program should be able to garner substantial support even there. The long-term fate of the residents of the Thirteenth Congressional District is not separate from that of Chicago and its inner suburbs but inextricably bound up with it. Almost half the residents of this district work in the central city. The corporations that have relocated to the district acquire business services and even a significant share of their workforce from Chicago; the Argonne National Laboratory recruits educated workers from its universities. If Chicago becomes a less attractive place, these services will deteriorate. Chicago presents an image for the entire region that is crucial if Naperville and other suburban communities are to prosper.

Residents of the Thirteenth Congressional District have a strong interest in controlling suburban sprawl, which has been eating away at their quality of life and is driven in part by a desire to escape the problems of concentrated poverty in Chicago. Fawell had pushed for the conservation of open land in metropolitan Chicago. By consolidating new development within existing built-up areas, including Chicago, the district can save substantial money and avoid the problems of excessively rapid development. Smart growth can help the suburban communities west of Chicago retain the green space that made them attractive in the first place. Controlling leapfrog development and enhancing public transit will reduce the level of highway congestion, or at least prevent it from growing worse. Moreover, as this area continues to grow economically, it too will need affordable housing and better public transportation so that it can support workers in entry-level jobs and lessen traffic jams and spot labor shortages. Shorter commutes mean more time for civic involvement and family life, including bonding with potentially troubled teens.

In between these two poles are the inner suburbs. Representative of such districts is Ohio's Tenth Congressional District.[35] It includes most of Cleveland's West Side, but more than half the district's population lives in the western and southern suburbs, mostly blue-collar, middle-class places such as Parma and Lakewood. Both the city and the suburban parts of the district are overwhelmingly white; overall, whites constituted 94.2 percent of the district population in 1990. (Cleveland's black central-city areas were excluded from this district to help form the majority black Eleventh District.) About 77 percent of the district's households own their homes. The voters in this district are typical of the increasingly independent voting patterns of the nation's older suburbs, where many unionized manufacturing jobs have disappeared and people feel caught between affluent suburbs and inner-city ghettos.

With many union members, the district has traditionally been heavily Democratic, but its voters are no longer loyal to the party. In 1988, 52 percent of its voters favored Republican George Bush over Democrat Michael Dukakis for president. The district also favored Republican George Voinovich, a former Cleveland mayor who ran successfully for governor. In 1992, Clinton captured the district by a narrow margin, winning 41 percent of the vote to 36 percent for Bush and 22 percent for Perot. Four years later, Clinton won 51 percent of the district, and Al Gore took 52.5 percent in 2000.

Although it has typically sent Democrats to Congress, in 1992, Republican Martin Hoke, a wealthy businessman, defeated incumbent Democrat Mary Rose Oakar, who had been involved in the House bank scandal, by 57 to 43 percent. Hoke was reelected, but his voting record in Congress was too conservative for this swing district.[36] In 1996, with strong union backing, former Cleveland mayor Dennis Kucinich, a liberal Democrat, narrowly beat Hoke and then won reelection by a wide margin in 1998 and in 2000 (with 75 percent of the vote).[37] Since his election, he has been one of the most liberal members of Congress, with a strong pro-labor and pro-environment record. In the 1996 elections, 227,885 district voters went to the polls, rising to 231,560 in 2000.

As the former mayor of Cleveland (1977–1979), Kucinich had presided over a fiscal crisis that ended up costing him reelection. He has seen the population and employment base fall on the West Side of Cleveland. Now most of his constituents live in the suburbs, where they moved to escape the problems of concentrated poverty in the city. Many are loath to cooperate with Cleveland, especially if that means moving poor people into their neighborhoods. But they strongly feel the negative effects of the last several decades of deindustrialization, stagnant wages, and blocked mobility. A populist liberal, Kucinich has focused on bread-and-butter issues that benefit his constituents, such as raising the minimum wage, improving health insurance, protecting American manufacturing jobs, and the like.

Districts like the one Kucinich represents are key for our argument. These "swing" districts, both in presidential elections and in the battle for the congressional majority, can be found in areas that span the older, inner-ring suburbs. If more is not done for relatively stable working- and middle-class suburbs such as Lakewood and Parma, they too will begin to deteriorate like the poor neighborhoods in Cleveland, which have suffered terribly in recent decades. Indeed, they already show signs of deterioration. Such trends induced "leaders of nine inner-ring suburbs to forge an alliance . . . calling themselves the First Suburbs Consortium."[38] This consortium has tried to get federal housing officials to repair and sell FHA-insured properties, fund redevelopment of their commercial districts, and restrain the use of tax benefits and freeway construction to promote suburban fringe development.

Kucinich well knows that the westward movement of constituents out of his district and the inner suburbs of Cleveland, together with Ohio's overall population decline, may open the way for the Republican state legislature to eliminate his district during the current reapportionment. He would receive ample backing from his constituents, as exemplified by the First Suburbs Consortium, for changing the rules that have heavily subsidized fringe suburban development, investing more in the rehabilitation of inner-ring suburbs, and forging a coalition with Cleveland for regional growth management and regional approaches to transportation, economic development, and labor market policies. Indeed, as a former mayor of Cleveland himself, Kucinich is an ideal person to work with Cleveland public officials to forge such a coalition. By uniting on policies that would strengthen working families and blue-collar neighborhoods, they could transcend the racial differences that, in earlier decades, so divided metropolitan Cleveland. This coalition would be strengthened as well by a strong emphasis on environmental protection and improvement.

THE SEEDS OF METROPOLITAN REVIVAL

In order for a new metropolitan political coalition to succeed, support must come from public opinion, organizations and elected officials that represent residents of central cities and inner suburbs, and political and economic elites and opinion shapers. Despite the strong tradition of localism in America and the pervasive skepticism about government's capacity to solve problems, the seeds of a new metropolitics for the twenty-first century have been planted in metropolitan areas across the country.

Elites and opinion shapers are especially important in moving these issues higher on the public agenda. The evident and increasing problems facing the cities and suburbs, the growing perception that old "solutions" did not resolve them and may even have aggravated them, and increasing understanding of the importance of regional interdependencies have led many of these elites to search for new metropolitan solutions. One obvious source of support can be found among corporate leaders who are interested in improving regional economic competitiveness. Their initiatives have taken many forms in the seven decades since the founding of the first corporate planning organization, the Regional Plan Association of metropolitan New York. Of particular interest has been the rise of corporate-backed organizations devoted specifically to solving problems that hamper regional economic competitiveness, such as Silicon Valley: Joint Venture, the Greater Baltimore Alliance, and the San Diego Regional Technology Alliance.[39]

As Rosabeth Moss Kanter reminds us, the rapidly changing business climate of the last several decades has undermined the old-fashioned "leading executive from the largest local corporations" form of business organization.[40] Deregulation, corporate reorganization, and a rapidly changing business environment have meant that even the core "place-bound" companies that once provided most local business leadership, such as newspapers and public utilities, are no longer locally owned, nor are their managers as focused on local public affairs. (This may be a good thing, as such elites backed some of the most destructive changes in American central cities and metropolitan regions in the postwar period, such as urban renewal and highway building.) At the same time, regions where local firms have been able to establish formal and informal ways to cooperate on common concerns often have been able to prosper through the transition from an industrial to a postindustrial economy, despite the pressures of globalization.[41] Although the conditions for organizing this constituency and the degree of leadership it requires vary considerably, it can be an important and powerful force for promoting regional cooperation to address issues of regional planning, affordable housing, transportation infrastructure investment, labor force development, and even regional equity.

The weight of this constituency will be all the more beneficial if it can meld with local trade unions and take the "high road" to local economic development. Instead of attempting to undercut local wages by moving production elsewhere, local employers can work with trade unions and local workforce development institutions (such as community colleges) to increase the skill levels of the labor pool and thereby increase regional competitiveness. The Center on Wisconsin Strategy pioneered this approach in Milwaukee.[42] In the context of tightening regional labor markets and an initiative by the Department of Labor to fund metropolitan planning for federal training programs, private-sector labor unions and employers have much to gain from such approaches. In addition, community-based organizations have begun to engage in worker training activities, often on a regional basis.[43] In southeastern Massachusetts, a coalition of twenty-two churches was a significant force behind a regional improvement plan.[44] In short, although many business-led regional initiatives have focused on economic competitiveness, with only a secondary emphasis on regional environmental quality and little or no attention to regional equity, it is clear that combining these dimensions can strengthen the overall initiative. Moreover, it appears that leaders of such organizations have begun to understand the synergies among them. As a recent report by the Greater Baltimore Committee said:

> Addressing the social and economic problems that are, at the moment, largely concentrated in Baltimore City is essential to the long term vitality of

the entire region. . . . We need to find policies and mechanisms and partnerships that bring the resources and capabilities of the entire region to bear on a set of problems that ultimately affect every single person living and working in the entire area.[45]

Trade unions are perhaps even more important than regionally oriented business elites for the future of a new metropolitan coalition. Though trade unions are usually based in central cities, the places where their members work and live stretch across the city line. Members who live in the central city often wish to move to the suburbs; workplaces where employees need union representation are also increasingly found there. As we have shown, higher levels of unionization are crucially associated with support for Democratic candidates and the creation of a sense of solidarity among workers that crosses city lines.

Since central labor councils conduct organizing drives and mobilize voters along county or multicounty lines, they are the natural locus for labor's efforts to build a new kind of regionalism. The labor movement needs to forge alliances with community organizations and other progressive forces on a regional basis. Labor-community alliances can play a central role in creating urban areas that are more humane as well as more competitive.[46] Most central labor councils have been neither as active at forging such alliances as they need to be nor as oriented toward operating on a regional basis as many metropolitan business leaders are.

Several exceptions point the way for the others, however. Particularly noteworthy is the South Bay Labor Council (SBLC), covering Santa Clara County, including Silicon Valley and the city of San Jose. The SBLC has been a national leader in promoting forms of regional growth that speak to the needs of workers, that slow the growth of inequality, and that adopt new forms of regional cooperation. Although Silicon Valley is one of the most prosperous regions in the country (when measured by indicators such as per capita income), the SBLC's affiliate, Working Partnerships, has shown that this has produced a severe housing squeeze, growing environmental problems, heightened inequality, and the threat that Latinos, a major portion of the county's population, will be excluded from these gains. In cooperation with local elected officials and academics, the SBLC has proposed a variety of creative approaches to these problems.[47]

The Los Angeles County Federation of Labor provides another notable example of the directions county labor councils should take. Over the last decade, it has become a powerful force not only for organizing new union members—especially janitors and health care workers—but also for supporting new and dynamic candidates to replace out-of-touch incumbents in Los Angeles County.[48] It is taken for granted that such candidates will be a major factor in mayoral races in Los Angeles, but they are also active in the San Gabriel Valley, the Harbor, and Glendale-Burbank. As the *Los Angeles Times* noted, "Los Angeles labor leaders are seeking to become key players in suburban politics."[49] With the election of new leadership in the Orange County Central Labor Council next door to Los Angeles County, this new labor activism may begin to operate on a truly regional basis. Although the Los Angeles labor federation has not yet taken up the challenge of regional economic development to the same degree as the SBLC has, it is headed in that direction. If these efforts can be replicated in more metropolitan areas across the country, then a labor dimension can clearly be a key ingredient in a new metropolitan coalition. Given that labor and business both have a strong interest in a well-educated, highly productive, well-housed, and well-paid labor force—the "high road" toward regional competitiveness—the prospects for a business-labor-community alliance are brighter than some might suspect.

Opinion shapers also count. Although it is easy to scoff at the lack of political power possessed by academics, planners, and policy advocates based in non-profit organizations, the outpouring of "new metropolitan thinking" over the last decade has been truly impressive. From the acclaimed books of David Rusk and Myron Orfield to the lucid syndicated columns of Neal Peirce, the prescient arguments of the National League of Cities under William Barnes, the careful policy assessments of the National Academy of Science, the provocative ideas of John Powell of the University of Minnesota, and the compelling studies by the Brookings Center for Urban and Metropolitan Policy led by Bruce Katz, the development of new metropolitan approaches to old urban problems has never been more squarely on the agenda of the nation's policy intellectuals. This thinking has informed new metropolitan initiatives being funded by major foundations and by HUD under Secretary Henry Cisneros. Fans of the free market have sought to belittle this new movement, but they have made little headway. It may take the advent of some new metropolitan crisis to provide the window of opportunity for their ideas to be put into action, but this emerging consensus is clearly an important precondition for policy innovation.

The "new regionalism" springing up across the country does not stem just from the words of public policy intellectuals, however. It has strong grassroots support, particularly on the environmental front. "Smart growth" has developed a political following among Republican as well as Democratic governors in states such as New Jersey and Maryland, and the Sierra Club has launched a successful national campaign around the need to control suburban sprawl and contain its negative environmental effects. Two dozen local communities have asked Myron Orfield and his Metropolitan Area Research Corporation to provide technical support for their efforts to understand regional inequities and develop new approaches for resolving them.[50]

Local elected officials are more ambivalent about regionalism. On the one hand, they understand that many of their basic problems can be solved only through regional cooperation. But they resist new metropolitan approaches when they feel that their fiefdoms would be threatened. This is true not only of those who represent the outer suburbs but also of those elected from the central city. (Indeed, in a misguided effort to win suburban support, the Democratic Speaker of the New York State Assembly, Manhattan's Sheldon Silver, even abandoned his support for the relatively modest commuter tax levied by New York City.)[51] As chapter 6 detailed, cooperation among elected officials has been weak in many metropolitan areas. In the New York metropolitan area, Mayor Giuliani and his predecessors have vocally opposed the predatory economic development efforts of nearby jurisdictions and called for a regional cease-fire, but despite superficial agreement, the competition continues. Indeed, conflict between the governors of New York and New Jersey has hampered the Port Authority, one of the strongest regional government agencies in the United States. Nor is this reluctance restricted to mayors and governors; representatives of minority communities fear that metropolitan approaches might dilute minority political power.[52] At the same time, however, leaders in many metropolitan areas are undertaking the hard work of overcoming these jurisdictional jealousies, as evidenced by the First Suburbs Consortium in greater Cleveland. New institutional frameworks that would stimulate greater dialogue among local elected officials, such as regional caucuses of House members and state legislators, would be most helpful.

Proponents of a new metropolitan majority can overcome the institutional jealousies among local elected officials only when these leaders finally realize that they can solve their pressing local problems only with support from political coalitions that cross city lines. Especially in the largest, most powerful jurisdictions, such as New York City, Los Angeles, and Chicago, this will be difficult to achieve, although the mayors of these cities understand the logic of regional cooperation well enough. Just as suburbs will have to look beyond their borders to see the collective interest of the region and support it in their day-to-day activities, so will the leaders of the big cities. As fate would have it, however, decades of competition from surrounding areas and other cities and decreasing support from the state and federal governments have led such big cities to become much more entrepreneurial.

The climate among elites is thus surprisingly favorable toward regionalism, particularly among the business, labor, and environmental organizations that have the most to gain from regional approaches to investing in the human and physical capital needed to promote regional competitiveness. For that matter, suburban public opinion also favors regionalism, at least insofar as regional growth management is concerned. For example, a survey of likely voters in Santa Clara County, California, found "widespread support for regional governance" among "residents of suburban areas who ostensibly covet the political independence of their suburban municipalities."[53] Clearly, successful coalitions for limiting sprawl have been forged among Democrats and Republicans; urban, suburban, and rural interests; state and local governments; and even developers in such disparate places as Oregon, Maryland, and New Jersey. In a careful review of how regional governance was successfully adopted and defended in Oregon and Minnesota, Margaret Weir concludes that "elements of an alternative approach to metropolitan problems are as yet faint and unassembled. But discontent from many quarters with the older model of metropolitan growth and urban abandonment suggests new possibilities for the future."[54]

At present, neither the rhetoric of "smart growth" nor that of "deconcentrating urban poverty" by tearing down decrepit public housing projects has been successfully coupled with the construction of affordable housing (for rent or ownership) in the middle and outer suburbs. Indeed, neither of the two "best" cases of metropolitan governance, Portland, Oregon, and the Twin Cities in Minnesota, has made much progress on this front.[55] Yet the creation of a regulatory framework for metropolitan development, when combined with the democratic representation of all the neighborhoods and constituencies within the metropolitan area, will inevitably place this issue on the agenda. In this way, the widespread suburban impulse to control growth, address traffic congestion and pollution, and provide more affordable housing will open the way to broader discussions of regional equity.

In the final analysis, a new metropolitan majority will be realized only if advocates of metropolitan cooperation can establish new institutional frameworks to amplify their voices. At present, many new voices can be heard speaking in favor of regional cooperation and equity. Missing is an institution that would consistently elicit such voices, provide the arena for metropolitan debate and consensus formation, and command wider public attention. Of all the recommendations in the previous chapter, therefore, establishing democratically elected metropolitan councils (stretching across state lines, where needed) is likely to have the greatest long-term impact on achieving a new metropolitan majority.

Even if such councils were no more than debating societies at first, they would serve extremely important purposes by representing constituencies within a common framework, articulating different views about the interests of the metropolitan region as a whole, and proposing policy solutions. (Analogous procedures for neighborhood participation within big cities have had an important impact, even when they have not had much formal authority.) [56] The most logical source for this kind of institutional innovation is the federal government. It need not impose such forms. As the history of federal-local relations shows, the federal government can induce the adoption of metropolitan councils by prescribing how they would be organized; requiring that federal domestic programs be reviewed, if not approved or even eventually operated, by these entities; and funding a minimum level of staffing. As these metropolitan councils prove they can address serious societal problems, localities might well decide to assign them additional operating responsibilities, as has occurred in the Portland and Minneapolis–St. Paul metropolitan areas. To some, this may seem like an insufficiently dramatic response to the growth of concentrated urban poverty and the blight of uncontrolled development on the suburban fringe. We respond that these problems took fifty years to emerge, and they will take fifty years to fix. Heavy-handed solutions imposed from above would not be desirable, even if feasible. Instead, we must gradually change the basic incentive structures that produced these twin problems, which will require us to create a durable new coalition between urban and suburban voters.

THE DEMOCRATIC STAKES

Our discussion has focused on how different economic and political interests can be mobilized behind a new metropolitan political agenda. We should not dismiss, however, the power of the broader moral point that the present system of economic segregation and sprawl is fundamentally unfair and anti-democratic. The dynamic that creates and sustains the growing concentration of urban poverty and subordination is, in the words of Owen Fiss, "a moral and constitutional betrayal that demands swift and effective remedial action, not just as a matter of policy, but as a requirement of justice." [57] This betrayal obviously has the most grievous effects on those who grow up in areas of concentrated poverty, but its ramifications spread out to the entire society.

Americans believe in equal opportunity. Economic segregation violates that bedrock value. We believe that where people live in relationship to jobs and other opportunities, especially education, is an important cause of rising economic inequality in the present period. Moreover, place accentuates inequalities in ways that are not captured by economic statistics, such as differential access to high-quality public services and retail shopping and differential exposure to crime and unhealthy environments. Liberal democracies can tolerate a great deal of economic inequality, but they cannot tolerate the combining of economic, political, and social inequalities into a vicious circle of rising inequality. This is exactly what we believe is happening in American metropolitan areas.

A "secession of the successful," as Robert Reich put it, threatens a central pillar of American democracy: the belief that we are all basically in the same boat.[58] In a metropolitan landscape characterized by economic segregation and sprawl, a rising tide does *not* lift all boats. In what is arguably the most prosperous economy ever on the face of the earth, many places (and the people who live in them) are being left behind. Not only are places becoming economically isolated from the mainstream; they are becoming politically cut off as well. The flight to the suburban fringe does not just sever social relations; it also severs political relations. Never before have economic classes sorted themselves into separate governments the way they have in the United States today. The result is a bland politics at the local level that short-circuits the normal processes of political conflict and compromise and undermines civic participation in both cities and suburbs. Stereotypes and mistrust thrive in such an environment, depleting precious stores of social trust that are necessary for democracy to function effectively. The revival of American democracy requires new political institutions at the metropolitan level. We all have a stake in this.

NOTES

CHAPTER 1. PLACE STILL MATTERS

1. The growth of distance learning is profiled in Karen W. Arenson, "More Colleges Plunging into Uncharted Waters of On-Line Courses," *New York Times,* November 2, 1998. For arguments about the obsolescence of traditional dense cities, see Peter O. Muller, "Are Cities Obsolete? The Fearful Symmetry of Post-Urban America," *Sciences* (March–April 1986): 43–46; Robert Fishman, "Megalopolis," *Wilson Quarterly* (winter 1990): 25–45; Tom Morganthau and John McCormick, "Are Cities Obsolete?" *Newsweek,* September 9, 1991, pp. 42–44.
2. For criticisms of the idea that technology is making cities obsolete, see Joseph Persky, Elliot Sclar, and Wim Wiewel, *Does America Need Cities? An Urban Investment Strategy for National Prosperity* (Washington, D.C.: Economic Policy Institute, 1991); Edward Glaeser, "Why Economists Still Like Cities," *City Journal* (spring 1996): 73–77. For a critical discussion of the "city obsolescence" thesis, see Manuel Castells, *The Rise of the Network Society* (Malden, Mass.: Blackwell Publishers, 1996), pp. 394–98.
3. The idea of "weak ties" was introduced by Mark Granovetter in "The Strength of Weak Ties," *American Journal of Sociology* 78, no. 6 (1972): 1360–80.
4. In 1998, only 12 percent of households earning $12,000 or less owned a computer; only 5 percent were connected to the Internet. For those earning over $60,000, 72 percent owned a computer, and 45 percent had access to the Internet. See U.S. Department of Commerce, National Telecommunications and Information Administration, *Falling Through the Net II: New Data on the Digital Divide* (Washington, D.C.: Government Printing Office, 1998).
5. Figures on manufacturing employment are from *Risen from the Ashes: An All-American City Plans for Its Future* (Bronx, N.Y.: Strategic Policy Statement for the Bronx, Borough President Fernando Ferrer, n.d.).
6. For a history of the South Bronx, see Jill Jonnes, *We're Still Here: The Rise, Fall, and Resurrection of the South Bronx* (Boston: Atlantic Monthly Press, 1986).
7. Quoted in Jonathan Kozol, *Amazing Grace: The Lives of Children and the Conscience of a Nation* (New York: Harper Perennial, 1995), p. 52.
8. Quoted in ibid., p. 125.
9. Paul Grogan and Tony Proscio, *Comeback Cities* (Boulder, Colo.: Westview Press, 2000).
10. For a sympathetic, scholarly analysis of the New York City Partnership, see Charles J. Orlebeke, *New Life at Ground Zero: New York, Home Ownership, and the Future of American Cities* (Albany, N.Y.: Rockefeller Institute Press, 1997).
11. As Rusk argues, only regional solutions can stem central-city decline. See David Rusk, *Cities Without Suburbs* (Washington, D.C.: Woodrow Wilson Center Press, 1993), and *Inside Game/Outside Game: Winning Strategies for Saving Urban America* (Washington, D.C.: Brookings Institution Press, 1999).

12. Edward W. Hill, "The Cleveland Economy: A Case Study of Economic Restructuring," in *Cleveland: A Metropolitan Reader,* ed. W. Dennis Keating, Norman Krumholz, and David C. Perry (Kent, Ohio: Kent State University Press, 1995), p. 55.

13. Ibid., p. 72.

14. Study by Thomas Bier, Cleveland State University, as reported in Karen Dewitt, "Older Suburbs Struggle to Compete with New," *New York Times,* February 26, 1995.

15. W. Dennis Keating, *The Suburban Racial Dilemma: Housing and Neighborhoods* (Philadelphia: Temple University Press, 1994), p. 149. For a discussion of the federal court case against Parma, see Phillip J. Cooper, *Hard Judicial Choices: Federal District Court Judges and State and Local Officials* (New York: Oxford University Press, 1988), chap. 3.

16. Gang activity in Parma is discussed in Tom Breckenridge, "The Gangs Are Here: Unlikely Seven Hills Leads Counterattack," *Cleveland Plain Dealer,* September 10, 1995.

17. Tom Bier, "Housing Dynamics of the Cleveland Area, 1950–2000," in *Cleveland: A Metropolitan Reader,* ed. W. Dennis Keating, Norman Krumholz, and David C. Perry (Kent, Ohio: Kent State University Press, 1995), p. 254.

18. Quoted in Alan Achkar, "Suburbs' Plight: Inner-Ring Communities Fight Loss of Funds, People to Outlying Areas," *Cleveland Plain Dealer,* March 23, 1998.

19. U.S. Bureau of the Census Web site: census. gov.

20. Joel Garreau, *Edge City: Life on the New Frontier* (New York: Doubleday, 1991), p. 428.

21. The results of the Zero Population Growth study and quotes are from Dan Rozek, "Naperville Rates as No. 1 'Kid-Friendly' City," *Chicago Sun-Times,* August 27, 1997.

22. Joanne Kanter, "Naperville's Tale of Two Counties: Housing Growth in '80s Boomtown Traveling South," *Chicago Sun-Times,* April 30, 1993. In fact, nonresidential growth may not be the fiscal money winner that people believe it is. One study of rapidly developing DuPage County concluded that "nonresidential development has an impact on total tax levy increases that is over three times greater than that of residential development." DuPage County Development Department, Planning Division, "Impacts of Development on DuPage County Property Taxes" (Wheaton, Ill.: DuPage County Development Department, 1991), p. 8, as reported in Persky et al., *Does America Need Cities,* p. 21.

23. Quoted in Becky Beaupre, "Suburbs Spread Further; More Residents Migrating to Kendall, Will Counties," *Chicago Sun-Times,* February 1, 1999.

24. The turnover rate in Naperville is discussed in Joanne Kanter, "Naperville Population Moves a Bit," *Chicago Sun-Times,* April 30, 1993.

25. Nicholas Lemann, "Naperville: Stressed out in Suburbia," *Atlantic* (November 1989): 34–48.

26. A cross-national comparison of per capita incomes, controlling for purchasing power, is found in Lawrence Mishel, Jared Bernstein, and John Schmitt, *The State of Working America 2000–01* (Ithaca, N.Y.: Cornell University Press, 2001), p. 374. We used advance proofs issued in September 2000 that may differ from the final version to be published in 2001.

27. Cox and Alm present persuasive evidence that, on average, Americans are much better off in terms of sheer consumption than they were twenty years ago. Most economists agree that the inflation rate, as low as it is, overstates inflation because it fails to take into account the technological improvements in the products we buy. See W. Michael Cox and Richard Alm, *Myths of Rich and Poor: Why We're Better Off than We Think* (New York: Basic Books, 1999). We disagree strongly, however,

with Cox and Alm's argument that economic inequality is nothing to be concerned about.

28. Mishel et al., *The State of Working America,* chap. 7.

29. Ibid., pp. 16–17.

30. The shift to greater inequality in the American economy is explored in Bennett Harrison and Barry Bluestone, *The Great U-Turn: Corporate Restructuring and the Polarizing of America* (New York: Basic Books, 1988).

31. Robert B. Reich, *The Work of Nations* (New York: Random House, 1991).

32. Unless otherwise noted, all figures on rising income and wealth inequality are from Mishel et al., *The State of Working America.*

33. "Special Report: Executive Pay," *Business Week,* April 17, 2000; "Executive Pay: It's out of Control," *Business Week,* April 21, 1997; Dean Foust, "CEO Pay: Nothing Succeeds Like Failure," *Business Week,* September 11, 2000; Sarah Anderson, John Cavanagh, Chuck Collins, Chris Hartman, and Felice Yeskel, *Executive Excess 2000: Seventh Annual CEO Compensation Survey* (Cambridge: United for a Fair Economy; Washington: Institute for Policy Studies, August 30, 2000).

34. Edward N. Wolff, "Recent Trends in Wealth Ownership, 1983–1998," Working Paper no. 300 (Jerome Levy Economics Institute, April 2000), p. 4.

35. U.S. Bureau of the Census, *1999 Income and Poverty Estimates Based on the March Supplement to the Current Population Survey,* available at http://www.census.gov/hhes/www/povty99.html.

36. U.S. Department of Housing and Urban Development (HUD), *The State of the Cities 2000: Megaforces Shaping the Future of the Nation's Cities* (Washington, D.C.: HUD, 2000), p. 11; Steven A. Holmes, "Income's Up and Poverty Is Down, Data Shows," *New York Times,* September 27, 2000.

37. HUD, *The State of the Cities 2000,* p. 21.

38. Nina Bernstein, "Family Needs Far Exceed the Official Poverty Line," *New York Times,* September 13, 2000.

39. *Making Ends Meet: How Much Does It Cost to Raise a Family in California?* (Sacramento: California Budget Project, October 1999); Paul More et al., *The Other Los Angeles: The Working Poor in the City of the 21st Century* (Los Angeles: Los Angeles Alliance for a New Economy, August 2000).

40. HUD, *The State of the Cities 2000,* pp. 33, ix.

41. Cushing Dolbeare, "Housing Affordability: Challenge and Context" (paper presented at Housing Policy in the New Millennium, Arlington, Va., October 2–3, 2000), table 4a.

42. The fair-market rent (FMR) is set for each metropolitan area by HUD. Currently, it is the 40th percentile of the rental housing distribution of two-bedroom units in the region. The FMR is thus a little below the median rent in the region.

43. Cushing Dolbeare, *Out of Reach* (Washington, D.C.: National Low-Income Housing Coalition, September 1999).

44. For conservative critiques of the literature on rising inequality, see Cox and Alm, *Myths of Rich and Poor,* and John H. Hindraker and Scott W. Johnson, "Inequality: Should We Worry?" *American Enterprise* (July–August 1996): 35–39.

45. Research on mobility is skillfully analyzed by Daniel P. McMurrer and Isabel V. Sawhill in *Getting Ahead: Economic and Social Mobility in America* (Washington, D.C.: Urban Institute Press, 1998).

46. Mishel et al., *The State of Working America,* pp. 77–79, citing Panel Study of Income Dynamics data tabulated by Peter Gottschalk. For a review of studies showing de-

clining economic mobility in America, see Aaron Bernstein, "Is America Becoming More of a Class Society?" *Business Week,* February 26, 1996, pp. 86–91.

47. Greg Duncan et al., "Poverty and Social Assistance Dynamics in the United States, Canada, and Europe" (paper presented at the Joint Center for Political and Economic Studies Conference on Poverty and Public Policy, Washington, D.C.), as reported in Mishel et al., *The State of Working America.* See also Bernstein, "Is America Becoming More of a Class Society?"

48. Hindraker and Johnson, "Inequality: Should We Worry?" p. 35.

49. The argument that American society is a meritocracy in which intelligence largely determines one's class position is made in Richard J. Herrnstein and Charles Murray, *The Bell Curve: Intelligence and Class Structure in American Life* (New York: Free Press, 1994). Herrnstein and Murray greatly exaggerate the role of IQ in economic success. See Claude S. Fischer et al., *Inequality by Design: Cracking the Bell Curve Myth* (Princeton, N.J.: Princeton University Press, 1996).

50. The increase in the work effort of the employable poor is found in Mishel et al., *The State of Working America,* p. 319.

51. Ibid., p. 320.

52. "The Wage Squeeze," *Business Week,* July 17, 1995, p. 62.

53. For the case that the poor are better off than ever, see Cox and Alm, *Myths of Rich and Poor,* pp. 14–17.

54. *The Politics of Aristotle,* ed. and trans. Ernest Barker (New York: Oxford University Press, 1962), p. 268.

55. Thomas Jefferson, letter to Reverend James Madison, President of William and Mary, First Bishop of the Protestant Episcopal Church in Virginia, October 28, 1785.

56. Franklin D. Roosevelt's "Four Freedoms" speech, in *Documents of American History,* 7th ed., ed. Henry Steele Commager (New York: Meredith, 1963), p. 448.

57. Amartya Sen, *Inequality Reexamined* (Cambridge, Mass.: Harvard University Press, 1992), p. 39.

58. Paul Jargowsky, *Poverty and Place: Ghettos, Barrios, and the American City* (New York: Russell Sage Foundation, 1997), p. 41. On white poverty concentration, see Stephen Mulherin, "Affordable Housing and White Poverty Concentration," *Journal of Urban Affairs* 22, no. 2 (2000): 139–56.

59. William Julius Wilson, *The Truly Disadvantaged: The Inner City, the Underclass, and Public Policy* (Chicago: University of Chicago Press, 1987).

60. The figure is much higher for minorities, who tend to live in more economically segregated settings. Thirty-three percent of all black poor people and 22.1 percent of all Hispanic poor lived in high-poverty census tracts in 1990, compared with only 6.2 percent of the white poor. But as we noted, the economic segregation of the white poor is increasing rapidly. Jargowsky, *Poverty and Place,* p. 41.

61. Katherine S. Newman debunks the myth that most poor people are lazy and do not want to work in *No Shame in My Game: The Working Poor in the Inner City* (New York: Alfred A. Knopf, 1999).

62. William H. Lucy and David L. Phillips, *Confronting Suburban Decline* (Washington, D.C.: Island Press, 2000). See also Myron Orfield's seminal work on the problems of inner-ring suburbs in *Metropolitics: A Regional Agenda for Community and Stability* (Washington, D.C.: Brookings Institution Press, 1997).

63. For data on improving social trends and the difficulties conservatives are having dealing with these facts, see the special issue of *American Enterprise* (January–February 1999) entitled "Is America Turning a Corner?"

64. Our critique of the failure of the underclass literature to consider the broader regional context borrows from Mark Allen Hughes, "Misspeaking Truth to Power: A Geographical Perspective on the 'Underclass' Fallacy," *Economic Geography* 65 (1989): 187–207.

65. Edward Banfield, *The Unheavenly City: The Nature and Future of Our Urban Crisis* (Boston: Little, Brown, 1968), p. 38.

66. Gunnar Myrdal, *An American Dilemma: The Negro Problem in Modern Democracy* (New York: Harper and Row, 1944), pp. 75–78.

67. The art of separation is discussed in Michael Walzer, "Liberalism and the Art of Separation," *Political Theory* 12, no. 3 (1984): 315–30, and in his *Spheres of Justice: A Defense of Pluralism and Equality* (New York: Basic Books, 1983). Similarly, democratic theorist Robert Dahl argues that pluralist democracies move from "cumulative" to "dispersed" inequalities in his classic *Who Governs? Democracy and Power in an American City* (New Haven, Conn.: Yale University Press, 1961), chap. 7.

68. The term "separate societies" originated in the 1968 Kerner Commission report on the urban riots of the 1960s.

69. See Grogan and Proscio, *Comeback Cities.*

70. Michael E. Porter, "The Competitive Advantage of the Inner City," *Harvard Business Review* (May–June 1995): 55–71.

71. Edward L. Glaeser and Matthew E. Kahn, "From John Lindsay to Rudy Giuliani: The Decline of the Local Safety Net?" *Federal Reserve Board of New York Economic Policy Review* (September 1999): 128.

72. P. Klite, R. A. Bardwell, and J. Salzmann, "Local Television News: Getting Away with Murder," *Harvard International Journal of Press/Politics* 2 (1997): 102–12, cited in Shanto Iyengar, "'Media Effects' Paradigms for the Analysis of Local Television News" (Palo Alto, Calif.: Department of Communication and Department of Political Science, Stanford University, 1998), available at http://pcl.stanford.edu/research/papers/effects.html.

73. Franklin D. Gilliam, Jr., Shanto Iyengar, Adam Simon, and Oliver Wright, "Crime in Black and White: The Violent, Scary World of Local News," Occasional Paper no. 95-1 (Los Angeles: UCLA Center for American Politics and Public Policy, September 1995); Jeffrey D. Alderman, "Leading the Public: The Media's Focus on Crime Shaped Sentiment," *Public Perspective* 5 (1994): 26–27; Robert Entman and Andrew Rojecki, *The Black Image in the White Mind: Media and Race in America* (Chicago: University of Chicago Press, 2000); M. Freeman, "Networks Doubled Crime Coverage in '93 Despite Flat Violence Levels in U.S. Society," *Mediaweek* 4 (1994): 3–4, cited in Gilliam et al., "Crime in Black and White;" and Martin Gilens, *Why Americans Hate Welfare* (Chicago: University of Chicago Press, 1999).

CHAPTER 2. THE FACTS OF ECONOMIC SEGREGATION AND SPRAWL

1. Timothy Egan, "Many Seek Security in Private Communities," *New York Times*, September 3, 1995. Over 30 million Americans live in common-interest developments, where residents must join a community association that owns common property (e.g., streets, swimming pools) and enforces rules governing the community. For a critical analysis, see Evan McKenzie, *Privatopia: Homeowner Associations and the Rise of Residential Private Government* (New Haven, Conn.: Yale University Press, 1994). An estimated 8 million Americans also live in communities with gates that

control public access. The best source on this growing trend is Edward J. Blakely and Mary Gail Snyder, *Fortress America: Gated Communities in the United States* (Washington, D.C.: Brookings Institution Press, 1997).

2. Data on the importance of exclusive neighborhoods are from *Town and Country* magazine (1994), as reported in Blakely and Snyder, *Fortress America*, p. 76.

3. For a discussion of different indices of segregation, see Douglas S. Massey and Nancy A. Denton, *American Apartheid: Segregation and the Making of the Underclass* (Cambridge, Mass.: Harvard University Press, 1993), chap. 3.

4. Jane Jacobs, *Cities and the Wealth of Nations: Principles of Economic Life* (New York: Random House, 1984), p. 32.

5. William R. Barnes and Larry C. Ledebur, *The New Regional Economies: The U.S. Common Market and the Global Economy* (Thousand Oaks, Calif.: Sage Publications, 1998), p. 3.

6. For a discussion of the importance of regions in global competition, see Neal R. Peirce, *Citistates: How Urban America Can Prosper in a Competitive World* (Washington, D.C.: Seven Locks Press, 1993).

7. Quoted in James L. Sundquist, *Dispersing Population: What America Can Learn from Europe* (Washington, D.C.: Brookings Institution, 1975), p. 1. Drawing from Europe, Sundquist makes a persuasive case for balanced regional growth policies in the United States. For an insightful analysis of why the United States failed to enact a national growth policy in the 1970s, see Sidney Plotkin, *Keep Out: The Struggle for Land Use Control* (Berkeley: University of California Press, 1987).

8. The Reagan administration's touting of convergence is found in U.S. Department of Housing and Urban Development, *The President's National Urban Policy Report* (Washington, D.C.: Government Printing Office, 1982), p. 28.

9. Lynn E. Browne, "Shifting Regional Fortunes: The Wheel Turns," *New England Economic Review* (May–June 1989): 27–40. For further evidence of regional income divergence, see Keith R. Phillips, "Regional Wage Divergence and National Wage Inequality," *Economic Review* (Federal Reserve Board of Dallas, fourth quarter 1992): 31–44; Matthew P. Drennan, Emanuel Tobier, and Jonathan Lewis, "The Interruption of Income Convergence and Income Growth in Large Cities in the 1980s," *Urban Studies* 33, no. 1 (1996): 63–82; Edward Nissan and George Carter, "Income Inequality Across Regions over Time," *Growth and Change* 24 (summer 1993): 303–19; C. Cindy Fan and Emilio Casetti, "The Spatial and Temporal Dynamics of U.S. Regional Income Inequality, 1950–1989," *Annals of Regional Science* 28 (1994): 177–96; Norman J. Glickman, "Does Economic Development 'Cause' Regional Inequality?" Working Paper no. 101 (Center for Urban Policy Research, Rutgers, March 1996). See also the Web-based presentation of inequality trends at the county level by James K. Galbraith and the University of Texas Inequality Project, available at http://utip.gov.utexas.edu/web/Web%20Presentations/usbycountiesweb/sld001.htm.

10. The contrast between New Orleans and Bridgeport is taken from census data as reported in Larry C. Ledebur and William R. Barnes, "'All in It Together'—Cities, Suburbs, and Local Economic Regions" (Washington, D.C.: National League of Cities, February 1993).

11. The pay of secretaries in different metropolitan areas is reported in U.S. Bureau of the Census, *Statistical Brief: How Much We Earn—Factors that Make a Difference* (June 1995).

12. Consumer price indices for different regions are reported in U.S. Bureau of the Cen-

sus, *Statistical Abstract of the United States: 1999* (Washington, D.C.: Government Printing Office, 1999), pp. 498–500.

13. Drennan et al., "The Interruption of Income Convergence," p. 71.

14. Statistics on income polarization are taken from Marc V. Levine, "Globalization and Wage Polarization in U.S. and Canadian Cities: Does Public Policy Make a Difference?" in *Cities in a Global Society,* ed. Richard V. Knight and Garry Gappert (Newbury Park, Calif.: Sage Publications, 1990).

15. DRI/McGraw-Hill, *America's Clusters: Building Industry Clusters* (Sedona, Ariz.: DRI/McGraw-Hill, June 1995).

16. The effect of amenities on regional growth is discussed in Nissan and Carter, "Income Inequality Across Regions over Time."

17. William H. Frey, "Immigration, Domestic Migration and Demographic Balkanization in America: New Evidence for the 1990s," *Population and Development Review* 22 (December 1996): 741–63, updated by the author with U.S. census estimates released March 20, 1997.

18. The link between economic growth and declining ghetto poverty is made by Paul Jargowsky, *Poverty and Place: Ghettos, Barrios, and the American City* (New York: Russell Sage Foundation, 1996), p. 162, and Drennan et al., "The Interruption of Income Convergence," pp. 75–79. Tight regional labor markets draw the ghetto poor into jobs. See Richard B. Freeman, "Employment and Earnings of Disadvantaged Young Men in a Labor Shortage Economy," and Paul Osterman, "Gains from Growth? The Impact of Full Employment on Poverty in Boston," in *The Urban Underclass,* ed. Christopher Jencks and Paul Peterson (Washington, D.C.: Brookings Institution, 1991), pp. 103–34; Jargowsky, *Poverty and Place,* pp. 191–93; Richard B. Freeman and William Rodgers III, "Area Economic Conditions and the Labor Market Outcomes of Young Men in the 1990s Expansion," Working Paper W7073 (Cambridge, Mass.: National Bureau of Economic Research, April 1999); the study was reported in Sylvia Nasar and Kirsten B. Mitchell, "Booming Job Market Draws Young Black Men into Fold," *New York Times,* May 23, 1999.

19. The connections between regional inequality and regional growth are explored in Larry C. Ledebur and William R. Barnes, *City Distress, Metropolitan Disparities and Economic Growth* (Washington, D.C.: National League of Cities, 1992); Hank V. Savitch et al., "Ties that Bind: Central Cities, Suburbs, and the New Metropolitan Region," *Economic Development Quarterly* 7, no. 4 (1993): 341–58; Richard Voith, "City and Suburban Growth: Substitutes or Complements," *Business Review* (Federal Reserve Bank of Philadelphia, September–October 1992): 21–33; Manuel Pastor, Peter Dreier, J. Eugene Grigsby III, and Marta Lopez-Garza, *Regions that Work* (Minneapolis: University of Minnesota Press, 2000).

20. The connection among regional inequality, reduced infrastructure investment, and declining regional growth is examined in Edward W. Hill, Harold W. Wolman, and Coit Cook Ford III, "Can Suburbs Survive Without Their Central Cities? Examining the Suburban Dependence Hypothesis," *Urban Affairs Review* 31, no. 2 (1995): 164–65.

21. Andrew F. Haughwout, "The Paradox of Infrastructure Investment: Can a Productive Good Reduce Productivity?" *Brookings Review* 18 (summer 2000): 40–43.

22. One study found that only 3.3 percent of the rise in national wage inequality between 1978 and 1987 could be attributed to increased inequality in wages across states. Phillips, "Regional Wage Divergence and National Wage Inequality," p. 37.

23. Ted Halstead and Michael Lind, "The National Debate over School Funding Needs a Federal Focus," *Los Angeles Times,* October 8, 2000.

24. Our discussion of the Haussmannization of Paris and Vienna relies on Robert Fishman, *Bourgeois Utopia: The Rise and Fall of Suburbia* (New York: Basic Books, 1987), pp. 111–16. For a discussion of how the government in Paris is still trying to exclude immigrants, the elderly, and the poor from central Paris, see Paul White, "Ideologies, Social Exclusion and Spatial Segregation in Paris," in *Urban Segregation and the Welfare State: Inequality and Exclusion in Western Cities,* ed. Sako Musterd and Wim Ostendorf (London: Routledge, 1998), pp. 148–67.

25. The data on housing prices in Kansas City are from Chris Lester and Jeffrey Spivak, "Buying Bigger Allows Better Housing Benefit," *Kansas City Star,* December 19, 1995. This article is part of an excellent six-part series on the costs of sprawl.

26. Oliver Byrum, *Old Problems in New Times* (Chicago: American Planning Association, 1992), p. 19.

27. An early statement of concentric zone theory is Ernest W. Burgess, "The Growth of the City," in Robert E. Park, Ernest W. Burgess, and Roderick McKenzie, *The City* (Chicago: University of Chicago Press, 1925).

28. The best historical account of the fragmentation of American urban areas is found in Jon C. Teaford, *City and Suburb: The Political Fragmentation of Metropolitan America, 1850–1970* (Baltimore: Johns Hopkins University Press, 1979).

29. G. Ross Stephens and Nelson Wikstrom, *Metropolitan Government and Governance: Theoretical Perspectives, Empirical Analysis, and the Future* (New York: Oxford University Press, 2000), p. 19.

30. David Rusk, *Cities Without Suburbs* (Washington, D.C.: Woodrow Wilson Center Press, 1993).

31. Figures for Atlanta, Albuquerque, and Anchorage are from U.S. Bureau of the Census, *State and Metropolitan Area Data Book, 1991* (Washington, D.C.: Government Printing Office, 1991), table D.

32. The study of 147 central cities is found in William H. Lucy and David L. Phillips, *Confronting Suburban Decline* (Washington, D.C.: Island Press, 2000), p. 119.

33. The poverty rates of cities and suburbs are found in U.S. Department of Housing and Urban Development (HUD), *The State of the Cities* (Washington, D.C.: HUD, June 1997), p. 5, and Joseph Dalaker and Bernadette Proctor, *Poverty in the United States: 1999* (Washington, D.C.: U.S. Bureau of the Census, P60-210, September 2000).

34. On the causes of the rising income gap between cities and suburbs, see Edward Hill and Harold Wolman, "Accounting for the Change in Income Disparities Between U.S. Central Cities and Their Suburbs from 1980 to 1990," *Urban Studies* 34, no. 1 (1997): 43–60; Janice Madden, "Changes in the Distribution of Poverty Across and Within the U.S. Metropolitan Areas, 1979–1989," *Urban Studies* 33, no. 9 (1996): 1581–1600.

35. Kathryn P. Nelson examines migration into cities in forty metropolitan areas in *Gentrification and Distressed Cities: An Assessment of Trends in Intrametropolitan Migration* (Madison: University of Wisconsin Press, 1988).

36. HUD, *State of the Cities 2000–01,* p. 11, and U.S. Bureau of the Census Web site: census.gov.

37. Data on the flight of middle-income and two-parent families out of cities is reported in John D. Kasarda, Stephen J. Appold, Stuart Sweeney, and Elaine Sieff, "Central City and Suburban Migration Patterns: Is a Turnaround on the Horizon?" *Housing Policy Debate* 8, no. 2 (1997): 307–58.

38. Rusk, *Cities Without Suburbs,* pp. 75–76.

39. Property tax rates in Harvey, Illinois, are reported in Lucy and Phillips, *Confronting Suburban Decline,* p. 2, based on John McCarron, "Tip of the Iceberg: Only a Matter of Time Before Some Suburbs Come Tumbling Down," *Chicago Tribune,* April 27, 1998.

40. Lucy and Phillips, *Confronting Suburban Decline,* pp. 170–77.

41. Tracie Rozhon, "Be It Ever Less Humble: American Homes Get Bigger," *New York Times,* October 22, 2000.

42. Gaines's insightful account of teenagers in downwardly mobile suburbs is found in *Teenage Wasteland: Suburbia's Dead End Kids* (Chicago: University of Chicago Press, 1998). See also Eric Bogosian's play *Suburbia,* which takes place in a 7-Eleven parking lot and depicts the despair of suburban teenagers.

43. The discussion of Countryside is based on Chris Lester and Jeffrey Spivak, "Divided We Sprawl," *Kansas City Star,* December 17, 1995.

44. Gregory R. Weiher, *The Fractured Metropolis: Political Fragmentation and Metropolitan Segregation* (Albany, N.Y.: SUNY Press, 1991).

45. The description of St. Louis County, including the quotation about Wellston, is from Rob Gurwitt, "Saving the Aging Suburb," *Governing* (May 1993): 36–42.

46. Olivier Zunz, *The Changing Face of Inequality: Urbanization, Industrial Development, and Immigrants in Detroit, 1880–1920* (Chicago: University of Chicago Press, 1982), p. 342.

47. Otis Dudley Duncan and Beverly Duncan, *The Negro Population of Chicago: A Study of Residential Succession* (Chicago: University of Chicago Press, 1957), as reported in Reynolds Farley, "Residential Segregation of Social and Economic Groups Among Blacks, 1970–1980," in *The Urban Underclass,* ed. Christopher Jencks and Paul E. Peterson (Washington, D.C.: Brookings Institution, 1991), p. 283.

48. Albert A. Simkus, "Residential Segregation by Occupation and Race in Ten Urbanized Areas, 1950–1970," *American Sociological Review* 43 (1978): 81–93, as reported in Douglas S. Massey, "The Age of Extremes: Concentrated Affluence and Poverty in the Twenty-first Century," *Demography* 33, no. 4 (1996): 398.

49. Claudia J. Coulton et al., "Geographic Concentration of Affluence and Poverty in 100 Metropolitan Areas, 1990," *Urban Affairs Review* 32, no. 2 (November 1996): 186–216.

50. Indices of isolation and dissimilarity for the poor are reported in Alan J. Abramson, Mitchell S. Tobin, and Matthew R. VanderGoot, "The Changing Geography of Metropolitan Opportunity: The Segregation of the Poor in U.S. Metropolitan Areas, 1970 to 1990," *Housing Policy Debate* 6, no. 1 (1995): 45–72. For a discussion of the different quantitative techniques for measuring segregation, see Massey and Denton, *American Apartheid,* chap. 3.

51. In *When Work Disappears: The World of the New Urban Poor* (New York: Alfred A. Knopf, 1996), William Julius Wilson substitutes the term *ghetto poverty* for the term *underclass,* apparently taking to heart the criticism that the word *underclass* has been used to stereotype the residents of poor neighborhoods as the undeserving poor. See Herbert J. Gans, "Deconstructing the Underclass: The Term's Danger as a Planning Concept," *Journal of the American Planning Association* (summer 1990): 271–77.

52. Paul Jargowsky, *Poverty and Place: Ghettos, Barrios, and the American City* (New York: Russell Sage Foundation, 1996).

53. Ibid., pp. 11, 85.

54. Ibid., p. 45.

55. Katherine S. Newman, *No Shame in My Game: The Working Poor in the Inner City* (New York: Alfred A. Knopf and Russell Sage Foundation, 1999), appendix 1, table 1. The source is the Chicago Urban and Family Life Survey, which was the basic source of information for Wilson's *When Work Disappears*.

56. Freeman, "Employment and Earnings of Disadvantaged Men"; Osterman, "Gains from Growth?"; Freeman and Rodgers, "Area Economic Conditions."

57. Jargowsky, *Poverty and Place*, p. 101.

58. Kathryn Edin and Laura Lein, *Making Ends Meet: How Single Mothers Survive Welfare and Low-Wage Work* (New York: Russell Sage Foundation, 1997), p. 44.

59. The argument about the importance of race in generating concentrated poverty is found in Douglas S. Massey and Mitchell L. Eggers, "The Ecology of Inequality: Minorities and the Concentration of Poverty, 1970–1980," *American Journal of Sociology* 95 (1990): 1153–88; Massey and Denton, *American Apartheid;* Douglas S. Massey, Andrew B. Gross, and Kumiko Shibuya, "Migration, Segregation, and the Geographic Concentration of Poverty," *American Sociological Review* 59 (1994): 424–45.

60. Jargowsky, *Poverty and Place*, pp. 38, 63.

61. Richard D. Alba and John R. Logan, "Analyzing Locational Attainments," *Sociological Methods and Research* 20, no. 3 (February 1992): 386. See also John R. Logan, Richard D. Alba, and Shu-Yin Leung, "Minority Access to White Suburbs: A Multiregional Comparison," *Social Forces* 74, no. 3 (March 1996): 851–81; John R. Logan, Richard D. Alba, Tom McNulty, and Brian Fisher, "Making a Place in the Metropolis: Locational Attainment in Cities and Suburbs," *Demography* 33, no. 4 (November 1996): 443–53. On changes in racial segregation, see Edward Glaeser and Jacob Vigdor, "Racial Segregation in the 2000 Census" (Washington, D.C.: Brookings Institution Press, April 2001).

62. This discussion draws heavily on Jargowsky, *Poverty and Place*, pp. 132–43.

63. Sprawl is an exceedingly complex concept. Galster and colleagues identified eight separate dimensions of sprawl. See George Galister, Royce Hanson, Hal Wolman, Stephen Coleman, and Jason Reihage, "Wrestling Sprawl to the Ground: Defining and Measuring an Elusive Concept" (paper presented at the Urban Affairs Association annual meeting, Los Angeles, May 5, 2000).

64. Barry Edmonton, Michael A. Goldberg, and John Mercer, "Urban Form in Canada and the United States: An Examination of Urban Density Gradients," *Urban Studies* 22 (1985): 213.

65. F. Kaid Benfield, Matthew D. Raimi, and Donald D. T. Chen, *Once There Were Greenfields: How Urban Sprawl Is Undermining America's Environment, Economy and Social Fabric* (New York: National Resources Defense Council, 1999), p. 12.

66. The free-market explanation of suburbanization is based on bid-rent curves. See William Alonso, "A Theory of the Urban Land Market," in *Urban Change and Conflict: An Interdisciplinary Reader,* ed. Andrew Blowers et al. (London: Harper and Row, 1981), pp. 63–67.

67. Thomas J. Sugrue, *The Origins of the Urban Crisis: Race and Inequality in Postwar Detroit* (Princeton, N.J.: Princeton University Press, 1996). See also Heather Ann Thompson, "Rethinking the Politics of White Flight in the Postwar City: Detroit, 1945–1980," *Journal of Urban History* 25, no. 2 (January 1999): 163–99.

68. For positive evidence on the push hypothesis, see William H. Frey, "Central City White Flight: Racial and Nonracial Causes," *American Sociological Review* 44 (June 1979): 425–48; Harvey Marshall and Kathleen O'Flaherty, "Suburbanization in the Seventies: The 'Push-Pull' Hypothesis Revisited," *Journal of Urban Affairs* 9, no. 3

(1987): 249–62. For contrary evidence, see David F. Bradford and Harry H. Kelejian, "An Econometric Model of Flight to the Suburbs," *Journal of Political Economy* 81 (January–June 1973): 566–89; Thomas M. Guterbock, "The Push Hypothesis: Minority Presence, Crime, and Urban Deconcentration," in *The Changing Face of the Suburbs*, ed. Barry Schwartz (Chicago: University of Chicago Press, 1976), pp. 137–61.

69. Charles F. Adams, Howard B. Fleeter, Yul Kim, Mark Freeman, and Imgon Cho, "Flight from Blight and Metropolitan Suburbanization Revisited," *Urban Affairs Review* 31, no. 4 (March 1996): 529–43.

70. Julie Berry Cullen and Steven D. Levitt, "Crime, Urban Flight, and the Consequences for Cities" (NBER Working Paper no. 5737, Cambridge, Mass., September 1996), as reported in William A. Fischel, "Does the American Way of Zoning Cause the Suburbs of Metropolitan Areas to Be Too Spread Out?" in *Governance and Opportunity in Metropolitan America*, ed. Alan Altshuler et al. (Washington, D.C.: National Academy Press, 1999), p. 158.

71. Fischel, "Does the American Way of Zoning," p. 161.

72. Based on a regression analysis using 150 variables, Anthony Downs concluded that there is no statistically significant relation between urban decline and sprawl. It is difficult to evaluate Downs's conclusion, however, because he has not yet made his detailed findings and data available to other scholars. Anthony Downs, "Some Realities About Sprawl and Urban Decline," *Housing Policy Debate* 10, no. 4 (1999): 955–74.

73. Notwithstanding his conclusion that sprawl and urban decline are not related, Downs thinks that limiting sprawl would "invigorate" the urban core ("Some Realities," p. 972), thereby helping efforts at community revitalization in poor urban neighborhoods. As David Rusk notes, like in basketball, we need both an inside game (community development) and an outside game (limits on sprawl). See his *Inside Game/Outside Game: Winning Strategies for Saving Urban America* (Washington, D.C.: Brookings Institution Press, 1999).

74. For an account of economic segregation that stresses global economic forces, see Saskia Sassen, *The Global City: New York, London, Tokyo* (Princeton, N.J.: Princeton University Press, 1991).

75. Our description of ghettos in France is based on Loic J. D. Wacquant, "Urban Outcasts: Stigma and Division in the Black American Ghetto and the French Urban Periphery," *International Journal of Urban and Regional Research* 17, no. 3 (1993): 366–83, and White, "Ideologies, Social Exclusion and Spatial Segregation in Paris."

76. Sophie Body-Gendrot cites the work of Edmond Preteceille on this point in *The Social Control of Cities: A Comparative Perspective* (Oxford: Blackwell Publishers, 2000), p. 184. Our comparison of French and American ghettos draws heavily from Gendrot's insightful analysis.

77. Ada Becchi, "The Changing Space of Italian Cities," *American Behavioral Scientist* 41, no. 3 (1997): 372.

78. Barbara Schmitter Heisler, "Housing Policy and the Underclass: The United Kingdom, Germany, and the Netherlands," *Journal of Urban Affairs* 16, no. 3 (1994): 212.

79. Wacquant makes the point that the ghetto poor are isolated from the rest of society in the United States, whereas in France, there has been a "closing of the economic, social, and cultural distance between immigrants and the stagnant or downwardly mobile fractions of the native working class stuck in the *banlieue*" ("Urban Outcasts," p. 379).

80. For an insightful account of the tensions between the working class and the ghetto

poor, see Jonathan Rieder, *Carnarsie: The Jews and Italians of Brooklyn Against Liberalism* (Cambridge, Mass.: Harvard University Press, 1985).

81. The point that strong welfare policies reduce resistance to economic integration is made throughout Musterd and Ostendorf, *Urban Segregation and the Welfare State*, and in Susan S. Fainstein, "The Egalitarian City: The Restructuring of Amsterdam," *International Planning Studies* 2, no. 3 (1997): 295–314.

82. Although the rich in Europe do not generally have the option of moving to a place with a separate government, Jeffrey Sellers shows that when economically advantaged groups live apart from the rest of society in both Europe and America, they are less likely to support shared amenities such as parks and public transportation. See his "Public Goods and the Politics of Segregation: An Analysis and Cross-National Comparison," *Journal of Urban Affairs* 21, no. 2 (1999): 237–62.

CHAPTER 3. THE COSTS OF ECONOMIC SEGREGATION AND SPRAWL

1. Edward Barnes, "Can't Get There from Here," *Time*, February 19, 1996, p. 33. Under the threat of a boycott from civil rights organizations and the Buffalo Teachers Federation, the owners of the Galleria and two other malls agreed to allow bus stops on their property, with one located just a few steps from Arthur Treacher's. In November 1999, the Galleria owners agreed to a $2.55 million settlement with Wiggins's heirs (*Washington Post*, November 18, 1999).

2. Neil Kraus, *Race, Neighborhoods and Community Power: Buffalo Politics, 1934–1997* (Albany, N.Y.: SUNY Press, 2000), p. 29.

3. A massive literature now exists on the "contextual effects" of living in areas of concentrated poverty. Some scholars have concluded that, after controlling for the effects of individual characteristics, the evidence on contextual effects is weak. After a comprehensive review of the research on children, Jencks and Mayer concluded that "The literature . . . does not . . . warrant any strong generalizations about neighborhood effects." Christopher Jencks and Susan Mayer, "The Social Consequences of Growing Up in a Poor Neighborhood," in *Inner-City Poverty in the United States*, ed. Laurence E. Lynn, Jr., and Michael G. H. McGeary (Washington, D.C.: National Academy Press, 1990), p. 176. Similarly, Galster and Zobel assert that the evidence that poverty concentration causes increased social problems beyond individual characteristics is "thin and contradictory." George Galster and Anne Zobel, "Will Dispersed Housing Programmes Reduce Social Problems in the US?" *Housing Studies* 13, no. 5 (1998): 605. We argue, on the contrary, that the evidence of contextual effects from poverty concentration is overwhelming, and we cite extensive research substantiating that point in the pages that follow. One problem with many studies is that they control for so many individual characteristics that are themselves related to context, such as education, that it is not surprising that contextual effects tend to wash out. Contextual effects interact with one another in complex ways that are difficult to study using statistical regression techniques. In many ways, urban ethnographies are a better way to study contextual effects. Having said this, we acknowledge that the exact social processes by which the context influences outcomes are not well understood. We also think that researchers on contextual effects need to move out of the ghetto to examine contextual effects in a wide range of communities, including inner-ring suburbs and low-density exurban communities.

4. The Urban Institute survey of former welfare recipients is discussed in Michael M. Weinstein, "When Work Is Not Enough," *New York Times,* August 26, 1999.

5. Katherine Allen and Maria Kirby, "Why Cities Matter to Welfare Reform" (Center for Urban and Metropolitan Policy, Brookings Institution, July 2000), available at www.brook.edu/es/urban/welfarecaseloads/2000report.htm. For further evidence on this point, see Sandra J. Newman, ed., *The Home Front: Implications of Welfare Reform for Housing Policy* (Washington, D.C.: Urban Institute, 2000), especially chap. 4 by Claudia Coulton, Laura Leete, and Neil Bania.

6. "Let Them Drive Cars: Wheels for the Poor," *New Republic,* March 20, 2000.

7. The commuting problems of single mothers in Los Angeles are described in Eric Bailey, "From Welfare Lines to Commuting Crush; Labor: Many Reentering Work Force Live Far from Jobs. Experts Fear Transit Woes May Slow Reform," *Los Angeles Times,* October 6, 1997, part A, p. 1; Paul Ong and Evelyn Blumenberg, "Job Access, Commuting, and Travel Burden Among Welfare Recipients," *Urban Studies* 31, no. 1 (January 1998): 77–93.

8. Martin Wachs, "Men, Women, and Urban Travel: The Persistence of Separate Spheres," in *The Car and the City: The Automobile, the Built Environment, and Daily Urban Life,* ed. Martin Wachs and Margaret Crawford (Ann Arbor: University of Michigan Press, 1992), pp. 86–100; Carol Lawson, "Distance Makes the Heart Skip for Commuter Moms," *New York Times,* November 7, 1991.

9. John F. Kain, "Housing Segregation, Negro Employment, and Metropolitan Decentralization," *Quarterly Journal of Economics* 82, no. 2 (1968): 175–97.

10. David T. Ellwood, "The Spatial Mismatch Hypothesis: Are There Teenage Jobs Missing in the Ghetto?" in *The Black Youth Employment Crisis,* ed. Richard B. Freeman and Harry J. Holzer (Chicago: University of Chicago Press, 1986), pp. 147–87; Norman Fainstein, "The Underclass/Mismatch Hypothesis as an Explanation for Black Economic Deprivation," *Politics and Society* 15 (1986): 403–51. William Julius Wilson found that racial discrimination by employers is an important factor, especially for black males; see *When Work Disappears: The World of the New Urban Poor* (New York: Alfred A. Knopf, 1996), chap. 5.

11. Keith Ihlanfeldt, "The Spatial Mismatch Between Jobs and Residential Locations Within Urban Areas," *Cityscape* 1, no. 1 (1994): 224.

12. Although people were not randomly chosen for the program (they had to voluntarily pursue admission), their assignment to city or suburban locations was on a first-come, first-served basis, determined by the availability of units. As a result, "the city and suburban groups were highly comparable." Leonard S. Rubinowitz and James E. Rosenbaum, *Crossing the Class and Color Lines* (Chicago: University of Chicago Press, 2000), p. 77.

13. Ibid., p. 189. See also James E. Rosenbaum, "Changing the Geography of Opportunity by Expanding Residential Choice: Lessons from the Gautreaux Program," *Housing Policy Debate* 6, no. 1 (1995): 231–69.

14. See John D. Kasarda, "Entry-Level Jobs, Mobility, and Urban Minority Unemployment," *Urban Affairs Quarterly* 19 (1983): 21–40; "Urban Change and Minority Opportunities," in *The New Urban Reality,* ed. Paul E. Peterson (Washington, D.C.: Brookings Institution, 1985); "Urban Industrial Transition and the Underclass," *Annals, AAPSS* 501 (1989): 26–47; Robert Lang, *Office Sprawl: The Evolving Geography of Business* (Washington, D.C.: Brookings Institution, Center for Urban and Metropolitan Policy, October 2000); Joseph Persky and Wim Wiewel, *When Cor-*

porations Leave Town: The Costs and Benefits of Metropolitan Job Sprawl (Detroit: Wayne State University Press, 2000).

15. Based on U.S. Bureau of the Census, *County Business Patterns,* as compiled in U.S. Department of Housing and Urban Development (HUD), *The State of the Cities 2000: Megaforces Shaping the Future of the Nation's Cities* (Washington, D.C.: HUD, June 2000), p. 2. See also Thomas Stanback, *The New Suburbanization* (Boulder, Colo.: Westview Press, 1991), p. 44, as cited in Joseph Persky, Elliott Sclar, and Wim Wiewel, *Does America Need Cities?* (Washington, D.C.: Economic Policy Institute, 1991), p. 12.

16. The figures on Westchester County jobs and residents are reported in Sam Roberts, "Migrant Labor: The McShuttle to the Suburbs," *New York Times,* June 14, 1990; Elsa Brenner, "It's in the Numbers: Waves of New Faces," *New York Times,* October 5, 1997. Housing price information is reported in Deborah West, "A Trailer Park with a View Worth Millions," *New York Times,* May 13, 2001.

17. Michael N. Danielson and Jameson W. Doig, *New York: The Politics of Urban Regional Development* (Berkeley: University of California Press, 1982), pp. 82–87.

18. Elsa Brenner, "As a Town Opts for Open Space, Not All Rejoice," *New York Times,* June 6, 1999.

19. Elsa Brenner, "The Many Faces of Hunger; Even in an Affluent County, Many Have Little to Spend on Food After Paying for Rent," *New York Times,* March 14, 1999.

20. Brad Kessler, "Down and Out in Suburbia," *Nation,* September 25, 1989.

21. Martin Commacho, interview with Todd Swanstrom, August 1991.

22. Dave Sheingold, "Renter's Dilemma," *Herald Statesman,* May 18, 1988; Bruce Lambert, "Raid on Illegal Housing Shows the Plight of Suburbs' Working Poor," *New York Times,* December 7, 1996.

23. Katherine M. O'Regan summarizes seven studies examining the search methods for finding jobs in "The Effect of Social Networks and Concentrated Poverty on Black and Hispanic Youth Unemployment," *Annals of Regional Science* 27 (1993): 329.

24. Wilson, *When Work Disappears,* pp. 133–35.

25. Ibid., p. 65.

26. Claude S. Fischer, *To Dwell Among Friends: Personal Networks in Town and City* (Chicago: University of Chicago Press, 1982). See also Manuel Pastor and Ara Robinson Adams, "Keeping Down with the Joneses: Neighbors, Networks, and Wages," *Review of Regional Economics* 26, no. 2 (1996): 115–45.

27. Edward Banfield, *The Unheavenly City* (Boston: Little, Brown, 1970); Charles Murray, *Losing Ground: American Social Policy, 1950–1980* (New York: Basic Books, 1984), p. 227.

28. Paul Osterman, "Gains from Growth? The Impact of Full Employment on Poverty in Boston," and Richard B. Freeman, "Employment and Earnings of Disadvantaged Young Men in a Labor Shortage Economy," in *The Urban Underclass,* ed. Christopher Jencks and Paul Peterson (Washington, D.C.: Brookings Institution, 1991), pp. 104–34.

29. Based on research on 322 metropolitan areas by Richard B. Freeman and William Rodgers III, "Area Economic Conditions and the Labor Market Outcomes of Young Men in the 1990s Expansion," Working Paper W7073 (Cambridge, Mass.: National Bureau of Economic Research, April 1999); the study was reported in Sylvia Nasar and Kirsten B. Mitchell, "Booming Job Market Draws Young Black Men into Fold," *New York Times,* May 23, 1999.

30. Katherine S. Newman, *No Shame in My Game: The Working Poor in the Inner City* (New York: Alfred A. Knopf, 1999), p. 62.

31. Paul Jargowsky, *Poverty and Place: Ghettos, Barrios, and the American City* (New York: Russell Sage Foundation, 1997), pp. 96, 101.

32. Joel Garreau, *Edge City: Life on the New Frontier* (New York: Doubleday, 1991), p. 92.

33. Dolores Hayden, *Redesigning the American Dream: The Future of Housing, Work, and Family Life* (New York: W. W. Norton, 1986), p. 148.

34. William A. Fischel, "Comment on Anthony Downs's 'The Advisory Commission on Regulatory Barriers to Affordable Housing: Its Behavior and Accomplishments,'" *Housing Policy Debate* 2, no. 4 (1991): 1139–60. The question of growth controls raises a number of issues that extend beyond the scope of our discussion. Efforts by communities to protect the environment or reduce traffic may be in the public interest, but if enacted by individual communities, growth controls often cause leapfrog development, worsen sprawl, and prevent people from moving closer to their jobs. For a review of the evidence on growth controls, see Anthony Downs, *New Visions for Metropolitan America* (Washington, D.C.: Brookings Institution, 1994), pp. 33–36.

35. Peter Dreier, David Schwartz, and Ann Greiner, "What Every Business Can Do About Housing," *Harvard Business Review* 66, no. 5 (September–October 1988): 52–58.

36. Richard Voith, "City and Suburban Growth: Substitutes or Complements?" in *Business Review* (Philadelphia: Federal Reserve Bank of Philadelphia, September–October 1992); Larry C. Ledebur and William R. Barnes, *Metropolitan Disparities and Economic Growth* (Washington, D.C.: National League of Cities, 1992); H. V. Savitch, David Collins, Daniel Sanders, and John P. Markham, "Ties that Bind: Central Cities, Suburbs, and the New Metropolitan Region," *Economic Development Quarterly* 7, no. 4 (November 1993): 341–58; Larry C. Ledebur and William R. Barnes, *"All in It Together": Cities, Suburbs and Local Economic Regions* (Washington, D.C.: National League of Cities, February 1993); David Rusk, *Cities Without Suburbs* (Washington, D.C.: Woodrow Wilson Center Press, 1993); Richard Voith, "Do Suburbs Need Cities," *Journal of Regional Science* 38, no. 3 (1998): 445–64; Stephanie Shirley Post and Robert M. Stein, "State Economies, Metropolitan Governance, and Urban-Suburban Dependence," *Urban Affairs Review* 36, no. 1 (September 2000): 46–60.

37. Edward W. Hill, Harold L. Wolman, and Coit Cook Ford III, "Can Suburbs Survive Without Their Central Cities? Examining the Suburban Dependence Thesis," *Urban Affairs Review* 31, no. 2 (November 1995): 147–74.

38. See Peter Muller, "Are Cities Obsolete? The Fearful Symmetry of Post-Urban America," *Sciences* (March–April 1986): 43–46; Anthony Pascal, "The Vanishing City," *Urban Studies* 24 (1987): 597–603; Robert Fishman, "Megalopolis," *Wilson Quarterly* (winter 1990): 25–45; Tom Morganthau and John McCormick, "Are Cities Obsolete?" *Newsweek,* September 9, 1991, pp. 42–44.

39. For a summary of the evidence on the continued need for face-to-face relations in the economy, see Keith Ihlanfeldt, "The Importance of the Central City to the Regional and National Economy: A Review of the Arguments and Empirical Evidence," *Cityscape* 1, no. 1 (1995): 219–44.

40. Garreau, *Edge City,* pp. 25, 4, 8. Muller, "Are Cities Obsolete?" and Robert Fishman, *Bourgeois Utopias* (New York: Basic Books, 1987), also argue that cities are becoming obsolete as suburbs take over their traditional functions.

41. Joseph Persky, Elliot Sclar, and Wim Wiewel, *Does America Need Cities? An Urban Investment Strategy for National Prosperity* (Washington, D.C.: Economic Policy Institute, 1991), p. 13.

42. Alex Schwartz, "Subservient Suburbia: The Reliance of Large Suburban Companies on Central City Firms for Financial and Professional Services," *Journal of the American Planning Association* (summer 1993): 302.

43. Antonio Ciccone and Robert E. Hall, "Productivity and the Density of Economic Activity," *American Economic Review* 86, no. 1 (March 1996): 54–70.

44. Michael Storper, "The Limits to Globalization: Technology Districts and International Trade," *Economic Geography* 68 (1992): 60–93.

45. AnnaLee Saxenian, *Regional Advantage: Culture and Competition in Silicon Valley and Route 128* (Cambridge, Mass.: Harvard University Press, 1994). See also Bennett Harrison, "Industrial Districts: Old Wine in New Bottles?" *Regional Studies* 26, no. 5 (1992): 469–83; Stephan Schrader, "Information Technology Transfers Between Firms: Cooperation Through Information Trading," *Research Policy* 20 (1991): 153–70.

46. The concept of flexible specialization was originated by Michael J. Piore and Charles F. Sabel in *The Second Industrial Divide: Possibilities for Prosperity* (New York: Basic Books, 1984).

47. For this reason, Mayor Richard Riordan's offer of costly incentives for the new DreamWorks studio was a waste of taxpayers' money. The studios are not about to relocate to St. Louis or any other metropolitan area.

48. Daniel J. Luria and Joel Rogers, *Metro Futures: Economic Solutions for Cities and Their Suburbs* (Boston: Beacon Press, 1999), p. 13. For further support of the proposition that high-wage manufacturing can prosper in central cities, see Joel Rast, *Remaking Chicago: The Political Origins of Urban Industrial Change* (De Kalb: Northern Illinois University Press, 1999).

49. *U.S. Metro Economies: The Engines of America's Growth* (Washington, D.C.: U.S. Conference of Mayors and the National Association of Counties, prepared by the Standard and Poor's DRI Division of the McGraw-Hill Companies, 1999).

50. Roberts, "Migrant Labor."

51. Laurie Kaye Abraham, *Mama might be better off dead: The Failure of Health Care in Urban America* (Chicago: University of Chicago Press, 1993), pp. 17–18.

52. U.S. Bureau of the Census, *Statistical Abstract of the United States: 1997* (Washington, D.C.: Government Printing Office, 1997), p. 833; U.S. Bureau of the Census, *Statistical Abstract of the United States: 2000* (Washington, D.C.: Government Printing Office, 1999), p. 832.

53. Amartya Sen, "The Economics of Life and Death," *Scientific American* (May 1993): 44.

54. Colin McCord and Harold P. Freeman, "Excess Mortality in Harlem," *New England Journal of Medicine* 322, no. 3 (January 18, 1990): 173.

55. G. B. Rodgers, "Income and Inequality as Determinants of Mortality: An International Cross-Section Analysis," *Population Studies* 33 (1979): 343–51.

56. John W. Lynch et al., "Income Inequality and Mortality in Metropolitan Areas in the United States," *American Journal of Public Health* 88, no. 7 (1998): 1074–80.

57. Yoav Ben-Shlomo, Ian R. White, and Michael Marmot, "Does the Variation in the Socioeconomic Characteristics of an Area Affect Mortality?" in *The Society and Population Health Reader: Income Inequality and Health,* ed. Ichiro Kawachi, Bruce P. Kennedy, and Richard G. Wilkinson (New York: New Press, 1999), pp. 47–49.

58. The increased risk of death persisted even after controlling for baseline health status, race, income, employment status, access to medical care, health insurance coverage, smoking, alcohol consumption, physical activity, body mass index, sleep patterns, social isolation, marital status, depression, and personal uncertainty. Because many of these conditions negatively associated with health are partly caused by residence in distressed neighborhoods, the Alameda study seriously underestimated the effect of place on the chances of dying. Mary Haan, George A. Kaplan, and Terry Camacho, "Poverty and Health: Prospective Evidence from the Alameda County Study," *American Journal of Epidemiology* 125, no. 6 (1987): 989–98. A more recent study based on a nationally representative sample of adults found that "a person's health is associated with the SES [socioeconomic status] characteristics of the community over and above one's income, education, and assets." Stephanie A. Robert, "Community-Level Socioeconomic Status Effects on Adult Health," *Journal of Health and Social Behavior* 39 (March 1998): 18. See also George A. Kaplan, "People and Places: Contrasting Perspectives on the Association Between Social Class and Health," *International Journal of Health Services* 26, no. 3 (1996): 507–19.

59. Robert I. Mills, *Health Insurance Coverage: 1999* (Washington, D.C.: U.S. Bureau of the Census, Current Population Reports, P60–211, September 2000). A higher proportion of central-city residents is uninsured compared with suburbanites. Among adults, for example, 25 percent of central-city residents are uninsured, compared with 17 percent of suburbanites. UCLA Center for Health and Policy Research, memo to the authors.

60. Data cited in James W. Fossett and Janet D. Perloff, *The "New" Health Reform and Access to Care: The Problem of the Inner City* (Washington, D.C.: Kaiser Commission on the Future of Medicaid, 1995), pp. 31–32.

61. Ibid., p. 32.

62. Jonathan Kozol, *Amazing Grace: The Lives of Children and the Conscience of a Nation* (New York: Harper Perennial, 1995), p. 172.

63. U.S. Bureau of the Census, *Statistical Abstract of the United States: 2000*, p. 382.

64. Jacob A. Riis, *How the Other Half Lives* (1890; reprint, New York: Hill and Wang, 1957), p. 81.

65. For a discussion of the parallels between New York slums in the 1890s and the 1990s, see Sam Roberts, "New York in the Nineties," *New York Times Magazine*, September 29, 1991, pp. 35–39.

66. One study found, for example, that the rate of traffic injuries to children was four times higher in the poorest neighborhoods of Montreal compared with the least poor neighborhoods. Geoffrey Dougherty, I. Barry Pless, and Russell Wilkins, "Social Class and the Occurrence of Traffic Injuries and Deaths in Urban Children," *Canadian Journal of Public Health* 81 (May–June 1990): 204–9.

67. Anthony P. Polednak, *Segregation, Poverty, and Mortality in Urban African Americans* (New York: Oxford University Press, 1991), p. 139.

68. According to Dr. Bernard Guyer of Johns Hopkins University, as reported in Lauran Neergaard, "Report Urges Improvement in Immunization System," *Albany Times Union*, June 16, 2000.

69. Paul Mushak, "Defining Lead as the Premiere Environmental Health Issue for Children in America: Criteria and Their Quantitative Application," *Environmental Research* 59 (1992): 281–309; Nick Farr and Cushing Dolbeare, "Childhood Lead Poisoning: Solving a Health and Housing Problem," *Cityscape* 2, no. 3 (September 1996): 176–82.

70. A 1992 U.S. Environmental Protection Agency report on environmental equity stated that "evidence indicates that racial minority and low-income populations are disproportionately exposed to lead, selected air pollutants, hazardous waste facilities, contaminated fish tissue, and agricultural pesticides in the workplace." It concluded that this population was "more likely to actually experience harm due to these exposures." U.S. Environmental Protection Agency (EPA), *Environmental Equity: Reducing Risks for All Communities,* vols. 1 and 2 (Washington, D.C.: EPA Policy, Planning and Evaluation Report no. PM-221, EPA 230-R-92-008, 1992), letter of transmittal and pp. 1–2. The literature on environmental equity is large and contentious. For an introduction to the issue, see Robert D. Bullard, *Dumping in Dixie: Race, Class and Environmental Quality* (Boulder, Colo.: Westview Press, 1990). For analyses of the literature, see J. Tom Boer, Manuel Pastor, Jr., James L. Sadd, and Lori D. Snyder, "Is There Environmental Racism: The Demographics of Hazardous Waste in Los Angeles County," *Social Science Quarterly* 78, no. 4 (December 1997): 793–810.

71. Kozol, *Amazing Grace,* p. 7; Kemba Johnson, "Big Stack Attack," *City Limits* (July–August 1999): 5.

72. Sheryl Gay Stolberg, "Poor People Are Fighting Baffling Surge in Asthma," *New York Times,* October 18, 1999.

73. Kozol, *Amazing Grace,* p. 171.

74. David L. Rosenstreich et al., "The Role of Cockroach Allergy and Exposure to Cockroach Allergen in Causing Morbidity Among Inner-City Children with Asthma," *New England Journal of Medicine* 336, no. 19 (May 8, 1997): 1356–63.

75. Kawachi et al., *Society and Population Health Reader,* comment by the editors, p. 158.

76. For an introduction to the literature, see the articles in ibid., part 3; Robert Putnam, *Bowling Alone: The Collapse and Revival of American Community* (New York: Simon and Schuster, 2000), chap. 20.

77. Loic J. D. Wacquant and William Julius Wilson, "The Cost of Racial and Class Exclusion in the Inner City," *Annals of the American Academy of Political and Social Science* 501 (January 1989): 22–24.

78. Research has established a firm connection between poor neighborhoods and early-adolescent sexual activity and failure to use contraceptives (controlling for individual characteristics). See Karin L. Brewster, John O. G. Billy, and William R. Grady, "Social Context and Adolescent Behavior: The Impact of Community on the Transition to Sexual Activity," *Social Forces* 71, no. 3 (March 1993): 713–40; Karin L. Brewster, "Race Differences in Sexual Activity Among Adolescent Women: The Role of Neighborhood Characteristics," *American Sociological Review* 59 (June 1994): 408–24; Karin L. Brewster, "Neighborhood Context and the Transition to Sexual Activity Among Black Women," *Demography* 31, no. 4 (November 1994): 603–14; John O. G. Billy, Karin L. Brewster, and William R. Grady, "Contextual Effects on the Sexual Behavior of Adolescent Women," *Journal of Marriage and Family* 56 (May 1994): 387–404.

79. Polednak, *Segregation, Poverty, and Mortality,* pp. 119, 122.

80. David Barboza, "Rampant Obesity: A Debilitating Reality for the Urban Poor," *New York Times,* December 26, 2000.

81. Paula Diehr et al., "Do Communities Differ in Health Behaviors?" *Journal of Clinical Epidemiology* 46, no. 10 (1993): 1141–49.

82. Maro Wilson and Martin Daly, "Life Expectancy, Economic Inequality, Homicide,

and Reproductive Timing in Chicago Neighborhoods," in Kawachi et al., *Society and Population Health Reader,* p. 299.

83. Geronimus argues that for poor women in poor neighborhoods who have short life expectancies and premature aging, teenage childbearing is rational because it increases the likelihood that the child will be healthy and have able-bodied caretakers. Geronimus also, however, argues that the risks and costs of teen childbearing are minimal. Arline T. Geronimus, "Teenage Childbearing and Personal Responsibility: An Alternative View," *Political Science Quarterly* 112, no. 3 (1997): 405–30.

84. Ana Correa Fick and Sarah Moody Thomas, "Growing Up in a Violent Environment: Relationship to Health-Related Beliefs and Behavior," *Youth and Society* 27, no. 2 (1996): 136–47.

85. For a review of some of this literature, see Shelley E. Taylor, Rena L. Repetti, and Teresa Seeman, "What Is an Unhealthy Environment and How Does It Get Under the Skin," in Kawachi et al., *Society and Population Health Reader,* pp. 351–78.

86. Bruce S. McEwen, "Protective and Damaging Effects of Stress Mediators," in Kawachi et al., *Society and Population Health Reader,* p. 386.

87. Rodrick Wallace, "A Synergism of Plagues: 'Planned Shrinkage,' Contagious Housing Destruction, and AIDS in the Bronx," *Environmental Research* 47 (1988): 1–33; Elmer L. Streuning, Rodrick Wallace, and Robert Moore, "Housing Conditions and the Quality of Children at Birth," *Bulletin of the New York Academy of Medicine* 66, no. 5 (1990): 463–78; Rodrick Wallace, "Urban Desertification, Public Health and Public Order: 'Planned Shrinkage,' Violent Death, Substance Abuse and AIDS in the Bronx," *Social Science Medicine* 31, no. 7 (1990): 801–13; Rodrick Wallace, "A Fractal Model of HIV Transmission on Complex Sociogeographic Networks. Part 2: Spread from a Ghettoized 'Core Group' into a More General Population," *Environment and Planning A* 29 (1997): 789–804; R. Wallace, A. J. Fisher, and R. Fullilove, "Marginalization, Information, and Infection: Risk Behavior Correlation in Ghettoized Sociogeographic Networks and the Spread of Disease to Majority Populations," *Environment and Planning A* 29 (1997): 1629–45; R. Wallace and D. Wallace, "The Destruction of US Minority Urban Communities and the Resurgence of Tuberculosis: Ecosystem Dynamics of the White Plague in the Developing World," *Planning and Environment A* 29 (1997): 269–91.

88. Sheryl Gay Stolberg, "U.S. Wakes to Epidemic of Sexual Diseases," *New York Times,* March 9, 1998.

89. R. Wallace, D. Wallace, and H. Andrews, "AIDS, Tuberculosis, Violent Crime, and Low Birth Weight in Eight U.S. Metropolitan Areas: Public Policy, Stochastic Resonance, and the Regional Diffusion of Inner-City Markers," *Environment and Planning A* 29 (1997): 525–55.

90. Allen Thein Durning, *The Car and the City* (Seattle: Northwest Environment Watch, 1996), p. 10.

91. Mark Delucchi, *Health Effects of Motor Vehicle Pollution* (Institute of Transportation Standards, University of California at Davis, 1995).

92. Durning, *The Car and the City,* p. 24.

93. For evidence and citations, see Meni Koslowsky, Avraham N. Kluger, and Mordechai Reich, *Commuting Stress: Causes, Effects, and Methods of Coping* (New York: Plenum Press, 1995), especially chap. 4; Steven M. White and James Rotton, "Type of Commute, Behavioral Aftereffects, and Cardiovascular Activity: A Field Experiment," *Environment and Behavior* 36, no. 6 (1998): 763–80.

94. Jeffrey P. Kaplan and William H. Dietz, "Caloric Imbalance and Public Health Policy," *Journal of the American Medical Association* 282, no. 16 (October 27, 1999): 1579–81.

95. Putnam, *Bowling Alone,* p. 213.

96. Jane Jacobs, *The Death and Life of Great American Cities* (New York: Random House, 1961), p. 72.

97. Richard D. Bingham and Zhongai Zhang, "Poverty and Economic Morphology of Ohio Central-City Neighborhoods," *Urban Affairs Review* 32, no. 6 (1997): 766–96.

98. U.S. Department of Housing and Urban Development, *New Markets: The Untapped Retail Buying Power in America's Inner Cities* (Washington, D.C.: Government Printing Office, July 1999), p. 23. These inner-city areas were defined as census tracts with poverty rates above 20 percent or with median family incomes 80 percent or less of the metropolitan area median.

99. David Caplovitz, *The Poor Pay More: Consumer Practices of Low-Income Families* (Glencoe, Ill.: Free Press, 1963).

100. Ibid., p. 13.

101. *Hearing Before the Select Committee on Hunger, House of Representatives, 102nd Congress,* September 30, 1992 (Washington, D.C.: Government Printing Office, 1992), p. 17. The percentage goes down in areas with high housing costs.

102. Reported in Alix M. Freedman, "The Poor Pay More for Food in New York, Survey Finds," *Wall Street Journal,* April 15, 1991.

103. James M. MacDonald and Paul E. Nelson, Jr., "Do the Poor Still Pay More? Food Price Variations in Large Metropolitan Areas," *Journal of Urban Economics* 30 (1991): 344–59.

104. As reported in *Hearing Before the Select Committee on Hunger,* p. 24.

105. Ibid., p. 1.

106. Michael E. Porter, "The Competitive Advantage of the Inner City," *Harvard Business Review* (May–June 1995): 58.

107. Testimony of Rev. Monsignor William J. Linder, in *Hearing Before the Select Committee on Hunger,* p. 185.

108. Bill Turque, "Where the Food Isn't," *Newsweek,* February 24, 1992, pp. 36–37.

109. Bingham and Zhang, "Poverty and Morphology of Ohio Central City Neighborhoods," p. 786.

110. John P. Caskey, *Fringe Banking: Check-Cashing Outlets, Pawnshops, and the Poor* (New York: Russell Sage Foundation, 1994).

111. Evelyn Nieves, "Poor Credit? Rent-to-Moan Is Wooing You," *New York Times,* January 15, 1998.

112. Edward C. Banfield, *The Unheavenly City Revisited* (Boston: Little, Brown, 1974), p. 61.

113. See the insightful discussion of the culture of poverty perspective in Caskey, *Fringe Banking,* pp. 81–83.

114. Ibid., p. 89.

115. The literature on redlining is voluminous. For a recent summary, see Margery Austin Turner et al., *What We Know About Mortgage Lending Discrimination in America* (Washington, D.C.: U.S. Department of Housing and Urban Development, September 1999).

116. John P. Caskey, "Bank Representation in Low-Income and Minority Communities," *Urban Affairs Quarterly* 29, no. 4 (June 1994): 617–38.

117. A two-tiered market also exists for insurance. Many insurance companies have re-

strictions on writing policies for older homes or homes below a certain value. Fewer insurance agents are located in central cities. As a result of insurance redlining, it is difficult to insure a home in many city neighborhoods, and when you can, the price is often higher. See Gregory D. Squires, ed., *Insurance Redlining: Disinvestment, Reinvestment, and the Evolving Role of Financial Institutions* (Washington, D.C.: Urban Institute Press, 1997). It also costs more for car insurance if you live in a city compared with a suburb. According to a survey by the *Chicago Sun-Times* of the three top insurance companies, the base rate in Chicago's Austin neighborhood is more than double that in Naperville, an outer-ring suburb. The difference can add up to $800 a year. Tim Novak and Jon Schmid, "Car Insurance Rides on Zip Codes: Cities Rates Higher than Most Suburbs," *Chicago Sun-Times,* November 30, 1997.

118. Chandrika Jayathirtha and Jonathan Fox, "Overspending Behavior of Households with and Without Vehicle Purchases," *Consumer Interests Annual* 43 (1997): 124–30.
119. U.S. Bureau of the Census, *Statistical Abstract of the United States: 2000,* pp. 458, 510, 511.
120. Leslie Earnest, "Household Debt Grows Precarious as Rates Increase," *Los Angeles Times,* May 13, 2000; Louis Uchitelle, "Equity Shrivels as Homeowners Borrow and Buy," *New York Times,* January 19, 2001; Edward N. Wolff, *Recent Trends in Wealth Ownership 1983–98,* Working Paper no. 300 (Annandale-on-Hudson, N.Y.: Jerome Levy Economics Institute of Bard College, April, 2000).
121. Juliet Schor, *The Overspent American* (New York: Basic Books, 1998), p. 72.
122. U.S. Bureau of the Census, *Statistical Abstract of the United States: 1999,* p. 563.
123. Dirk Johnson, "For Teenagers, Fast Food Is a Snack, Not a Job," *New York Times,* January 8, 2001.
124. U.S. Bureau of the Census, *Statistical Abstract of the United States: 2000,* p. 516.
125. Ibid., p. 640.
126. Jayathirtha and Fox, "Overspending Behavior of Households."
127. For this reason, "location-efficient mortgages" have been proposed that allow households with less automobile dependence to qualify for larger mortgages and thus buy more expensive homes. Durning, *The Car and the City,* p. 19.
128. John Kenneth Galbraith, *The Affluent Society* (New York: Mentor Books, 1958).
129. Evan McKenzie, *Privatopia: Homeowner Associations and the Rise of Residential Private Government* (New Haven, Conn.: Yale University Press, 1994).
130. Alladi Venkratesh, "Changing Consumption Patterns: The Transformation of Orange County Since World War II," in *The Consumer Society,* ed. Neva R. Goodwin, Frank Ackerman, and David Kiron (Washington, D.C.: Island Press, 1997), p. 74.
131. Reported in Schor, *The Overspent American,* p. 87.
132. Tom Wolfe, *The Bonfire of the Vanities* (Toronto: Bantam Books, 1987), p. 87.
133. Myron Orfield, *Metropolitics: A Regional Agenda for Community and Stability* (Washington, D.C.: Brookings Institution Press, 1997), pp. 20–21.
134. Crime rate data are from FBI Uniform Crime Reports, as analyzed in U.S. Department of Housing and Urban Development (HUD), *The State of the Cities 2000: Megaforces Shaping the Future of the Nation's Cities* (Washington, D.C.: HUD, 2000), p. 47. For a discussion of the extent of the crime drop in cities and the debate about its causes, see Paul Grogan and Tony Proscio, *Comeback Cities* (Boulder, Colo.: Westview Press, 2000), chap. 7, and Fox Butterfield, "Reason for Dramatic Drop in Crime Puzzles Experts," *New York Times,* March 29, 1998.
135. U.S. Bureau of the Census, *Statistical Abstract of the United States: 2000,* p. 210.
136. Robert J. Sampson and Janet L. Lauritsen, "Violent Victimization and Offending:

Individual-, Situational-, and Community-Level Risk Factors," in *Understanding and Preventing Violence,* vol. 3, *Social Influences,* ed. Albert J. Reiss, Jr., and Jeffrey A. Roth (Washington, D.C.: National Academy Press, 1994), pp. 41–42.

137. For a subcultural view of crime, see Murray, *Losing Ground,* chap. 8. In that chapter, Murray uses "blacks as our proxy for that group" (p. 116) — that is, the group of people who were drawn into a culture of poverty by federal welfare spending and misguided programs to prevent crime instead of punish it.

138. The evidence on this point is cited in John Hagan and Ruth D. Peterson, "Criminal Inequality in America: Patterns and Consequences," in *Crime and Inequality,* ed. John Hagan and Ruth D. Peterson (Stanford, Calif.: Stanford University Press, 1995), p. 20.

139. Allen E. Liska and Paul E. Bellair, "Violent Crime Rates and Racial Composition: Convergence over Time," *American Journal of Sociology* 101, no. 3 (November 1995): 578–610.

140. Michiko Kakatuni, "Bananas for Rent," *New York Times Magazine,* November 9, 1997, p. 32.

141. Schor, *The Overspent American,* p. 78.

142. Ibid., p. 39.

143. Caplovitz, *The Poor Pay More,* p. 180.

144. In a review of William Julius Wilson's *When Work Disappears,* Joe Klein points out that "this new poverty — the chronic anarchy and dependency that began to manifest itself in the 1960s — is primarily a disease of affluence." It is disastrous, Klein argues, for the poor to seek to imitate the lifestyle choices of the upper middle class. *New Republic,* October 28, 1996, p. 32.

145. Carol W. Kohfeld and John Sprague, "Urban Unemployment Drives Urban Crime," *Urban Affairs Quarterly* 24, no. 2 (December 1988): 215–41.

146. Studies on how much crime pays are summarized in Richard B. Freedman, "Crime and the Employment of Disadvantaged Youths," in *Urban Labor Markets and Job Opportunity,* ed. George E. Peterson and Wayne Vroman (Washington, D.C.: Urban Institute Press, 1992), pp. 227–31.

147. Wilson, *When Work Disappears,* chap. 5.

148. Philippe Bourgois, "Office Work and the Crack Alternative Among Puerto Rican Drug Dealers in East Harlem," in *Urban Life: Readings in Urban Anthropology,* 3d ed., ed. George Gmelch and Walter P. Zenner (Prospect Heights, Ill.: Waveland Press, 1996), p. 425.

149. Daniel Goleman, "Black Scientists Study the 'Pose' of the Inner City," *New York Times,* April 29, 1992. Dr. Majors is the coauthor of *Cool Pose: The Dilemmas of Black Manhood in America* (Lexington, Mass.: Lexington Books, 1992).

150. Elijah Anderson, "The Code of the Streets," *Atlantic Monthly* (May 1994): 81–94.

151. Douglas S. Massey, "The Age of Extremes: Concentrated Affluence and Poverty in the Twenty-first Century," *Demography* 33, no. 4 (November 1996): 408.

152. Robert J. Sampson, Stephen W. Raudenbush, and Felton Earls, "Neighborhoods and Violent Crime: A Multilevel Study of Collective Efficacy," in Kawachi et al., *Society and Population Health Reader,* pp. 336–50.

153. William Julius Wilson, *The Truly Disadvantaged: The Inner City, the Underclass, and Public Policy* (Chicago: University of Chicago Press, 1987).

154. For evidence on this point, see Sampson and Lauritsen, "Violent Victimization and Offending," p. 76.

155. For evidence on the relationship between crime and population loss, see William

Frey, "Central City White Flight: Racial and Non-Racial Causes," *American Sociological Review* 44 (1979): 425–48; Robert J. Sampson and J. Wooldredge, "Evidence that High Crime Rates Encourage Migration Away from Central Cities," *Sociology and Social Research* 70 (1986): 310–14; Wesley Skogan, "Fear of Crime and Neighborhood Change," in *Communities and Crime*, ed. A. J. Reiss and M. Tonry (Chicago: University of Chicago Press, 1986), pp. 203–29; Liska and Bellair, "Violent Crime Rates and Racial Composition." For a review of the literature on this point, see Sampson and Lauritsen, "Violent Victimization and Offending," pp. 75–78.

156. Dan Korem, *Suburban Gangs: The Affluent Rebels* (Richardson, Tex.: International Focus Press, 1994); Daniel J. Monti, *Wannabe: Gangs in Suburbs and Schools* (Cambridge, Mass.: Blackwell Publishers, 1994).

157. There are about 49,000 completed or attempted carjackings each year. Bureau of Justice Statistics Special Report, *Carjackings in the United States 1992–96* (March 1999). Under Section 2119(2) of Title 18 of the United States Code, carjacking is a federal crime punishable by up to twenty-five years in prison in the case of "serious bodily injury."

158. Kathleen Maguire and Ann L. Pastore, eds., *Sourcebook of Criminal Justice Statistics 1999* (Washington, D.C.: U.S. Department of Justice, Bureau of Justice Statistics, Government Printing Office, 2000), pp. 277–78.

159. HUD, *State of the Cities 2000*, p. 47. For further evidence on the converging rates of crime in cities and suburbs, see *Sourcebook of Criminal Justice Statistics* (Washington, D.C.: U.S. Department of Justice, Bureau of Justice Statistics, Government Printing Office, various years).

160. A study examining 244 suburban communities in northern New Jersey found that the 1980 property crime rate varied from 343 to 25,582 crimes per 100,000 population, and the violent crime rate varied from zero to 9,544 per 100,000 population. Richard D. Alba, John R. Logan, and Paul E. Bellair, "Living with Crime: The Implications of Racial/Ethnic Differences in Suburban Location," *Social Forces* 73, no. 2 (1994): 403, 406.

161. The data are based on a nationally representative sample of students reported in Bureau of Justice Statistics, *School Crime Supplement to the National Crime Victimization Survey,* January–June 1989, 1995, 1999, pp. 35–37.

162. Quoted in Laurel Shaper Walters, "School Violence Enters Suburbs," *Christian Science Monitor,* April 19, 1993.

163. Douglas Smith, "The Neighborhood Context of Police Behavior," in *Communities and Cities,* ed. Albert J. Reiss, Jr., and Michael Tonry (Chicago: University of Chicago Press, n.d.), as reported in Robert J. Sampson, "Effects of Socioeconomic Context on Official Reaction to Juvenile Delinquency," *American Sociological Review* 51, no. 6 (1986): 877.

164. Ibid.

165. Monti, *Wannabe: Gangs in Suburbs and Schools.*

166. See Janny Scott, "Working Hard, More or Less," *New York Times,* July 10, 1999.

167. Lawrence Mishel, Jared Bernstein, and John Schmitt, *State of Working America 2000–01* (Ithaca, N.Y.: Cornell University Press, 2001). Schor reports that between 1969 and 1987 the average employed person worked the equivalent of an extra month a year. Juliet Schor, *The Overworked American: The Unexpected Decline of Leisure* (New York: Basic Books, 1992), p. 29.

168. Reported in Sylvia Ann Hewlett, "Running Hard Just to Keep Up," *Time,* special issue, "Women: The Road Ahead" (fall 1990), p. 54.

169. Schor, *The Overworked American,* p. 21.

170. Reported in Hewlett, "Running Hard," p. 54.

171. Reported in Fox Butterfield, "Survey Finds that Crimes Cost $450 Billion a Year," *New York Times,* April 9, 1999.

172. Alan Farnham, "U.S. Suburbs Are Under Seige," *Fortune,* December 28, 1992, p. 43.

173. Edward J. Blakely and Mary Gail Snyder, *Fortress America: Gated Communities in the United States* (Washington, D.C.: Brookings Institution Press, 1997), p. 126.

174. James D. Wright, Joseph F. Sheley, and M. Dwayne Smith, "Kids, Guns, and Killing Fields," *Society* (November–December 1992): 88.

175. Allen E. Liska, Andrew Sanchirico, and Mark D. Reed, "Fear of Crime and Constrained Behavior: Specifying and Estimating a Reciprocal Effects Model," *Social Forces* 66, no. 3 (1988): 827–37.

176. Linda Heath and John Petraitis, "Television Viewing and Fear of Crime: Where Is the Mean World?" *Basic and Applied Social Psychology* 8, nos. 1 and 2 (1987): 97–123; Shanto Iyengar, "'Media Effects' Paradigms for the Analysis of Local Television News" (Departments of Communication and Political Science, Stanford University, 1998), available at http://pcl.stanford.edu/research/papers/effects.html; Franklin D. Gilliam, Jr., Shanto Iyengar, Adam Simon, and Oliver Wright, "Crime in Black and White: The Violent, Scary World of Local News," Occasional Paper no. 95-1 (Los Angeles: UCLA Center for American Politics and Public Policy, September 1995); Robert Entman and Andrew Rojecki, *The Black Image in the White Mind: Media and Race in America* (Chicago: University of Chicago Press, 2000).

177. See Orfield, *Metropolitics,* pp. 22–25.

178. Manuel Pastor, Jr., Peter Dreier, J. Eugene Grigsby III, and Marta Lopez-Garza, *Regions that Work: How Cities and Suburbs Can Grow Together* (Minneapolis: University of Minnesota Press, 2000), p. 32.

179. Our estimate is based on a study of 1,333 zip codes in thirty-three metropolitan areas. Robert W. Klein, "Availability and Affordability Problems in Urban Homeowners Insurance Markets," in *Insurance Redlining: Disinvestment, Reinvestment, and the Evolving Role of Financial Institutions,* ed. Gregory D. Squires (Washington, D.C.: Urban Institute Press, 1997), p. 56.

CHAPTER 4. THE ROADS NOT TAKEN

1. Rebecca Trouson and John Johnson, "Housing Strain Unravels Community Ties," *Los Angeles Times,* January 7, 2001; *Raising the Roof: California Housing Development Projections and Constraints 1997-2000* (Sacramento: California Department of Housing and Community Development, 2000), exhibit 45, "Housing Cost Burden by Income and Tenure for Selected California Metropolitan Areas: 1988–1995," p. 164; Chris Brenner, *Growing Together or Drifting Apart? A Status Report on Social and Economic Well-Being in Silicon Valley* (San Jose, Calif.: Working Partnerships and Economic Policy Institute, January 1998).

2. Robert Fishman, "The American Metropolis at Century's End: Past and Future Influences," *Housing Policy Debate* 11, no. 1 (2000): 199–213. The survey was conducted for the Fannie Mae Foundation among members of the Society for American City and Regional Planning History; the article can be found at www.fanniemaefoundation.org/research/facts/wi99s1.html.

3. Llewellyn H. Rockwell, Jr., "The Ghost of Gautreaux," *National Review,* March 7, 1994, pp. 57–59.

4. Ibid.

5. Fred Siegel, "The Sunny Side of Sprawl," *New Democrat* (March–April 1999): 20–21. See also Fred Siegel, "Is Regional Government the Answer?" *Public Interest* (fall 1999): 85–98; Fred Barnes, "Suburban Beauty: Why Sprawl Works," *Weekly Standard,* May 22, 2000, pp. 27–30.

6. Howard Husock, "Mocking the Middle Class: The Perverse Effects of Housing Subsidies," *Heritage Foundation Policy Review* (spring 1991): 96–101. Bovard agrees that federal government programs to help the poor escape the ghetto "amount to a project to dictate where welfare recipients live in every county, city and cranny across the nation." James Bovard, "Suburban Guerilla," *American Spectator* (September 1994): 26–32.

7. Nevertheless, 76 percent of transit riders had a total trip time of less than thirty minutes, 57 percent less than twenty minutes, and 25 percent less than ten minutes. David F. Schulz, "Urban Transportation System Characteristics, Condition and Performance" (paper prepared for the Conference on Transportation Issues in Large U.S. Cities, Transportation Research Board, Detroit, June 28–30, 1998).

8. Gregg Easterbrook, "Suburban Myth: The Case for Sprawl," *New Republic,* March 15, 1999, pp. 18–21.

9. Joel Garreau, *Edge City: Life on the New Frontier* (New York: Doubleday, 1991), p. 242. See also Philip Langdon, *A Better Place to Live: Reshaping the American Suburb* (New York: Harper, 1994).

10. Tamar Jacoby and Fred Siegel, "Growing the Inner City?" *New Republic,* August 23, 1999.

11. Michael E. Porter, "The Competitive Advantage of the Inner City," *Harvard Business Review* (May–June 1995): 55–71. Porter's article triggered a major debate on this topic. See Thomas Boston and Catherine Ross, eds., *The Inner City: Urban Poverty and Economic Development in the Next Century* (New Brunswick, N.J.: Transaction Books, 1997). Also see Bennett Harrison and Amy K. Glasmeier, "Why Business Alone Won't Redevelop the Inner City," *Economic Development Quarterly* 11, no. 1 (1997): 28–38; Timothy Bates, "Michael Porter's Conservative Agenda Will Not Revitalize America's Inner Cities," *Economic Development Quarterly* 11, no. 1 (February 1997): 39–44.

12. The same argument is applied to business location decisions, but here we focus on residential choice (or the lack thereof).

13. Charles M. Tiebout, "A Pure Theory of Local Expenditure," *Journal of Political Economy* 64, no. 5 (October 1956): 418.

14. Robert Bish and Robert Warren, "Scale and Monopoly Problems in Urban Government Services," *Urban Affairs Quarterly* 8 (September 1972): 99.

15. Tiebout, "A Pure Theory of Public Expenditure," pp. 416–24; Vincent Ostrom, Charles Tiebout, and Roland Warren, "The Organization of Government in Metropolitan Areas," *American Political Science Review* 55 (1961): 835–42; Vincent Ostrom, Robert Bish, and Elinor Ostrom, *Local Government in the United States* (San Francisco: Institute for Contemporary Analysis, 1988); Paul Peterson, *City Limits* (Chicago: University of Chicago Press, 1981); Mark Schneider, *The Competitive City: The Political Economy of Suburbia* (Pittsburgh: University of Pittsburgh Press, 1989). For an excellent summary of the public choice perspective, see G. Ross Stephens and

Nelson Wikstrom, *Metropolitan Government and Governance: Theoretical Perspectives, Empirical Analysis, and the Future* (New York: Oxford University Press, 2000).

16. Robert Warren, "A Municipal Services Market Model of Metropolitan Organization," *Journal of the American Institute of Planners* 30 (August 1964): 198–99.

17. Werner Z. Hirsch, "Local Versus Areawide Urban Government Services," *National Tax Journal* 17 (December 1964): 331–39.

18. Douglas S. Massey and Nancy A. Denton, *American Apartheid: Segregation and the Making of the Underclass* (Cambridge, Mass.: Harvard University Press, 1993), pp. 96–114, 187–212. Margery Austin Turner and Ron Wienk, "The Persistence of Segregation in Urban Areas: Contributing Causes," in *Housing Markets and Residential Mobility,* ed. G. Thomas Kingsley and Margery Austin Turner (Washington, D.C.: Urban Institute Press, 1993), pp. 193–216.

19. Gary J. Miller, *Cities by Contract: The Politics of Incorporation* (Cambridge, Mass.: MIT Press, 1981).

20. William Fulton, *The Reluctant Metropolis: The Politics of Urban Growth in Los Angeles* (Point Arena, Calif.: Solano Press, 1997), p. 279.

21. John E. Anderson and Robert W. Wassmer, *Bidding for Business: The Efficacy of Local Economic Development Incentives in a Metropolitan Area* (Kalamazoo, Mich.: W. E. Upjohn Institute for Employment Research, 1999), available at http://www.csus.edu/ indiv/w/wassmerr/upjohn.htm.

22. See, for example, United Nations Center for Human Settlements (HABITAT), *An Urbanizing World: Global Report on Human Settlements: 1996* (London: Oxford University Press, 1996); Charles Abrams, "The Uses of Land in Cities," *Scientific American* (September 1965): 225–31.

23. See Gerald E. Frug, "The City as a Legal Concept," *Harvard Law Review* 93, no. 6 (April 1980): 1057–1154; Gerald E. Frug, "Decentering Decentralization," *University of Chicago Law Review* 60, no. 2 (spring 1993): 253–73; Gerald E. Frug, "The Geography of Community," *Stanford Law Review* 48, no. 5 (May 1996): 1047–94; Gerald E. Frug, *City Making: Building Communities Without Building Walls* (Princeton, N.J.: Princeton University Press, 1999); Sidney Plotkin, *Keep Out: The Struggle for Land Use Control* (Berkeley: University of California Press, 1987); Harvey M. Jacobs, "Fighting over Land," *Journal of the American Planning Association* 65, no. 2 (spring 1999): 141–49.

24. Kenneth Jackson, *Crabgrass Frontier* (New York: Oxford University Press, 1985); David Rusk, *Cities Without Suburbs,* 2d ed. (Washington, D.C.: Woodrow Wilson Center Press, 1995).

25. Rusk, *Cities Without Suburbs.*

26. The Court struck down racial zoning in *Buchanan v. Warley,* 245 U.S. 60 (1917).

27. Gwendolyn Wright, *Building the Dream* (Cambridge, Mass.: MIT Press, 1983), p. 213.

28. Mary K. Nenno and Paul C. Brophey, *Housing and Local Government* (Washington, D.C.: National Association of Housing and Redevelopment Officers, n.d.), p. 7.

29. Among many others on this topic, see Alan Mallach, *Inclusionary Housing Programs* (New Brunswick, N.J.: Rutgers University Center for Urban Policy Research, 1984).

30. Ann R. Markusen, "The Urban Impact Analysis: A Critical Forecast," in *The Urban Impact of Federal Policies,* ed. Norman Glickman (Baltimore: Johns Hopkins University Press, 1979).

31. We borrow this term from Bernard H. Ross and Myron A. Levine, *Urban Politics: Power in Metropolitan America,* 5th ed. (Itasca, Ill.: F. E. Peacock, 1996), p. 434.

32. Harold Wolman, "The Reagan Urban Policy and Its Impacts," *Urban Affairs Quarterly* 21, no. 3 (March 1986): 311–35.

33. Bruce Katz and Kate Carnevale, "The State of Welfare Caseloads in America's Cities" (Washington, D.C.: Brookings Institution Center of Urban and Metropolitan Policy, May 1998).

34. James Flink, *The Car Culture* (Cambridge, Mass.: MIT Press, 1975); Kenneth Jackson, *Crabgrass Frontier: The Suburbanization of the United States* (New York: Oxford University Press, 1985); Jane Holtz Kay, *Asphalt Nation: How the Automobile Took over America and How We Can Take It Back* (New York: Crown Publishers, 1997); Helen Leavitt, *Superhighway-Superhoax* (New York: Doubleday, 1970); Pietro S. Nivola, *Laws of the Landscape: How Policies Shape Cities in Europe and America* (Washington, D.C.: Brookings Institution Press, 1999).

35. By the mid-1920s, 56 percent of American families owned an automobile, according to Nivola, *Laws of the Landscape*, p. 11.

36. See Bradford C. Snell, "American Ground Transport: A Proposal for Restructuring the Automobile, Truck, Bus, and Rail Industries" (presented to the Subcommittee on Antitrust and Monopoly of the Committee on the Judiciary, U.S. Senate, February 26, 1974).

37. Nivola, *Laws of the Landscape*, p. 13.

38. Howard P. Chudacoff and Judith E. Smith, *The Evolution of American Urban Society*, 4th ed. (Englewood Cliffs, N.J.: Prentice-Hall, 1994), p. 260.

39. Fishman, "American Metropolis," p. 3.

40. Ibid., p. 2.

41. U.S. Bureau of the Census, *Statistical Abstract of the United States: 2000*, p. 625.

42. Texas Transportation Institute, *Urban Mobility Study* (College Station: Texas A&M University, November 1999).

43. Kay, *Asphalt Nation*, p. 14.

44. Ibid.

45. Nivola, *Laws of the Landscape*, p. 15.

46. Timothy Egan, "The Freeway, Its Cost and 2 Cities' Destinies," *New York Times*, July 14, 1999.

47. Nivola, *Laws of the Landscape*, p. 15.

48. John H. Mollenkopf, *The Contested City* (Princeton, N.J.: Princeton University Press, 1983), p. 105.

49. See ibid., pp. 102–9, on World War II; Ann Markusen, Peter Hall, Scott Campbell, and Sabrina District, *The Rise of the Gunbelt: The Military Remapping of Industrial America* (New York: Oxford University Press, 1991).

50. Ann Markusen and Joel Yudken, *Dismantling the Cold War Economy* (New York: Basic Books, 1992); Markusen et al., *Rise of the Gunbelt*. Military research and development and weapons production have spawned new industries and new fields, but in doing so, much of the nation's resources and scientific expertise have been diverted from civilian production and research. Likewise, military production and research and the siting of facilities help some areas but drain others.

51. *Report to the Boston Redevelopment Authority* (Lansing, Mich.: Employment Research Associates, 1992), reported in Steven Greenhouse, "Study Says Big Cities Don't Get Fair Share of Military Spending," *New York Times*, May 12, 1992, p. A20, and in Marion Anderson and Peter Dreier, "How the Pentagon Redlines America's Cities," *Planners Network* (May 1993): 3–4.

52. Markusen and Yudken, *Dismantling the Cold War Economy*, p. 173.

53. For example, in September 1992, President Bush, far behind Governor Clinton in the Missouri polls, traveled to St. Louis to announce the sale to Saudi Arabia of F-15 jet fighters, which are manufactured by McDonnell-Douglas, the state's largest employer. The sale was highly questionable on defense and foreign policy grounds, but Bush made little pretense of discussing geopolitics. He emphasized the 7,000 local jobs generated by the weapon.

54. Howard Schuman, Charlotte Steeh, and Lawrence Bobo, *Racial Attitudes in America: Trends and Interpretations* (Cambridge, Mass.: Harvard University Press, 1985); Massey and Denton, *American Apartheid;* Reynolds Farley, "Neighborhood Preferences and Aspirations Among Blacks and Whites," in *Housing Markets and Residential Mobility,* ed. G. Thomas Kingsley and Margery Austin Turner (Washington, D.C.: Urban Institute Press, 1993); George Galster, "Research on Discrimination in Housing and Mortgage Markets: Assessment and Future Directions," *Housing Policy Debate* 3, no. 2 (1992): 639–83; David Dent, "The New Black Suburbs," *New York Times Magazine,* July 14, 1992.

55. Massey and Denton, *American Apartheid;* Arnold Hirsch, *Making the Second Ghetto: Race and Housing in Chicago 1940–1960* (New York: Cambridge University Press, 1983); Arnold R. Hirsch, "Searching for a 'Sound Negro Policy': A Racial Agenda for the Housing Acts of 1949 and 1954," *Housing Policy Debate* 11, no. 2 (2000): 393–442; Thomas J. Sugrue, *The Origins of the Urban Crisis: Race and Inequality in Postwar Detroit* (Princeton, N.J.: Princeton University Press, 1996).

56. Margery Turner, "Achieving a New Urban Diversity: What Have We Learned?" *Housing Policy Debate* 8, no. 2 (1997): 295–305; John Yinger, "Housing Discrimination Is Still Worth Worrying About," *Housing Policy Debate* 9, no. 4 (1998): 893–927; *What We Know About Mortgage Lending Discrimination in America* (Washington, D.C.: U.S. Department of Housing and Urban Development and the Urban Institute, September 1999); Gregory Squires, ed., *Insurance Redlining* (Washington, D.C.: Urban Institute Press, 1997).

57. Joe Darden, "Choosing Neighbors and Neighborhoods: The Role of Race in Housing Preference," in *Divided Neighborhoods: Changing Patterns of Racial Segregation,* ed. Gary Tobin (Newbury Park, Calif.: Sage, 1987); W. Dennis Keating, *The Suburban Racial Dilemma: Housing and Neighborhoods* (Philadelphia: Temple University Press, 1994); Hirsch, "Searching for a 'Sound Negro Policy.'"

58. Rose Helper, *Racial Policies and Practices of Real Estate Brokers* (Minneapolis: University of Minnesota Press, 1969); Jackson, *Crabgrass Frontier.*

59. Charles Abrams, *Forbidden Neighbors* (New York: Harper and Brothers, 1955); Julia Saltman, *Open Housing as a Social Movement: Challenge, Conflict and Change* (Lexington, Mass.: Heath, 1971); Keating, *Suburban Racial Dilemma;* Hirsch, "Searching for a 'Sound Negro Policy.'"

60. Massey and Denton, *American Apartheid*, p. 54.

61. Cited in Dennis Judd and Todd Swanstrom, *City Politics* (New York: Longman, 1998), p. 198. The U.S. Supreme Court ruled that state courts could not enforce racial covenants in *Shelly v. Kraemer* in 1948. The FHA was forced to change its official policy. It took the FHA until 1950 to revise its underwriting manual so that it no longer recommended racial segregation or restrictive covenants. But the FHA continued to favor racial segregation. It did nothing to challenge racial steering or redlining against blacks. As a result, the Supreme Court's ruling had little impact on racial segregation in private housing. See Keating, *Suburban Racial Dilemma*, p. 8.

62. Barry Checkoway, "Large Builders, Federal Housing Programs, and Postwar Suburbanization," in *Critical Perspectives on Housing,* ed. Rachel Bratt, Chester Hartman, and Ann Meyerson (Philadelphia: Temple University Press, 1986).

63. Fishman, "American Metropolis," p. 4.

64. Jackson, *Crabgrass Frontier,* pp. 196–213; Massey and Denton, *American Apartheid,* pp. 42–57.

65. Fishman, "American Metropolis," p. 4.

66. Cited in Judd and Swanstrom, *City Politics,* p. 197.

67. Massey and Denton, *American Apartheid,* p. 53.

68. Jackson, *Crabgrass Frontier,* p. 207.

69. Nathan Glazer and David McEntire, eds., *Housing and Minority Groups* (Berkeley: University of California Press, 1960), p. 140.

70. Massey and Denton, *American Apartheid,* p. 55.

71. Tax reform legislation passed by Congress in 1997 sweetened the capital gains provisions enormously: such home sale profits are now, under most conditions, completely untaxed up to $500,000 for a couple and $250,000 for an individual, and the benefit is available repeatedly. The previous provision, which allowed home owners to defer capital gains taxes only if they purchased a more expensive home, encouraged the purchase of larger homes, typically in suburbs farther from the central city.

72. During the 1978–1997 period, the federal government also provided $16 billion in low-income housing subsidies through the low-income-housing tax credit and $89 billion in low-income housing subsidies through the Department of Agriculture. These figures, calculated from a variety of government sources, are reported and explained in Peter Dreier, "The Truth About Federal Housing Subsidies," in *Housing: Foundation of a New Social Agenda,* ed. Rachel Bratt, Chester Hartman, Mary Ellen Hombs, and Michael Stone (Philadelphia: Temple University Press, forthcoming).

73. Only 22.1 percent of the 134 million taxpayers took the mortgage interest deduction, but this varied significantly with income. For example, 73 percent of taxpayers with incomes over $200,000 took the mortgage interest deduction, with an average benefit of $6,073. By contrast, only 24.8 percent of those in the $40,000 to $50,000 bracket took the deduction; those who did so saved an average of $737 on their taxes. Among those in the $20,000 to $30,000 income category, only 5.5 percent took the deduction and received an average benefit of only $411. Among households with incomes under $20,000, slightly more than half own their own homes. Of those that own their homes, only 28.5 percent have mortgages. Of those that have mortgages, only 6.8 percent itemize (taxpayers taking the standard deduction get no benefit from these tax breaks). Among households in the $60,000 to $100,000 income bracket, more than 80 percent own their own homes. Of those that own their homes, 78 percent have mortgages. Of those that have mortgages, 66 percent itemize. Among households in the $120,000 to $140,000 income bracket, 91 percent own their homes. Of those, 82 percent have mortgages. Among this group, 92 percent itemize. Mortgage interest and property tax deductions are available for a second or vacation home as well as for one's primary residence (and until 1986 were available for as many secondary residences as the taxpayer owned—clearly adding to its regressivity).

74. Joseph Gyourko and Richard Voith, "Does the U.S. Tax Treatment of Housing Promote Suburbanization and Central City Decline?" (Philadelphia: Wharton School, University of Pennsylvania, Real Estate and Finance Departments, September 24, 1997); Thomas Bier and Ivan Meric, "IRS Homeseller Provision and Urban Decline,"

Journal of Urban Affairs 16, no. 2 (1994): 141–54; Richard Voith, "The Determinants of Metropolitan Development Patterns: Preferences, Prices, and Public Policies," in *Metropolitan Development Patterns: Annual Roundtable 2000* (Cambridge, Mass.: Lincoln Institute of Land Policy, 2000).

75. Jeffrey Birnbaum and Alan Murray, *Showdown at Gucci Gulch: Lawmakers, Lobbyists, and the Unlikely Triumph of Tax Reform* (New York: Random House, 1987); Christopher Howard, *The Hidden Welfare State: Tax Expenditures and Social Policy in the United States* (Princeton, N.J.: Princeton University Press, 1997).

76. Abrams, *Forbidden Neighbors;* Richard Davies, *Housing Reform During the Truman Administration* (Columbia: University of Missouri Press, 1966); Nathaniel Keith, *Politics and the Housing Crisis Since 1930* (New York: Universe Books, 1973).

77. National Advisory Commission on Civil Disorders (the Kerner Commission), *Report* (New York: Bantam, 1968).

78. The housing and lending industries argue that even if they do not discriminate, consumers "vote with their feet." Whites move out of a neighborhood when they perceive that it is, or could become, "too black." Surveys indicate that although whites have generally become more tolerant of racially mixed neighborhoods, they define a neighborhood as acceptably integrated when a small number of blacks (usually no more than 10 percent) live there. There is much debate about whether there are "tipping" points when whites begin to flee.

79. James Kushner, "Federal Enforcement and Judicial Review of the Fair Housing Amendments Act of 1988," *Housing Policy Debate* 3, no. 2 (1992): 537–99.

80. Keating, *Suburban Racial Dilemma,* p. 14.

81. Keating, in *Suburban Racial Dilemma,* discusses suburbs that have utilized these approaches. See also Philip Nyden, Michael Maly, and John Lukehart, "The Emergence of Stable Racially and Ethnically Diverse Urban Communities: A Case Study of Nine U.S. Cities," *Housing Policy Debate* 8, no. 2 (1997): 491–534.

82. For a good overview, see Robert Halperin, *Rebuilding the Inner City: A History of Neighborhood Initiatives to Address Poverty in the United States* (New York: Columbia University Press, 1995).

83. Alice O'Connor, "Swimming Against the Tide: A Brief History of Federal Policy in Poor Communities," in *Urban Problems and Community Development,* ed. Ronald Ferguson and William Dickens (Washington, D.C.: Brookings Institution Press, 1999). See also Raymond Mohl, "Shifting Patterns of American Urban Policy Since 1900," in *Urban Policy in Twentieth-Century America,* ed. Arnold Hirsch and Raymond Mohl (New Brunswick, N.J.: Rutgers University Press, 1993).

84. Steven Hayward, "Broken Cities: Liberalism's Urban Legacy," *Policy Review* (March–April 1998): 18.

85. Frances Piven and Richard Cloward, *Poor People's Movements* (New York: Pantheon, 1977).

86. Mark Gelfand, *A Nation of Cities: The Federal Government and Urban America, 1933–1965* (New York: Oxford University Press, 1975).

87. Judd and Swanstrom, *City Politics,* p. 121.

88. Davies, *Housing Reform During the Truman Administration.*

89. Mohl, "Shifting Pattern," pp. 11–13.

90. See the 1997 "Picture of Subsidized Housing" at www.huduser.org/datasets/assthsg/statedata98/us.html. The U.S. Department of Agriculture also provides housing subsidies, but these are primarily in rural areas and account for a very small proportion of federal housing assistance.

91. Peter Dreier, "Philanthropy and the Housing Crisis: Dilemmas of Private Charity and Public Policy in the United States," in *Shelter and Society: Theory, Research and Policy for Nonprofit Housing,* ed. C. Theodore Koebel (Albany, N.Y.: SUNY Press, 1998), pp. 91–137; E. L. Birch and D. S. Gardner, "The Seven Percent Solution: A Review of Philanthropic Housing, 1870–1910," *Journal of Urban History* 7 (1981): 403–38; Roy Lubove, *The Progressives and the Slums: Tenement House Reform in New York City, 1890–1917* (Pittsburgh: University of Pittsburgh Press, 1962); Gail Radford, *Modern Housing for America: Policy Struggles in the New Deal Era* (Chicago: University of Chicago Press, 1996); Gwendolyn Wright, *Building the Dream: A Social History of Housing in America* (New York: Pantheon, 1981).

92. Radford, *Modern Housing for America.*

93. Michael Danielson, *The Politics of Exclusion* (New York: Columbia University Press, 1976), cited in Edward Goetz, "From Policy Option to Policy Problem: The Federal Government and Restrictive Housing Regulation" (Washington, D.C.: Fannie Mae Foundation, 1999).

94. Hirsch, *Making the Second Ghetto.*

95. Martin Meyerson and Edward Banfield, *Politics, Planning and the Public Interest: The Case of Public Housing in Chicago* (New York: Free Press, 1955).

96. Michael Schill and Susan Wachter, "The Spatial Bias of Federal Housing Law and Policy: Concentrated Poverty in Urban America," *University of Pennsylvania Law Review* 143, no. 5 (May 1995): 1285–1342; Massey and Denton, *American Apartheid;* Douglas Massey and S. M. Kanaiaupuni, "Public Housing and the Concentration of Poverty," *Social Science Quarterly* 74 (1993): 109–22; Steven Holloway, Deborah Bryan, Robert Chabot, Donna Rogers, and James Rulli, "Exploring the Effect of Public Housing on the Concentration of Poverty in Columbus, Ohio," *Urban Affairs Review* 33, no. 6 (July 1998): 767–89.

97. John Goering, Ali Kamely, and Todd Richardson, *The Location and Racial Composition of Public Housing in the United States* (Washington, D.C.: U.S. Department of Housing and Urban Development, 1994). Most housing developments created with the federal Low-Income-Housing Tax Credit (a program begun in 1986) are in high-poverty neighborhoods, mostly in central cities. Preliminary research indicates that most of these developments are in predominantly minority neighborhoods, although the racial characteristics of the projects' residents is not identified. See Jean Cummings and Denise DePasquale, *Rebuilding Affordable Rental Housing: An Analysis of the Low Income Housing Tax Credit* (Boston: City Research, 1998).

98. Goering et al., *Location and Racial Composition of Public Housing;* Holloway et al., "Exploring the Effect of Public Housing"; Sandra Newman and Ann Schnare, "'. . . And a Suitable Living Environment': The Failure of Housing Programs to Deliver on Neighborhood Quality," *Housing Policy Debate* 8, no. 4 (1997): 755–67.

99. Only 45.3 percent of vouchers and certificates are in central cities, 32.4 percent in census tracts with median household incomes below $20,000, 14.8 percent in census tracts with poverty rates of 30 percent or more, and 21 percent in census tracts where minorities constitute at least half the population (Newman and Schnare, "Suitable Living Environment"). Harris has documented that the affordable apartments available to Section 8 certificate holders are segregated in poor, black, central-city neighborhoods — far from suburban locations with more job opportunities and good schools. Laura Harris, "A Home Is More than Just a House: A Spatial Analysis of Housing for the Poor in Metropolitan America" (Ph.D. diss., State University of New York at Albany, 1999).

100. For discussion of urban growth coalitions, see John Mollenkopf, "The Post-War Politics of Urban Development," *Politics and Society* 5, no. 2 (winter 1975): 247–95; Mollenkopf, *Contested City;* Harvey Molotch, "The City as a Growth Machine," *American Journal of Sociology* 82, no. 2 (1976):309–32; John Logan and Harvey Molotch, *Urban Fortunes* (Berkeley and Los Angeles: University of California Press, 1987).

101. Mohl, "Shifting Pattern," p. 16.

102. Cited in O'Connor, "Swimming Against the Tide," p. 96.

103. Susan Fainstein and Norman Fainstein, eds., *Restructuring the City: The Political Economy of Urban Development* (New York: Longman, 1986), p. 49; Mollenkopf, *Contested City.*

104. See, for example, Herbert Gans, *The Urban Villagers* (New York: Free Press, 1965); Thomas Hines, "Housing, Baseball, and Creeping Socialism: The Battle of Chavez Ravine, Los Angeles," *Journal of Urban History* 8 (February 1982): 123–45; Chester Hartman, *Yerba Buena: Land Grab and Community Resistance in San Francisco* (San Francisco: Glide Publications, 1974); Alan Lupo, Frank Colcord, and Edward Fowler, *Rites of Way* (Boston: Little, Brown, 1971); and Jon C. Teaford, "Urban Renewal and Its Aftermath," *Housing Policy Debate* 11, no. 2 (2000): 443–65.

105. Chester Hartman, "The Housing of Relocated Families," and Herbert Gans, "The Failure of Urban Renewal," in *Urban Renewal: The Record and the Controversy,* ed. James Q. Wilson (Cambridge, Mass.: MIT Press, 1966).

106. Mohl, "Shifting Pattern," p. 15.

107. Robert Caro, *The Power Broker* (New York: Vintage, 1975); Mollenkopf, *Contested City.*

108. Martin Anderson, *The Federal Bulldozer* (Cambridge, Mass.: MIT Press, 1964).

109. Gans, *Urban Villagers,* describes the destruction of Boston's West End neighborhood by urban renewal.

110. Bruce Ehrlich and Peter Dreier, "The New Boston Discovers the Old: Tourism and the Struggle for a Livable City," in *The Tourist City,* ed. Dennis R. Judd and Susan S. Fainstein (New Haven, Conn.: Yale University Press, 1999).

111. Hartman, *Yerba Buena.*

112. Judd and Swanstrom, *City Politics,* p. 193.

113. Cited in Kevin Boyle, "Little More than Ashes: The UAW and American Reform in the 1960s," in *Organized Labor and American Politics, 1894–1994,* ed. Kevin Boyle (Albany, N.Y.: SUNY Press, 1998). See also Nelson Lichtenstein, *The Most Dangerous Man in Detroit: Walter Reuther and the Fate of American Labor* (New York: Basic Books, 1995). William Julius Wilson's *The Bridge over the Racial Divide: Rising Inequality and Coalition Politics* (Berkeley: University of California Press, 1999), updates many of Reuther's arguments.

114. Sar Levitan, Garth Mangum, and Stephen Mangum, *Programs in Aid of the Poor,* 7th ed. (Baltimore: Johns Hopkins University Press, 1998); James T. Patterson, *America's Struggle Against Poverty 1900–1980* (Cambridge, Mass.: Harvard University Press, 1981).

115. Judd and Swanstrom, *City Politics,* p. 217.

116. During the 1950s and early 1960s, big-city mayors, the liberal National Housing Conference, and a coalition of labor unions and public housing advocates supported unsuccessful efforts by congressional Democrats to create a cabinet-level agency to deal with urban problems. The 1960 Democratic platform called for replacing the Housing and Home Finance Agency (HHFA) with a new cabinet-level agency.

Upon his election, President Kennedy tried to create such a department, but he was stymied by southern Democrats, who feared that Kennedy would appoint HHFA administrator Robert Weaver (the highest-ranking black in the federal government) to be the new secretary. Rachel Bratt and W. Dennis Keating, "Federal Housing Policy and HUD: Past Problems and Future Prospects of a Beleaguered Bureaucracy," *Urban Affairs Quarterly* 29, no. 1 (September 1993): 3–27.

117. Morton Schussheim, "The Federal Government, the Central City, and Housing" (Washington, D.C.: Congressional Research Service, September 29, 1992).

118. Kerner Commission, *Report*.

119. In 1970, Nixon proposed a welfare reform plan drafted by Daniel Patrick Moynihan. The Family Assistance Plan (FAP) was a guaranteed minimum income for all families with children, a radical notion at the time. Conservatives in Congress opposed it because they disagreed with the principle of a federal guaranteed income. Liberals and welfare advocacy groups opposed it because the FAP's income floor— $1,600 per family—was far below the poverty line. For Moynihan's perspective, see Daniel P. Moynihan, *The Politics of a Guaranteed Income: The Nixon Administration and the Family Assistance Plan* (New York: Random House, 1973).

120. Morton Schussheim, "Housing the Poor: Federal Housing Programs for Low-Income Families" (Washington, D.C.: Congressional Research Service, October 20, 1998), p. 16.

121. Ibid.

122. Ibid., p. 18.

123. Ibid., p. 17. See also Michael Rich, *Federal Policymaking and the Poor: National Goals, Local Choices, and Distributional Outcomes* (Princeton, N.J.: Princeton University Press, 1993).

124. Cited in Mohl, "Shifting Pattern," p. 21.

125. This wave of plant closings and its consequences are brilliantly chronicled in Barry Bluestone and Bennett Harrison, *The Deindustrialization of America* (New York: Basic Books, 1982).

126. "Ford to City: Drop Dead," *New York Daily News*, October 29, 1975.

127. Mohl, "Shifting Pattern," p. 22.

128. Carter terminated the state component of revenue sharing in 1980. See John Kincaid, "De Facto Devolution and Urban Defunding: The Priority of Persons over Places," *Journal of Urban Affairs* 21, no. 2 (1999): 135–67.

129. President's Commission on a National Agenda for the Eighties, *Urban America in the 1980s* (Washington, D.C.: Government Printing Office, 1980).

130. For a review of the Nixon, Ford, and Carter approaches to urban policy, see the articles in Marshall Kaplan and Franklin James, eds., *The Future of National Urban Policy* (Durham, N.C.: Duke University Press, 1990).

131. Reagan did not reduce federal spending in either absolute terms or as a proportion of GNP. Increases in federal military spending more than offset declines in domestic spending.

132. George Peterson and Carol Lewis, eds., *Reagan and the Cities* (Washington, D.C.: Urban Institute Press, 1986); Harold Wolman, "The Reagan Urban Policy and Its Impacts," *Urban Affairs Quarterly* 21 (March 1986): 311–35; Frances Fox Piven and Richard Cloward, *The New Class War: Reagan's Attack on the Welfare State and Its Consequences* (New York: Pantheon, 1982); Kevin Phillips, *The Politics of Rich and Poor* (New York: Random House, 1990).

133. U.S. President's Commission on Housing, *The Report of the President's Commission*

on Housing (Washington, D.C.: Government Printing Office, 1982); U.S. Department of Housing and Urban Development, *The President's National Urban Policy Report* (Washington, D.C.: Government Printing Office, 1982).

134. The figures on the Reagan and Bush administrations draw on Demetrios J. Caraley, "Washington Abandons the Cities," *Political Science Quarterly* 107, no. 1 (spring 1992): 1–30, and Demetrios J. Caraley, "Dismantling the Federal Safety Net: Fictions Versus Realities," *Political Science Quarterly* 111, no. 2 (summer 1996): 225–58.

135. The number of AFDC recipients increased from 7.4 million in 1970 to 10.6 million in 1980 to 11.5 million in 1990. See "Historical Trends in AFDC Enrollments and Average Payments, Fiscal Years 1970–96," in Committee on Ways and Means, U.S. House of Representatives, *1998 Green Book* (Washington, D.C.: Government Printing Office, May 19, 1998), p. 413.

136. Since AFDC and food stamp benefits differ from state to state, this figure is the median of all states. See "Gross Income Limit, Need Standard, and Maximum Monthly Potential Benefits, AFDC and Food Stamps, One-Parent Family of Three Persons," in Committee on Ways and Means, U.S. House of Representatives, *1992 Green Book* (Washington, D.C.: Government Printing Office, 1992), pp. 636–37.

137. Actual expenditures (or outlays) for housing actually increased during the early Reagan years because of spending commitments made during the Carter administration. HUD's contracts with developers, landlords, and public housing authorities are spread out over many years. But Reagan dramatically cut HUD's ability to enter into new contracts by reducing its overall budget authority. See R. Allen Hays, *The Federal Government and Urban Housing*, 2d ed. (Albany, N.Y.: SUNY Press, 1995).

138. Jennifer Daskal, *In Search of Shelter: The Growing Shortage of Affordable Rental Housing* (Washington, D.C.: Center on Budget and Policy Priorities, June 15, 1998).

139. Joel Blau, *The Visible Poor: Homelessness in the United States* (New York: Oxford University Press, 1992); Martha Burt, *Over the Edge: The Growth of Homelessness in the 1980s* (New York: Russell Sage Foundation, 1992); Bruce Link, Ezra Susser, Ann Stueve, Jo Phelan, Robert Moore, and Elmer Struening, "Lifetime and Five-Year Prevalence of Homelessness in the United States," *American Journal of Public Health* 84, no. 12 (1994): 1907–12; U.S. Conference of Mayors, *A Status Report on Hunger and Homelessness in American Cities: 1993* (Washington, D.C., December 1993).

140. "Poverty Rates for Individuals in Selected Demographic Groups, 1959–1994," in Committee on Ways and Means, U.S. House of Representatives, *1996 Green Book* (Washington, D.C.: Government Printing Office, November 4, 1996), p. 1226.

141. "Percentage of Persons in Poverty in NonMetro and Metro Areas, 1978–1994," in *1996 Green Book*, p. 1233.

142. William O'Hare, *A New Look at Poverty in America* (Washington, D.C.: Population Reference Bureau, September 1996), p. 14; "The Economic Crisis of Urban America," *Business Week*, May 18, 1992; "Poverty of People, by Residence: 1959 to 1998," U.S. Bureau of the Census, Current Population Survey, 1999, available at http://www.census.gov/pub/income/histpov/hstpov08.txt.

143. Billy Tidwell, *Playing to Win: A Marshall Plan for America* (Washington, D.C.: National Urban League, July 1991); Richard Nathan, *A New Agenda for Cities* (Washington, D.C.: National League of Cities, 1992); Joseph Persky, Elliott Sclar, and Wim Wiewel, *Does America Need Cities? An Urban Investment Strategy for National Prosperity* (Washington, D.C.: U.S. Conference of Mayors and Economic Policy Institute, 1991); Urban Institute, *Confronting the Nation's Urban Crisis* (Washington, D.C.:

Urban Institute, September 1992); "The Economic Crisis of Urban America," *Business Week,* May 18, 1992.

144. The Moving to Opportunity program is based on the successful Gautreaux program in Chicago, which began in the 1970s as a result of a federal court settlement against the city's segregated public housing program. See James Rosenbaum, "Changing the Geography of Opportunity by Expanding Residential Choice," *Housing Policy Debate* 6, no. 1 (1995): 231–69; Peter Dreier and David Moberg, "Moving from the 'Hood': The Mixed Success of Integrating Suburbia," *American Prospect* (winter 1996): 75–79; Jason DeParle, "An Underground Railroad from Projects to Suburbs," *New York Times,* December 1, 1993; U.S. Department of Housing and Urban Development, Office of Policy Development and Research, "Residential Mobility Programs," *Urban Policy Brief* 1 (September 1994): 1.

145. Bridges to Work was modeled on several successful local programs in Chicago and Philadelphia. Rochelle Stanfield, "The Reverse Commute," *National Journal,* November 23, 1996; Penelope Lemov, "The Impossible Commute," *Governing* (June 1993): 32–35; Rick Wartman, "New Bus Lines Link the Inner-City Poor with Jobs in Suburbia," *Wall Street Journal,* September 24, 1993; Mark Alan Hughes, "A Mobility Strategy for Improving Opportunity," *Housing Policy Debate* 6, no. 1 (1995): 271–97; Margaret Pugh, *Barriers to Work: The Spatial Divide Between Jobs and Welfare Recipients in Metropolitan Areas* (Washington, D.C.: Brookings Institution Center on Urban and Metropolitan Policy, September 1998).

146. Christina FitzPatrick and Edward Lazere, *The Poverty Despite Work Handbook* (Washington, D.C.: Center on Budget and Policy Priorities, April 1999). For a history of the earned income tax credit, see Christopher Howard, *The Hidden Welfare State: Tax Expenditures and Social Policy in the United States* (Princeton, N.J.: Princeton University Press, 1997).

147. The law also made changes in federal aid for child care, food stamps, Supplemental Security Income for children, benefits for legal immigrants, child nutrition programs, child-support enforcement, and other low-income programs.

148. Bruce Katz and Kate Carnevale, "The State of Welfare Caseloads in America's Cities" (Washington, D.C.: Brookings Institution Center on Urban and Metropolitan Policy, May 1998).

149. Most families leaving welfare for work earn poverty-level wages. One study found that single mothers who were working five years after leaving welfare earned an average of $10,315 a year. In eighteen of the nation's twenty largest metropolitan areas in 1995, the typical hourly wage of single working mothers who had recently received AFDC was about $6 an hour, far below the poverty line. Barbara Sard and Jennifer Daskal, "Housing and Welfare Reform: Some Background Information" (Washington, D.C.: Center on Budget and Policy Priorities, February 1998). Harry Holzer, "Unemployment Insurance and Welfare Recipients: What Happens When the Recession Comes?" (Washington, D.C.: Urban Institute, December 2000).

150. During the summer and fall, Clinton toured major cities and rural areas across the country to draw attention to persistent poverty in the midst of low unemployment. David Sanger, "In Visit to Northeast, Clinton Calls for Investment in Cities," *New York Times,* November 5, 1999. See also *Now Is the Time: Places Left Behind in the New Economy* (Washington, D.C.: U.S. Department of Housing and Urban Development, April 1999); *The New Markets: The Untapped Retail Buying Power in America's Inner Cities* (Washington, D.C.: U.S. Department of Housing and Urban Develop-

ment, July 1999); *The State of the Cities: 1998* (Washington, D.C.: U.S. Department of Housing and Urban Development, June 1998).

151. Louis Uchitelle, "Rising Incomes List 1.1 Million out of Poverty," *New York Times,* October 1, 1999; Joseph Dalaker and Bernadette Proctor, "Poverty in the United States: 1999" (Washington, D.C.: U.S. Bureau of the Census, Current Population Reports, P 60-210, September, 2000).

152. Dalaker and Proctor, "Poverty in the United States: 1999."

153. Daniel H. Weinberg, "A Brief Look at Postwar U.S. Income Inequality" (Washington, D.C.: U.S. Bureau of the Census, Current Population Reports, P60-191, June 1996); Edward N. Wolff, "Recent Trends in the Size Distribution of Household Wealth," *Journal of Economic Perspectives* 12, no. 3 (summer 1998): 131-50.

154. Robert Pear, "More Americans Were Uninsured in 1998, U.S. Says," *New York Times,* October 4, 1999; Robert I. Mills, "Health Insurance Coverage, 1999" (Washington, D.C.: U.S. Bureau of the Census, Current Population Reports, P 60-211, September 2000).

CHAPTER 5. WHAT CITIES CAN AND CANNOT DO TO ADDRESS POVERTY

1. Nancy Cleeland, "Lives Get a Little Better on a Living Wage," *Los Angeles Times,* February 7, 1999.

2. David Reynolds, "The Living Wage Movement Sweeps the Nation," *Working USA* 3, no. 3 (September–October 1999): 61–80; Isaac Martin, "Dawn of the Living Wage: The Diffusion of a Redistributive Municipal Policy," *Urban Affairs Review* 36, no. 4 (March 2001): 470–96; Robert Pollin and Stephanie Luce, *The Living Wage: Building a Fair Economy* (New York: New Press, 1998).

3. States can enact minimum wage laws covering all employees. In 2000, the California minimum wage, $5.75 an hour, exceeded the federal threshold of $5.15. Although business leaders think that this puts the state at a competitive disadvantage, research suggests otherwise. David Card and Alan Krueger, *Myth and Measurement: The New Economics of the Minimum Wage* (Princeton, N.J.: Princeton University Press, 1995).

4. See Amy Ellen Schwartz and Ingrid Gould Ellen, "Cautionary Notes for Competitive Cities," (New York: New York University Wagner School of Public Service, March 1, 2000); Natalie Cohen, "Business Location Decision-Making and Cities: Bringing Companies Back," (Washington, D.C.: Brookings Institution Center on Urban and Metropolitan Policy, April 2000).

5. Paul Peterson, *City Limits* (Chicago: University of Chicago Press, 1981).

6. Quoted in Robin Soslow, "Cleveland: A Special Report," *World Trade* (October 1992), as cited in Michael H. Shuman, *Going Local: Creating Self-Reliant Communities in a Global Age* (New York: Routledge, 2000), p. 1.

7. U.S. Bureau of the Census, *Statistical Abstract of the United States: 2000,* p. 301.

8. Robert L. Lineberry, *Equality and Urban Policy: The Distribution of Municipal Public Services* (Beverly Hills, Calif.: Sage, 1974), p. 10.

9. Helen Ladd and John Yinger, *America's Ailing Cities: Fiscal Health and the Design of Urban Policy,* updated ed. (Baltimore: Johns Hopkins University Press, 1989), p. 9.

10. Ibid., p. 292.

11. *The State of the Cities 2000: Megaforces Shaping the Future of the Nation's Cities* (Washington, D.C.: U.S. Department of Housing and Urban Development, 2000).

12. A detailed study of the distribution of public services in San Antonio by Lineberry

concluded that they were characterized by "unpatterned inequalities." Some areas got more than others, but not on the basis of race or class. See Lineberry, *Equality and Urban Policy*. Also discussing this question are Frank S. Levy, Arnold Meltsner, and Aaron Wildavsky, *Urban Outcomes* (Berkeley: University of California Press, 1974); Bryan D. Jones et al., "Service Delivery Rules and the Distribution of Local Government Services: Three Detroit Bureaucracies," *Journal of Politics* 40 (1978): 334–68; Kenneth R. Mladenka, "The Urban Bureaucracy and the Chicago Political Machine: Who Gets What and Limits to Political Reform," *American Political Science Review* 74 (1980): 991–98; and Michael J. Rich, *Federal Policymaking and the Poor: National Goals, Local Choices, and Distributional Outcomes* (Princeton, N.J.: Princeton University Press, 1993).

13. Edward W. Hill and Jeremy Nowack, "Nothing Left to Lose," *Brookings Review* 18, no. 3 (summer 2000): 22–26; Neil Smith, Paul Caris, and Elvin Wyly, "The Camden Syndrome and the Menace of Urban Decline: Residential Disinvestment in Camden County, N.J." *Urban Affairs Review* 36, no. 4 (March 2001): 497–531.

14. Losers include New York, Chicago, Philadelphia, Detroit, Baltimore, Cleveland, St. Louis, Washington, Boston, San Francisco, Pittsburgh, Milwaukee, Buffalo, New Orleans, Minneapolis, Cincinnati, Kansas City, and Newark; gainers include Los Angeles, Houston, San Antonio, Dallas, Indianapolis, Seattle, and Denver. Cities that were not in the top twenty-five in 1950 but were in 1990 include San Diego, San Jose, Jacksonville, Columbus, El Paso, Memphis, Austin, Charlotte, and Nashville. Campbell Gibson, *Population of the 100 Largest Cities and Other Urban Places in the United States: 1950 to 1999* (Washington, D.C.: U.S. Census Bureau, June 1998), at http://www.census.gov/population/documentation/twps0027.html, and "Population Estimates for Cities with Populations of 100,000 and Greater (Size Rank in U.S.): July 1, 1999" (Washington, D.C.: U.S. Census Bureau, October 2000), at http://www.census.gov/population/estimates/metro-city/SC100K-T1.txt.

15. John Brennan and Edward W. Hill, "Where Are the Jobs? Cities, Suburbs, and the Competition for Employment" (Washington, D.C.: Brookings Institution, Center on Urban and Metropolitan Policy, November 1999).

16. Howard Chernick and Andrew Reschovsky, "The Long-Run Fiscal Health of Central Cities," *Chicago Policy Review* 4, no. 1 (spring 2000): 6.

17. Ibid.

18. Mark S. Rosentraub, *Major League Losers* (New York: Basic Books, 1999).

19. Chernick and Reschovsky, "Long-Run Fiscal Health," p. 6.

20. Richard Perez-Pena, "Court Upholds Law to Repeal Commuter Tax," *New York Times,* April 5, 2000.

21. Susan MacManus, "Financing Federal, State and Local Governments in the 1990s," *Annals of the American Academy of Political and Social Science* 509 (May 1990): 22–35; Joseph Zimmerman, "Regulating Intergovernmental Relations in the 1990s," *Annals of the American Academy of Political and Social Science* 509 (May 1990): 48–59; Michael Pagano, "State-Local Relations in the 1990s," *Annals of the American Academy of Political and Social Science* 509 (May 1990): 94–105; Janet M. Kelly, *State Mandates* (Washington, D.C.: National League of Cities, February 1992); Timothy Conlan and David R. Beam, "Federal Mandates," *Intergovernmental Perspective* 18, no. 4 (fall 1992): 7–11; *Intergovernmental Relations: Changing Patterns in State-Local Finances* (Washington, D.C.: General Accounting Office, HRD-92-87FS, March 1992); *Federal Statutory Preemption of State and Local Authority: History, Inventory, and Issues* (Washington, D.C.: U.S. Advisory Commission on Intergovernmental Re-

lations, A-121, September 1992); *Impact of Unfunded Federal Mandates on U.S. Cities: A 314 City Survey* (Washington, D.C.: U.S. Conference of Mayors and Price Waterhouse, October 26, 1993).

22. *Impact of Unfunded Federal Mandates on U.S. Cities.*

23. This discussion draws on Joel Blau, *The Visible Poor: Homelessness in the United States* (New York: Oxford University Press, 1992).

24. The number of shelter beds in New York City has declined to about 25,000. Nina Bernstein, "Shelter Population Reaches Highest Lead since 1980s," *New York Times,* February 8, 2001.

25. *The Oxford Dictionary of Quotations,* 3d ed. (New York: Oxford University Press, 1979), p. 217.

26. Jonathan Kozol, *Amazing Grace: The Lives of Children and the Conscience of a Nation* (New York: Harper Perennial, 1995), pp. 99–108.

27. Annette Kondo, "City Revises Code Enforcement but Adds No Staff," *Los Angeles Times,* November 29, 2000.

28. William E. Simon, *A Time for Truth* (New York: Berkeley Books, 1979), p. 193. See also Steven Hayward, "Broken Cities: Liberalism's Urban Legacy," *Policy Review* (March–April 1998): 14–22; Stephen Moore and Dean Stansel, "The Myth of America's Underfunded Cities," *Policy Analysis* 188 (1993): 1–20. Anthony Downs shows that urban decline is driven more by concentrated poverty and other objective conditions than by profligate spending and taxing decisions in *New Vision for Metropolitan America* (Washington, D.C.: Brookings Institution, 1994), appendix B.

29. Janet Rothenberg Pack, "Poverty and Urban Public Expenditures," *Urban Studies* 35, no. 11 (1998): 1995–2019. In their study of eighty-six cities, Ladd and Yinger showed that old housing and poverty drive up the costs of city services. A city with a poverty rate that is just one percentage point higher than that of another city will have police costs that are 5.5 percent higher, and a ten percentage point difference in the share of old housing causes a 6.9 percent increase in the cost of fire protection. Ladd and Yinger, *America's Ailing Cities,* pp. 85–86.

30. According to data compiled by the Advisory Commission on Intergovernmental Relations in 1981, the central-city tax burden relative to income was 50 percent higher than in the suburbs. In Washington, D.C., central-city residents paid 15 percent more in taxes, but creating a shared metropolitan tax base would have only a small effect on the after-tax distribution of income. Replacing local taxes with an areawide income tax would nonetheless increase the incomes of low-income households by 20 percent. See Seth B. Sacher, "Fiscal Fragmentation and the Distribution of Metropolitan Area Resources: A Case Study," *Urban Studies* 30, no. 7 (1993): 1225–39.

31. For a summary of the evidence of how suburban commuters drive up the cost of central-city services more than they contribute in taxes, see Dennis R. Judd and Todd Swanstrom, *City Politics: Private Power and Public Policy,* 2d ed. (New York: Longman, 1998), p. 316.

32. Paul Jargowsky, *Poverty and Place: Ghettos, Barrios, and the American City* (New York: Russell Sage Foundation, 1997), p. 36.

33. Myron Orfield, *Metropolitics: A Regional Agenda for Community and Stability* (Washington, D.C.: Brookings Institution Press, 1997), p. 162.

34. Robert Rafuse, "Fiscal Disparities in Chicagoland," *Intergovernmental Perspective* 17, no. 3 (1991): 14–19.

35. David Rusk, *Cities Without Suburbs,* 2d ed. (Washington, D.C.: Woodrow Wilson Center Press, 1995).

36. John D. Kasarda, "Industrial Restructuring and the Changing Location of Jobs," in *The State of the Union: America in the 1980s,* vol. 1, *Economic Trends,* ed. Reynolds Farley (New York: Russell Sage Foundation, 1995), pp. 215–67; William H. Frey, "The New Geography of Population Shifts," in ibid., vol. 2, *Social Trends,* pp. 271–336.

37. William Frey, "Immigration, Domestic Migration, and Demographic Balkanization in America: New Evidence for the 1990s," *Population and Development Review* 22, no. 4 (December 1996): 741–63.

38. Jargowsky, *Poverty and Place.*

39. Reynolds Farley, Charlotte Steeh, Tara Jackson, Maria Krysan, and Keith Reeves, "Continued Racial Residential Segregation in Detroit: Chocolate City, Vanilla Suburbs Revisited," *Journal of Housing Research* 4, no. 1 (1993): 1–38.

40. Calculated from data in Lawrence Mishel, Jared Bernstein, and John Schmitt, *The State of Working America, 2000–01* (Ithaca, N.Y.: ILR Press, an imprint of Cornell University Press, 2001), p. 153.

41. U.S. Bureau of the Census, *Statistical Abstract of the United States: 2000,* p. 299.

42. As reported in statistical profiles of New York State school districts, New York State Education Department, April 1999, at http://www.emsc.nysed.gov/irts/ch655_99/D660405.html.

43. Kenneth B. Wong, *Funding Public Schools: Politics and Policies* (Lawrence: University Press of Kansas, 1999), p. 12.

44. The controversy over the impact of spending on student achievement is reflected in two opposing studies: Eric Hanushek, "School Resources and Student Performance," in *Does Money Matter: The Effect of School Resources on Student Achievement and Adult Success,* ed. Gary Burtless (Washington, D.C.: Brookings Institution Press, 1996), and Richard Rothstein, *The Way We Were? The Myths and Realities of America's Student Achievement* (New York: Century Foundation Press, 1998).

45. For a good summary, see James Traub, "What No School Can Do," *New York Times Magazine,* January 16, 2000.

46. Xavier de Souza Briggs, "Moving up Versus Moving out: Neighborhood Effects in Housing Mobility Programs," *Housing Policy Debate* 8, no. 1 (1997): 195–234.

47. As reported by the General Accounting Office in 1994 and cited in Richard Rothstein, "Inner-City Nomads Follow a Track to Lower Grades," *New York Times,* January 20, 2000.

48. Kozol, *Amazing Grace,* p. 216.

49. Xavier de Souza Briggs, "Brown Kids in White Suburbs: Housing Mobility and the Many Faces of Social Capital," *Housing Policy Debate* 9, no. 1 (1998): 177–221.

50. James E. Rosenbaum, "Changing the Geography of Opportunity by Expanding Residential Choice: Lessons from the Gautreaux Program," *Housing Policy Debate* 6, no. 1 (1995): 231–70.

51. In the late 1960s, black residents of the small town of Shaw, Mississippi, filed a class action suit alleging that the town government had discriminated against them in providing city services. The town was 60 percent black, but black households accounted for 98 percent of those whose homes fronted unpaved streets and 97 percent of those not served by sanitary sewers. In 1971, a federal appeals court found that these practices violated the equal protection clause of the Fourteenth Amendment and ordered the town to correct the inequities. *Time* trumpeted the decision, saying that it would "force big as well as small cities across the U.S. to reallocate everything from police patrols to garbage pickups to park space." Subsequent to *Shaw,* however, the courts have largely withdrawn from overseeing local public service distribution.

Federal courts have ruled that plaintiffs must prove racially discriminatory *intent*, not just discriminatory effects. Courts have also found it difficult to judge what level of inequality across neighborhoods is impermissible or whether equality should be measured by spending, output, or results. The courts have thus generally followed the dissenting justice in *Shaw,* who wrote, "Such problems as plaintiffs have disclosed by the evidence . . . are to be resolved at the ballot box." See "New Attacks on Discrimination," *Time,* February 22, 1971, p. 59; Ralph A. Rossum, "The Rise and Fall of Equalization Litigation," *Urban Interest* 2, no. 1 (1980): 2; *Hawkins v. Shaw,* 461 F.2d 1169 (1972).

52. John Kincaid, "De Facto Devolution and Urban Funding: The Priority of Persons over Places," *Journal of Urban Affairs* 21, no. 2 (1999): 136.

53. U.S. Bureau of the Census, *Finances of Municipal and Township Governments 1997* (Washington, D.C.: Government Printing Office, September 2000), table 1, p. 13.

54. Thomas R. Swartz and John E. Peck, eds., *The Changing Face of Fiscal Federalism* (Armonk, N.Y.: M. E. Sharpe, 1990), especially Richard Child Hill, "Federalism and Urban Policy," pp. 35–55.

55. For a description of these organizations, see *Taking Care of Civic Business: How Formal CEO-Level Business Leadership Groups Have Influenced Civic Progress in Key American Cities* (Grand Rapids, Mich.: Frey Foundation, March 1993). John Mollenkopf, Harvey Molotch, and others sought to explain how and why these alignments arose. Mollenkopf coined the phrase "pro-growth coalition" in "The Post-War Politics of Urban Development," *Politics and Society* 5, no. 3 (winter 1975): 247–96, and *The Contested City* (Princeton, N.J.: Princeton University Press, 1983). Molotch used the phrase "growth machine" in "The City as a Growth Machine," *American Journal of Sociology* 82, no. 2 (1976): 309–32. Andrew Jonas and David Wilson, eds., *The Urban Growth Machine: Critical Perspectives Two Decades Later* (Albany: SUNY Press, 1999).

56. Michael Useem, *The Inner Circle* (New York: Oxford University Press, 1984); G. William Domhoff, *Who Rules America? Power and Politics in the Year 2000,* 3d ed. (Mountain View, Calif.: Mayfield, 1998).

57. See Raymond Mohl, "Planned Destruction: The Interstates and Central City Housing," in *From Tenements to the Taylor Homes: In Search of an Urban Housing Policy in Twentieth Century America,* ed. John F. Bauman, Roger Biles, and Kristin M. Szylvian (University Park: Pennsylvania State University Press, 2000), pp. 226–45.

58. C. H. Heying, "Civic Elites and Corporate Delocalization, *American Behavioral Scientist* 40, no. 5 (March 1997): 656–67. Joel Kotkin, "Cities Need Leaders . . . and Businessmen Are Indispensable," *American Enterprise* 9, no. 5 (September–October 1998): 12–18.

59. Rob Gurwitt, "The Rule of the Absentocracy," *Governing* (September 1991): 54.

60. This approach was pioneered by Clarence Stone. See his "Urban Regimes and the Capacity to Govern: A Political Economy Approach," *Journal of Urban Affairs* 15, no. 1 (1993): 1–28, and *Regime Politics: Governing Atlanta 1946–1988* (Lawrence: University Press of Kansas, 1989). For additional discussions, see Stephen Elkin, *City and Regime in the American Republic* (Chicago: University of Chicago Press, 1987); Susan Fainstein and Norman Fainstein, eds., *Restructuring the City: The Political Economy of Urban Redevelopment* (New York: Longman, 1986); David Judge, Gerry Stoker, and Harold Wolman, eds., *Theories of Urban Politics* (Thousand Oaks, Calif.: Sage Publications, 1995); Mickey Lauria, ed., *Reconstructing Urban Regime Theory: Regulation and Urban Politics in a Global Economy* (Thousand Oaks, Calif.: Sage Publica-

tions, 1997); John Logan and Todd Swanstrom, eds., *Beyond the City Limits* (Philadelphia: Temple University Press, 1990); Adolph Reed, "Demobilization in the New Black Political Regime: Ideological Capitulation and Radical Failure in the Post-segregation Era," in *The Bubbling Cauldron: Race, Ethnicity and the Urban Crisis,* ed. Michael Peter Smith and Joe R. Feagin (Minneapolis: University of Minnesota Press, 1995).

61. Stone, "Urban Regimes and the Capacity to Govern." For a comparison of local government capacity in the United States and elsewhere, see Judge et al., *Theories of Urban Politics;* Hal Wolman and Michael Goldsmith, *Urban Politics and Policy: A Comparative Approach* (Cambridge: Blackwell Publishers, 1992).

62. Kelly Candaele and Peter Dreier, "LA's Progressive Mosaic: Beginning to Find Its Voice," *Nation,* August 21-28, 2000, pp. 24-29. Harold Meyerson, "Why Liberalism Fled the City . . . and How It Might Come Back," *American Prospect,* March/April 1998.

63. Norman Fainstein and Susan Fainstein, "Regime Strategies, Communal Resistance, and Economic Forces," in Fainstein and Fainstein, *Restructuring the City;* and Stephen Elkin, *City and Regime in the American Republic.* Stone developed a typology of maintenance regimes, development regimes, middle-class progressive regimes, and regimes devoted to lower-class opportunity expansion in *Regime Politics* and "Urban Regimes and the Capacity to Govern." See also Mollenkopf, "Post-War Politics of Urban Development."

64. We borrow this typology from Judd and Swanstrom, *City Politics,* chap. 13, and replace their phrase "urban populism" with "urban progressivism."

65. Howard Chudacoff and Judith Smith, *The Evolution of American Urban Society* (Englewood Cliffs, N.J.: Prentice-Hall, 1994), p. 156.

66. Steven P. Erie, *Rainbow's End: Irish-Americans and the Dilemmas of Urban Machine Politics, 1840-1985* (Berkeley: University of California Press, 1988), p. 242.

67. The literature on political machines is vast. For thoughtful perspectives, see M. Craig Brown and Charles Halaby, "Machine Politics in America, 1870-1945," *Journal of Interdisciplinary History* 17, no. 3 (winter 1987): 587-612; Erie, *Rainbow's End;* Alan DiGaetano, "The Rise and Development of Urban Political Machines," *Urban Affairs Quarterly* 24, no. 2 (December 1988): 243-67; Amy Bridges, *A City in the Republic: Antebellum New York and the Origins of Machine Politics* (New York: Cambridge University Press, 1994); Martin Shefter, "The Electoral Foundations of the Political Machine: New York City, 1884-1897," in *The History of American Electoral Behavior,* ed. Joel Silbey et al. (Princeton, N.J.: Princeton University Press, 1978), pp. 263-98.

68. William Julius Wilson, *When Work Disappears: The World of the New Urban Poor* (New York: Alfred A. Knopf, 1996).

69. The Boston school busing wars and New York's Ocean Hill–Brownsville "community control" school controversy provide two dramatic examples of these divisions. Ralph Formisano, *Boston Against Busing: Race, Class, and Ethnicity in the 1960s and 1970s* (Chapel Hill: University of North Carolina Press, 1991); D. Garth Taylor, *Public Opinion and Collective Action: The Boston School Desegregation Conflict* (Chicago: University of Chicago Press, 1986); Alan Lupo, *Liberty's Chosen Home: The Politics of Violence in Boston* (Boston: Beacon Press, 1988); Maurice R. Berube and Marilyn Gittell, eds., *Confrontation at Ocean Hill–Brownsville: The New York School Strike of 1968* (New York: Praeger, 1969); Diane Ravitch, *The Great School Wars* (New York: Basic Books, 1974); Barbara Carter, *Pickets, Parents and Power: The Story Behind the New York City Teachers' Strike* (New York: Citation Press, 1971).

70. Harold Baron, "Black Powerlessness in Chicago," *Transaction* (November 1968): 32–38; Gregory Squires, Larry Bennett, Kathleen McCourt, and Phillip Nyden, *Chicago: Race, Class and the Response to Urban Decline* (Philadelphia: Temple University Press, 1987); Paul Kleppner, *Chicago Divided: The Making of a Black Mayor* (De Kalb: Northern Illinois University Press, 1985); Dianne M. Pinderhughes, "An Examination of Chicago Politics for Evidence of Political Incorporation and Representation," in *Racial Politics in American Cities*, 2d ed., ed. Rufus Browning, Dale R. Marshall and David Tabb (New York: Longman, 1997).

71. Jim Sleeper, "The End of the Rainbow? America's Changing Urban Politics," *New Republic*, November 1, 1993, pp. 20–25.

72. Twenty of these cities had African American mayors. Another five (Miami, El Paso, Albuquerque, Sacramento, and Santa Ana) had Hispanic mayors. In Dallas, Houston, San Francisco, Seattle, Kansas City, Baltimore, Memphis, St. Louis, Minneapolis, Rochester, Sacramento, and Birmingham, voters elected their first black or Hispanic mayor. In Detroit, Washington, New Orleans, Cleveland, Atlanta, Oakland, Newark, Albuquerque, Miami, and Denver, voters elected their second or third black or Hispanic mayor. Denver voters elected Hispanic Federico Pena as mayor in 1983 and 1987; when he declined to run for reelection, they elected Wellington Webb, an African American, to replace him. Among black mayors in 1999, Ron Kirk led Dallas, where 29.5 percent of the population is black, 20.9 percent is Hispanic, and 2.2 percent is Asian. Lee Brown led Houston, where 28.1 percent of the population is black, 27.6 percent Hispanic, and 4.1 percent Asian. Black mayors Willie Brown of San Francisco (10.9 percent black, 13.9 percent Hispanic, and 29.1 percent Asian), Norman Rice of Seattle (10.1 percent black, 3.6 percent Hispanic, and 0.8 percent Asian), Sharon Belton of Minneapolis (13 percent black, 3.1 percent Hispanic, and 4.3 percent Asian), Emanuel Cleaver of Kansas City (29.6 percent black, 3.9 percent Hispanic, and 1.2 percent Asian), Elzie Odom of Arlington, Texas (8.4 percent black, 8.9 percent Hispanic, and 3.9 percent Asian), and William Johnson of Rochester (31.5 percent black, 8.7 percent Hispanic, and 1.8 percent Asian) all led large cities where blacks do not make up the majority of the population or the electorate and where blacks are not always the largest minority group. Albuquerque, a majority white city of 385,000 (3 percent black, 34.5 percent Hispanic, and 1.7 percent Asian), elected Martin Chavez, a Hispanic, as mayor in 1993. Voters in Sacramento, a majority of whose 369,000 residents are white (15.3 percent black, 16.2 percent Hispanic, and 15 percent Asian), elected Joseph Serna, a Hispanic, as their mayor in 1992 and 1996. Many other smaller cities with white majorities have also elected black and Hispanic mayors. See Neil Kraus and Todd Swanstrom, "Minority Mayors and the Hollow Prize Problem," *PS: Political Science* 24, no. 1 (March 2001): 99–105.

73. U.S. Bureau of the Census, *Statistical Abstract of the United States: 2000*, p. 288. These figures do not include individuals elected to local school boards or special district boards.

74. Georgia A. Persons, ed., *Dilemmas of Black Politics* (New York: HarperCollins, 1993); Richard A. Keiser, *Subordination or Empowerment? African-American Leadership and the Struggle for Urban Political Power* (New York: Oxford University Press, 1997); Browning et al., *Racial Politics in American Cities*, essays by Sonenshein and by Browning, Marshall, and Tabb.

75. Browning et al., *Racial Politics in American Cities*; Persons, *Dilemmas of Black Politics*; Huey L. Perry, *Race, Politics, and Governance in the United States* (Gainesville: University Press of Florida, 1996); Sharon Wright, "The Mayoral Elections of the

Nineties: An Analysis of a New Generation of Black Mayors" (paper presented to the annual meeting of the American Political Science Association, August 1996).

76. Some urban liberals changed city charters from at-large to district election of city councils, giving minority areas a greater voice.

77. Jeffrey R. Henig, "Black Leaders, White Businesses: Racial Tension and the Construction of Public-Private Partnerships" (paper presented to the annual meeting of the American Political Science Association, September 1996).

78. James Button's study of Florida cities, *Blacks and Social Change: The Impact of the Civil Rights Movement in Southern Communities* (Princeton, N.J.: Princeton University Press, 1989), found that an increase in black police officers was correlated with a reduction in incidents of police misconduct and brutality. W. Marvin DeLaney, *Black Police in America* (Bloomington: Indiana University Press, 1996), found that cities with more black police officers have fewer citizen complaints against police and are more likely to institute community-based police programs.

79. Reed, "Demobilization in the New Black Political Regime."

80. Peter K. Eisinger, "Black Mayors and the Politics of Racial Economic Advancement," in *Urban Politics: Past, Present, and Future,* 2d ed., ed. Harlan Hahn and Charles H. Levine (New York: Longman, 1984), p. 257. See also Peter K. Eisinger, "Black Employment in Municipal Jobs: The Impact of Black Political Power," *American Political Science Review* 76, no. 2 (June 1982): 380–92.

81. Edward Greer, *Big Steel: Black Politics and Corporate Power in Gary, Indiana* (New York: Monthly Review Press, 1979).

82. Peter Dreier and Bruce Ehrlich, "Downtown Development and Urban Reform: The Politics of Boston's Linkage Policy," *Urban Affairs Quarterly* 26, no. 3 (March 1991): 345–75; Barbara Ferman, *Governing the Ungovernable City: Political Skill, Leadership, and the Modern Mayor* (Philadelphia: Temple University Press, 1985); Phillip Clay, "Boston: The Incomplete Transformation," in *Big City Politics in Transition,* ed. H. V. Savitch and John Clayton Thomas (Newbury Park, Calif.: Sage Publications, 1991); Cynthia Horan, "Coalition, Market, and State: Postwar Development Politics in Boston," in Lauria, *Reconstructing Urban Regime Theory.*

83. Stone, *Regime Politics.* See also Clarence Stone and Carol Pierannunzi, "Atlanta and the Limited Reach of Electoral Control," in Browning et al., *Racial Politics in American Cities;* Adolph Reed, "A Critique of Neo-Progressivism in Theorizing About Local Development Policy: A Case from Atlanta," in *The Politics of Urban Development,* ed. Clarence N. Stone and Haywood T. Sanders (Lawrence: University Press of Kansas, 1987).

84. Douglas S. Massey and Nancy A. Denton, *American Apartheid and the Making of the Underclass* (Cambridge: Harvard University Press, 1993), especially chap. 6.

85. Bryan Jackson and Michael Preston, "Race and Ethnicity in Los Angeles Politics," in *Big-City Politics, Governance and Fiscal Constraints,* ed. George Peterson (Washington, D.C.: Urban Institute Press, 1994); Alan Saltzstein and Raphael Sonenshein, "Los Angeles: Transformation of a Governing Coalition," in Savitch and Thomas, *Big City Politics in Transition;* H. Eric Schockman, "Is Los Angeles Governable?" in *Rethinking Los Angeles,* ed. Michael Dear, H. Eric Schockman, and Greg Hise (Thousand Oaks, Calif.: Sage Publications, 1996); Raphael Sonenshein, *Politics in Black and White* (Princeton, N.J.: Princeton University Press, 1993); Raphael Sonenshein, "Post-Incorporation Politics in Los Angeles," in Browning et al., *Racial Politics in American Cities.*

86. Latino Edward Roybal was elected the city's first minority council member in 1949.

He subsequently served as a congressman. In 1986, Gloria Molina won in a neighboring district created in the wake of a voting rights challenge by Latino activists. In 1993, Richard Alarcon was elected from the San Fernando Valley.

87. In 1992, following the city's devastating riots, the voters approved a Bradley-endorsed charter reform that eliminated the police chief's civil service protection. Blacks, Latinos, and white liberal voters overwhelmingly supported the measure. Bradley then forced Gates to resign and replaced him with Willie Williams, the African American police chief of Philadelphia, who pledged more cooperation between the police department and community groups. After Richard Riordan became mayor in 1993, it took him three years to force Williams to resign and to replace him with a more conservative black chief, Bernard Parks.

88. Mike Davis, *City of Quartz* (New York: Vintage, 1989); Saltzstein and Sonenshein, "Los Angeles: Transformation of a Governing Coalition"; Sonenshein, *Politics in Black and White;* Sonenshein, "Post-Incorporation Politics in Los Angeles."

89. James Johnson, Jones Farrell, and Melvin Oliver, "The Los Angeles Rebellion: A Retrospective View," *Economic Development Quarterly* 6, no. 4 (November 1992): 356–72.

90. Stone, *Regime Politics,* p. 87.

91. Reed, "A Critique of Neo-Progressivism."

92. "Atlanta's Mayor Defies Threat to Affirmative Action," *New York Times,* July 16, 1999.

93. Stone, *Regime Politics.* Preferential procurement programs have been damaged by evidence that some minority-owned firms are actually "fronts" for white-owned businesses or that they do not employ more minorities than white-owned firms do. See Timothy Bates and Darrell Williams, "Preferential Procurement Programs and Minority-Owned Business," *Journal of Urban Affairs* 17, no. 1 (1995): 10–17. In 1989, in *City of Richmond v. J. A. Croson Co.,* the U.S. Supreme Court ruled that Richmond's policy requiring that 30 percent of city contracts be set aside for minority-owned businesses violated the equal protection clause of the Fourteenth Amendment. To enact a constitutional program, cities must document prior discrimination by city government and demonstrate that race-neutral approaches will not solve the problem. This decision and other rulings in the 1990s limited the ability of municipal governments to enact laws designed to expand minority participation in public employment and publicly subsidized contracts.

94. Gary Orfield and Carole Ashkinaze, *The Closing Door: Conservative Policy and Black Opportunity* (Chicago: University of Chicago Press, 1991). See also Stone and Pierannunzi, "Atlanta and the Limited Reach of Electoral Control."

95. Bill Dedman, "The Color of Money," *Atlanta Journal-Constitution,* May 1–4, 1988; Larry Keating, Lynn Brazen, and Stan Fitterman, "Reluctant Response to Community Pressure in Atlanta," in *From Redlining to Reinvestment: Community Responses to Urban Disinvestment,* ed. Gregory Squires (Philadelphia: Temple University Press, 1992). Almost a decade after the initial uproar, little progress had been made in addressing racial disparities in lending. See Elvin K. Wyly and Steven R. Holloway, "'The Color of Money' Revisited: Racial Lending Patterns in Atlanta's Neighborhoods," *Housing Policy Debate* 10, no. 3 (1999): 555–600.

96. Joe Darden, Richard Child Hill, June Thomas, and Richard Thomas, *Detroit: Race and Uneven Development* (Philadelphia: Temple University Press, 1987); Richard Child Hill, "Crisis in the Motor City: The Politics of Economic Development in Detroit," in Fainstein and Fainstein, *Restructuring the City;* June Thomas, "Detroit: The Centrifugal City," in *Unequal Partnerships: The Political Economy of Urban Re-*

development in Postwar America, ed. Gregory D. Squires (New Brunswick, N.J.: Rutgers University Press, 1989).

97. Wilbur Rich, "Detroit: From Motor City to Service Hub," in Savitch and Thomas, *Big City Politics in Transition;* Marion E. Orr and Gerry Stoker, "Urban Regimes and Leadership in Detroit," *Urban Affairs Quarterly* 30, no. 1 (September 1994): 48–73.

98. Bill Vlasic, "Motown in Motion," *Business Week,* April 21, 1997. Japanese and European competition and the shift of U.S. production to the "global assembly line" meant layoffs and plant closings in Detroit, according to Hill, "Crisis in the Motor City," and Richard Child Hill and Joe R. Feagin, "Detroit and Houston," in *The Capitalist City,* ed. Michael Peter Smith and Joe R. Feagin (Cambridge: Basil Blackwell, 1987). In the mid-1960s, manufacturing accounted for 42.4 percent of the area's jobs; by 1988, it represented only 24.2 percent. Blacks constituted 43 percent of Detroit's population in 1970, rising to 76 percent in 1990, and 82 percent in 2000. Middle-class black professionals and auto workers began leaving Detroit to escape its property taxes, schools, and crime. The city poverty rate increased dramatically during the 1970s and 1980s, becoming the highest among the nation's 100 largest cities. Banks redlined the city, landlords and home owners abandoned their buildings, and many residential neighborhoods came to resemble bombed-out areas. In 1993, only one building permit was taken out for a new house, as reported in Vlasic, "Motown." Detroit's downtown core hollowed out as businesses closed or fled. Meanwhile, federal funds, as a percentage of Detroit's general revenue, declined from 27.5 percent in 1976 to 5.9 percent in 1988, according to Rich, "Detroit: From Motor City to Service Hub."

99. Rich, "Detroit: From Motor City to Service Hub."

100. Frank Washington and Bill Turque, "New Deal in Detroit," *Newsweek,* September 12, 1994.

101. Vlasic, "Motown."

102. John King, "Whining Doesn't Work Any More, Mayors Learning," *San Francisco Chronicle,* June 27, 1996.

103. Vlasic, "Motown."

104. Jon Pepper, "Power Elite Designing a New Downtown," *Detroit News,* March 10, 1996. Chrysler agreed to invest $2.1 billion in the city, about half in a new engine plant on the decaying East Side, for which the city granted an $87 million tax abatement. General Motors pledged to spend $250 million to upgrade its facilities and $72 million to purchase the Renaissance Center, a partly vacant riverfront office complex that had been a failure from the time it was built in 1976. Archer supported the construction of new professional football and baseball stadiums downtown to keep the Lions and Tigers in Detroit, according to Vlasic, "Motown." The UAW agreed to move its education and training program, run in collaboration with General Motors, from suburban Oakland County into Detroit. See also Gary Heinlein and Suzette Hackney, "City on the Rebound," *Detroit News,* January 5, 1997. Business support helped the city improve its junk bond rating, according to Tom Henderson, "Calculating the Archer Effect," *Corporate Detroit Magazine* (June 1994): 34–43. Archer gave minority entrepreneurs a share in the private economic growth. The Detroit Tigers agreed to award 20 percent of the construction work on their new $235 million stadium to minority businesses, at least one-quarter based in Detroit, and half the construction workers will be Detroit residents, as reported in Washington and Turque, "New Deal." See also Valarie Basheda and Tricia Serju, "Minority Firms Will Get Share of Stadium Work," *Detroit News,* November 21, 1995.

105. Washington and Turque, "New Deal."

106. Ibid.

107. Melinda Wilson, "Archer's Biggest Donors Are in the 'Burbs," *Detroit News,* March 9, 1997.

108. Tim Kiska, Judy DeHaven, and Suzette Hackney, "Archer Win Strengthens City's Ties with Suburbs: Tricounty Leaders Praise Mayor's Ability to Reach out, Create Coalition," *Detroit News,* September 10, 1997.

109. Robyn Meredith, "Demand for Single-Family Homes Helps Fuel Inner-City Resurgence," *New York Times,* July 5, 1997.

110. Suzette Hackney, "Archer Gets Chance to Take a Bow," *Detroit News,* January 27, 1997.

111. Washington and Turque, "New Deal."

112. Reed, "A Critique of Neo-Progressivism"; Rich, "Detroit: From Motor City to Service Hub"; Stone, *Regime Politics;* Stone and Pierannunzi, "Atlanta and the Limited Reach of Electoral Control"; Thomas, "Detroit: The Centrifugal City"; Arnold Fleischmann, "Atlanta: Urban Coalitions in a Suburban Sea," in Savitch and Thomas, *Big City Politics in Transition.*

113. Peter Beinart, "The Pride of the Cities," *New Republic,* June 30, 1997, pp. 16–22; Sleeper, "End of the Rainbow?"

114. Pierre Clavel, *The Progressive City* (New Brunswick, N.J.: Rutgers University Press, 1986); Norman Krumholz, John Forester, and Alan A. Altshuler, *Making Equity Planning Work* (Philadelphia: Temple University Press, 1990); Norman Krumholz and Pierre Clavel, *Reinventing Cities: Equity Planners Tell Their Stories* (Philadelphia: Temple University Press, 1994).

115. For unions' recent involvement in urban progressivism, see Steven Greenhouse, "The Innovative Figure in Silicon Valley? Maybe This Labor Organizer," *New York Times,* November 14, 1999; David Moberg, "Union Cities," *American Prospect,* September 11, 2000; Douglas Foster, "Unions.com," *Mother Jones* 25, no. 5 (September–October 2000): 74–79; and Candaele and Dreier, "LA's Progressive Mosaic."

116. This discussion of Pingree and his counterparts is summarized in Judd and Swanstrom, *City Politics,* pp. 69–70. See also Melvin G. Holli, *Reform in Detroit: Hazen S. Pingree and Urban Politics* (New York: Oxford University Press, 1969).

117. In Milwaukee, Socialists were elected to the mayor's office, the city council, the school board, other city and county posts, and Congress. Milwaukee's third and last Socialist mayor held office as late as 1960, but the Socialists' heyday was the first two decades of the twentieth century. See James Weinstein, *The Decline of Socialism in America 1912–1925* (New York: Vintage Books, 1967), pp. 93–108.

118. Ibid., p. 108.

119. On progressive urban reformers, see Roy Lubove, *The Progressives and the Slums* (Pittsburgh: University of Pittsburgh Press, 1962); John Buenker, *Urban Liberalism and Progressive Reform* (New York: W. W. Norton, 1973); Allan F. Davis, *Spearheads for Reform* (New York: Oxford University Press, 1967).

120. Mark Gelfand, *A Nation of Cities: The Federal Government and Urban America, 1933–1965* (New York: Oxford University Press, 1975), p. 36; see also Francis Fox Piven and Richard Cloward, *Poor People's Movements* (New York: Pantheon, 1977).

121. Thomas Kessner, *Fiorello H. LaGuardia and the Making of Modern New York* (New York: McGraw-Hill, 1989); Josh Freeman, *Working-Class New York: Life and Labor Since World War II* (New York: New Press, 2000).

122. Margaret Weir, "Power, Money, and Politics in Community Development," and

Peter Dreier, "Comment," in *Urban Problems and Community Development,* ed. Ronald Ferguson and William Dickens (Washington, D.C.: Brookings Institution Press, 1999).

123. Harry Boyte, *The Backyard Revolution* (Philadelphia: Temple University Press, 1980); Harry Boyte, *CommonWealth: A Return to Citizen Politics* (New York: Free Press, 1989); Gary Delgado, *Beyond the Politics of Place: New Directions in Community Organizing in the 1990s* (Oakland, Calif.: Applied Research Center, 1994); Peter Dreier, "Community Empowerment: The Limits and Potential of Community-Based Organizing in Urban Neighborhoods," *Cityscape* 2, no. 2 (1996): 121–59; Jeffrey M. Berry, Kent E. Portney, and Ken Thomson, *The Rebirth of Urban Democracy* (Washington, D.C.: Brookings Institution, 1993); Michael Lipsky, *Protest in City Politics* (Chicago: Rand McNally, 1970); Mary Beth Rogers, *Cold Anger: A Story of Faith and Power in Politics* (Denton: University of North Texas Press, 1990); Mark Warren, *Dry Bones Rattling* (Princeton, N.J.: Princeton University Press, 2001); Peter Medoff and Holly Sklar, *Streets of Hope* (Boston: South End Press, 1994); Piven and Cloward, *Poor People's Movements.*

124. Christopher J. Walker and Mark Weinheimer, *Community Development in the 1990s* (Washington, D.C.: Urban Institute, 1998); Edward Goetz, "Local Government Support for Nonprofit Housing: A Survey of U.S. Cities," *Urban Affairs Quarterly* 27, no. 3 (1992): 420–35; Edward Goetz, *Shelter Burden: Local Politics and Progressive Housing Policy* (Philadelphia: Temple University Press, 1993).

125. Peter Dreier, "Redlining Cities: How Banks Color Community Development," *Challenge* 134, no. 6 (1991): 15–23; Squires, *From Redlining to Reinvestment;* Susan White Haag, *Community Reinvestment and Cities: A Literature Review of CRA's Impact and Future* (Washington, D.C.: Brookings Institution Center on Urban and Metropolitan Policy, March 2000). To ensure that the federal government will accept applications to open branches or to buy other banks, banks frequently reach agreements with community groups to expand their lending activities in poor neighborhoods. According to one estimate, more than 300 community reinvestment agreements have added $350 billion in private investment in low-income areas, primarily for housing rehabilitation and new construction. See Alex Schwartz, "From Confrontation to Collaboration? Banks, Community Groups, and the Implementation of Community Reinvestment Act Agreements," *Housing Policy Debate* 9, no. 3 (1998): 631–62.

126. Stella Capek and John Gilderbloom, *Community Versus Commodity: Tenants and the American City* (Albany, N.Y.: SUNY Press, 1992).

127. Carlos Munoz, Jr., "Mexican Americans and the Promise of Democracy: San Antonio Mayoral Elections," in Peterson, *Big-City Politics, Governance, and Fiscal Constraints.*

128. Carmine Scavo, "The Use of Regulative Mechanisms by Large U.S. Cities," *Journal of Urban Affairs* 15, no. 1 (1993): 100.

129. Mary Brooks, *A Status Report on Housing Trust Funds in the United States* (Washington, D.C.: Center for Community Change, 1997); Mary Brooks, "Housing Trust Funds: A New Approach to Funding Affordable Housing," in *Affordable Housing and Urban Redevelopment in the United States,* ed. Willem van Vliet (Thousand Oaks, Calif.: Sage Publications, 1997).

130. Capek and Gilderbloom, *Community Versus Commodity;* Church Collins and Kirby White, "Boston in the 1980s: Toward a Social Housing Policy," in *The Affordable City,* ed. John E. Davis (Philadelphia: Temple University Press, 1994); Peter Dreier, "The Landlords Stage a Rent Strike," *Nation,* June 23, 1997, pp. 17–22; Goetz, *Shelter Bur-*

den; Mark Kann, *Middle Class Radicalism in Santa Monica* (Philadelphia: Temple University Press, 1986); W. Dennis Keating, "Linking Downtown Development to Broader Community Goals: An Analysis of Linkage Policy in Three Cities," *Journal of the American Planning Association* 52, no. 2 (1986): 133–46.

131. Richard DeLeon, *Left Coast City: Progressive Politics in San Francisco, 1975–1991* (Lawrence: University Press of Kansas, 1992).

132. For discussion of progressive urban regimes, see Clavel, *Progressive City;* Krumholz and Clavel, *Reinventing Cities;* Donald Rosdil, "The Context of Radical Populism in U.S. Cities: A Comparative Analysis," *Journal of Urban Affairs* 13, no. 1 (1991): 77–96; David Imbroscio, *Reconstructing City Politics: Alternative Economic Development and Urban Regimes* (Newbury Park, Calif.: Sage Publications, 1997). For Portland, see Carl Abbott, "The Portland Region: Where City and Suburbs Talk to Each Other—and Often Agree," *Housing Policy Debate* 8, no. 1 (1997): 65–73. For Chicago, see Stephen Alexander, Robert Giloth, and Joshua Lerner, "Chicago's Industry Task Forces: Joint Problem Solving for Local Economic Development," *Economic Development Quarterly* 1, no. 4 (1987): 352–57; Pierre Clavel and Wim Wiewel, eds., *Harold Washington and the Neighborhoods: Progressive City Government in Chicago* (New Brunswick, N.J.: Rutgers University Press, 1991); Robert Mier, *Social Justice and Local Development Policy* (Newbury Park, Calif.: Sage Publications, 1993); Dianne M. Pinderhughes, "An Examination of Chicago Politics for Evidence of Political Incorporation and Representation," in Browning et al., *Racial Politics in American Cities;* Michael Preston, "The Politics of Economic Redistribution in Chicago: Is Balanced Growth Possible?" in *Regenerating Cities,* ed. Michael Parkinson, Bernard Foley, and Dennis Judd (Glenview, Ill.: Scott, Foresman, 1989); and Barbara Ferman, *Challenging the Growth Machine* (Lawrence: University Press of Kansas, 1996). For Boston, see Peter Dreier, "Ray Flynn's Legacy: American Cities and the Progressive Agenda," *National Civic Review* (fall 1993): 380–403; Dreier and Ehrlich, "Downtown Development and Urban Reform"; Peter Dreier and W. Dennis Keating, "The Limits of Localism: Progressive Municipal Housing Policies in Boston," *Urban Affairs Quarterly* 26, no. 2 (1996); Peter Dreier, "Urban Politics and Progressive Housing Policy: Ray Flynn and Boston's Neighborhood Agenda," in *Revitalizing Urban Neighborhoods,* ed. W. Dennis Keating, Norman Krumholz, and Philip Star (Lawrence: University Press of Kansas, 1996); and Peter Medoff and Holly Sklar, *Streets of Hope* (Boston: South End Press, 1994). For Burlington, see William Conroy, *Challenging the Boundaries of Reform: Socialism in Burlington* (Philadelphia: Temple University Press, 1990). For San Francisco, see Randy Shilts, *The Mayor of Castro Street* (New York: St. Martin's Press, 1982); Richard DeLeon, *Left Coast City: Progressive Politics in San Francisco, 1975–1991* (Lawrence: University Press of Kansas, 1992); Richard DeLeon, "Progressive Politics in the Left Coast City: San Francisco," in Browning et al., *Racial Politics in American Cities.* For Pittsburgh, see Louise Jezierski, "Neighborhoods and Public-Private Partnerships in Pittsburgh," *Urban Affairs Quarterly* 26, no. 2 (December 1990): 217–49; John Metzger, "The Community Reinvestment Act and Neighborhood Revitalization in Pittsburgh," in Squires, *From Redlining to Reinvestment;* John Metzger, "Reinventing Housing in Pittsburgh: A Former CDC Director Becomes Mayor," *Shelterforce* (March–April 1996): 13–18; John Metzger, "Remaking the Growth Coalition: The Pittsburgh Partnership for Neighborhood Development," *Economic Development Quarterly* 12, no. 1 (February 1998): 112–29; Ferman, *Challenging the Growth Machine.* For Santa Monica, see Derek Shearer,

"How the Progressives Won in Santa Monica," *Social Policy* 12, no. 3 (1982): 7–14; Kann, *Middle Class Radicalism in Santa Monica;* John Gilderbloom and Stella Capek, "Santa Monica a Decade Later," *National Civic Review* (spring 1992). For Cleveland, see Krumholz et al., *Making Equity Planning Work;* Todd Swanstrom, *The Crisis of Growth Politics: Cleveland, Kucinich, and the Challenge of Urban Populism* (Philadelphia: Temple University Press, 1985).

133. DeLeon, *Left Coast City;* DeLeon, "Progressive Politics in the Left Coast City."

134. DeLeon, *Left Coast City.*

135. See Ferman, *Challenging the Growth Machine.* Information on recent political trends in Pittsburgh was provided by John Metzger in a personal communication, August 11, 1997.

136. Pinderhughes, "Examination of Chicago Politics," p. 113.

137. Medoff and Sklar, *Streets of Hope.*

138. Dreier and Keating, "Limits of Localism."

139. Paul Osterman, "Gains from Growth? The Impact of Full Employment on Poverty in Boston," in *The Urban Underclass,* ed. Christopher Jencks and Paul E. Peterson (Washington, D.C.: Brookings Institution Press, 1991).

140. At the first Conference for Good City Government in 1894, President Theodore Roosevelt urged the delegates to make local government more "practical and efficient," according to Melvin G. Holli, "Urban Reform in the Progressive Era," in *The Progressive Era,* ed. Louis Gould (Syracuse, N.Y.: Syracuse University Press, 1974), p. 144. The U.S. Chamber of Commerce initially provided office space and paid the executive secretary of the City Managers Association. Judd and Swanstrom, *City Politics,* p. 101.

141. George Mowry, *The Era of Theodore Roosevelt, 1900–1912* (New York: Harper and Row, 1958); Ernest S. Griffith, *A History of American City Government, 1900–1920* (New York: Praeger, 1974); James Weinstein, *The Corporate Ideal in the Liberal State, 1900–1918* (Boston: Beacon Press, 1968); Samuel Hayes, "The Politics of Reform in Municipal Government in the Progressive Era," in *Social Change and Urban Politics: Readings,* ed. Daniel N. Gordon (Englewood Cliffs, N.J.: Prentice-Hall, 1972), pp. 107–27.

142. Previously, voters could just show up at polling places on the day of an election. Reformers also endorsed the secret ballot. Before it was introduced in the 1880s, parties printed the ballots, and they were often cast publicly. Illiterate immigrants could ask for help in reading and filling out the ballot—something the machine's precinct captains were happy to do.

143. Willis D. Hawley, *Nonpartisan Elections and the Case for Party Politics* (New York: Wiley, 1973), pp. 14–18.

144. Weinstein, *Decline of Socialism in America;* Hayes, "The Politics of Reform."

145. John Mollenkopf, *A Phoenix in the Ashes* (Princeton, N.J.: Princeton University Press, 1994); John Mollenkopf, "New York: The Great Anomaly," in Browning et al., *Racial Politics in American Cities.*

146. Los Angeles Mayor Sam Yorty (elected in 1961) and Philadelphia Mayor Frank Rizzo (the city's former police chief, elected in 1971) were among the most visible big-city mayors vaulted into office by a conservative backlash. They called for "law and order," a thinly veiled call for tougher police practices in poor minority areas. Although neither Yorty nor Rizzo pretended to show concern for the plight of the poor, the urban conservatives of the 1980s and 1990s justified their policies by arguing

that "big government" liberalism had trapped the poor in the welfare safety net. See Richard A. Keiser, "After the First Black Mayor: Fault Lines in Philadelphia's Biracial Coalition," in Browning et al., *Racial Politics in American Cities.*

147. Edward Banfield, *The Unheavenly City* (Boston: Little, Brown, 1970). Heirs to Banfield include Fred Siegel, *The Future Once Happened Here: New York, DC, LA, and the Fate of America's Big Cities* (New York: Free Press, 1997); Stephen Goldsmith, *The Twenty-first Century City: Resurrecting Urban America* (New York: Rowman and Littlefield, 1999); John O. Norquist, *The Wealth of Cities: Revitalizing the Centers of American Life* (Reading, Mass.: Addison-Wesley, 1998); Steven Hayward, "Broken Cities: Liberal's Urban Legacy," *Policy Review* (March–April 1998); Senator Dan Coats and Senator Spencer Abraham, "Liberalism's Mean Streets: How Conservatives Can Reverse Urban Decline," *Policy Review* (July–August 1998): 36–40; James Q. Wilson and George L. Kelling, "Broken Windows," *Atlantic Monthly* (March 1982): 29–39; Tamar Jacoby, "Mandate for Anarchy," *New Democrat* 10, no. 3 (May–June 1998): 18–23.

148. Fred Siegel and Kay Hymowitz, "Why Did Ed Rendell Fizzle Out?" *City Journal* 9, no. 4 (autumn 1999): 1–27.

149. Heather MacDonald, "Gotham's Workforce Woes," *City Journal* 7, no. 3 (summer 1997): 41–49.

150. For critiques of Siegel's book, see Elliot Currie, "The Liberals Done It," *Dissent* 45, no. 1 (winter 1998): 114–17; Adam Yarmolinsky, "Looking Backwards," *Washington Monthly* 29, no. 10 (October 1997): 59–60; and Sean Wilentz, "The Rise and Fall of Racialized Liberalism," *American Prospect* 40 (September–October 1998): 82–86.

151. Quoted in James Traub, "Giuliani Internalized," *New York Times Magazine,* February 11, 2001, p. 66.

152. Tucker, whose work was funded by right-wing think tanks and published by several conservative magazines, went so far as to argue that rent control caused homelessness during the 1980s. William Tucker, "America's Homeless: Victims of Rent Control," *Heritage Foundation Backgrounder* 685 (January 12, 1989): 1–14; William Tucker, "Home Economics: The Housing Crisis that Over-regulation Built," *Policy Review* 50 (fall 1989): 20. For a critique of Tucker's work and his backers, see Richard P. Appelbaum, Michael Dolny, Peter Dreier, and John Gilderbloom, "Scapegoating Rent Control: Masking the Causes of Homelessness," *Journal of the American Planning Association* 57, no. 2 (spring 1991): 153–64. For a conservative critique of public housing, see Howard Husock, "We Don't Need Subsidized Housing," *City Journal* 7, no. 1 (winter 1997): 50–58.

153. Joe Feagin, *Free Enterprise City: Houston in Political and Economic Perspective* (New Brunswick, N.J.: Rutgers University Press, 1988); Peter Dreier, "The Landlords Stage a Rent Strike," *Nation,* June 23, 1997, pp. 17–22; Rob Gurwitt, "Indianapolis and the Republican Future," *Governing* (February 1994); Peter Beinart, "The Pride of the Cities," *New Republic,* June 30, 1997.

154. Tracy Shryer and Marc Lacey, "Riordan Studies Privatization in Indianapolis," *Los Angeles Times,* June 22, 1993. See also Louise Simmons, "A New Urban Conservatism: The Case of Hartford, Connecticut," *Journal of Urban Affairs* 20, no. 2 (1998): 175–98; E. J. Dionne, "Saving Cities: Is 'Kojak Liberalism' the Answer?" *Washington Post,* June 28, 1993; Dan Finnigan, "Philadelphia Turnaround May Offer Lessons for L.A.," *Los Angeles Times,* July 15, 1993; Charles Mahtesian, "Maybe Philadelphia Is Governable After All," *Governing* (April 1993): 34–38.

155. Jonathan Walters, "Who Needs Civil Service?" *Governing* (August 1997): 17–21.

156. Evelyn Nieves, "Homeless Defy Cities' Drives to Move Them," *New York Times,* December 7, 1999. See also Elliott Currie, *Reckoning: Drugs, the Cities, and the American Future* (New York: Hill and Wang, 1993); Adele Harrell and George Peterson, eds., *Drugs, Crime, and Social Isolation* (Washington, D.C.: Urban Institute Press, 1992); Jeffrey Reiman, *The Rich Get Richer and the Poor Get Prison* (Needham Heights, Mass.: Allyn and Bacon, 1995); Wesley Skogan, *Disorder and Decline* (Berkeley: University of California Press, 1990); Michael Tomasky, "The Left and Crime," *Dissent* (fall 1997): 85–96, with comments by Elliott Currie, Ester Fuchs, and Randall Kennedy; Neal Peirce, "Community Policing that Works," *National Journal,* October 12, 1996, p. 2190; James Lardner, "Can You Believe the New York Miracle?" *New York Review of Books,* August 14, 1997, pp. 54–58.

157. Goldsmith ran unsuccessfully for governor in 1996 and was George W. Bush's chief domestic policy adviser in the 2000 presidential campaign, positioning the Texas governor as a "compassionate conservative" who cares about the poor. Frank Bruni, "Bush Unveils a Proposal to Encourage Development in Struggling Neighborhoods," *New York Times,* April 19, 2000; Alison Mitchell, "Bush Draws Campaign Theme from More than 'the Heart,'" *New York Times,* June 12, 2000. On Goldsmith's tenure as mayor, see Michael Grunwald, "The Myth of the Supermayor," *American Prospect* 9, no. 40 (September–October 1998): 20–29; Beinart, "The Pride of the Cities"; Rob Gurwitt, "Indianapolis and the Republican Future," *Governing* (February 1994): 24–28; Stephen J. McGovern, "Urban Populism: The Case of Indianapolis" (paper presented to the annual meeting of the American Political Science Association, Washington, D.C., August 1997); Sleeper, "End of the Rainbow?" Goldsmith, *Twenty-first Century City;* Siegel, *The Future Once Happened Here.* On Mayor Rendell, see Buzz Bissinger, *A Prayer for the City* (New York: Random House, 1997); Stephen J. McGovern, "Mayoral Leadership and Economic Development Policy: The Case of Ed Rendell's Philadelphia," *Policy and Politics* 25, no. 2 (April 1997): 153–72.

158. Sonenshein, "Post-Incorporation Politics in Los Angeles."

159. "The Times Poll: Profile of the City Electorate," *Los Angeles Times,* April 10, 1997. Sixty-seven percent of all white voters supported Riordan. White conservatives, who represented a fifth of the vote and were concentrated in the San Fernando Valley area, gave him 92 percent of their votes. Moderate whites, a third of the vote, gave Riordan 75 percent of their votes, primarily over racial concerns. Riordan even made inroads into Woo's natural constituency of Bradley supporters. Several high-profile black and Latino political figures endorsed Riordan. Thirty-nine percent of Democrats and 31 percent of self-identified white liberals supported Riordan, as well as 70 percent of independents. Riordan even won 49 percent of the Jewish vote and 31 percent of the Asian vote. In addition, 43 percent of Latino voters supported Riordan. Turnout was low among Woo constituencies. Whites were only 37 percent of the population but constituted 65 percent of registered voters and 72 percent of votes cast. Although 86 percent of blacks supported Woo, blacks accounted for only 14 percent of the population, 15 percent of registered voters, and 12 percent of the mayoral vote. Latinos gave Woo 57 percent of their vote, but they represented only 10 percent of the vote. (Asians accounted for 4 percent of the total vote.) Four years later, Riordan flattened his progressive white challenger, Tom Hayden, 61 to 39 percent. Riordan improved his minority vote with 19 percent of the black vote, 60 percent of the Latino vote, and 62 percent of the Asian vote. See Karen M. Kaufman, "Racial Conflict and Political Choice: A Study of Mayoral Voting Behavior in Los Angeles

and New York," *Urban Affairs Review* 33, no. 5 (May 1998): 655–85; and Sonenshein, "Post-Incorporation Politics in Los Angeles."

160. Schockman, "Is Los Angeles Governable?" p. 69.

161. Marla Cone, "Smog Plan Would Harm Economy," *Los Angeles Times,* August 30, 1994; Marla Cone, "State Scales Back Clean-Air Plan to Bow to Oil, Trucking Industries," *Los Angeles Times,* November 10, 1994; Marla Cone, "Wilson, Riordan Criticize EPA's Delay on Smog Rules," *Los Angeles Times,* January 14, 1995; Marla Cone, "U.S. Unveils Scaled-Back Clean-Air Plan," *Los Angeles Times,* February 15, 1995; Marla Cone, "Economy Found Undamaged by L.A. Smog Rules," *Los Angeles Times,* April 3, 1995; Marla Cone, "Southland Smog Levels Are Lowest in 4 Decades," *Los Angeles Times,* October 21, 1995.

162. Riordan failed to get Los Angeles designated as a federal empowerment zone, but he persuaded the Clinton administration to give Los Angeles federal funds to establish a community development bank to lend to inner-city businesses. He supported Clinton and Senator Dianne Feinstein for reelection, remained neutral on Proposition 187 (restricting benefits to immigrants) in 1994 and Proposition 209 (eliminating state affirmative action laws) in 1995, and marched in the city's gay pride parade.

163. Mollenkopf, *Phoenix in the Ashes;* Mollenkopf, "New York: The Great Anomaly"; William Sites, "The Limits of Urban Regime Theory: New York City Under Koch, Dinkins and Giuliani," *Urban Affairs Review* 32, no. 4 (March 1997): 536–57; Jim Sleeper, *The Closest of Strangers: Liberalism and Politics of Race in New York* (New York: W. W. Norton, 1990).

164. Mollenkopf, *Phoenix in the Ashes;* Mollenkopf, "New York: The Great Anomaly."

165. Ibid.

166. Mollenkopf, "New York: The Great Anomaly," p. 100.

167. Ibid., p. 111.

168. Thomas L. McMahon, Larian Angelo, and John Mollenkopf, *Hollow in the Middle: The Rise and Fall of New York City's Middle Class* (New York: Finance Division, City Council, December 1997); Kathryn Larin and Elizabeth McNichol, *Pulling Apart: A State-by-State Analysis of Income Trends* (Washington, D.C.: Center of Budget and Policy Priorities, December 1997); Gregg Van Ryzin and Andrew Genn, "Neighborhood Change and the City of New York's Ten-Year Housing Plan," *Housing Policy Debate* 10, no. 4 (1999): 799–838; Alex Schwartz, "New York City and Subsidized Housing: Impacts and Lessons of the City's $5 Billion Capital Budget Housing Plan," *Housing Policy Debate* 10, no. 4 (1999): 839–77; Edward L. Glaeser and Matthew E. Kahn, "From John Lindsay to Rudy Giuliani: The Decline of the Local Safety Net?" *Economic Policy Review* 5, no. 3 (September 1999): 117–30.

169. When the consolidation law took effect in 1970, Indianapolis's jurisdiction swelled from 82 to 402 square miles and its population from 480,000 to 740,000. The consolidation occurred over opposition from Democrats and African Americans, who feared that the inclusion of a large segment of suburban Republicans in the local electorate would undermine their influence. See McGovern, "Urban Populism: The Case of Indianapolis."

170. McGovern, "Urban Populism: The Case of Indianapolis"; Grunwald, "The Myth of the Supermayor."

171. McGovern, "Urban Populism: The Case of Indianapolis," p. 8.

172. Ibid., pp. 17–18.

173. See William Julius Wilson, *The Bridge over the Racial Divide: Rising Inequality and Coalition Politics* (Berkeley: University of California Press, 1999).

174. McMahon et al., *Hollow in the Middle,* p. 5.

175. Booming urban economies have had a downside for the poor: the housing burden has soared. Since 1975, median renter income (adjusted for inflation) in New York City went up 3 percent, while median rent increased 33 percent. Bruce Lambert, "Housing Crisis Confounds a Prosperous City," *New York Times,* July 9, 2000.

176. The best analysis of distressed suburbs is William Lucy and David Phillips, *Confronting Suburban Decline: Strategic Planning for Metropolitan Revival* (Washington, D.C.: Island Press, 2000). It concentrates more on documenting suburban decline than on analyzing how distressed suburban governments are responding to the crisis.

CHAPTER 6. REGIONALISMS OLD AND NEW

1. Kenneth Neubeck and Richard Ratcliff, "Urban Democracy and the Power of Corporate Capital," in *Business Elites and Urban Development,* ed. Scott Cummings (Albany, N.Y.: SUNY Press, 1988).

2. Ibid., p. 322.

3. Shipman's plan is described in Vicki Kemper, "Operation Urban Storm," *Common Cause Magazine* (July–August 1991): 10–16, 39–40.

4. At the time, at least thirty cities across the country had adopted zoning laws to restrict social service agencies. A growing number of cities, responding to the increase in homelessness, adopted laws to restrict homeless people from panhandling or from sleeping in public places. Evelyn Nieves, "Homeless Defy Cities' Drives to Move Them," *New York Times,* December 7, 1999; William Claiborne, "From Champion to Chief Critic of the Homeless," *Washington Post,* December 9, 1997.

5. Michael Matza, "Social Service Groups Caught in the Middle," *Houston Chronicle,* August 22, 1996; "Hartford Restricts Social Services to Stem Flow of Poor People," *New York Times,* August 14, 1996; Colman McCarthy, "Heartless Go After Services for Homeless," *Washington Post,* May 14, 1996.

6. Ronald Smothers, "City Seeks to Grow by Disappearing," *New York Times,* October 18, 1993; Woody Baird, "Memphis' Black Mayor Fears a Bleak Future: Leader Wants to Merge City with Majority-White Suburbs to Relieve the Strain on Tax Base," *Los Angeles Times,* October 3, 1993.

7. Baird, "Memphis' Black Mayor Fears Bleak Future."

8. The term is "favored quarter" from Myron Orfield, *Metropolitics: A Regional Agenda for Community and Stability,* rev. ed. (Washington, D.C., and Cambridge, Mass.: Brookings Institution Press and Lincoln Institute of Land Policy, 1997), p. 5.

9. Gerald Frug, *City Making* (Princeton, N.J.: Princeton University Press, 1999), p. 80.

10. Robert D. Putnam, *Bowling Alone: The Collapse and Revival of American Community* (New York: Simon and Schuster, 2000), chap. 12; J. Eric Oliver, "The Effects of Metropolitan Economic Segregation on Local Civic Involvement," *American Journal of Political Science* 43 (January 1999): 186–212; J. Eric Oliver, "City Size and Civic Involvement in Metropolitan America," *American Political Science Review* 94, no. 2 (June 2000): 361–73.

11. Frug, *City Making,* p. 137.

12. Carl Sussman, ed., *Planning the Fourth Migration: The Neglected Vision of the Regional Planning Association of America* (Cambridge, Mass.: MIT Press, 1976), p. 89.

13. Regional Plan Association, *Regional Plan of New York and Its Environs* (1927); Na-

tional Resources Committee, *Our Cities: Their Role in the National Economy* (Washington, D.C.: Government Printing Office, 1937).

14. Paul Studentski, *The Government of Metropolitan Areas in the United States* (New York: National Municipal League, 1930), p. 64.

15. An overview of their work is provided by G. Ross Stephens and Nelson Wikstrom, *Metropolitan Government and Governance* (New York: Oxford University Press, 2000), chap. 2. That volume, together with David K. Hamilton, *Governing Metropolitan Areas: Response to Growth and Change* (New York: Garland Publishing, 1999), and Alan Altshuler, William Morrill, Harold Wolman, and Faith Mitchell, eds., *Governance and Opportunity in Metropolitan America* (Washington, D.C.: National Academy Press, 1999), offer the most thorough reviews of the history, theory, and contemporary practice of metropolitan government.

16. Neal R. Peirce, "Louisville Votes Merger — First Since Indy in 1969," syndicated column, December 3, 2000.

17. The report reflected a new sophistication among environmentalists regarding urban fragmentation. Real Estate Research Corporation, *The Costs of Sprawl* (Washington, D.C.: Government Printing Office, 1974), prepared for the Council on Environmental Quality, HUD, and the Environmental Protection Agency.

18. See Peter Calthorpe, *The Next American Metropolis: Ecology, Community, and the American Dream* (New York: Princeton Architectural Press, 1993), and Andres Duany, Elizabeth Plater-Zyberk, and Jeff Speck, *Suburban Nation: The Rise of Sprawl and the Decline of the American Dream* (New York: North Point Press, 2000).

19. A representative critique is Alex Anas, "The Costs and Benefits of Fragmented Metropolitan Governance and the New Regionalist Policies" (paper presented to the symposium "Regionalism: Promise and Problems," SUNY Buffalo Law School, March 6, 1999), available at www.pam.usc.edu. For a systematic review of the evidence on the costs and benefits of sprawl, see Robert W. Burchell, David Listokin, Naveed A. Shad, Hilary Phillips, Anthony Downs, Samuel Seskin, Judy S. Davis, Terry Moore, David Helton, and Michelle Gall, *Costs of Sprawl Revisited: The Evidence of Sprawl's Negative and Positive Impacts* (New Brunswick, N.J.: Rutgers University Center for Urban Policy Research, 1998). Robert W. Burchell, "State of the Cities and Sprawl" (paper presented to the U.S. Department of Housing and Urban Development conference "Bridging the Divide," December 8, 1999), estimates that a more consolidated form of metropolitan growth would generate $250 billion in savings over ten years. A good short statement of this consensus is Bruce Katz and Jennifer Bradley, "Divided We Sprawl," *Atlantic Monthly* (December 1999): 26–42.

20. Metro Chicago Information Center, 1998 annual survey; Larry N. Gerston and Peter J. Haas, "Political Support for Regional Government in the 1990s: Growing in the Suburbs?" *Urban Affairs Quarterly* 29, no. 1 (September 1993): 154–63.

21. Todd Purdum, "Suburban Sprawl Takes Its Place on the Political Landscape," *New York Times*, February 6, 1999; Daniel Pedersen, Vern E. Smith, and Jerry Adler, "Sprawling . . . ," *Newsweek*, July 19, 1999; Bruce Katz and Jennifer Bradley, "Divided We Sprawl," *Atlantic*, December 1999; Julie Cart, "Rapidly Growing Phoenix Finds Dust Unsettling," *Los Angeles Times*, September 7, 1999; William Fulton and Paul Shifley, "Operation Desert Sprawl," *Governing*, August 1999; Mark Arax, "Putting the Brakes on Growth," *Los Angeles Times*, October 6, 1999; Rob Gurwitt, "The Quest for Common Ground," *Governing*, June 1998; Rob Gurwitt, "The State vs. Sprawl," *Governing*, January 1999; Alan Ehrenhalt, "The Czar of Gridlock," *Governing*, May 1999; *Smart Growth, Better Neighborhoods: Communities Leading the*

Way (Washington, D.C.: National Neighborhood Coalition, 2000); Neal R. Peirce, "Smarth Growth, Smart Regions—Smart Politics?" syndicated column, January 16, 2000; Neal R. Peirce, "Sprawl Debate Warms Up," syndicated column, March 5, 2000; Neal R. Peirce, "Smart Growth 2000, Bumps and Breakthroughs," syndicated column, December 31, 2000.

22. For documentation, see www.smartgrowth.org.

23. Annalee Saxenian, *Regional Advantage: Culture and Competition in Silicon Valley and Route 128* (Cambridge, Mass.: Harvard University Press, 1994).

24. Pivotal statements in this discussion include Joel Garreau, *Edge Cities: Life on the New Frontier* (New York: Doubleday, 1991); David Rusk, *Cities Without Suburbs* (Washington, D.C.: Woodrow Wilson Center Press, 1993); Neal Peirce, Curtis Johnson, and John Hall, *Citistates* (Washington, D.C.: Seven Locks Press, 1993); Henry Cisneros, ed., *Interwoven Destinies: Cities and the Nation* (New York: W. W. Norton, 1993); H. V. Savitch et al., "Ties that Bind: Central Cities, Suburbs, and the New Metropolitan Region," *Economic Development Quarterly* 7, no. 4 (1993): 341–58; Edward Hill, Harold Wolman, and William Ford, "Can Suburbs Survive Without Their Central Cities?" *Urban Affairs Review* 31, no. 2 (November 1995): 147–74; H. V. Savitch, "Straw Men, Red Herrings, and Suburban Dependence," *Urban Affairs Review* 31, no. 2 (November 1995): 175–79; Keith Ihlanfeldt, "The Importance of the Central City to the Regional and National Economy: A Review of the Arguments and Empirical Evidence," *Cityscape* 1, no. 2 (June 1995): 125–50; Todd Swanstrom, "Ideas Matter: Reflections on the New Regionalism," *Cityscape* 2, no. 2 (May 1996): 5–23; Manuel Pastor, Peter Dreier, Eugene Grigsby, and Marta Lopez-Garza, *Regions that Work: How Cities and Suburbs Can Grow Together* (Minneapolis: University of Minnesota Press, 2000); William Barnes and Larry Ledebur, *The New Regional Economies* (Thousand Oaks, Calif.: Sage, 1998); David Rusk, *Inside Game/Outside Game* (Washington, D.C.: Brookings Institution, 1999).

25. Neal Peirce and Curtis Johnson, *Boundary Crossers: Community Leadership for a Global Age* (College Park, Md.: Academy of Leadership, University of Maryland, 1997), synthesize lessons from a number of case studies included in Bruce Adams, John Parr, et al., *Boundary Crossers: Case Studies of How Ten of America's Metropolitan Regions Work* (College Park, Md.: Academy of Leadership, University of Maryland, 1997), available at http://civicsource.org/KLFP/boundary.htm. Peirce and Johnson's Web site is at http://www.citistates.com/index.htm. Other important regionalism sites include http://www.cnt.org/mi/index.htm, the Metropolitan Initiative of the Center for Neighborhood Technology, and http://www.brookings.edu/es/urban/urban.html, the Brookings Institution Center on Urban and Metropolitan Policy. See also Allan Wallace, "The Third Wave: Current Trends in Regional Governance," *National Civic Review* 83 (summer–fall 1994): 292–93; he characterizes the trends of the 1990s as stressing governance and business-government partnerships as opposed to purely public initiatives, with collaboration, process, and networks of trust more important than formal structure.

26. *The Regionalist* is published by the National Association of Regional Councils in conjunction with the Schaefer Center of the University of Baltimore, at http://scpp.ubalt.edu. See also the Institute for the Regional Community, at http://narc.org/narc.itrec.

27. Michael Porter, *The Competitive Advantage of Nations* (New York: Basic Books, 1990); ICF Kaiser Consulting, *America's New Economy and the Challenge of the Cities* (Washington, D.C.: U.S. Department of Housing and Urban Development, October

1996). A summary of this report can be found at www.hud.gov/nmesum.html. But see Bennett Harrison, Jon Gant, and Maryellen R. Kelly, "Specialization vs. Diversity in Local Economies: The Implications for Innovative Private Sector Behavior" (Heinz School of Public Policy and Management, Carnegie Mellon University, January 1995), for an argument that diversity of proximate companies and urbanization shape innovation, whereas proximity of like firms does not.

28. http://www.sdrta.org/sdrta/clusterdata/industriescluster.html.

29. Michael H. Schill, "Deconcentrating the Inner City Poor," *Chicago-Kent Law Review* 67, no. 3 (1992): 852.

30. In addition to Rusk's previously cited work, see Anthony Downs, *New Visions for Metropolitan America* (Washington, D.C.: Brookings Institution, 1994); Orfield, *Metropolitics;* Gary Orfield and Carole Ashkinaze, *The Closing Door: Conservative Policy and Black Opportunity* (Chicago: University of Chicago Press, 1991).

31. For a description of these activities, see the Web site of the Metropolitan Area Research Corporation at http://www.metroresearch.org/.

32. Midwest Consortium for Economic Development Alternatives, *Metro Futures: A High-Wage, Low-Waste, Democratic Alternative Development Strategy for America's Cities and Inner Suburbs* (New York and Madison: Sustainable America and Center on Wisconsin Strategy, 1996); Daniel D. Luria and Joel Rogers, *Metro Futures: Economic Solutions for Cities and Their Suburbs* (Boston: Beacon Press, 1999), pp. 11–39 (also available at www.bostonreview.mit.edu/BR22.1/ and www.cows.org).

33. H. V. Savitch and Ronald K. Vogel, eds., *Regional Politics: America in a Post-City Age* (Thousand Oaks, Calif.: Sage Publications, 1996).

34. National Resources Committee, *Our Cities: Their Role in the National Economy* (Washington, D.C.: Government Printing Office, 1937).

35. Alice O'Connor, "Swimming Against the Tide: A Brief History of Federal Policy in Poor Communities," in *Urban Problems and Community Development,* ed. Ronald Ferguson and William Dickens (Washington, D.C.: Brookings Institution Press, 1999).

36. Cited in Sidney Plotkin, *Keep Out: The Struggle for Land Use Control* (Berkeley: University of California Press, 1987), p. 160.

37. Cited in ibid., pp. 160–61.

38. Ibid., p. 161.

39. Cited in ibid., p. 162.

40. National Commission on Urban Problems, *Building the American City* (Washington, D.C.: Government Printing Office, 1969), p. 211.

41. Plotkin, *Keep Out,* p. 26.

42. In 1960, for example, the Committee for Economic Development (CED), a business-sponsored policy group, issued a report calling for greater metropolitan coordination and national laws to regulate local land use and zoning. The CED noted that "most American communities lack any instrumentality of government with legal powers, geographic jurisdiction, and independent revenue sources necessary to conduct self-government in any valid sense." See Plotkin, *Keep Out,* pp. 155–59. See also Shelby Green, "The Search for a National Land Use Policy: For the Cities' Sake," *Fordham Urban Law Journal* 26, no. 1 (November 1998): 69–119.

43. See Advisory Commission on Regulatory Barriers to Affordable Housing, *"Not in My Back Yard": Removing Barriers to Affordable Housing* (Washington, D.C.: U.S. Department of Housing and Urban Development, July 1991).

44. Chicago's Gautreax program is the best known of several local housing "mobility"

programs that sought to help poor and minority residents find rental housing in suburban areas. It resulted from a 1966 lawsuit brought by attorney Alexander Polikoff on behalf of public housing tenants (led by Dorothy Gautreaux) against the city's housing authority for siting public housing projects in segregated black neighborhoods. In 1969, U.S. District Court judge Richard Austin ordered the Chicago Housing Authority to build low-rise, scattered-site public housing throughout the city, but the housing authority failed to comply. In response, the U.S. Supreme Court ordered HUD in 1976 to create a Section 8 rent subsidy program throughout the six-county Chicago area and to fund the nonprofit Leadership Council for Metropolitan Open Communities to manage it. This pathbreaking decision defined the metropolitan area, not just the city of Chicago, as the relevant context for remedying the city's practices. Five years later, a consent decree required HUD to continue the rent subsidy program until 7,100 black families had been placed in areas with less than 30 percent black population. Originally, participants could move to predominantly white neighborhoods in Chicago or to the suburbs; since 1991, however, all participants have been required to move to the suburbs. Smaller Gautreaux-like programs exist in Cincinnati, Memphis, Dallas, Milwaukee, Hartford, and a few other cities, often brought about by court order. The success of the Gautreaux program led Congress in 1992 to create a federal version, called Moving to Opportunity. HUD selected five cities in 1994 to test the program, which included providing tenants with housing search and counseling services, but congressional opposition forced HUD to scale back the program.

45. In 1968, New York State created an urban development corporation (UDC) to develop new towns and mixed-income housing (mostly for middle-income families) on a major scale. The legislature gave it the authority to override local zoning codes, if necessary, to construct its projects. Suburban political opposition led the legislature to revoke the UDC's zoning override authority.

In 1969, Massachusetts passed an antisnob zoning law. If localities denied permits to developers of low- and moderate-income housing, the developers could, under certain circumstances, appeal to a state appeals board, which could order the municipality to issue the permit. Massachusetts was one of the few states with its own low-income rental housing construction program, as well as a major conduit for federally subsidized housing. State officials assumed that the antisnob zoning law would promote the siting of developments in suburbs and open them up to minorities. After more than two decades, the state claimed that the law had facilitated the construction of 20,000 units. Critics argued that many of these developments were targeted for the elderly, not families, and that the number was still relatively small. By the late 1980s, the city of Boston had 20 percent of the metropolitan population but 40 percent of its poor people and 42 percent of the subsidized housing.

California requires local governments to develop and periodically update a comprehensive master plan, including a so-called housing element, that is subject to review by state agencies. As part of the housing element, every city and county must show how it will comply with a regional "fair-share" allocation for low-income housing. The state has failed to enforce this law. In fact, under Republican Governors Deukmejian and Wilson in the 1980s and 1990s, it opposed local inclusionary housing programs. Most municipalities with such policies have favored moderate-income over low-income housing.

New Jersey has the most expansive state program, resulting from a series of court cases known as *Mt. Laurel, Mt. Laurel II,* and *Mt. Laurel III.* In 1971, the NAACP sued the small suburb of Mt. Laurel on the grounds that its zoning regulations excluded housing that was affordable to poor minorities. (Discrimination against the poor is not a violation of the Fair Housing Act, but discrimination against racial minorities is.) In 1975, the state supreme court unanimously ruled that Mt. Laurel and every municipality in the state were obligated by the state constitution to allow all economic groups access to housing. The decision declared a "fair share" doctrine, requiring each region to assess its housing needs and, in effect, set a quota for each municipality to meet. When the state government and municipalities dragged their feet, the state supreme court ruled in *Mt. Laurel II* in 1983 that the state government had a responsibility to monitor and enforce the decision. A Council on Affordable Housing (COAH) was set up to implement the policy. *Mt. Laurel III* in 1986 added new provisions to the policy. The COAH had an original goal of adding 145,000 affordable housing units by 1993. By 1992, only 25,000 Mt. Laurel units had been approved, but fewer than 10,000 had actually been started or completed. Moreover, few occupants of Mt. Laurel units were racial minorities or low-income families. In other states, a few metropolitan areas adopted voluntary fair-share housing policies without the impetus of court orders or state legislation. In the 1970s, the Dayton, Ohio, region did so, using federal housing programs to build about 8,000 units and reducing the central city's share of the region's low-income housing inventory. The Minneapolis–St. Paul metropolitan area adopted a similar policy in the early 1970s with modest success. Other voluntary fair-share plans during the 1970s — in Chicago, San Francisco, and Washington, D.C. — failed, in part because of the Nixon administration's moratorium on federally assisted developments and in part because suburban areas were reluctant to cooperate. In 1988, Connecticut created a pilot program for voluntary regional fair-share housing compacts. Two years later, twenty-six of the twenty-nine municipalities in the greater Hartford region approved the Capital Region Fair Housing Compact on Affordable Housing, with a goal of creating at least 5,000 units of affordable housing over a five-year period. To assist this plan, HUD let Hartford use its Section 8 subsidies in the suburbs, and local foundations (drawing on the Gautreaux program model) provided funds to counsel low-income Hartford residents about the program. In the 1990s, the Twin Cities adopted another regional fair-share plan, this time with the support of state legislation. See W. Dennis Keating, *The Suburban Racial Dilemma: Housing and Neighborhoods* (Philadelphia: Temple University Press, 1994); Nico Calavita, Kenneth Grimes, and Alan Mallach, "Inclusionary Housing in California and New Jersey: A Comparative Analysis," *Housing Policy Debate* 8, no. 1 (1997): 109–42; and Orfield, *Metropolitics*.

46. Calavita et al., "Inclusionary Housing in California and New Jersey"; David Kirp, John Dwyer, and Larry Rosenthal, *Our Town: Race, Housing, and the Soul of Suburbia* (New Brunswick, N.J.: Rutgers University Press, 1995).

47. *Removing Regulatory Barriers to Affordable Housing: How States and Localities Are Moving Ahead* (Washington, D.C.: U.S. Department of Housing and Urban Development, Office of Policy Development and Research, December 1992); Dwight Merriam, David Brower, and Philip Tegeler, *Inclusionary Zoning Moves Downtown* (Chicago: American Planning Association, 1985); Alan Altshuler and Jose A. Gomez-Ibanez, *Regulation for Revenue: The Political Economy of Land Use Exactions* (Washington, D.C.: Brookings Institution, 1993).

48. Savitch and Vogel, *Regional Politics.*

49. Rusk, *Cities Without Suburbs.*

50. This section draws on Bruce Berg and Paul Kantor, "New York: The Politics of Con-

flict and Avoidance," in Savitch and Vogel, *Regional Politics;* U.S. Bureau of the Census at census.gov.

51. Robert D. Yaro and Tony Hiss, *A Region at Risk: The Third Regional Plan for the New York–New Jersey–Connecticut Metropolitan Area* (Washington, D.C.: Island Press, 1996).

52. Berg and Kantor, "New York," p. 42.

53. The St. Louis discussion draws on Donald Phares and Claude Louishomme, "St. Louis: A Politically Fragmented Area," in Savitch and Vogel, *Regional Politics;* and Andrew Glassberg, "St. Louis: Racial Transition and Economic Development," in *Big City Politics in Transition,* ed. H. V. Savitch and John Clayton Thomas (Newbury Park, Calif.: Sage Publications, 1991).

54. This term was coined by Robert Fogelson, *The Fragmented Metropolis: Los Angeles 1850–1930* (Cambridge, Mass.: Harvard University Press, 1967).

55. The Los Angeles discussion draws on Alan Saltzstein, "Los Angeles: Politics Without Governance," in Savitch and Vogel, *Regional Politics;* Scott A. Bollens, "Fragments of Regionalism: The Limits of South California Governance," *Journal of Urban Affairs* 19, no. 1 (1997): 105–22; Charles Lockwood and Christopher Leinberger, "Los Angeles Comes of Age," *Atlantic Monthly* (January 1988); Pastor et al., *Regions that Work;* William Fulton, *The Reluctant Metropolis: The Politics of Urban Growth in Los Angeles* (Point Arena, Calif.: Solano Press Books, 1997).

56. James P. Allen and Eugene Turner, *The Ethnic Quilt: Population Diversity in Southern California* (Northridge: Center for Geographical Studies, California State University–Northridge, 1997).

57. Steven Erie, "How the West Was Won: The Local State and Economic Growth in Los Angeles, 1880–1932," *Urban Affairs Quarterly* 27, no. 4 (June 1992): 519–54.

58. Marla Cone, "State Scales Back Clean-Air Plan in Bow to Oil, Trucking Industries," *Los Angeles Times,* November 10, 1994; Marla Cone, "U.S. Unveils Scaled-Back Clean-Air Plan," *Los Angeles Times,* February 15, 1995; Linda Wade and Gail Ruderman Feuer, "'Good News' that Means Dirtier Air," *Los Angeles Times,* August 5, 1996; James Lents and William Kelly, "Clearing the Air in Los Angeles," *Scientific American* (October 1993).

59. John J. Harrigan, "Minneapolis–St. Paul: Structuring Metropolitan Government," in Savitch and Vogel, *Regional Politics;* Orfield, *Metropolitics.*

60. Orfield gives a detailed description of his efforts in *Metropolitics.* See also Rusk, *Inside Game/Outside Game,* pp. 222–48.

61. This discussion draws on Arthur Nelson, "Portland: The Metropolitan Umbrella," in Savitch and Vogel, *Regional Politics,* pp. 253–74; Carl Abbott, "The Portland Region" (and comments by Henry Richmond and William Fischel), *Housing Policy Debate* 8, no. 1 (1997): 11–73; Christopher Leo, "Regional Growth Management Regime: The Case of Portland, Oregon," *Journal of Urban Affairs* 20, no. 4 (1998): 363–94; Orfield, *Metropolitics,* pp. 157–59; Rusk, *Inside Game/Outside Game,* pp. 153–77. See also Timothy Egan, "Urban Sprawl Strains Western States," *New York Times,* December 29, 1996; Timothy Egan, "Drawing the Hard Line on Urban Sprawl," *New York Times,* December 30, 1996; Kim Murphy, "Portland Struggles to Draw Line on Growth," *Los Angeles Times,* December 10, 1997.

62. Arthur C. Nelson, "Smart Growth = Central City Vitality and a Higher Quality of Life" (paper presented to the U.S. Department of Housing and Urban Development conference "Bridging the Divide," Washington, D.C., December 8, 1999).

63. Orfield, *Metropolitics,* p. 102.

64. Abbott, "Portland Region," p. 24.

65. Ibid., p. 35.

66. Scott A. Bollens, "Concentrated Poverty and Metropolitan Equity Strategies," *Stanford Law and Policy Review* 8, no. 2 (summer 1997): 13.

67. Schill, "Deconcentrating," p. 836.

68. Considerable attention has also been paid to equalizing the financial basis for school systems and creating metropolitan school districts, as discussed in Schill, "Deconcentrating," pp. 847–52. In general, spending per pupil has become more equal within states but has increased across states, according to William J. Hussar and William Sonnenberg, "Trends in Disparities in School District Level Expenditures per Pupil" (Washington, D.C.: National Center for Education Statistics in Early Childhood, 1999). High levels of disparities among districts within states and within districts have persisted in many cases, however. The trend on school desegregation and district consolidation has been toward what Gary Orfield has described as "re-segregation." See Gary Orfield, Susan Eaton, and the Harvard Project on School Desegregation, *Dismantling Desegregation: The Quiet Reversal of Brown v. Board of Education* (New York: New Press, 1996).

69. Schill, "Deconcentrating," pp. 845–47.

70. Charles T. Clotfelter, "Are Whites Still 'Fleeing'? Racial Patterns and Enrollment Shifts in Urban Public Schools, 1987–1996" (Working Paper W7290, National Bureau of Economic Research, August 1999), found that "white losses appear to be spurred both by interracial contact in districts where their children attend school and by the opportunities available in metropolitan areas for reducing that contact."

71. These efforts were inspired by the successes of the Gautreaux program in Chicago (see note 44, as well as the discussion in chapter 3). In 1994, HUD launched a five-city, ten-year social experiment in which 4,610 families were randomly assigned to an "MTO [Moving to Opportunity] treatment group," which moved to more suburban settings (1,820 families); a "Section 8 comparison group," which moved out of projects but remained in central-city settings (1,350 families); and an "in place control group" (1,440 families). A preliminary report on the project (John Goering, Joan Kraft, Judith Feins, Debra McInnis, Mary Joel Holin, and Huda El-hassan, *Moving to Opportunity for Fair Housing Demonstration Program: Current Status and Initial Findings* [Washington, D.C.: Policy Development and Research, U.S. Department of Housing and Urban Development, September 1999], available at http://www.huduser.org) found that counseling played an important role in the success of the program, and those who moved out of the projects experienced improved security from crime and more support for finding jobs (pp. 32–33). All the mobility programs report positive results, but the numbers involved are tiny compared with the need.

72. Discussion of the Montgomery County program is drawn from Alexander Poli-koff, ed., *Housing Mobility: Promise or Illusion?* (Washington, D.C.: Urban Institute, 1995); George E. Peterson and Kale Williams, eds., *Housing Mobility: What Has It Accomplished and What Is Its Promise?* (Washington, D.C.: Urban Institute, October 1994); David Rusk, *Inside Game/Outside Game* (Washington, D.C.: Brookings Institution Press, 1999); Christie I. Baxter, *Moderately Priced Dwelling Units in Montgomery County, Maryland* (Cambridge, Mass.: Kennedy School of Government, Case Program, c16-91-1043.0, 1991). Data were also drawn from the Web sites of Montgomery County (http://www.co.mo.md.us), the Montgomery County Planning Board (http://www.mc-mncppc.org), the Montgomery County Housing

Opportunity Commission (http://www.hocweb.org), and the Innovative Housing Institute (http://www.inhousing.org/MPDUNarr.htm), and from a telephone interview with Erik Larsen, section chief with the Moderately Priced Dwelling Units program, October 11, 2000.

73. These income targets increased steadily over the years, parallel to changes in the county's median household income, as did the sales prices and rents of the units.

74. In 1974, Maryland enacted legislation to create a Montgomery County Housing Opportunity Commission to acquire, own, lease, and operate housing. The seven-member board is appointed by the county executive and approved by the county council.

75. Polikoff, *Housing Mobility*, p. 74.

76. Brian D. Taylor and Paul M. Ong, "Spatial Mismatch or Automobile Mismatch? An Examination of Race, Residence, and Community in U.S. Metropolitan Areas," *Urban Studies* 32 (1995): 1453–73; Evelyn Blumenburg and Paul Ong, "Job Access, Commute, and Travel Burden Among Welfare Recipients," *Urban Studies* 35 (1998): 1–43; Martin Wachs and Brian D. Taylor, "Can Transportation Strategies Help to Meet the Welfare Challenge?" *Journal of the American Planning Association* 64, no. 1 (1998): 15–19; Margy Waller and Mark Alan Hughes, "Working Far from Home: Transportation and Welfare Reform in the Ten Big States" (Washington, D.C.: Progressive Policy Institute, August 1, 1999); Carol Harbaugh and Theresa Smith, "Welfare Reform and Transportation: There Is a Connection," *Public Roads* (January–February 1998), at http://www.bts.gov/NTL/DOCS/Welfare_Reform/Welfare_Reform.htm.

77. Discussion of this program draws on Mark Alan Hughes and Julie E. Sternberg, *The New Metropolitan Reality: Where the Rubber Meets the Road in Antipoverty Policy* (Washington, D.C.: Urban Institute, December 1992); Rochelle Stanfield, "The Reverse Commute," *National Journal* (November 23, 1996), pp. 2546–49.

78. Stanfield, "Reverse Commute," pp. 2547–48.

79. Ibid., p. 2548.

80. Ibid.; Rick Wartzman, "New Bus Lines Link the Inner-City Poor with Jobs in Suburbia," *Wall Street Journal*, September 24, 1993.

81. Descriptions and initial evaluations of JobLinks can be found at http://www.ctaa.org/ntrc/atj/joblinks; for Bridges to Work, see http://www.huduser.org/publications/pvosoc/btw.html.

82. Waller and Hughes, "Working Far from Home," p. 1.

83. See also the editorial "Let Them Drive Cars," *New Republic*, March 20, 2000.

84. In October 2000, the Clinton administration proposed increasing the car and housing allowances used to calculate food stamp eligibility. The proposal lifts the $4,650 limit that a family is allowed to deduct for the value of its car. See Janet Hook, "Food Stamp Expansion Gets Surprising Boost," *Los Angeles Times*, October 11, 2000.

85. Bennett Harrison and Marcus Weiss, *Workforce Development Networks: Community-Based Organizations and Regional Alliances* (Thousand Oaks, Calif.: Sage Publications, 1998), p. 2.

86. Mark Drayse, Dan Flaming, and Peter Force, *The Cage of Poverty* (Los Angeles: Economic Roundtable, September 2000); Nicholas Riccardi, "Post-Welfare Jobs No Cure for Poverty, Study Finds," *Los Angeles Times*, September 7, 2000; Kate Shatzkin, "Study Finds Workers Off Welfare Often Remain in Need of Assistance," *Baltimore Sun*, October 6, 2000.

87. This discussion of Project Quest draws on Jay Walljasper, "A Quest for Jobs in San

Antonio," *Nation,* July 21, 1997, pp. 30–32; and Harrison and Weiss, *Workforce Development Networks.*

88. Walljasper, "Quest for Jobs," p. 30.

89. Harrison and Weiss, *Workforce Development Networks,* p. 72.

90. See also *Organizations and Regional Alliances* (Thousand Oaks, Calif.: Sage Publications, 1998); Marcus Weiss, "Regional Workforce Development Networks" (paper presented to the U.S. Department of Housing and Urban Development conference "Bridging the Divide," Washington, D.C., December 8, 1999); Bennett Harrison, "It Takes a Region (or Does It?): The Material Basis for Metropolitanism and Metropolitics," in *Urban-Suburban Interdependencies,* ed. Rosalind Greenstein and Wim Wiewel (Cambridge, Mass.: Lincoln Institute of Land Policy, 2001).

91. Rick McDonough, "Merger Wins with Solid Majority," *Louisville Courier-Journal,* November 8, 2000. See www.louky.org/merger/default.htm for the city Web site on the merger. Juliet F. Gainsborough, *Fenced Off: The Suburbanization of American Politics* (Washington, D.C.: Georgetown University Press, 2001).

CHAPTER 7. METROPOLICIES FOR THE TWENTY-FIRST CENTURY

1. For a defense of free markets in housing and a critique of government interference, see Peter D. Salins, *The Ecology of Housing Destruction: Economic Effects of Public Intervention in the Housing Market* (New York: New York University Press, 1980), and Peter D. Salins and Gerard C. S. Mildner, *Scarcity by Design: The Legacy of New York City's Housing Policies* (Cambridge, Mass.: Harvard University Press, 1992). For a general argument that poor areas can be revitalized by markets with little help from government, see Michael E. Porter, "The Competitive Advantage of the Inner City," *Harvard Business Review* (May–June 1995): 55–71. For the free-market defense of fragmented local governments, see the works cited in chapter 4 by Charles Tiebout, Elinor Ostrom, Robert Bish, and others.

2. The classic statement of an urban culture of poverty is found in Edward Banfield, *The Unheavenly City: The Nature and Future of Our Urban Crisis* (Boston: Little, Brown, 1968). Charles Murray argues that welfare policies are a major cause of the culture of poverty. See his influential *Losing Ground: American Social Policy 1950–1980* (New York: Basic Books, 1984). For a recent statement that enhancing the mobility of poor households would spread the culture of poverty, see Howard Husock, "Let's End Housing Vouchers," *City Journal* (autumn 2000): 84–91.

3. The classic statement that the problems of concentrated poverty are caused mainly by deindustrialization and should be addressed primarily by economic policies is William Julius Wilson's *The Truly Disadvantaged: The Inner City, the Underclass, and Public Policy* (Chicago: University of Chicago Press, 1987). In *When Work Disappears: The World of the New Urban Poor* (New York: Alfred A. Knopf, 1996), Wilson emphasizes spatial policies as well as macroeconomic policies.

4. The literature on enterprise zones and CDCs is voluminous. One of the first advocates for enterprise zones was Stuart Butler in his *Enterprise Zones: Greenlining the Inner City* (New York: Universe Publishers, 1981). See also Karen Mossberger, *The Politics of Ideas and the Spread of Enterprise Zones* (Washington, D.C.: Georgetown University Press, 2000). Congress created the Enterprise Zone/Empowerment Community program in 1993; many states have enacted enterprise zone programs of their own. For a sampling of the literature on CDCs, see Rachel G. Bratt, *Rebuild-*

ing a Low-Income Housing Policy (Philadelphia: Temple University Press, 1989); Avis Vidal, "CDCs as Agents of Neighborhood Change: The State of the Art," in *Revitalizing Urban Neighborhood*, ed. W. Dennis Keating, Norman Krumholz, and Philip Star (Lawrence: University Press of Kansas, 1996), pp. 149–63; Theodore Koebel, ed., *Shelter and Society: Theory, Research, and Policy for Nonprofit Housing* (Albany, N.Y.: SUNY Press, 1998); Herbert J. Rubin, *Renewing Hope Within Neighborhoods of Despair: The Community-Based Development Model* (Albany, N.Y.: SUNY Press, 2000). The National Congress for Community Economic Development (NCCED) is the trade organization for CDCs and publishes an annual survey of their accomplishments (www.ncced.org). For a critical history of the movement, see Robert Halpern, *Rebuilding the Inner City: A History of Neighborhood Initiatives to Address Poverty in the United States* (New York: Columbia University Press, 1995).

5. The classic argument for the importance of race in causing problems of concentrated poverty is Douglas D. Massey and Nancy A. Denton, *American Apartheid: Segregation and the Making of the Underclass* (Cambridge, Mass.: Harvard University Press, 1993).

6. William A. Fischel, "Does the American Way of Zoning Cause the Suburbs of Metropolitan Areas to Be Too Spread Out?" in *Governance and Opportunity in Metropolitan America*, ed. Alan Altshuler, William Morrill, Harold Wolman, and Faith Mitchell (Washington, D.C.: National Academy Press, 1999).

7. See, for example, Pietro S. Nivola, *Laws of the Landscape: How Policies Shape Cities in Europe and America* (Washington, D.C.: Brookings Institution Press, 1999). See also John Mollenkopf, "Assimilating Immigrants in Amsterdam: A Perspective from New York," *Netherlands Journal of Social Science* (forthcoming), with comments from Malcolm Cross, Susan Fainstein, Robert Kloosterman, Enzo Mingione and Enrico Pugliese, Kees van Kerksbergen, and Hans Vermeulen and Tijno Venema; Sako Musterd and Wim Ostendorf, eds., *Urban Segregation and the Welfare State: Inequality and Exclusion in Western Cities* (London: Routledge, 1996).

8. Timothy Smeeding, "Why the U.S. Anti-Poverty System Doesn't Work Very Well," *Challenge* (January–February 1992): 30–36; Janet Gornick and Marcia Meyers, "Support for Working Families: What the United States Can Learn from Europe," *American Prospect* (January 1–15, 2001): 3–7; Peter Dreier and Elaine Bernard, "Kinder, Gentler Canada," *American Prospect* 12 (winter 1992): 85–88.

9. Jacques van de Ven, "Urban Policies and the 'Polder Model': Two Sides of the Same Coin" (Amsterdam Center for the Metropolitan Environment, University of Amsterdam, May 1998).

10. Jay Forrester, *Urban Dynamics* (Cambridge, Mass.: MIT Press, 1969); President's Commission on a National Agenda for the Eighties, *Urban American in the Eighties* (Washington, D.C.: Government Printing Office, 1980). Paul Peterson's *City Limits* (Chicago: University of Chicago Press, 1981) reflects a similar perspective.

11. *New Yorker*, October 16, 1995, p. 83.

12. Henry R. Richmond, "Metropolitan Land Use Reform: The Promise and Challenge of Majority Consensus," in *Reflections on Regionalism*, ed. Bruce Katz (Washington, D.C.: Brookings Institution, 2000), p. 36, available at www.brook.edu/es/urban.

13. For representative agendas, see Altshuler et al., *Governance and Opportunity in Metropolitan America*, chaps. 4 and 5 (see www.nap.edu/html/governance_opportunity/); David Rusk, *Inside Game/Outside Game* (Washington, D.C.: Brookings Institution Press, 1999), chaps. 12 and 14; Myron Orfield, *Metropolitics: A Regional Agenda for Community and Stability*, rev. ed. (Washington, D.C.: Brookings

Institution Press, 1998), chap 6; Katz, *Reflections on Regionalism*. The Brookings Center on Urban and Metropolitan Policy (at www.brook.edu/ES/Urban/) has been particularly effective in stimulating discussion of these issues. See also the Metropolitan Initiative of the Center for Neighborhood Technology at www.cnt.org/mi/, *The Regionalist* at scpp.ubalt.edu/public/regional/regional.htm, the Citistates site at www.citistates.com, and Myron Orfield's Metropolitan Area Research Corporation site at www.metroresearch.org.

14. Harold Wolman and Elizabeth Agius, eds., *National Urban Policy and the President's National Urban Policy Report* (Detroit: Wayne State University Press, 1996), p. 26.

15. Ann Markusen, Peter Hall, Scott Campbell, and Sabina Deitrick, *The Rise of the Gunbelt: The Military Remapping of Industrial America* (New York: Oxford University Press, 1991); Steven Greenhouse, "Study Says Big Cities Don't Get Fair Share of Military Spending," *New York Times,* May 12, 1992.

16. Our thinking on these matters has been influenced by Scott Bollens, "Concentrated Poverty and Metropolitan Equity Strategies," *Stanford Law and Policy Review* 8, no. 2 (summer 1997): 11–23; Michael Schill, "Deconcentrating the Inner City Poor," *Chicago-Kent Law Review* 67, no. 3 (1992): 795–853; the work of Bruce Katz and his colleagues at the Brookings Center on Urban and Metropolitan Problems; and the writings of Neal Peirce. For parallel discussions, see Bruce Katz, "The Limits of Urban Revival: The Case for Metropolitan Solutions to Urban Problems" (Washington, D.C.: Center on Urban and Metropolitan Problems, Urban Institute, March 1998); the Forum on Forging Metropolitan Solutions to Urban and Regional Problems, May 28, 1997, at www.brook.edu/es/urbancen/metnif.htm; Bruce Katz, "Beyond City Limits: A New Metropolitan Agenda" in *Setting National Priorities: The 2000 Election and Beyond,* ed. Henry Aaron and Robert Reischauer (Washington, D.C.: Brookings Institution Press, 1999). For the views of Peirce and his colleague Curtis Johnson, see *Boundary Crossers: Community Leadership for a Global Age* (College Park, Md.: Academy of Leadership, University of Maryland, 1997). Additional perspectives are provided in Tony Hiss, "Outlining the New Metropolitan Initiative," and Clement Dinsmore, "The Federal Role in Metropolitan Cooperation" (Chicago: Center for Neighborhood Technology, March 1997), at www.cnt.org/mi; DeWitt John et al., *Building Stronger Communities and Regions: Can the Federal Government Help?* (Washington, D.C.: National Academy of Public Administration, April 1998), at www.napawash.org. For an analysis of the link between regional economic inequality and urban poverty, see Manuel Pastor, Peter Dreier, Eugene Grigsby, and Marta Lopez-Garcia, *Regions that Work: How Cities and Suburbs Can Grow Together* (Minneapolis: University of Minnesota Press, 2000).

17. Peter D. Salins, "Metropolitan Areas: Cities, Suburbs, and the Ties that Bind," in *Interwoven Destinies: Cities and the Nation,* ed. Henry Cisneros (New York: W. W. Norton, 1993), pp. 147–66.

18. For a discussion of how the federal government can limit bidding wars, see Melvin Burstein and Arthur Rolnick, "Congress Should End the Economic War for Sports and Other Business," *Region* 10, no. 2 (June 1996): 35–36. This issue of the Federal Reserve Bank of Minneapolis publication was devoted to the topic of bidding wars. It is available at http://minneapolisfed.org/sylloge/econwar.

19. For the text of the Minge bill, see http://minneapolisfed.org/sylloge/econwar/HR1060.html.

20. See William Schwenke, "Curbing Business Subsidy Competition: Does the EU Have an Answer?" *Accountability: The Newsletter of the Business Incentives Clearinghouse*

2, no. 9 (September 2000): 1–4. This newsletter is an excellent source of ideas and information about this issue.

21. Joseph Gyourko and Richard Voith, "Does the U.S. Tax Treatment of Housing Promote Suburbanization and Central City Decline?" (Working Paper 97-13, Federal Reserve Bank of Philadelphia, September 1997); Joseph Gyourko and Todd Sinai, "The Spatial Distribution of Housing-Related Tax Benefits in the United States" (Philadelphia: University of Pennsylvania, Wharton School, Real Estate Department, April 11, 2000).

22. John et al., *Building Stronger Communities and Regions.*

23. Mark Alan Hughes, "The Administrative Geography of Devolving Social Welfare Programs" (Joint Occasional Paper 97-1, Center for Public Management and Center on Urban and Metropolitan Policy, Brookings Institution, 1997), available at www.brook.edu/ES/Urban/admgeo.htm.

24. There have been a few efforts to administer the Section 8 voucher and certificate program on a regional basis. For one good approach to this problem, see Bruce Katz and Margery Austin Turner, "Who Should Run the Housing Voucher Program? A Reform Proposal" (Brookings Institution Center on Urban and Metropolitan Policy, November 2000), at www.brook.edu/ES/Urban/.

25. Many studies have shown that Section 8 households tend to be clustered in established zones of concentrated poverty; see Hughes, "Administrative Geography." One way to expand choices may be through the "split subsidy" approach advocated by Jill Khadduri, Marge Martin, and Larry Buron, "Split Subsidy: The Future of Rental Housing Policy?" (paper presented to the annual meeting of the American Political Science Association, Washington, D.C., September 2, 2000).

26. For ideas on how best to do this, see Center on Budget and Policy Priorities (CBPP), "Section 8 Utilization and the Proposed Housing Voucher Success Fund" (Washington, D.C.: CBPP, March 22, 2000), at www.cbpp.org/3-22-00hous2.htm.

27. David K. Hamilton, *Governing Metropolitan Areas: Response to Growth and Change* (New York: Garland Publishing, 1999), p. 160.

28. See John et al., *Building Stronger Communities and Regions;* Robert Puentes, "Flexible Funding for Transit: Who Uses It?" (Brookings Institution Center on Urban and Metropolitan Policy, May 2000).

29. This echoes points made in Rusk, *Inside Game/Outside Game,* and Katz, "Beyond City Limits."

30. Christopher Edley, "The Next Phase of the Clinton Urban Policy: Metropolitan Empowerment Zones" (draft memorandum, Office of Management and Budget, Executive Office of the President, October 1993).

31. Paul G. Lewis, "Regionalism and Representation: Measuring and Assessing Representation in Metropolitan Planning Organizations," *Urban Affairs Review* 33, no. 6 (July 1998): 839–53.

32. Arthur C. Nelson counters this view by arguing that housing costs in Portland are high because people want to live there, so they are willing to pay more. See his "Smart Growth = Central City Vitality and Higher Quality of Life" (paper presented to the U.S. Department of Housing and Urban Development conference "Bridging the Divide," Washington, D.C., December 8, 1999).

33. Hamilton, *Governing Metropolitan Areas,* p. 232.

34. U.S. Code, Title 23, Section 134, at www4.law.cornell.edu/uscode/23/134.text.html.

35. See Rusk, *Inside Game/Outside Game,* for an evaluation of the limited role that community development efforts have played in reducing concentrated poverty.

36. Edward Hill and Jeremy Nowak recommend a program of federally funded tax relief, administrative reform, massive land acquisition and clearance, and wage subsidies for such cities in "Nothing Left to Lose," *Brookings Review* 18, no. 3 (summer 2000): 22–26.

37. For a discussion of the experiences of racially and economically diverse neighborhoods, see the following articles, all contained in a special issue of *Housing Policy Debate* 8, no. 2 (1997): Margery Austin Turner, "Achieving a New Urban Diversity: What Have We Learned?"; Roberto G. Quercia and George C. Galster, "Threshold Effects and the Expected Benefits of Attracting Middle-Income Households to the Central City"; Robert E. Lang, James W. Hughes, and Karen A. Danielsen, "Targeting the Suburban Urbanite: Marketing Central-City Housing"; Philip Nyden, Michael Maly, and John Lukehart, "The Emergence of Stable Racially and Ethnically Diverse Urban Communities: A Case Study of Nine U.S. Cities."

38. For varying perspectives on these initiatives, see Joan Walsh, "Community Building and the Future of Urban America" (New York: Rockefeller Foundation, January 1997), at www.Rockfound.Org/Reports/community/renewal.html; Karen Fulbright-Anderson, Anne C. Kubish, and James P. Connell, eds., *New Approaches to Evaluating Community Initiatives* (Washington, D.C.: Aspen Institute, 1998); Rebecca Stone and Benjamin Butler, *The Core Issues in Comprehensive Community-Building Initiatives: Exploring Power and Race* (Chicago: Chapin Hall Center for Children, February 2000).

39. Jeremy Nowak, "Neighborhood Initiative and the Regional Economy," *Economic Development Quarterly* 11, no. 1 (February 1997: 3–11); Pastor et al., *Regions that Work;* Edwin Melendez and Bennett Harrison, "Matching the Disadvantaged to Job Opportunities: Structural Explanations for the Past Successes of the Center for Employment Training," *Economic Development Quarterly* 12, no. 1 (February 1998: 3–11); Bennett Harrison and Marcus Weiss, *Workforce Development Networks: Community-Based Organizations and Regional Alliances* (Thousand Oaks, Calif.: Sage Publications, 1998).

40. Daniel P. McMurrer and Isabel V. Sawhill, *Getting Ahead: Economic and Social Mobility in America* (Lanham, Md.: University Press of America, 1998).

41. Richard Rothstein, "The Myth of Public School Failure," *American Prospect* 13 (spring 1993), available at http://epn.org/prospect/13/13roth.html; Richard Rothstein, "LA's School District Doesn't Deserve to Be Called a Failure," *Los Angeles Times,* May 11, 1997.

42. Rothstein, "Myth of Public School Failure."

43. Robert A. Levine, "Schools: Standards Are Important, but Money Is Vital," *Los Angeles Times,* May 21, 2000.

44. Nick Anderson, "Smaller Classes Aid Test Schools, Results Show," *Los Angeles Times,* December 29, 1998.

45. Richard Rothstein with Karen Hawley Miles, *Where's the Money Gone? Changes in the Level and Composition of Education Spending, 1967–1991* (Washington, D.C.: Economic Policy Institute, 1995); Richard Rothstein, *Where's the Money Going? Changes in the Level and Composition of Education Spending 1991–96* (Washington, D.C.: Economic Policy Institute, 1997); Richard Rothstein, *The Way We Were? The Myths and Realities of America's Student Achievement* (New York: Century Foundation Press, 1998); Richard Rothstein, "Does Money Not Matter? The Data Suggest It Does," *New York Times,* January 17, 2001; Abby Goodnough, "New York Is Shortchanged in School Aid, State Judge Rules," *New York Times,* January 11, 2001; John Gold-

man, "N.Y.'s School Funding Illegal, Judge Rules," *Los Angeles Times,* January 11, 2001.

46. James Traub, "What No School Can Do," *New York Times Magazine,* January 17, 2000.

47. Dennis Shirley, *Community Organizing for Urban School Reform* (Austin: University of Texas Press, 1997); Harrison and Weiss, *Workforce Development Networks;* Jay Walljasper, "A Quest for Jobs in San Antonio," *Nation,* July 21, 1997.

48. Gary Orfield, Susan Eaton, and the Harvard Project on School Desegregation, *Dismantling Desegregation* (New York: New Press, 1996); Gary Orfield with Jennifer Arenson, Tara Jackson, Christine Bohrer, Dawn Gavin, Emily Kalejs, and many volunteers for the Harvard Project on School Desegregation, "City-Suburban Desegregation: Parent and Student Perspectives in Metropolitan Boston" (report of a research conference sponsored by the Harvard Civil Rights Project, September 1997).

49. See, for example, Stephen Burd, "In Some Federal Aid Programs, Not all Campuses Are Treated Alike," *Chronicle of Higher Education* 46, no. 41 (June 16, 2000): A27.

50. Jared Bernstein, "Two Cheers for the Earned Income Tax Credit," *American Prospect* (June 19–July 3, 2000): 64. The original study is Jared Bernstein and Heidi Hartmann, "Defining and Characterizing the Low-Wage Labor Market," in *The Low-Wage Labor Market: Challenges and Opportunities for Economic Self-Sufficiency* (Washington, D.C.: Urban Institute, December 1999), available at http://aspe.hhs.gov/hsp/lwlm99/index.htm.

51. Jared Bernstein, Chauna Brocht, and Maggie Spade-Aguilar, *How Much Is Enough: Basic Family Budgets for Working Families* (Washington, D.C.: Economic Policy Institute, 2000).

52. "Is America's Economy Really Failing: The Backlash Against the *New York Times* Scare," *American Enterprise* (July–August 1996): 26–31, excerpting op-ed pieces by Robert J. Samuelson, Jonathan Marshall, Irwin Stelzer, John Cassidy, James K. Glassman, and Herbert Stein.

53. Robert J. Samuelson, *The Good Life and Its Discontents: The American Dream in the Age of Entitlement, 1945–1995* (New York: Times Books, 1995).

54. Janet C. Gornick, Marcia K. Meyers, and Katherin E. Ross, "Supporting the Employment of Mothers: Policy Variation Across Fourteen Welfare States," *Journal of European Social Policy* 7, no. 1 (1997): 45–70.

55. For the case of New York, see the *New York Times* series on welfare reform: Alan Binder, "Evidence Is Scant that Workfare Leads to Full Time Jobs," April 12, 1998; Rachel Swarns, "Mothers Poised for Workfare Face Acute Lack of Day Care," April 14, 1998; Vivian Toy, "Tough Workfare Rules Used as a Way to Cut Welfare Rolls," April 15, 1998.

56. For a history of the EITC, see Christopher Howard, *The Hidden Welfare State: Tax Expenditures and Social Policy in the United States* (Princeton, N.J.: Princeton University Press, 1997). For recent EITC experience, see Bernstein, "Two Cheers."

57. "Earned Income Tax Credit and Other Tax Benefits," at www.makingwageswork.org.

58. Bernstein, "Two Cheers."

59. Bruce Meyer and Dan Rosenbaum, "Welfare, the Earned Income Tax Credit, and the Labor Supply of Single Mothers" (Working Paper 7363, National Bureau of Economic Research, September 1999).

60. Peter Dreier, "Low-Wage Workers Miss a Tax Break," *Los Angeles Times,* January 24, 1999.

61. See Robert Greenstein, "Should EITC Benefits Be Enlarged for Families with Three or More Children?" (Washington, D.C.: Center for Budget and Policy Priorities,

July 10, 2000), available at http://www.cbpp.org/3-14-00tax.htm; Robert Greenstein, "Should the EITC for Workers Without Children Be Abolished, Maintained, or Expanded?" (Washington, D.C.: Center for Budget and Policy Priorities, July 7, 2000), available at http://www.cbpp.org/6-22-00eitc.htm.

62. Max Sawicky and Robert Cherry, "Giving Credit Where Credit Is Due: A 'Universal Unified Child Credit' that Expands the EITC and Cuts Taxes for Working Families" (Washington, D.C.: Economic Policy Institute, April 2000).

63. See Bernstein, "Two Cheers," for this critique.

64. "The Minimum Wage," on the Web site of Making Wages Work, at http://www.makingwageswork.org/minimum.htm; Lawrence Mishel, Jared Bernstein, and John Schmitt, *The State of Working America 1998–1999* (Ithaca, N.Y.: Cornell University Press, 1998).

65. Oren M. Levin-Waldman, *Automatic Adjustment of the Minimum Wage: Linking the Minimum Wage to Productivity,* Public Policy Brief no. 42 (Annandale-on-Hudson, N.Y.: Jerome Levy Economics Institute of Bard College, 1998).

66. Kathryn Porter, "Proposed Changes in the Official Measure of Poverty" (Washington, D.C.: Center on Budget and Policy Priorities, November 15, 1999); Bernstein et al., *How Much Is Enough.*

67. This paragraph draws on the following: Owen M. Levin-Waldman and George McCarthy, *Small Business and the Minimum Wage* (Annandale-on-Hudson, N.Y.: Jerome Levy Economics Institute of Bard College, 1998); Jared Bernstein and John Schmitt, *Making Work Pay: The Impact of the 1997 Minimum-Wage Increase* (Washington, D.C.: Economic Policy Institute, 1998); *Raising the Minimum Wage: Talking Points and Background* (Washington, D.C.: AFL-CIO, July 1999); David Card and Alan Krueger, *Myth and Measurement: The New Economics of the Minimum Wage* (Princeton, N.J.: Princeton University Press, 1995).

68. Jennifer Campbell, *Health Insurance Coverage: 1998* (Washington, D.C.: U.S. Census Bureau, Current Population Reports, October 1999); Robert I. Mills, *Health Insurance Coverage: 1999* (Washington, D.C.: U.S. Bureau of the Census, Current Population Reports, P60–211, September 2000).

69. Campbell, *Health Insurance Coverage.*

70. Sharon Bernstein and Robert Rosenblatt, "More Recipients of Medicare to Be Cut from HMOs," *Los Angeles Times,* July 25, 2000.

71. Calculated and updated from 1995 figures found in Gary Burtless, "Growing American Inequality," in *Setting National Priorities: The 2000 Election and Beyond,* ed. Henry Aaron and Robert Reischauer (Washington, D.C.: Brookings Institution Press, 1999).

72. See Steven Greenhouse, "Why Paris Works," *New York Times Magazine,* July 19, 1992; Timothy Smeeding, "Why the U.S. Anti-Poverty System Doesn't Work Very Well," *Challenge* (January–February 1992): 30–36.

73. All the information in the previous two paragraphs is drawn from the Children's Defense Fund, "Overview of Child Care, Early Education, and School-Age Care" (1999).

74. Barbara R. Bergmann, "Reducing Poverty Among American Children Through a 'Help for Working Parents' Program" (Foundation for Child Development Working Paper Series, November 1997); Barbara R. Bergmann, "Decent Child Care at Decent Wages," *American Prospect* (January 1–15, 2001): 8–9.

75. Center for the Future of Children, David and Lucile Packard Foundation, "Children and Poverty," *Future of Children* 7, no. 2 (summer–fall 1997).

76. Margaret Weir, "Coalition-Building for Regionalism," in Katz, *Reflections on Regionalism.*

77. According to the March 1999 Current Population Survey of the Bureau of the Census, the median central-city poor person lives in a household with four people in it. Thus, these calculations assume that there are four persons in each low-income household.

78. Alan Abramson, Mitchell Tobin, and Matthew VanderGoot, "The Segregation of the Poor in U.S. Metropolitan Areas," *Housing Policy Debate* 6, no. 1 (1995): 46. Houston population figures are from *Metropolitan Areas and Cities,* 1990 Census Profile, no. 3 (Washington, D.C.: Bureau of the Census, September 1991).

79. Abramson et al., "Segregation of the Poor."

80. A typical Section 8 voucher—which allows low-income families to pay for apartments in the private rental market by paying the difference between 30 percent of a family's income and market-level rents—costs about $6,000 per year.

81. See Harrison and Weiss, *Workforce Development Networks.*

82. According to HUD's evaluation report, except for Baltimore, "there was no further political opposition in low-poverty areas we are aware of, and few instances of suspected discrimination were reported." John Goering, Joan Draft, Judith Feins, Debra McInnis, Mary Joel Holin, and Hudu Elhassan, *Moving to Opportunity for Fair Housing Demonstration Program: Current Status and Initial Findings* (Washington, D.C.: U.S. Department of Housing and Urban Development, Office of Policy Development and Research, September 1999), p. 53. See also John Goering, Helene Stebbins, and Michael Siewert, *Promoting Housing Choice in HUD's Rental Assistance Programs: A Report to Congress* (Washington, D.C.: U.S. Department of Housing and Urban Development, Office of Policy Development and Research, April 1995); John Goering and Judith Feins, "The Moving to Opportunity Social 'Experiment': Early Stages of Implementation and Research Plans," *Poverty Research News* 1, no. 2 (spring 1997): 46–48; Thomas Waldron, "Parading Politicians Hear Critics of Housing Program," *Baltimore Sun,* September 12, 1994; Larry Carson, "City Vows to Proceed on Housing," *Baltimore Sun,* September 21, 1994; Peter Dreier and David Moberg, "Moving from the 'Hood': The Mixed Success of Integrating Suburbia," *American Prospect* (winter 1996): 75–80; Llewellyn Rockwell, Jr., "The Ghost of Gautreaux," *National Review,* March 7, 1994; Margery Austin Turner, Susan Popkin, and Mary Cunningham, *Section 8 Mobility and Neighborhood Health: Emerging Issues and Policy Challenges* (Washington, D.C.: Urban Institute, April 2000).

83. Timothy M. Smeeding and Peter Gottschalk, "Cross-National Income Inequality: How Great Is It and What Can We Learn From It?" *Focus* (Institute for Research on Poverty, University of Wisconsin-Madison) 19, no. 3 (summer–fall 1998): 15–19.

84. Paul Jargowsky, *Poverty and Place: Ghettos, Barrios, and the American City* (New York: Russell Sage Foundation, 1997).

85. Ibid.

86. These studies are summarized in Douglas S. Massey and Nancy A. Denton, *American Apartheid: Segregation and the Making of the Underclass* (Cambridge, Mass.: Harvard University Press, 1993).

87. See Richard Engstrom, "The Voting Rights Act: Disfranchisement, Dilution, and Alternative Election Systems," *PS: Political Science and Politics* 27, no. 4 (December 1994): 685–88; Frances Fox Piven and Richard Cloward, *Why Americans Don't Vote* (New York: Pantheon, 1998).

88. A study of turnout in 5,400 electoral districts in New York City concluded that

neighborhood instability depressed turnout even more than concentrated poverty (though poor neighborhoods tend to be more unstable than middle-income areas). This is not just because of low registration rates but because unstable neighborhoods lack the social capital to link citizens to the political process. David Olson, "Place Matters: Explaining Turnout in New York City Elections, 1988–1994" (Ph.D. diss., Department of Political Science, State University of New York at Albany, 1997).

89. Raymond Wolfinger, "Improving Voter Registration" (unpublished paper, University of California at Berkeley, March 1994).

90. According to the Federal Election Commission (FEC), most states require voters to register at least twenty-eight days before an election. See the FEC Web site at www.fec.gov/pages/faqs.htm.

91. Raymond E. Wolfinger and Steven J. Rosenstone, *Who Votes?* (New Haven, Conn.: Yale University Press, 1980); Jan Leighley and Jonathan Nagler, "Individual and Systemic Influences on Turnout: Who Votes?" *Journal of Politics* 54 (1992): 718–40; Glen Mitchell and Christopher Wlezien, "The Impact of Legal Constraints on Voter Registration, Turnout, and the Composition of the American Electorate" (paper presented at the annual meeting of the Midwest Political Science Association, 1989), cited in Wolfinger, "Improving Voter Participation."

92. See Douglas Amy, *Real Choices, New Voices: The Case for Proportional Representation Elections in the United States* (New York: Columbia University Press, 1993); Robert Richie and Steven Hill, *Reflecting All of Us: The Case for Proportional Representation* (Boston: Beacon Press, 1999); Lani Guinier, *Tyranny of the Majority: Fundamental Fairness in Representative Democracy* (New York: Free Press, 1994).

93. Ruy Teixeira, *The Disappearing American Voter* (Washington, D.C.: Brookings Institution Press, 1992); David Callahan, "Ballot Blocks: What Gets the Poor to the Polls?" *American Prospect* (July–August 1998): 68–76; Robert Dreyfus, "The Turnout Imperative," *American Prospect* (July–August 1998): 76–82; Marshall Ganz, "Motor Voter or Mobilized Voter?" *American Prospect* (September–October 1996): 41–50.

94. See, for example, Carol Swain, *Black Faces, Black Interests: The Representation of African Americans in Congress* (Cambridge, Mass.: Harvard University Press, 1993).

95. Bureau of Labor Statistics, "Labor Force Statistics from the Current Population Survey," January 18, 2001, at http://stats.bls.gov/newsrel.htm.

96. Richard Rothstein, "Toward a More Perfect Union: New Labor's Hard Road," *American Prospect* (May–June 1996): 47–54; Richard Freeman, ed., *Working Under Different Rules* (New York: Russell Sage Foundation, 1994); Kate Bronfenbrenner, Sheldon Friedman, Richard Hurt, Rudolph Oswald, and Ronald Seeber, *Organizing to Win: New Research on Union Strategies* (Ithaca, N.Y.: ILR Press, 1998); Lawrence Mishel, Jared Bernstein, and John Schmitt, *The State of Working America 2000–01* (Ithaca, N.Y.: Cornell University Press, 2001); Peter Dreier and Kelly Candaele, "Canadian Beacon," *Nation*, December 16, 1996, p. 20.

CHAPTER 8. CROSSING THE CITY LINE

1. See Christopher R. Conte, "The Boys of Sprawl," *Governing* (May 2000): 28–33; David Rusk, *Inside Game/Outside Game* (Washington, D.C.: Brookings Institution Press, 1999).

2. William Schneider, "The Suburban Century Begins," *Atlantic* (July 1992): 33–43. See also Juliet F. Gainsborough, *Fenced Off: The Suburbanization of American Politics* (Washington, D.C.: Georgetown University Press, 2001), chap. 5. Lee Sigelman and

Lars Willnat, "Attitudinal Differentiation Between African-American Urbanites and Suburbanites: A Test of Three Accounts," *Urban Affairs Review* 35, no. 5 (May 2000): 677–94, suggest that the urban-suburban differences among blacks are relatively minor, however.

3. J. Phillip Thompson, "Beyond Moralizing," reacting to Owen Fiss, "What Should Be Done for Those Who Have Been Left Behind," *Boston Review* (summer 2000).

4. Robert Coles, "Better Neighborhoods," Jennifer Hochschild, "Creating Options," and Gary Orfield, "Exit and Redevelopment," symposium on "Moving Out," *Boston Review* (summer 2000).

5. David R. Harris, "All Suburbs Are Not Created Equal: A New Look at Racial Differences in Suburban Location" (Research Report 99–440, Population Studies Center, Institute for Social Research, University of Michigan, September 1999); William Lucy and David Phillips, *Confronting Suburban Decline: Strategic Planning for Metropolitan Renewal* (Washington, D.C.: Island Press, 2000).

6. Gainsborough, *Fenced Off,* chap. 6.

7. For the case of New York City, see John R. Logan et al., "Global Neighborhoods" (unpublished manuscript); more generally, see William H. Frey and Douglas Geverdt, "Changing Suburban Demographics: Beyond the 'Black-White, City-Suburb' Typology" (Research Report 98-422, Population Studies Center, Institute of Social Research, University of Michigan, June 1998).

8. Orfield, "Exit and Redevelopment." William Julius Wilson, *The Bridge over the Racial Divide* (Berkeley: University of California Press, 1999); Mark R. Warren, *Dry Bones Rattling* (Princeton: Princeton University Press, 2001).

9. Thomas Byrne Edsall and Mary D. Edsall, *Chain Reaction: The Impact of Race, Rights, and Taxes on American Politics* (New York: W. W. Norton, 1991), pp. 228, 229.

10. Schneider, "Suburban Century Begins."

11. Richard Sauerzopf and Todd Swanstrom, "The Urban Electorate in Presidential Elections, 1920–1996," *Urban Affairs Review* 35, no. 1 (September 1999): 72–91; 2000 figures updated by the authors.

12. Gerald M. Pomper, "The Presidential Election," in *The Elections of 1992,* ed. Michael Nelson (Washington, D.C.: CQ Press, 1993), p. 139; "Who Voted: A Portrait of American Politics, 1976–2000," *New York Times,* November 12, 2000, p. 4.

13. Peter Nardulli, Jon Dalager, and Donald Greco, "Voter Turnout in U.S. President Elections: An Historical View and Some Speculation," *PS* 29, no. 3 (September 1996): 480–90.

14. Ibid., p. 484.

15. Sauerzopf and Swanstrom, "Urban Electorate," p. 78; 2000 figures updated by the authors.

16. Harold Wolman and Lisa Marckini, "Changes in Central City Representation and Influence in Congress Since the 1960s," *Urban Affairs Review* 34, no. 2 (November 1998): 294. See also Gainsborough, *Fenced Off,* chap. 7.

17. Wolman and Marckini, "Changes in Central City Representation," p. 310.

18. Margaret Weir, "Central Cities' Loss of Power in State Politics," *Cityscape* 2, no. 2 (May 1996): 23–40.

19. Stanley B. Greenberg, *Middle Class Dreams: The Politics and Power of the New American Majority* (New York: Times Books, 1995), pp. 278–83. See also Al From, "The Next Battleground: Suburbs Are the Key to Democratic Victories in 2000," *New Democrat* (March–April 1999): 35–36.

20. Chris Black, "Clinton Links Suburbanites to Solutions for Urban Ills," *Boston Globe,*

May 10, 1992, p. 9; David Lauter, "Clinton Tells Orange County Not to Ignore Cities," *Los Angeles Times,* May 31, 1992, p. A1.

21. Pomper, "Presidential Election," pp. 138–39.

22. Neal Peirce, "Sprawl Control: A Political Issue Comes of Age" (syndicated column, November 15, 1998); Todd Purdum, "Suburban Sprawl Takes Its Place on the Political Landscape," *New York Times,* February 6, 1999; Margaret Kriz, "The Politics of Sprawl," *National Journal,* February 6, 1999.

23. John Mollenkopf, *The Contested City* (Princeton, N.J.: Princeton University Press, 1983), chap. 2. Arguably, the Nixon administration launched or proposed some of the most important urban policies, but this was at a time when the strength of non-southern Democrats in the House was at a post–New Deal high point.

24. See Wolman and Marckini, "Changes in Central City Representation," for a discussion of the limited circumstances under which a cohesive urban delegation was able to influence contested House votes in this period. See also Nicol C. Rae, *Southern Democrats* (New York: Oxford University Press, 1994).

25. For an excellent discussion of the interplay of policy and politics in this period, see Margaret Weir, ed., *The Social Divide: Political Parties and the Future of Activist Government* (Washington, D.C., and New York: Brookings Institution Press and Russell Sage Foundation, 1998).

26. See Charles Cameron, David Epstein, and Sharyn O'Halloran, "Do Majority-Minority Districts Maximize Substantive Black Representation in Congress?" *American Political Science Review* 90, no. 4 (December 1996): 794–812, for a related argument concerning the concentration of black voters in majority-black districts.

27. For a well-documented argument to this effect, see Ruy Teixeira and Joel Rogers, *America's Forgotten Majority: Why the White Working Class Still Matters* (New York: Basic Books, 2000).

28. The correlation is .134 with 1996 Democratic presidential votes and .262 with 1998 Democratic votes in contested House races, according to our analysis of Mollenkopf's Congressional District Database constructed from 1990 census population statistics (Summary Tape Files 1D and 3D, Census of Population and Housing, 1990, Congressional Districts of the United States, 104th Congress, on CD-ROM) and election results from various editions of Michael Barone and Grant Ujifusa, *Almanac of American Politics* (Washington, D.C.: National Journal), as confirmed by data compiled from official sources by Robin H. Carle, Clerk of the House of Representatives, at http://clerkweb.house.gov/elections/elections.htm.

29. The unstandardized coefficient between the percentage voting for the House Democratic candidate in 1998 and the unionized percentage of the labor force was .759 after controlling for the log of density, median household income, and percentage black, according to our analysis of Mollenkopf's Congressional District Database. The standardized coefficient was .228, and the standardized coefficient for density vote was .452. These variables were significant at the .05 level, and the adjusted R squared for the model was .368.

30. Teixeira and Rogers, *America's Forgotten Majority.*

31. This discussion draws on Michael Barone and Grant Ujifusa, *Almanac of American Politics, 1998* (Washington, D.C.: National Journal, 1997), pp. 1009–11.

32. Asher Arian, Arthur Goldberg, John Mollenkopf, and Edward Rogowsky, *Changing New York City Politics* (New York: Routledge, 1991), p. 145. See also Robert Caro, *The Power Broker: Robert Moses and the Fall of New York* (New York: Random House, 1974).

33. In 1998 and 1999, Serrano had a 100 percent voting record in rankings by the United Auto Workers, National Council of Senior Citizens, Consumer Federation of America, and National Abortion and Reproductive Rights Action League; he had a 95 percent ranking from the liberal Americans for Democratic Action, 93 percent from the American Civil Liberties Union, and 90 percent from the National Education Association. *Voter's Self-Defense Manual: 2000 Elections Edition* (Phillipsburg, Mont.: Project Vote Smart, 2000).

34. Barone and Ujifusa, *Almanac of American Politics, 1998,* pp. 502–3.

35. Ibid., pp. 1132–34.

36. In 1994, he earned a 14 percent rating from Americans for Democratic Action, a 13 percent rating from the AFL-CIO, a 29 percent rating from the American Civil Liberties Union, a 20 percent rating from the Consumer Federation of America, and an 11 percent rating from the League of Conservation Voters. He also voted for Speaker Newt Gingrich's "Contract with America."

37. Kucinich had been elected mayor in 1977 at age thirty-one and was defeated after two stormy years in office during which he challenged the city's business establishment, which then mobilized to undermine his agenda. Todd Swanstrom, *The Crisis of Growth Politics: Cleveland, Kucinich, and the Challenge of Urban Populism* (Philadelphia: Temple University Press, 1985).

38. Alan Achkar, "Suburbs' Plight: Inner-Ring Communities Fight Loss of Funds, People to Outlying Cities," *Cleveland Plain Dealer,* March 23, 1998, p. 1A.

39. See http://www.jointventure.org, www.greaterbaltimore.org, and www.sdrta.org.

40. Rosabeth Moss Kanter, "Business Coalitions as a Force for Regionalism," in *Reflections on Regionalism,* ed. Bruce Katz (Washington, D.C.: Brookings Institution Press, 2000), pp. 154–81.

41. Annalee Saxenian, *Regional Advantage: Culture and Competition in Silicon Valley and Route 128* (Cambridge, Mass.: Harvard University Press, 1994), compares the former favorably to the latter, noting that Silicon Valley benefited from a network of specialized firms that, while competing intensely, also collaborated in formal and informal ways with one another and with local universities and governments. See also Stephen S. Cohen and Gary Fields, "Social Capital and Capital Gains in Silicon Valley," *California Management Review* 41, no. 2 (1999): 108–26, available at socrates.berkeley.edu/~briewww/pubs/wp/wp132.htm; Rosabeth Moss Kanter, *World Class: Thriving Locally in the Global Economy* (New York: Simon and Schuster, 1995). Louise Jezierski, "Political Limits to Development in Two Declining Cities: Cleveland and Pittsburgh," *Research in Politics and Society* 3 (1993): 173–89, makes a similar point regarding these two cities.

42. For the Milwaukee case, see David Wood, Josh Whitford, and Joel Rogers, *At the Center of It All* (Center on Wisconsin Strategy, University of Wisconsin, June 2000), at http://www.cows.org/pdf/metro/mvp-report.pdf. More generally, see Eric Parker and Joel Rogers, "Building the High Road in Metro Areas: Sectoral Training and Employment Projects" (Center on Wisconsin Strategy, University of Wisconsin, May 2000).

43. Bennett Harrison and Marcus Weiss, *Workforce Development Networks: Community-Based Organizations and Regional Alliances* (Thousand Oaks, Calif.: Sage Publications, 1998).

44. Kanter, "Business Coalitions," p. 159.

45. The Greater Baltimore Committee, "'One Region, One Future': A Report on Regionalism" (July 1997), at www.gbc.org/reports/regionalism.htm.

46. For more extended discussion, see Peter Dreier, "Labor's Love Lost? Rebuilding Unions' Involvement in Federal Housing Policy," *Housing Policy Debate* 11, no. 2 (2000): 327–92, especially 366–81.

47. For a perspective on Silicon Valley developed by the Working Partnerships program of the South Bay Labor Council, see Chris Benner, *Growing Together or Drifting Apart: Working Families and Business in the New Economy—A Status Report on Social and Economic Well Being in Silicon Valley* (San Jose, Calif.: Working Partnerships USA and Economic Policy Institute, 1998), at http://www.atwork.org/wp/cei/gtda. pdf.

48. For a discussion of both the Los Angeles County Labor Federation and the South Bay Labor Council, see Harold Meyerson, "Rolling the Union On: John Sweeney's Movement Four Years Later," *Dissent* (winter 2000), at http://www.dissentmagazine.org/ archive/wi00/meyerson.html; Steven Greenhouse, "The Most Innovative Figure in Silicon Valley? Maybe This Labor Organizer," *New York Times,* November 14, 1999; Kelly Candaele and Peter Dreier, "LA's Progressive Mosaic: Beginning to Find Its Voice," *Nation,* August 21–28, 2000; Douglas Foster, "Unions.com: Silicon Valley Isn't Exactly Known as a Stronghold of Organized Labor; Amy Dean Is Working to Change That," *Mother Jones* (September–October 2000).

49. Antonio Olivo and Jean Merl, "Unions Seeking to Increase Clout in Suburban Races," *Los Angeles Times,* March 12, 2000.

50. See the Metropolitan Area Research Corporation Web site at www.metroresearch. org/about.html. For a variety of case studies of progressive smart-growth initiatives, see *Smart Growth, Better Neighborhoods: Communities Leading the Way* (Washington, D.C.: National Neighborhood Coalition, 2000).

51. Ester R. Fuchs, "The City Already Pays More Than Its Fair Share," *New York Times,* May 22, 1999.

52. john a. powell, "Addressing Regional Dilemmas for Minority Communities," in Katz, *Reflections on Regionalism,* pp. 218–46. For an eloquent defense of this perspective, see John O. Calmore, "Racialized Space and the Culture of Segregation: 'Hewing a Stone of Hope from a Mountain of Despair,'" *University of Pennsylvania Law Review* 143 (1995): 1233–71.

53. Larry N. Gerston and Peter J. Haas, "Political Support for Regional Government in the 1990s: Growing in the Suburbs?" *Urban Affairs Quarterly* 29, no. 1 (September 1993): 154. See also "Sprawl: The Revolt in America's Suburbs," *New Democrat* 11, no. 2 (March–April 1999); "Crossing the Line: The New Regional Dynamics," *Governing* (January 2000): 44–50; "Smart Growth," *Planning* (January 2000): 5–29.

54. Margaret Weir, "Coalition Building for Regionalism," in Katz, *Reflections on Regionalism,* 148.

55. Thomas Kamber, "The Politics of Section 8 in Portland and New York City" (Ph.D. diss., Political Science Program, CUNY Graduate Center, 2000); Edward G. Goetz, "The Politics of Poverty Concentration and Housing Demolition," *Journal of Urban Affairs* 22, no. 2 (2000): 157–73.

56. Jeffrey M. Berry, Kent E. Portney, and Ken Thomson, *The Rebirth of Urban Democracy* (Washington, D.C.: Brookings Institution, 1993).

57. Owen Fiss, "A Task Unfinished," symposium on "Moving Out," *Boston Review* (summer 2000).

58. Robert Reich, *The Work of Nations* (New York: Random House, 1992).

INDEX

Bronx: CDCs in, 6; investment in, 6; population decline for, 4. *See also* South Bronx

Brookings Institution, 124, 181, 256, 315n25

Brown, Lee, 151, 302n72

Brown, Willie, 302n72

Buchanan, Pat, 169

Buchanan v. Warley (1917), 286n26

Buckley v. Valeo (1976), 20

BUILD, living wage law and, 134

Bureau of Economic Research, 33

Bush, George, xii, 127, 128, 288n53; support for, 128, 237, 239, 250, 251, 252

Bush, George W., 240, 311n157

Business alliances, 216, 315n25

Businesses, 65; attracting, 100, 135; minority-owned, 152, 304n93

Business leaders, 161, 255

Business Week, 13, 19, 156

Byrum, Oliver, 37

Campbell, William, 154

Capital Region Fair Housing Compact on Affordable Housing, 317n45

Caplovitz, David, 77, 84

Car culture, 103–5, 206. *See also* Automobiles

Carey, Jim, 41

Carjackings, 87, 283n157

Carter, Jimmy, 4, 124, 125, 126, 236, 293n128

Cato Institute, 165

CDBG. *See* Community Development Block Grant

CDCs. *See* Community development corporations

CED. *See* Committee for Economic Development

Census Bureau, 32, 46

Center on Wisconsin Strategy, 182, 254

Central Atlanta Progress, 145

Central cities: comebacks by, 26; deterioration of, 27, 113; flight from, 53; protecting, 94

Chain Reaction (Edsall and Edsall), 234

Chavez, Martin, 302n72

Check-cashing outlets, 79, 80, 90

Chevrolet, 7

Chicago Housing Authority, 58, 316n44

Chicago Sun-Times, 280n117

Chief executive officers (CEOs), 15

Child care, 55, 221–22, 229, 295n147

Child labor, 157

Children: health issues and, 70; poverty and, 4–5, 11; traffic injuries for, 277n66

Christopher Commission, 168

Chrysler, 155, 305n104

Cisneros, Henry, 128, 159, 256

Cities: aid to, 113, 115; competitive advantage for, 26, 96; economic segregation and, 173; elastic/inelastic, 38; electoral clout of, 234–35; as engines of prosperity, 24–27; fiscal crisis for, 125; political isolation for, 234, 235; population decline for, 39; sprawl and, 173;

suburbs and, 38, 52, 232, 234–37, 239, 243; urban problems and, 26; wealth and, 26. *See also* Central cities

Cities Without Suburbs (Rusk), 37–38

City managers, 165

City Managers Association, 309n140

"City obsolescence" thesis, 261n2

City workers, 145, 166

Civic engagement, 166, 225–29

Civil rights movement, 47, 151, 156, 160, 165, 177, 236; housing and, 112, 149; political/legal strategy for, 226; urban renewal and, 120; voting rights and, 225

Class divisions, 18, 31, 50, 185, 236, 264n49

Clean Air Act (1990), 168, 212

Cleaver, Emanuel, 302n72

Cleveland, east side of, 8

Cleveland, west side of, 6, 7, 8, 252

Clinton, Bill, 29, 84, 288n53; cities and, 128–29; coalition for, 239, 240; "common ground" message of, 237; EITC and, 220; HUD and, 129; middle class and, 239; poverty and, 129, 130; suburban districts and, 239; support for, 233, 237, 244, 250, 251–52; urban policy of, 128–30; welfare and, 130

COAH. *See* Council on Affordable Housing

Coalitions: antiurban, 243; assembling, 229, 231–32; governing, 147, 152; metropolitan, 246–47, 253, 255; political, xi, 28, 147, 168, 257; pro-growth, 118, 146, 149, 152, 159, 300n55; urban-suburban, 232, 237–38, 240–45, 247

Coastal-interior gap, 34

Codes, 60, 139–40, 158

COGs. *See* Councils of government

Coles, Robert, 231

Columbine High School, 87

Commission on Urban Problems, 126

Committee for Economic Development (CED), 316n42

Committee of 25, 145

Communities Organized for Public Service (COPS), 159, 197–98

Community-based organizations, 96, 171, 197, 216, 254, 265n1; lack of, 159; low-income people and, 215; neighborhood improvement and, 170

Community development, 28, 123, 183, 223; poverty and, 203–4, 325n35; regional economy and, 214–16, 223; sprawl and, 271n73

Community Development Block Grant (CDBG), 124, 127, 210, 211

Community development corporations (CDCs), 6, 159–61, 163, 204, 214, 216, 249

Community groups, 160

Community policing, 168, 303n78

Community Reinvestment Act (CRA), 125, 126, 129, 159

Commuting, 62, 92, 93, 132, 133, 186, 298n31. *See also* Reverse commuting

Earned income tax credit (EITC), 121, 129, 130, 203, 220

Easterbrook, Gregg, 95–96, 98

East-West Tollway, 10

E-commerce, 2

Economic competitiveness, 35, 66, 93, 176, 177, 187, 253, 254

Economic concentration, 55, 64

Economic development, 7–8, 27, 35, 161, 187, 200, 203, 211, 214, 253, 254; community-based approaches to, 171; industrial clusters and, 65; neighborhood, 204; regional, 247, 256; urban, 157

Economic diversity, 29, 41

Economic elites, 253

Economic growth, 16–17, 61, 123, 136–37, 162, 178, 189, 228–29, 249; benefit from, 14; poverty and, 17, 207, 267n18; regional, 33, 188, 209, 233; sprawl and, 62–66, 96, 131–32

Economic inequality, 1, 23, 53, 259; addressing, 134, 203, 209; city/suburban, 36–40; growth of, 12, 24, 181, 228; health issues and, 67; liberal democracies and, 260

Economic Policy Institute, 220

Economic problems, 40, 57, 205, 207, 250; addressing, 254–55; urban, 183

Economic productivity, 24, 64, 104

Economic segregation, 1, 31, 44, 116, 142, 171, 247, 260; addressing, 28, 94, 196, 202, 250; concentrated poverty and, 23, 52; costs of, 28, 55, 80; impact of, 3, 57, 233, 259; increase in, 32, 46, 90, 94, 99, 131, 199, 209; neighborhood-level, 45–50; problem of, 12–27, 198, 206; source of, 28, 91; sprawl and, 51–53, 63; suburban, 41–45, 81; in United States, 53–55; urban programs and, 113; urban revival and, 171

Edge cities, 11, 64, 96, 98

Edge City (Garreau), 10, 62

Edsall, Mary and Thomas, 234

Education, xii, 59, 200, 203, 222; concentrated poverty and, 216, 217, 219; employment and, 218; housing vouchers and, 144; local governments and, 93, 99; place and, 2; poverty and, 144, 216, 217, 219; providing, 55, 136, 143–45; spending on, 36, 137, 217; strengthening, 143, 216–18. *See also* Public schools; Schools

Eisenhower, Dwight D., 118

EITC. *See* Earned income tax credit

Elections, 309n142; cities and, 234–35; nonpartisan, 165; presidential, 234, 235, 241–42; union, 228. *See also* Voter turnout

Eleventh Congressional District (Ohio), 251

Elkin, Stephen, 301n61

Embry, Robert, xiii

Emergency Quota Act, 114

Emergency Relief and Construction Act, 114

Employment, 64–65, 91, 187, 273n10; black males and, 62; commuting and, 33; edu-

cation and, 218; entry-level, 51–52, 59, 60, 61, 62, 171, 212, 251; gains in, 141; income and, 57–62; location of, 61; metropolitan, 36; part-time, 81; pay for, 219–22; place and, 2, 60; poverty and, 203; public, 304n93; regional, 66; service, 85, 143; suburban, 196; war mobilization and, 106. *See also* Job training; Unemployment

Empowerment zones (EZs), 129, 215, 249, 312n162

Enterprise zones (EZs), 129, 204, 322n4

Environmental issues, 23, 72, 91, 124, 132, 166, 176–77, 194, 208, 233, 250, 253–56; curing, 98; money for, 138; regional, 179; sprawl and, 95, 176

Environmental Protection Agency, 168, 314n17

Equality, 24, 231, 299n51; economic segregation and, 19, 68; sprawl and, 68

Equal opportunity, 18, 19, 29, 121

Equal protection clause, 143, 304n93

Erlenborn, John, 250

Ethnic groups, 161; occupational segregation and, 45; relations among/politics of, 232; urban liberalism and, 148–49

Euclid v. Ambler (1926), 101

Exclusion, 196, 233; racial dimension of, 194; social, 26, 206; suburban, 198. *See also* Zoning, exclusionary

EZs. *See* Empowerment zones; Enterprise zones

Fair Housing Act (1968), 111, 112, 317n45

Fair housing laws, segregation and, 111–13

Fair-market rent (FMR), 17, 263n42

Falling Down (movie), 104

Family Assistance Plan (FAP), 293n119

Family Research Council, 89

Fannie Mae Foundation, 284n2

Favored quarters, 175, 200, 247

Fawell, Harris, 250, 251

Federal Election Commission (FEC), 330n90

Federal Highway Act (1962), 184

Federal Housing Administration (FHA), 122; loans from, 109, 110, 212, 248; redlining and, 109, 288n61; suburbanization and, 108, 109; Twin Cities and, 190

Federalism, 145, 223, 229

Federal Reserve Bank of New York, 207

Federal Signal Corporation, 9

Feinstein, Dianne, 312n162

Fermi National Accelerator Laboratory, 132

FHA. *See* Federal Housing Administration

Fielding, Elaine, xiii

Fire protection, 91, 298n29

First Chicago Trust Company, 187

First Suburbs Consortium, 9, 252, 253, 257

Fiscal capacity, 140–43, 207

Fiscal crisis, 136, 145, 168–69, 250, 252

Fiscal Disparities Act (1971), 190

Fischel, William, 52

Fishman, Robert, 109
Fiss, Owen, 231, 259
Flexible specialization, 64–65, 276n46
Flight, 4, 8, 39, 41, 103, 120, 143, 232,
    260; black, 305n98; crime and, 52, 87;
    motivations for, 52–53; preventing, 208; race
    and, 52; riots and, 155; tipping points for,
    290n78
Flynn, Ray, 162, 163
FMR. *See* Fair-market rent
Food stamps, 103, 114, 121, 127, 148, 166, 197,
    294n136
Ford, 7, 155
Ford, Gerald, 125
Ford Foundation, 183
Forrester, Jay, 207
Fortunate fifth, 14
1400 Governments (Wood), 44, 178
Fourteenth Amendment, 143, 304n93
Free markets, 103; geographical avoidance
    behavior and, 31; myth of, 98–99; support
    for, 201–2
Free-market theory, 51–52, 202
Freeways, 8–9, 44, 93, 178, 254; automobile
    travel and, 104; construction of, 117, 248,
    252; suburbs and, 132, 176; urban renewal
    and, 118, 119, 146. *See also* Automobiles;
    Highway lobby; Road building
Frey, William, 232
Front National, 54
Frug, Gerald, 176, 177
Fulton County Housing Authority, 117
Future Once Happened Here, The (Siegel), 166

Gaines, Donna, 43
Gainsborough, Juliet, 199
Galbraith, John Kenneth, 82
Gangs, 8, 26, 262n16; suburban, 86, 87, 88
Garreau, Joel, 10, 62, 63, 64, 65, 96, 98
Gated communities, 30, 266n1
Gates, Daryl, 153, 304n87
Gautreaux, Dorothy, 316n44
Gautreaux program, 61, 144, 185, 224, 294n144,
    316n44
General Motors, 155, 305n104
Gentrification, 39, 152, 166
Geronimus, Arline T., 278n83
Ghettos, 3–6, 54, 88, 100, 196; crime and, 90;
    dismantling, 98, 181, 223–24; health issues
    in, 73; low density of, 48; supermarkets and,
    78
GHP. *See* Greater Hartford Process
Gingrich, Newt, 169, 239, 333n36
Giuliani, Rudolph W., 166, 171; administra-
    tion of, 168, 169–70; affirmative action and,
    169; economic development and, 257; Port
    Authority and, 186; reinvestment and, 249
Global economy, 35, 254, 266n6, 305n98;
    regionalism and, 180, 200, 214
Godard, Jean Luc, 104

Goldberg, Jackie, 133
Goldschmidt, Neal, 193
Goldsmith, Stephen, 167, 170, 311n157
Goode, Wilson, 151
Good government groups, 164
Gore, Al, xii, 180, 233, 240
Governments: county, 179; differences be-
    tween, 140; district, 187; in fifteen largest
    metropolitan areas, 39(table); influence of,
    93–94; private, 30; state, 236; suburban, 44–
    45, 233, 313n176. *See also* Councils of gov-
    ernment; Local governments; Metropolitan
    governments; Regional governments
Grands ensembles, 54
Grant programs, 121–22, 124, 127, 143, 213. *See
    also* Block grants
Great Depression, 34, 114, 235
Greater Baltimore Alliance, 253
Greater Baltimore Committee, 254–55
Greater Downtown Partnership, 156
Greater Hartford Process (GHP), 173, 174
Greater New York, 177
Great Society, 120–23, 149, 159, 214
Greco, Donald, 235
Greenberg, Stanley, 237
Grosse Point Farms, 124
Gross national product (GNP), 67
Growth: economic segregation and, 63;
    managed, 162; population, 52, 189; private-
    sector, 164; rates of, 32, 49; regional, 36,
    64, 131, 176, 266n7, 267nn19,20; unplanned,
    178, 179. *See also* Economic growth; Smart
    growth
Growth boundaries, 179; regional, 35, 190, 192
Growth management, 33, 81, 159, 160, 192, 193,
    194, 253, 258
Gulick, Luther, 178
Guns, 89, 129
Gwinnett Place mall, 96

Harlem, 67
Harvey, 41, 44
Hatcher, Richard, 123, 151, 152
Haussmann, Baron, 36–37
Hayden, Tom, 311n159
Hayward, Steven, 113
Head Start, 121, 149, 159
Health, 91; inequality and, 67–68; life expec-
    tancy and, 69; wealth and, 66–67, 276n58
Health care, 127, 198, 229; access to, 68–69;
    children and, 222
Health insurance, 68, 74, 114, 129, 130; child
    care and, 222; expanding, 221–22; lack of,
    221; means-tested, 121
Health issues, 55, 66–75; automobile and, 74;
    children and, 70; concentrated poverty and,
    68, 69, 70, 72–73; economic inequality and,
    67; immigrants and, 69; poor neighbor-
    hoods and, 140; sprawl and, 73; suburban,
    73–75

National Academy of Sciences, 73, 256
National Advisory Commission on Civil
  Disorders, 183–84
National Association of Real Estate Boards,
  116
National Bureau of Economic Research, on
  EITC, 220
National Commission on Urban Problems,
  184
National Institute of Justice, 89
National Labor Relations Board, 228
National Land Use Policy bill, 184
National League of Cities, 256
National Municipal League, 164, 178
National Origins Act (1924), 114
National Resources Committee, 178, 183, 184
National Review, 94
National Urban Policy Report (1982), 34, 126
National Voter Registration Act (1993), 225–26
National Welfare Rights Organization, 159
NCC. *See* New Community Corporation
Neighborhood movements, 159; urban pro-
  gressive regimes and, 158
Neighborhoods; advantages of, 56–57;
  bad/good, 202–3; deterioration of, 191, 225;
  ethnic, 100; exclusive, 30, 44, 266n2; good,
  202; high-poverty, 86, 225; low-income, 22,
  204; minority, 119, 199; racially segregated,
  107–8, 326n37; revitalization of, 215; stability
  for, 108–9
Neighborhood Youth Corps, 122
Nelson, Arthur C., 325n32
Nelson, Kathryn P., 268n35
New Community Corporation (NCC), 77
New Deal, 113–15, 120, 158, 178
New Detroit Committee, 145
New Federalism, 123–26
New Haven, 119
New Left, 160
Newman, Katherine S., 22, 264n61
New regionalism, 175, 233, 256–57
New Republic, 95
New urbanism, movement for, 179
New York City, 186, 189
New York City Department of Consumer
  Affairs, 77
New York City Partnership, 6
New York Daily News, 125
New York Times, 219
Nicholson, Richard, 60
Nike, 84, 193
Nixon, Richard M., 317n45; growth policy and,
  33; land use and, 184; New Federalism and,
  123–26; Section 8 program and, 122; silent
  majority and, 165; urban renewal and, 118,
  332n23; welfare reform and, 293n119
Nonprofit organizations, 138, 146, 196
North American Free Trade Agreement, 239
North-South gap, 34
Nowak, Jeremy, 216, 325n36

Oakar, Mary Rose, 252
Oak Brook, 10, 132, 250
O'Connor, Alice, 113
Office of Economic Opportunity, 122
Office of Management and Budget, 213
Olympic Games, 154
"Open occupancy" law, 111
Open spaces, 29, 180, 251
Opinion shapers, public agenda and, 253
Orange County Central Labor Council, 256
Orfield, Gary, 320n68; on diversity, 232; re-
  gionalism and, 181; on resegregation, 218;
  on suburbanites/school policy, 231
Orfield, Myron, 210, 257; housing bills of,
  191; on inner suburbs, 199; metropolitan
  approaches and, 256; Metropolitan Council
  and, 191; regionalism and, 181, 193, 232, 247
Ostrom, Elinor and Vincent, 97
Our Cities: Their Role in the National Economy,
  183
Outer-ring suburbs, 22–23, 74
Out-of-wedlock births, 21, 22. *See also* Teen
  pregnancies
Overconsumption, 80–82
Overcrowding, 114, 140

Panhandling, 167, 169, 313n4
Parma, 6, 7, 8, 9, 251, 252, 262n16
Parmatown Mall, gangs at, 8
Pastor, Manuel, xiii
Pataki, George, 138, 169
Pathmark supermarket, 77, 78
Pawnshops, 78–79, 80
Peirce, Neal, xiii, 180–81, 256, 324n16
Pena, Federico, 128, 302n72
Per capita income, 12, 34, 36, 38, 39, 40(fig.),
  60, 262n26
Pericom, 92
Perot, Ross, 128, 250, 252
Personal Responsibility and Work Opportu-
  nity Reconciliation Act (1996), 57, 130
Peterson, Paul, 97
Phillips, David, 41, 43
Physical environment, 69–71
Pingree, Hazen, 158, 306n116
Place: crime and, 83; importance of, 3–12, 35,
  92–94, 202, 203, 205–8; income and, 57; jobs
  and, 60; poor and, 21–22; race and, 204–5;
  technology and, 1–2; unhealthy, 69–71
Place-based inequalities, 20–24; addressing,
  203, 205; racial segregation and, 204–5
Place-based programs, 208, 231, 240
Planning, 136; centralized, 33; environmental,
  194; equity, 157; government, 36; metropoli-
  tan, 178, 212, 254; neighborhood, 162; new
  forms of, 177. *See also* Land-use planning;
  Regional planning
Plano, drug problem in, 86
Plant closing laws, 134
Poletown, 155

Race: class/place and, 204–5; concentrated poverty and, 49, 50; crime and, 83–84; employment and, 273n10; flight and, 52; poverty and, 270n59, 323n5

Racial discrimination, 23, 49, 107, 155, 273n10, 304n95; economic segregation and, 204

Racial diversity, increase in, 29

Racial segregation, 24, 112, 116, 155, 171, 185, 247; countering, 94, 98; decline of, 199, 232; economic segregation and, 32, 50, 204, 205; majority minority districts and, 226; place-based inequalities and, 204–5; poor and, 47; promoting, 117, 209; riots and, 183

Racial tensions, 26, 167–68; progressivism and, 161–62

Racial transition, 113, 120, 143

Racism, 107, 128, 205

Reagan, Ronald: federal aid and, 127, 293n131; HUD and, 125; public housing and, 127; tax reform plan and, 111; urban programs and, 126–28

Reapportionment, 9, 253

Reason Foundation, 165

Redevelopment, 145–46, 155, 161, 188, 190

Redistribution, 161, 206, 208

Redistricting, 226, 245

Redlining, 109, 112, 125–26, 248, 280nn115,117, 288n61, 305n98

Reform movements, 149, 164

Regime theory, 147

Regional agencies, creation of, 187

Regional approaches, 130, 198–99; benefits of, 113, 258; obstacles for, 173

Regional competitiveness, 181, 210, 254; economic downturn and, 188; promoting, 182, 258

Regional cooperation, 28, 181, 182, 187, 200, 213, 258; economic segregation and, 25; logic of, 257; problems in, 188, 189; promoting, 208

Regional development, 161, 182; sprawl and, 25, 175, 190; tax breaks and, 187

Regional economy, 324n16; cities and, 66; community development and, 214–16, 223; integration of, 25

Regional equity, 29, 258; addressing, 254, 257; promoting, 194–95

Regional governments, 176, 214; experiments in, 190–94; fiscal capacity of, 140–41; forming, 179; plan for, 174; promoting, 188; strength of, 194

Regional Housing Mobility Program, 185

Regional inequality, 32–36, 93, 194, 267nn19,20; death rates and, 67; increase in, 34–35; urban poverty and, 324n16

Regionalism, 209, 247; ambivalence about, 257; economic competitiveness arguments for, 180–81; efficiency arguments for, 178–79; environmental arguments for, 179–80;

equity arguments for, 181–82; global economy and, 180, 200, 214; origins of, 177–82; politics of, 199–200; support for, 255, 257–58

Regionalist, The, 181, 315n26

Regional planning, 180, 185, 186, 189, 192; addressing, 188, 254

Regional Planning Association, 59, 177, 178, 180, 186, 253

Regional prosperity, central-city performance and, 65

Regional Technology Alliance, 181, 253

Registration, 165, 225–26

Regulations, reducing, 135, 166

Reich, Robert, 14, 260

Rent control, 134, 152, 163, 166, 169, 310n152

Rent-to-own stores, 79, 80

Report of the President's Commission of Housing, 126

Restrictive covenants, 107

Retail gaps, 76, 76(table)

Retail outlets, 75, 80, 91

Reuther, Walter, 120, 121

Revenue capacities, 143

Reverse commuting, 195, 196, 212, 224; growth of, 197; programs for, 182. *See also* Commuting

Reynold, Malvina, 43

Rich, the, 13, 22, 30, 31, 32, 37

Richmond, Henry, 207

Richmond County, Louisville and, 179

Rich-poor gap, 15, 19, 20, 31

Riis, Jacob, 69

Riordan, Richard, 147, 171; campaign of, 167–68, 311n159; downtown development and, 168; DreamWorks and, 276n47; federal empowerment zone and, 312n162; living wage law and, 133, 168

Riots, 123, 155, 166, 168, 183

Rizzo, Frank, 123, 309n146

Road building, 103; sprawl and, 105, 212; urban, 104. *See also* Freeways

Road rage, 74–75

Robberies, drop in, 83, 87

Rockwell, Llewellyn, 94

Rodriguez, Bernardo, 139

Rodriguez, Nestor, xiii

Rogan, James, 227

Rogers, Joel, 65

Roosevelt, Franklin D., 106, 114, 183

Roosevelt, Theodore, 20, 309n140

Rothstein, Richard, 217

Route 128, 35, 64, 180

Roybal, Edward, 303n86

Rusk, David, 316n30; on community development/sprawl, 271n73; on economic disparities, 40; on elastic cities, 37, 185; metropolitan approaches and, 256; on movement to suburbs, 6; regionalism and, 181

251, 250, 256, 258; costs of, 28, 55, 80; defenders of, 95–96; free-market perspective on, 131; impact of, 3, 57, 131–32, 198, 233, 259; land markets and, 202; problems with, xi, 198, 205, 206; progressivism and, 164; promoting, 93, 94, 99, 131, 208; suburban, 205; in United States, 53–55; urban decline and, 271nn72,73; urban programs and, 113

Standard City Planning Enabling Act (1928), 101

Standard State Zoning Enabling Act (1924), 101

Steffens, Lincoln, 157

Stereotypes, 41, 49, 260

Sticky capital, 35

St. Louis, 107, 187, 189

St. Louis County, 45

Stokes, Carl, 123, 151

St. Paul, 190

Street, John, 151

Stress, 72, 73

Studentski, Paul, 178

Subculture, 87, 88

Subsidies: housing/home ownership, 115–17, 121, 122, 139, 176, 189, 194, 207, 210; local, 210; providing, 135; taxing, 210

Suburban districts: conditions in, 242–43; heterogeneity of, 243; median household income in, 243; Republicans and, 241; support in, 236–37

Suburbanites, 237, 244; cities and, 138, 232, 239, 243; fears of, 53

Suburbanization, 100–101, 103, 140, 226; central-city densities and, 51; federal government and, 131–32; FHA/VA and, 109; impact of, 25; marketplace and, 94; as natural market phenomenon, 52; political terrain and, 234–35; promotion of, 93, 95–96, 108, 111, 117–18, 131; pull/push factors in, 51; state/national politics and, 235; tax codes and, 210; urban renewal and, 120

Suburban JobLink, 196, 197

Suburban Maryland Fair Housing, 195

"Suburban Myth: The Case for Sprawl" (Easterbrook), 95–96

Suburbs: aging of, 199; black, 199, 232; competition among, 99–100, 206; decline of, 43, 313n176; development of, 9–12; diversity of, 41; Hispanic, 199; identity of, 44; income export to, 25; low-density, 2; outer city/edge city and, 64; poor, 43; rich, 37, 42; urbanization of, 64. See also Inner-ring suburbs

Subways, 105, 189

Sugrue, Thomas, 52

Supermarkets, 77–78

Superstores, 75

Supplemental Security Income, 295n147

Sweeney, John, 228

Swing districts, 7, 227, 252

Tale of Three Counties, A (League of Women Voters), 192

TANF. See Temporary Assistance to Needy Families

Tax base: lowering, 138, 174; metropolitan, 298n30

Tax breaks, 96, 100, 135, 149, 161, 189, 210, 219, 237, 289n2; geographic/social consequences of, 111; using, 186–87

Tax codes, 27, 111, 210

Taxes, 136, 137, 138, 207; business, 134, 166, 170; capital gains, 289n71; commuter, 257; gas, 104, 105; income, 138, 192; linkage, 153, 163; local, 93, 97; payroll, 169; reducing, 135, 166; sales, 188, 192. See also Property taxes

Tax Reform Act (1986), 111

Tax revenues, 99; distribution of, 210; expanding, 135; maximizing, 176

Tax sharing, 94, 124, 144, 200, 209, 210, 247; regional, 190; suburban growth and, 213

TEA-21. See Transportation Equity Act for the Twenty-first Century

Technology, 142, 143, 261n2; place and, 1–2; space and, 2

Teen pregnancies, 21, 26. See also Out-of-wedlock births

Temporary Assistance to Needy Families (TANF), 130

Tennessee Valley Authority, 209

Tensions: progressivism and, 161–62; racial, 26, 161–62, 167–68; urban/suburban, 185

Tenth Congressional District (Ohio), 251–52; compared, 3(table); described, 6–9; federal policy and, 248; highway construction in, 132; map of, 7; urban decline in, 8

Ten-Year Housing Program, 248

Texas Industrial Areas Foundation, 247

Thatcher, Margaret, 54

Think tanks, 35, 64, 128, 165, 166

Thirteenth Congressional District (California), 227

Thirteenth Congressional District (Illinois), 9–12, 249–50; Chicago and, 250; compared, 3(table); federal policy and, 248; highway construction in, 132; map of, 10; median family income in, 9; sprawl and, 251

Thompson, J. Phillip, 231

Tiebout, Charles, 97

Time, 13, 299n51

Tipping point, 225, 290n78

Tocqueville, Alexis de, ix, 233

Tourism, 138, 192

Traffic congestion, 29, 74–75, 95, 104, 118, 132, 160, 180, 206, 210, 212, 233, 251, 258

Transportation, 97, 124, 179, 182, 189, 190, 192, 197, 200, 211, 216, 247, 253; car-dominated, 105; costs of, 77; funds for, 185, 212; improvements in, 31, 56, 184, 188, 193, 198, 212; individualism in, 96; policy, 27, 103–5, 193; problems with, 58; regional, 186; truck,